SOCIAL Pulse

von
Isobel Williams

sowie
Megan Hadgraft

unter Mitarbeit der Verlagsredaktion

Dieses Buch gibt es auch auf www.scook.de

Es kann dort nach Bestätigung der Allgemeinen Geschäftsbedingungen genutzt werden.

Buchcode: **k6hzf-9tmxw**

VORWORT

Social Pulse ist einer der vier Titel in der komplett neuen Lehrwerksreihe *Pulse*, die den mittleren Schulabschluss voraussetzt und auf den Erwerb der Fachhochschulreife an Fachoberschulen, Berufskollegs und Höheren Berufsfachschulen hinarbeitet. Das Lehrwerk deckt die grundlegenden Anforderungen der Stufe B1 des Europäischen Referenzrahmens ab und führt zu Stufe B2.

Jede der zwölf Units in *Social Pulse* behandelt sachlich aber dennoch sensibel die wichtigsten Themen im Bereich Soziales. Dabei steht die Kommunikation im Mittelpunkt. Insofern bildet der direkte Berufsbezug die didaktische Grundlage des Lehrwerks und der Reihe (**handlungsorientierter Ansatz**).

Aufbau der Units

Die zwölf Units sind wie folgt aufgebaut:

 Einstieg

In jeder Unit bietet Ihnen diese Doppelseite anhand von Fotos, Cartoons, Illustrationen, Zitaten und Statistiken einen stark **visuellen** und **kommunikativen** Einstieg in die Unit.

Ein *What's to come*-Kästchen hält Ausblick auf die Inhalte/Kompetenzen der Unit zur Unterstützung des **eigenverantwortlichen Lernens**.

 Part A/B/C

Diese drei stark **kompetenzorientierten** Doppelseiten sind durch ihre in Handlungsrahmen eingebetteten Themen klar lernerfolgsorientiert und transparent.

Jede dieser drei Doppelseiten beginnt mit einem Situations-Kästchen **S**, das den Handlungsrahmen beschreibt und Lernende dazu anregt, sich aktiv mit dem Unterrichtsstoff auseinanderzusetzen.

- Alle Aufgabenüberschriften weisen die Kompetenz und den Inhalt aus, z. B. *Writing: termination or adoption?*
- *Situational grammar* wird in jede Unit integriert.
- Durch gezielte Übungen wird der **Wortschatz** trainiert, erweitert und gefestigt.
- Das Hör-/Sehverstehen wird durch **Augmented Reality** trainiert. (Mehr Informationen zu *Augmented Reality* finden Sie auf Seite 3.)
- **Binnendifferenzierung** wird durch GUIDANCE-Karten (die mehr Unterstützung anbieten) und CHALLENGE-Karten (die eine zusätzliche Herausforderung bereithalten) gefördert.

Vorwort

 Part D – *Practice and projects*

Auf dieser Doppelseite werden die in die Units situativ eingebetteten Grammatikübungen **konsolidiert** und weitere **Projektarbeit** angeboten, um das selbstgesteuerte Lernen zu fördern.
Ein *Checking progress*-Kästchen – eine **Checkliste zur Selbstevaluation** – rundet die Unit ab und ermöglicht es den Lernenden, über ihren persönlichen Lernerfolg zu reflektieren.

Exam skills and strategies

Zwischen den Units befindet sich eine Doppelseite zur Entwicklung **methodischer Kompetenzen**. Hier beschäftigen sich die Lernenden anhand von kurzen **Tipps** und dazu passenden **Aufgaben** mit verschiedenen Lernstrategien. Insofern bereiten diese Seiten von Anfang an auf die Abschlussprüfung vor. Das *Wichtig-für*-Kästchen macht den **Prüfungsbezug** noch klarer und transparenter, damit gezielt geübt werden kann.

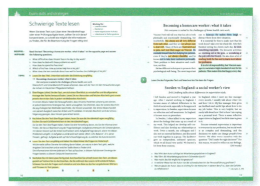

Am Puls der Technik – mit *Augmented Reality*

Social Pulse bietet Lehrenden und Lernenden die Möglichkeit, durch *Augmented Reality* ganz einfach mit ihren Smartphones oder Tablets auf alle digitalen Inhalte des Schülerbuchs (Audio- und Video-Dateien) zuzugreifen – ohne CD oder DVD! Schnell, intuitiv und komfortabel – *Augmented Reality* ist die flexible und modernste Art, das Hör- und Sehverstehen auch unterwegs zu trainieren.

So einfach funktioniert es: Nachdem Sie die notwendige App heruntergeladen haben (siehe unten), können Sie ihr Handy oder Tablet über jede Seite mit einem Audio-Symbol oder Video-Symbol halten und mit einem einfachen Klick auf „Play" die Audio- bzw. Video-Datei abspielen. *There's nothing to it!*

 Los geht's! Scannen Sie den QR-Code (links) mit Ihrem Smartphone oder Tablet (oder gehen Sie auf www.cornelsen.de/pulse-ar), um die für *Augmented Reality* notwendige App herunterzuladen, und dann … *enjoy*![1]

Alternativ können Sie die Medien für die Nutzung ohne mobile Geräte unter www.cornelsen.de/webcodes mit dem folgenden Webcode aufrufen: ▶ SP-MEDIA

Wir hoffen, dass Ihnen die Arbeit mit *Social Pulse* Freude bereitet und das Lehrwerk zu einem gelungenen und erfolgreichen Unterricht beiträgt.

Die Autoren und der Verlag 2014

---

[1] *Onlineverbindung notwendig. Die Systemvoraussetzungen finden Sie unter dem QR-Code bzw. unter www.cornelsen.de/pulse-ar.*

TABLE OF CONTENTS

1 Caring for people			**6**
A **Who cares?**	Speaking: caring professionals at work Listening: three caring professionals Interaction: interviews and introductions	Talking about what people do (*Simple present*) Asking for information (*Question words / Simple present /* *Simple past*)	
B **Why care?**	Reading: three caring organizations Talking about your workplace		
C **Self-care**	Talking about stress Reading: professional supervision Interaction: conducting a survey	Designing a website: from research to presentation	

Exam skills and strategies: Schwierige Texte lesen			**16**

2 Applying for a job			**18**
A **Getting started**	Reading: a job advertisement Reading: how to write a CV in English Internet research: finding a placement	Giving advice (*Modal auxiliary verbs*)	
B **Doing the paperwork**	Writing: preparing your CV Reading and writing: a covering letter	Get that job! From job advert to interview	
C **No sweat!**	Mediation: tips for telephone interviews Role-play: a telephone interview Listening: tips for face-to-face interviews		

Exam skills and strategies: Mit unbekannten Wörtern umgehen			**28**

3 Supporting families			**30**
A **Meet the family**	Reading: defining the family Video: "Just a family" Writing: the changing family	Describing change (*Present perfect / Simple past /* *Used to + infinitive*) Talking about behaviour (*Adverbs of frequency*)	
B **Problems and patterns**	Reading: What is a dysfunctional family? Listening: describing the dysfunctional family Discussing two cases Presentation: supporting dysfunctional families		
C **Making decisions**	Reading and summarizing case notes Discussion: assessing adoptive parents Writing: termination or adoption?	Producing a scene from a scripted reality show	

Exam skills and strategies: Textproduktion – Umgang mit Operatoren			**40**

4 Learning to listen			**42**
A **Listening between the lines**	Reading: understanding unspoken signs Listening: the cycle of violence in domestic abuse Writing: domestic abuse	Talking about how people look and behave (*Adjectives and adverbs*) Talking about possible solutions and expected results (*If-sentences type I*)	
B **School violence and victimization**	Reading: violence and victimization in schools Listening: finding causes Discussion: establishing a violence-free environment Giving a talk: school violence and victimization		
C **I'm listening**	Discussion: making referrals Reading: skills for active listening Role-play: helpline calls	Writing and acting out a helpline dialogue	

Exam skills and strategies: Mit Hör-/Sehverstehensaufgaben umgehen			**52**

5 Reaching out to at-risk teens			**54**
A **Teams for teens**	Listening: greetings and small talk Role-play: introducing yourself Listening: Outreach's mission and a personal success story Mediation: street kids in Germany	Talking about current activities and regular schedules (*Simple present / Present* *progressive*)	
B **Programmes and activities**	Reading: supporting homeless teenagers Video: "Young and homeless" Writing: asking for contributions	Presenting facts and figures: homeless teens in your area	
C **Drug facts and figures**	Describing a graph: drug use Reading: decriminalizing drugs Debate: the pros and cons of legalizing drugs		

Exam skills and strategies: Einen Text zusammenfassen			**64**

6 Solving problems at work			**66**
A **Case 1: harassment**	Mediation: understanding what harassment is Listening: scenes from a session Mediation and role-play: dealing with harassment	Reporting what someone says (*Reported speech*) Talking about circumstances over which people have no control (*The passive*)	
B **Case 2: assessment**	Reading: analysing a stress checklist Listening: the challenging client Role-play and writing: the follow-up appointment		
C **Case 3: Closure**	Reading: effects of downsizing Writing: how (not to) restructure	Guidelines: preventing problems among staff	

Exam skills and strategies: Mindmaps und Gliederungen erstellen			**76**

Video-Symbol / Grammatik-Symbol / Projekt-Symbol

7 Working with clients with special needs			78
A Why this school?	Reading: for and against inclusion Video: "Graduation day at the Rise School" Writing: inclusion – both sides of the story	Adding extra information (*Relative clauses*)	
B The right to work	Reading: disabilities – definitions and rights Listening: assisting disabled people looking for work Presentation: employment opportunities for the disabled	Developing and presenting a concept for a facility for clients with special needs	
C A visit to a sheltered workshop	Reading and mediation: preparing for the visit Listening: a tour of the workshop Giving an oral report: the Eider Werkstätten GmbH		

Exam skills and strategies: Einen Aufsatz oder eine Stellungnahme schreiben			**88**

8 Staying healthy, keeping fit			90
A You are what you eat	Discussion: the types of food kids eat Listening: an interview with a nutritionalist Writing: the impact of fast food	Talking about making changes (*If-sentences type II*)	
B Dying to be slim	Reading: the end result of anorexia Discussion: it's a matter of opinion …	Designing an advertising campaign to promote health and fitness	
C The influence of the media	Reading: dreams for sale Research and discussion: messages in magazines Video: "Boot camps boom in Australian outdoors"		

Exam skills and strategies: Präsentieren			**100**

9 Volunteering abroad			102
A Learning for life	Reading: voluntourism Video: "Youth in Action – EVS for refugees" Writing: the pros and cons of volunteering	Describing past actions and events (*Past progressive / Simple past / Past perfect / Past perfect progressive / Present perfect*)	
B Getting down to work	Reading: the Outdoor Experience Centre Listening: taking a message		
C Dealing with an emergency	Listening and discussion: being prepared for all eventualities Role-play: emergency! Writing: a report of the accident	Planning and presenting an outdoor adventure excursion	

Exam skills and strategies: Bilder und Cartoons beschreiben und analysieren			**112**

10 Helping people cope with change			114
A Settling down in a new country	Reading: schooling for young immigrants Listening: coping with problems Writing: towards successful integration	Talking about strategies (*Gerunds/Infinitive*)	
B Working with elderly migrants	Reading and writing: reports from the field Listening: developing cultural competence	Making a poster: options for working with migrants in your area	
C Supporting asylum seekers	Mediation: looking for a volunteer mentor Listening and speaking: voicemail messages		

Exam skills and strategies: An Diskussionen teilnehmen			**124**

11 Giving support at times of loss			126
A When a child dies	Reading: working with bereaved families Writing: working at a hospice	Giving an objective report (*Other passive forms*)	
B "What should we do with Grandad?"	Listening: the background to the case Reading and discussion: ailments and diseases of the elderly Role-play: answering a relative's questions	Research and presentation: celebrations of life	
C Death in Germany	Reading: burial vs cremation – the environmental aspects Video: "High-tech headstones"		

Exam skills and strategies: Schaubilder und Statistiken beschreiben und analysieren			**136**

12 Looking ahead			138
A Developments in the health sector	Reading: investment in professional care Listening: the global challenge Writing: an enquiry or an unsolicited job application	Making predictions and describing plans (*The future*)	
B Technological advances	Reading: the smart home Mediation: the smart environment	Mapping the future: an infographic about the social and health care sectors in the year 2025	
C Where are we heading?	Reading: the future for professional carers Writing: caring professions in 2025		

Exam skills and strategies: Mediation			**148**

Partner files	152	Basic word list	228
Guidance and challenge files	172	Unit word list	234
Correspondence	186	A–Z word list	268
Phrase bank	190	Exam skills and strategies – answer key	290
Skills file	202	Irregular verbs	294
Grammar summary	212	Quellenverzeichnis	295

5

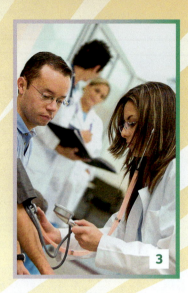

1 Caring for people

1 What words and phrases do you think of when you talk about the caring professions? Collect ideas in the class.

2 Match six of the headlines (a–h) to the photos. There are two more headlines than you need.

a. Good job chances for trained assistants in general hospital

b. Substance abuse on the increase among unemployed

c. Rise in number of students training to be social administrators

d. Midwives report fewer home births

e. GERIATRIC CARE WORKERS IN DEMAND

f. Positive developments in care in the community

g. Need for more youth clubs in inner cities

h. STILL NOT ENOUGH MALE KINDERGARTEN NURSES

4

5

6

3 What field interests you? Where would you like to work when you have finished your studies?

I'm not sure, but … could be interesting.

I'm hoping to find a job in …

I don't know. Perhaps I'll go into …

What's to come

In this unit, you will …
- meet some carers and hear their thoughts about their jobs.
- take a look at some organizations that are in the business of caring.
- consider some suggestions which might help you in your role as a caring professional.

At the end of the unit, you will do research and produce material for a website.

Before you begin, think about how the pages that follow might help you move towards your goal of becoming a caring professional. Make notes about what you expect to learn.

A Who cares?

> In this section, you will meet several people who work in caring professions and will find out what they do and what they like about their jobs.

1 Speaking: caring professionals at work
> Job titles, p. 191

A Look at this extract from a job advert in a magazine for carers and choose the best heading.

a   Ready to work hard? Become a carer!
b   Motivated? Committed? We need YOU!
c   Carers in demand
d   Social support services

> In the UK today, around 2.5 million people receive social care. This care ranges from children's services to support for teens and adults of all ages. With people working harder and living longer, the demands on our social support services are immense. That's why we continually need highly motivated and committed carers to provide support to the people who need it most. Could one of these carers be you?

B Which caring professionals from the list below work with adults, which work with children, and which with both? Draw a table and sort the jobs into the right categories.

> community support worker • day care centre assistant • geriatric carer • midwife •
> nursery/kindergarten nurse • occupational therapist • paediatric assistant •
> physiotherapist • social administrator • social worker • telephone counsellor

C Who does what? Match the caring professionals to the tasks they might do.

I think that a geriatric carer assists the elderly.

I agree. He or she also works with people and helps them do everyday things.

1   support people with problems
2   help people live in their community
3   help people do everyday things
4   manage a team of care workers
5   work with people
6   assist the elderly
7   help a mother with a child

Talking about what people do

Midwives **work** with pregnant women.
- We use the simple present to describe what someone does regularly. > *Simple present, p. 212*

A nursery nurse **works** with children. NOT: ~~She work~~ …
- He, she, it – das „s" muss mit!

2 Listening: three caring professionals
> Mit Hörverstehensaufgaben umgehen, S. 207

The Social Pulse team talks to people from all sectors of the caring professions and brings you information, opinions and tips that will be useful for you at work. In this week's podcast, Fran and Mark interview three carers: Adya, Bill and Cass. Our first question: "Why did you decide to work as a carer?"

Unit 1　Caring for people

1/2

A Listen to the interviews and note down anything you find interesting about the speakers.

B Collect the information on the board and try to reconstruct the carers' stories. Then listen again and check.

C Which of the speakers say the following personal qualities are necessary for their work? Make a list of other qualities that carers need.

1　being able to stick to decisions　　3　being pragmatic　　5　being strict
2　being easy-going　　　　　　　　　4　being sensitive　　　6　having patience

D Work with a partner. Can you remember the questions that Fran and Mark asked? Write down three more questions you would like to ask the carers.

Asking for information

Where are you from? – I'm from Birmingham.
- Question words (*who/what/where*, etc.) come at the start of the question.

Do carers **work** long hours? – Well, some carers **do**, but some **don't**.
Did you **go** to college full-time? – No, I **didn't**. I went part-time.
- We use *do/does* to ask questions and give short answers in the simple present, and *did* in the simple past.
- For negative statements we use *don't/doesn't* or *didn't*.
  > *Simple present, p. 212; Simple past, p. 213*

3　**Interaction: interviews and introductions**

A Talk to a partner. Ask what he/she hopes to do and where he/she would like to work. Find out about personal qualities that will help your partner at work.

B Introduce your partner to the class.

Introducing people

- I would like to introduce … / This is …
- He/She decided to be a carer because …
- He/She hopes to work as a/an …
- He/She would like to work with adults …
  > *Introductions, p. 190*

9

B Why care?

> You are going to compare and contrast three organizations in the field of caring.

1 Reading: three caring organizations
> *Schwierige Texte lesen, S. 202*

A First, look at the web pages and study the headings and photos. Work with a partner and try to predict what you will learn from the pages. Note down a few points.

B Now skim the texts (= read them quickly). Which points on your list have been covered?

TALK IT OVER

We are a charity providing relationship support to couples and families.
Our vision is a future in which healthy relationships are the basis of a thriving society.
Our highly skilled counsellors support clients at times of crisis and help them make decisions about their relationships. This support has an impact on people's ability to work or go to school, to maintain a stable home life and to get involved in their community.

Our mission is to:
- help couples, families and individuals to make relationships work better.

Our organization was set up in Edinburgh in 1962 when its aim was to help married couples with relationship problems.
Today, we help people in all kinds of relationships. We have over 50 centres all over the UK and a network of trained counsellors working face-to-face as well as by phone and online.

MULTICULTURAL ELDERLY CARE, Birmingham

We offer advice and assistance to the elderly and provide activities in our day care centre. We also offer home support or home help services and undertake crisis management for clients who are isolated or ill.

Culturally sensitive support in a caring community

Our aims are to:
- establish culturally appropriate care services for elderly people from Birmingham's black and minority ethnic communities.
- respond to needs for personal care, domestic care, carer support and crisis care.

We are a non-profit organization.

Our centre was founded in 1994 to help the many ethnic families who had problems dealing with bureaucracy. Our day care facilities are aimed particularly at those from the black and minority ethnic (BME) communities.

We train our hand-picked team to respond to the needs of BME elders. We also aim to recruit and train more people from BME communities as home carers.

Our school was founded in 1992 by a group of parents who wanted child-centred education for their children.

Our highly qualified staff guide and support the young in a nurturing environment.

SWANSEA STEINER SCHOOL

We are a thriving Steiner Waldorf School in the Welsh city of Swansea. With over 1,000 schools in 60 different countries, and 36 in the UK alone, Swansea Steiner School is part of the largest independent school system in the world.

We have two mixed-age kindergartens for 3- to 6-year-olds and classes for children aged 6 to 10.

We are accredited by the Steiner Waldorf Schools Fellowship and registered with the Welsh Government as an independent day school.

Inspiring education for children aged 3 to 10

C Do the tasks below using your own words as often as possible.   ▸ *Umgang mit Operatoren, S. 202*

1 Describe the clientele each of the organizations is aimed at.
2 Explain why each organization was set up.
3 Outline the services each organization offers.
4 Find evidence in the texts to show that each organization offers a competent and professional service.

D Find phrases in the texts to describe the following:

1 a an organization which is funded by gifts of money given by private individuals.
  b an organization which does not earn any money.
  c a place of education which is not run by the government.
2 a people who know how to give advice.
  b employees who have been carefully chosen for the job.
  c trained workers.
3 a people living and working together successfully.
  b a group of people that help and respect each other.
  c a situation or place where people can develop and grow.

2 Comparing and contrasting

Compare and contrast the three organizations for a friend of yours who would like to apply for a job in the UK.

All three organizations aim to …

The … is an organization dealing with …

In contrast, the …

GUIDANCE *If you would like guidance, turn to file G1 on page 172.*

3 Talking about your workplace

You are going to prepare a short talk about your place of work. Introduce yourself, say what you do and describe the organization you work for. Choose one of the options below.

Option 1 If you have done practical training or have work experience, make notes about one of the places where you have worked. Use your notes to describe that workplace.

Option 2 If you have no work experience, imagine you work for one of the places mentioned on these pages. Use information from the web page to describe your place of work. Invent more information where you need to, e.g. *there are 16 carers and three therapists*.

Talking about your workplace

- My name is …
- I'm a/an (*job title*) at (*name of organization*).
- It's located in …
- I work for … (*e.g. the city council*)
- (*Name of organization*) was set up in … by … to …
- We look after …
- We have a staff of (*number*).
- I'm responsible for …
- My responsibilities include …

  ▸ *Introductions, p. 190*

Remember!

I work **for** the NHS (National Health Service).
NOT: I work ~~by~~ the NHS.

C Self-care

> **S** How can a caring professional cope with stress at work? One way of coping is to get supervision. You are going to talk about stress and learn about professional supervision, then conduct a survey.

1 Talking about stress

How do people cope with stress in everyday life? Talk in groups, then make a list of the top five stress-busters on the board.

2 Reading: professional supervision

A Before you read, sort the items below into positive and negative aspects of working as a carer.

1. being unable to switch off after work
2. coping with challenges
3. feeling balanced
4. experiencing a feeling of despair
5. solving problems
6. suffering from stress

B How might a supervisor help you cope with the negative aspects of your job?
Scan (= quickly look for information in) the advertisement below to find the answers.

Are you suffering from stress as a result of challenges at work?

John Hardy,
Licensed Counsellor
10 years of clinical experience

A
You are a responsible caring professional.
You are looking for ways to cope with stress at work.

Have you ever experienced
- difficulties separating work and private life?
- the inability to cool down and switch off after work?
- a feeling of despair when you're faced with challenging clients and responsibilities?

If you've answered yes to at least one of these questions, you might like to think about professional supervision.

B
- Supervision can help professionals become balanced carers, aware of what they are doing and able to cope with the challenges of the job.
- Supervision provides support for professionals who frequently work with difficult and stressful cases.

C
- Professional supervision is a way to get to know yourself properly. When you know yourself properly, you become a more balanced carer.

- Professional supervision will help you to reflect on how you interact with others. When you are aware of how you interact with others, you become a more conscious carer.
- Professional supervision can teach you how to solve problems at work. When you learn how to solve problems at work, you will be able to cope with day-to-day stress much more easily.

D
I provide a safe, confidential environment in which you can talk freely about your concerns.
I will guide you towards solutions and help you develop and maintain a balance in your professional and private life.

E
- Awareness, balance, coping
- Work-life balance with professional supervision

Unit 1   Caring for people

C The headings are missing in the advert. Match the questions to the paragraphs (A–E).

1 How can a licensed counsellor support you?
2 How can professional supervision improve the quality of your care?
3 What is professional supervision?
4 What will you achieve with professional supervision?
5 Who are you?

D Answer the questions above in your own words to summarize the advertisement.

E Which English words in the text match these German words?

1 berufliche Anforderungen
2 verantwortungsbewusst
3 ausgeglichen
4 belastende Fälle
5 mit anderen umgehen
6 sich selbst kennenlernen
7 vertraulich
8 Sorgen
9 Gleichgewicht halten

3 Reading: pros and cons of professional supervision

A Read some opinions from carers who have experience of professional supervision. Describe how professional supervision helped Jose. Point out what Angie and Mary dislike about supervision. What techniques for beating stress do they prefer?

> My supervisor has helped me develop into a caring carer. He is a good listener and asks the kind of questions that lead me to find the solution to my problems myself. I trust him completely, so I can talk to him about everything in an open way.
> *Jose, nursing assistant*
>
> Talking about problems might be good for some people, but professional supervision is not for me. If I've had a stressful day at work, I prefer to go to the gym or go for a run. If you eat a healthy diet and get enough exercise, you won't suffer from burnout.
> *Angie, social worker*
>
> Supervision didn't work for me. The supervisor reminded me of a nasty teacher I once had, and it was clear that she didn't like me either. That's one of the problems with supervision. Personalities can get in the way. I meditate regularly and I do relaxation exercises, and that's enough to keep me in balance.
> *Mary, auxiliary nurse*

B Is professional supervision an option for you? Respond to one or two of the writers above and give your opinion.

 I agree/disagree with …
 In my opinion, …
 I feel/think that …

GUIDANCE If you would like guidance, turn to file G2 on page 172.

4 Interaction: conducting a survey

A Work in groups. Make up a questionnaire to find out how people in the class actively cope with stress and what they do to achieve work-life balance.

B Ask a member of another group the questions. Note down the answers, then pool and summarize the results and present them to the class.

13

D Practice and projects

1 Saying what people do

A Match the sentence halves and use the correct form of the verb to produce job descriptions.

1. A geriatric care worker
2. A nursery nurse
3. A nutritionist
4. Physiotherapists
5. Substance abuse counsellors
6. Community learning and development workers

a ... (advise) people on how and what to eat.
b ... (help) with mobility problems.
c ... (look after) the elderly.
d ... (support) people who have addictions.
e ... (take care of) children.
f ... (aim to) help people to gain new skills and expand their horizons.

B Put the verbs into the simple present. Be careful with questions and negative statements.

1. Ian (work) hard all day at the nursery so he (not go out) in the evenings during the week.
2. Bob and Mary (be) trainee social workers. They (go) to college once a week.
3. (you / get on) well with old people? A geriatric nurse (need) a lot of patience.
4. David (enjoy) his job. He (be) a physiotherapist.
5. Claire (be) a nurse, but she (not work) in a hospital. She (have) a job in a private clinic.
6. (the youth worker / know) what Tommy (do) every evening?

> Simple present, p. 212

2 Asking questions

Read the answers that one carer gave about herself and her job. Use the WH-questions in the box and the words in brackets to make the questions we asked her.

> How • What (x2) • Where • Who • Why

1. I like helping people. (become a carer)
2. I work in a residence for the elderly. (work)
3. I serve meals, I make beds, I help the residents get washed and dressed. (do at work)
4. I am patient and I have respect for older people. (personal qualities help at work)
5. I go running and I meditate. (cope with stress at work)
6. My colleagues give me support. (give support)

> Simple present, p. 212; Simple past, p. 213

3 Odd one out

Which personal quality does not fit with the others? Say why. Use your dictionary if you need to.

1. friendly • good • sociable
2. gentle • happy • kind
3. balanced • calm • talkative
4. helpful • interested • supportive

4 Writing a profile

You did an internship with Beth, an English carer in a residence for the elderly. She asks you to describe her on her Xing page. Use your notes to write a short description of Beth.

> engagierte Altenpflegerin
> unkompliziert, aber auch sensibel
> verantwortungsbewusst und fleißig
> hat Geduld und Respekt gegenüber Senioren

14

Unit 1 Caring for people

5 **Making a mind map** › *Mindmaps erstellen, S. 207*

Start a mind map in your notebook describing ways to achieve work-life balance. Add more words to your mind map as you work through the book.

> **Remember!**
>
> **do** sport
> NOT: ~~make~~ sport

  Designing a website: from research to presentation

Your task is to work in groups and design a website that trainee carers in your area can use to decide on their career path. Your website should show opportunities for work, and describe the qualifications and personal qualities needed for the jobs on offer.

Before you start, decide how your group wants to do the first three steps. Do you want to work in three teams (each doing one step) or together?

Step 1 Research opportunities for work in your area. Find out about types of jobs and types of workplaces.

Step 2 Think about the personal qualities carers need for work.

Step 3 Think about the drawbacks of working as a carer and ways to deal with them.

Step 4 As a group, gather all your information, decide who writes what, then work with a partner to write your part of the content.

> **Presenting a website**
>
> - We've divided the website into the following pages: …
> - On our home page we have …
> - As you can see, most of the jobs are in the … sector.
> - If you click on …, you can see a list of …
> - So, that's our website. Does anyone have any questions?
>
> › *Presentations, p. 195*

Step 5 Come together and design your website. What information will you put on the home page? Where will you put the other content? What kind of headings do you want in your menu?

Step 6 Present your website and its contents to the class. › *Präsentieren, S. 209*

Checking progress

Browse through the previous pages in the unit, looking at headings and pictures.
What have you learned? What can you do now that you have learned these things?
  ✔ I can introduce myself, talk about what I am doing and where I would like to work. (Part A)
  ✔ I can describe my workplace. (Part B)
  ✔ I can write my own opinion in a forum entry. (Part C)
  ✔ I can do research and design a website about working as a carer. (Part D)

Write down two more statements of your own.

How has this unit helped you towards your goal of becoming a caring professional?

15

Exam skills and strategies

Schwierige Texte lesen

Wenn Sie einen Text zum Lösen einer Verständnisfrage oder einer Prüfungsaufgabe lesen, sollten Sie sich darauf konzentrieren, so schnell wie möglich die Informationen zu finden, die für die Beantwortung der Fragen nötig sind.

Wichtig für:
- Leseverstehen
- Mediation
- materialgestützten Aufsatz
- rollenbasierte Stellungnahme

BEISPIEL-AUFGABE

Read the text "Becoming a homecare worker: what it takes" on the opposite page and answer the following questions.

a What difficulties does Vincent face in his day to day work?
b How does he deal with these problems at work?
c How does he spend his free time?
d Which of his free-time activities help him in his job?
e What does the text conclude about how well he handles the challenges of his job?

TIPPS

1 Lesen Sie den Titel, Untertitel und/oder die Einleitung sorgfältig.
→ **Becoming a homecare worker: what it takes**
    Not everyone is suited to the challenges of home health care work.
Überschrift und Unterüberschrift lassen erkennen, dass sich der Text mit den Herausforderungen der Arbeit im Häuslichen Pflegedienst befasst.

2 Überfliegen (skim) Sie den Text, um sich einen Überblick zu verschaffen und die allgemeine Aussage des Textes herauszufinden. Lesen Sie nur den ersten und letzten Abschnitt ganz sowie jeweils den ersten Satz in jedem verbleibenden Abschnitt.
Im ersten Absatz haben Sie herausgefunden, dass Vincents Patienten schwierig sein können, er jedoch bestimmte Strategien hat, damit umzugehen. Sie erkennen, dass der zweite Abschnitt die psychologischen Methoden beschreibt, die Vincent anwendet. Der dritte Absatz handelt von seinem Ausgleich zwischen Arbeit und Privatleben. Im letzten Abschnitt wird die Schlussfolgerung gezogen, dass Vincent gute Arbeit leistet.

3 Nachdem Sie den Text überflogen haben, lesen Sie nun die Verständnisfragen sorgfältig. Suchen Sie nach Schlüsselwörtern in den Verständnisfragen.
Da Sie den Text überflogen haben, haben Sie eine Vorstellung davon, wo Sie die Informationen finden, die Sie zur Beantwortung der Frage benötigen. Aufgabe **a** untersucht die Schwierigkeiten, mit denen Vincent auf der Arbeit konfrontiert wird. Aufgabe **b** fragt danach, wie er mit diesen Problemen umgeht. In Aufgaben **c** und **d** wird nach seiner „Work-Life-Balance", d. h. seiner Freizeit, gefragt. Aufgabe **e** zielt auf die Schlussfolgerung ab, zu welcher die Autorin kommt.

4 Lesen Sie den Text sorgfältig und haben Sie dabei immer die Fragen im Hinterkopf.
Mittlerweile sollten Sie eine Vorstellung davon haben, um was es in dem Text geht, welche Angaben Sie brauchen und an welcher Stelle diese zu finden sind.
Die Informationen können jederzeit im Text auftauchen. In diesem Fall könnten Sie einige der Fragen bereits zu diesem Zeitpunkt beantworten.

5 Nachdem Sie mit dem Lesen fertig sind, durchsuchen Sie schnell (scan) den Text, um diesen gezielt auf Antworten zu durchsuchen, die Sie während des Lesens nicht entdeckt haben. Schauen Sie sich die Fragen noch einmal an und wie diese zu den hervorgehobenen Wörtern und Phrasen im Text passen.

Exam skills and strategies

Becoming a homecare worker: what it takes

Not everyone is suited to the challenges of home health care work.

Vincent Ford will tell you that his job is both physically and emotionally demanding, but worthwhile. His clients are all very different from each other, and they are not always easy to deal with. Many of them are frustrated and in pain, and vent their anger on Vincent. He reminds himself that he's helping his patients, even if they're not always thankful, and he knows not to take their outbursts personally. Their problem is their situation and condition, not him.

He has different techniques to promote their psychological well-being. The most important one is humour. He makes them laugh to distract them from their situation.

It is essential for him to make sure that his work doesn't take over his whole life. After he's finished seeing his clients each day, he does something enjoyable. His favourite activities are working out at the gym, or socialising at the pub with his friends. He also does a lot of reading, both for fun and to learn more about his profession.

It is a lot of responsibility, but Vincent manages to maintain a high standard of care for his patients. This makes him feel happy every day.

---

1 Lesen Sie den folgenden Text und beantworten Sie dann die Fragen.

Sweden vs England: a social worker's view

Erik Lindberg talks about differences in supervision style.

I left Sweden and moved to England a year ago. After I started working in England, I became aware of cultural differences in the field of social work, especially in the approach to supervision. In Sweden, supervision focuses on reflection and self-awareness. In England, it focuses more on procedure.

In Sweden, I often talked to my supervisor about the feelings that came up as a result of my work. This helped me develop self-confidence and also develop my relationships at work. Twice a month, my colleagues and I also met an external facilitator, and discussed our work together in a group. The facilitator gave us independent, unbiased opinions, which we all found very useful. We learned a lot from these sessions.

In England, when I meet my line manager every month, I usually talk about what I do and how I do it. My line manager then gives me feedback and useful tips about how to do my job better. This is very helpful, but we rarely talk about how I feel or how I am coping on a personal level. There is some reflective supervision in England, but little time is given to it.

Process-oriented supervision is important to everyone in our profession, but social work is so complex and demanding, and the decisions we make can change people's lives forever. We often worry ourselves with the question: "Did I make the right decision?" For this reason, we need to reflect on our feelings.

(260 words)

a Was fehlt dem Autor zufolge bei Mitarbeitergesprächen in England?
b Wer führt die Mitarbeitergespräche in Schweden durch?
c Was macht der/die englische Vorgesetzte?
d In welcher Weise hat der Autor von der schwedischen Art der Personalführung profitiert?
e Warum glaubt der Autor, dass es wichtig für die Menschen in seinem Beruf ist, über die Gefühle zu reflektieren?

> *Lösungen, S. 290*

CV and covering letter (or letter of application)

Dear Ms Haslam
Work placement
I would like to apply for a work placement at your organization as advertised in the March edition of the magazine *Caring for People*.

job centre

2 Applying for a job

1

A Describe the activities above, then put them in the order you would do them when looking for employment.

Putting things in sequence
- First, …
- Second, …
- Then, …
- After that, …
- Next, …
- Finally, …

First, I would check the paper or the internet to find job advertisements. Then, …

B Discuss in small groups. Say which of these activities you have already done and describe what happened. Which activities have you not done yet?

I've written a few applications, but I've never done a telephone interview.

Same here. I haven't …, but I have …

2 What jobs do people in the class want to do when they finish school or training? Do a survey. Go round the class and collect ideas on the board under the heading "Jobs".

18

 A Work with a partner. Look at the list of jobs on the board and make a list of the top six skills or qualities you think an employee in these places of work should have.

B Compare your lists in class and add your ideas to the board under the heading "Skills/Qualities".

What's to come

In this unit, you will …
- study some job advertisements.
- write your CV and a covering letter.
- prepare yourself for job interviews.

At the end of the unit, you will apply for a job and attend an interview.

Before you begin, check the Europass website and download the English CV template which you will need for a later task. You should also download one example of an English CV and the German instructions for completing the Europass. Here is the link:
http://europass.cedefop.europa.eu/en/home

19

A Getting started

> In this unit, you will go through the steps of applying for a job. The first steps are understanding job advertisements and writing your CV.

1 Brainstorming: the ideal work placement

What would be your ideal work placement? Where would you like to work and what would you like to do? Make a list.

> I'd like to …
> use English   work in the health sector
> gain experience   work with children

2 Reading: a job advertisement

A Scan the advert below and see if you can find any of the aspects from your list in exercise 1.

B Read the advertisement carefully and make notes on the following: the job sector, what the employer is looking for, types of duties, what the employer offers.

C How should an applicant apply for the job? What will happen if the application is successful?

Trainee care worker for work placement

Are you interested in working in one of the caring professions? Why not do your work placement with us?

Who we are
Care Disability supports thousands of disabled people all over the UK. We help people with physical impairments, learning difficulties and long-term health conditions, as well as their carers, friends and families.

Who you are
You are reliable, motivated and flexible. You speak good English and at least one other language. You are already studying or hope to study social and health care. A full driving licence is an advantage.

Work placement
Our work placement lasts for four weeks. During this time, you may be asked to:
- accompany disabled people who are taking part in leisure and social activities.
- support disabled people with their education or training opportunities.
- help the family of a disabled person with their daily routine.

How we support you
Your time at Care Disability will be an enjoyable and rewarding experience.

We offer:
- a training programme for you to learn new skills.
- support and supervision to help you carry out your tasks.
- a small token payment to help you with your day-to-day expenses.

Apply now!
Send your CV and covering letter to:

Care Disability
Attn: Ann Haslam
62 Calder Street
Glasgow G42 7NQ
Great Britain

If your application is successful, we will contact you by telephone.

Unit 2 Applying for a job

3 Reading: how to write a CV in English

You have decided to apply for the job and you find some advice online about writing a CV in English. There is something wrong with the website, and some of the words are missing from the article.

A Work with a partner and complete the article with the words below.

- a you must not give
- b you could include
- c you don't have to say this
- d it must grab
- e can do
- f ought to be
- g you should leave out
- h you should write
- i you must always ask
- j you needn't attach
- k you should keep
- l you should state that

How to write your CV

Your CV is a summary of your abilities, work experience, education and qualifications. There is no set format for a British CV but ●¹ it short, using headings to guide the reader. Make sure your CV is honest and factual.

Personal details: Start your CV with your name and address, telephone number(s) (home/mobile) and email address. However, unlike a German CV, ●² a photo to your British CV.

Profile: This is a short message which summarizes your skills and experience relevant to the job you are applying for. Make it eye-catching – ●³ the reader's attention.

Work experience: This information ●⁴ in reverse chronological order, with the most recent position first. Provide dates of the start and end of employment, employer's name and address, job title, main responsibilities and achievements.

Education: Give a brief description of your qualifications and the names of schools or colleges in reverse chronological order. ●⁵ in English, but ●⁶ what the equivalent is, e.g. "Fachoberschule is equivalent to vocational college".

Skills: Write about what you are good at and ●⁷ well. Describe the skills you gained throughout your education and work experience. Describe your character using words like team-orientated, flexible, energetic, etc.

Interests: This section is optional, but ●⁸ something more personal to discuss at an interview. Be careful about what you write; ●⁹ things like partying every evening!

References: Due to data protection laws, ●¹⁰ names or any contact details on CVs, but ●¹¹ the details are available on request. Remember, ●¹² for permission before you give someone's contact details.

B How is a German CV different from a British one? Work with a partner to write some tips on how to write a German CV.

C Use advice from the text above to make notes for your own CV.

GUIDANCE *If you would like guidance, turn to file G10 on page 176.*

> **Giving advice**
>
> You **shouldn't** include copies of your certificates with your application.
> You **mustn't** use a silly email address on your CV.
>
> - We use modal verbs such as *should*, *ought to* and *must* to give advice.
> > Modal auxiliary verbs, p. 216

---

4 Internet research: finding a placement

Using your notes from exercise 1, do an internet search for work placements. Make notes about the three most interesting ones you find and tell your group about the jobs. Say which one you might like to apply for and why.

21

B Doing the paperwork

> It is important to adapt your CV and covering letter to the job you are applying for. Below you will see how Leonie Kuhn has prepared her job application for the position at Care Disability.

1 Writing: preparing your CV

A Compare the information on Leonie's CV with the advertisement on page 20. Say why Leonie might be a good candidate for the job.

B Use the notes you made for exercise 3C on page 21 to prepare your own CV. Copy the layout of Leonie's CV and use any words and phrases from her CV that are appropriate.

Leonie Kuhn
Domkloster 6, 50667 Cologne, Germany
Phone (+49) 0221 34589
Mobile (+49) 0176 28948610
Email leokuhn@gmx.com

Profile
Highly-motivated student of social and health care seeks practical experience in the UK.
Fluent English speaker who is friendly, flexible and good at working under pressure.

Education

August 20.. – present	Fachoberschule, Cologne (equivalent to British vocational college) Main subjects: English, German, Biology, Health Studies, Social Studies and Home Economics
August 20.. – June 20..	Kölner Realschule, Cologne (equivalent to British secondary school)

Work experience

September 20.. – June 20..	Au pair, Münster, Germany. Temporary position taking care of three primary school-aged children for visiting American Professor

Skills
German (native speaker), English (fluent: oral and written), Polish (conversational)
MS Office
Good at working under pressure, friendly, flexible
Full driving licence, first-aid certificate

Interests
Sport, cooking

References
Names of referees available on request

22

Unit 2 Applying for a job

2 Reading and writing: a covering letter

A Read Leonie's covering letter to Care Disability and say in which order she did the following.

a ask to be considered for an interview
b refer to details on the CV
c refer to the position

d say why she is applying for the position
e state why she is the best person
for the job

Domkloster 6
50667 Cologne
Germany

25 March 20..

Care Disability
Attn: Ann Haslam
62 Calder Street
Glasgow G42 7NQ
Great Britain

Dear Ms Haslam

Work placement

I would like to apply for a work placement at your organization as advertised in the March edition of the magazine *Caring for People*.

I am very interested in gaining experience with disabled people and their families as I feel sure this will give me the opportunity to develop both personally and professionally. I am particularly keen to work in an English-speaking country where I can apply my knowledge of English on a daily basis.

As you can see from the enclosed CV, I am currently studying at a German vocational college. My studies include Health Studies, Biology, Social Studies, Home Economics and English.

Through the experience I gained working as an au pair, I know that I enjoy helping people and can fit in well with families. My language abilities will also make me an asset to your team. My English is excellent, I am a native German speaker and, because of family ties, I also have conversational Polish.

I hope that you will consider my application and grant me an interview.

I look forward to hearing from you soon.

Yours sincerely

Leonie Kuhn

Leonie Kuhn

Enc: curriculum vitae

B Choose one of the jobs you found online (see page 21, exercise 4) and write a covering letter.
> *Writing formal letters, p. 186*

❗ Remember!

I **am interested in gaining** experience ...
● *to be interested in + -ing*

23

C No sweat!

> The final step in the application process is the interview. Here you will learn how to have a successful interview.

1 Mediation: tips for telephone interviews
> Mediation, S. 211

You have found some interesting tips about telephone interviews in a magazine. Read the text below and make notes in German. Use your notes to explain the tips to a friend who is going to do a telephone interview soon.

No sweat! It's only a telephone interview

Your first telephone interview needn't be scary. Just make sure that your interviewer hears that this phone call is as meaningful to you as if it were a face-to-face interview. Follow the tips below.

Always dress carefully for a telephone interview
Studies show that interviewees who take the call wearing appropriate clothing do better than interviewees wearing casual wear. Even though the interviewer cannot see you, you will feel – and sound – more confident and will make a better impression.

Understand the questions
By asking just a few questions, an interviewer can quickly decide if you are a likely candidate for the job. Here are the top five interview questions, and what the interviewer really wants to find out.

	Question	What the interviewer wants to find out
1	Can you tell me something about yourself? What are your hobbies, for example?	What kind of person are you? Should I spend time on this interview?
2	What made you apply for this position?	Why do you think you're the right person for the job?
3	What would you like to be doing five years from now?	If we take you on, will we be making an investment in the future of the company?
4	Is there anything you'd like to ask me?	Have you done any research on our company?
5	Would you be interested in coming in and talking with us face-to-face?	Are you still interested in the job?

Be prepared!
Have these things ready beside your phone:
> a copy of the job description
> a copy of your covering letter and your CV
> a notepad and a couple of pens so that you can take notes during the interview
> a list of your strengths and weaknesses
> a list of questions you want to ask the interviewer

Practice makes perfect!
Before the interview, role-play a telephone interview with a friend.

Unit 2　Applying for a job

2　Role-play: a telephone interview

Use the flow chart and the phrases below to role-play a telephone interview.

CHALLENGE! If you would prefer a challenge, Partner A turn to file C1 on page 184; Partner B turn to file C8 on page 185.

Partner A: Candidate　**Partner B:** Interviewer

- Answer the phone.
- Greet the interviewer and say you will be happy to answer his/her questions.
- Give your own answers to the questions.
- Ask the interviewer your questions.
- Thank the interviewer for calling and say goodbye.

- Greet the candidate when he/she answers the phone and give your own name. Say that you would like to ask a few questions.
- Ask five or six questions and respond appropriately to the replies.
- Ask the candidate if he/she has any questions and respond appropriately.
- Thank the candidate and say goodbye.

Telephoning

- Hello, this is … (speaking).
- I'm calling from … .
- Can I speak to … , please? / Is this … ?
- Speaking. / This is … .
- I'm sorry, I didn't understand that.
- Could you repeat that, please?
- I'm sorry, you're breaking up.
- Thank you for calling.

> Telephoning, p. 192

3　Listening: tips for face-to-face interviews

> Mit Hörverstehensaufgaben umgehen, S. 207

1/3

The next step in the process is the personal interview. You find an interesting podcast.

In this week's podcast, Mark, from the Social Pulse team, talks to Ann Haslam about face-to-face interviews. Ann is in charge of recruitment at Care Disability. She is an experienced interviewer and gives Mark a lot of useful tips.

A What do you think Ann will say about the following? Brainstorm with a partner, then listen and check.

dress • panic • handshake • eyes • body language • small talk • questions • research

B Listen again and take notes on the dos and don'ts of face-to-face interviews.

GUIDANCE If you would like guidance, turn to file G3 on page 173.

4　Writing an email: giving advice

> Writing emails, p. 188

A friend of yours who does not speak German is applying for a job for the first time. Write your friend an email describing the most important tips for telephone and face-to-face interviews.

D Practice and projects

1 Using modal verbs

A Choose the most suitable modal verb from the brackets to complete the sentences.

1 You (could / might / should) always prepare questions for the interviewer.
2 The interview is at ten. It's only nine o'clock now, so I (can / could / need not) hurry.
3 I (needn't / could / must) ask a question about training opportunities.
4 You (ought to / might / could not) find out where the interview will take place.
5 You (can't / mustn't / needn't) be late for the interview.
6 You (might not / could not / should not) give details about your parents' professions on your CV.
7 When you have a permanent job, you (mustn't / needn't / couldn't) borrow money any more.

B A friend of yours would like to volunteer at a nearby community centre. Give him/her tips using each modal verb from the box at least once.

> Modal auxiliary verbs, p. 216

> can • might (not) • must (not) • need (not) • ought to • should (not)

2 Writing a covering letter

Complete the covering letter with phrases from the box.

> a certificate • advertised • doing a work placement • enclose •
> I am currently studying • I studied • I look forward to • qualified

Dear Sir or Madam

Trainee Nursery Nurse – Work Placement

I refer to the offer of a work placement as a Trainee Nursery Nurse ●¹ in *The Daily Times* of 12 October.

●² Social and Health Care at the Dortmund Vocational College. Part of my course involves ●³.

As I hope to work in childcare after I have ●⁴, a work placement at your nursery would be ideal for me.

●⁵ English for six years at secondary school and did a first-aid and rescue course at my local swimming club. This course was given by the General Health Insurance Company and I received ●⁶ showing details about the course. A copy is available on request.

I ●⁷ a copy of my CV.

I believe I can add value to your nursery and ●⁸ hearing from you soon.

Yours faithfully

Unit 2 Applying for a job

3 In preparation for the project below, complete the Europass Curriculum Vitae that you downloaded from the Europass website with your personal details. Print out the final version.

Get that job! From job advert to interview

You are going to write a job advertisement, then apply for a work placement and practise an interview. Work with a partner to do all the steps below.

Step 1 You and your partner work for a local organization which offers work placements to social and health care students. Write an advertisement in English for the website. Include the following points:
- the name of your organization
- details of the work placement (number of weeks, what the student will have to do, etc.)
- how to apply
- a request for a copy of a Europass CV

Proofread your advertisement, write your names on it, then pin it up on the wall.

Step 2 With your partner, take a job advert from the wall and apply for the job. First write a draft of a covering letter and proofread it. Then "send" a final draft of your letter and a copy of both of your CVs to the pair who wrote the advert.
> *Writing formal letters, S. 186*

Step 3 The pair who advertised the job you have applied for will invite you and your partner to an interview. Remember to take your CV with you to the interview; you will be asked to go through it by the interviewers. Take turns to be interviewed. During your partner's interview, make notes on how he/she handles the questions.
> *Job interviews, p. 194*

Step 4 After the interview, work in groups of four to say how the interviews went. Did the candidates handle the questions confidently? Could they communicate effectively (vocabulary, grammar)? What about body language? Suggest where your partners might improve.

Step 5 Now swap roles so candidates become interviewers and vice versa. Do steps 3 and 4 in your new group.

Checking progress

Browse through the previous pages in the unit, looking at headings and pictures. What have you learned? What can you do now that you have learned these things?
- ✔ I can read and understand job advertisements. (Part A)
- ✔ I can complete the paperwork needed for a job application. (Part B)
- ✔ I can understand what is needed for a successful interview. (Part C)
- ✔ I can take part in a simulated job interview. (Part D)

Write down two more statements of your own.

How much has this unit helped you present yourself at your best? Work with a partner and make a list of criteria for successful interactions with others. Here are some ideas to start you off: sound friendly and polite, use appropriate vocabulary, etc.

Exam skills and strategies

Mit unbekannten Wörtern umgehen

Wichtig für:
- Leseverstehen
- schriftliche Mediation
- materialgestützten Aufsatz
- rollenbasierte Stellungnahme

Mit unbekannten Wörtern umgehen zu können ist eine sehr wichtige Kompetenz. Wenn Sie einen Text lesen, werden Sie sicherlich auf Wörter stoßen, die Sie nicht kennen. Das ist jedoch kein Grund, in Panik zu geraten. Man muss nicht jedes einzelne Wort kennen, um den ganzen Text zu verstehen.

Verbringen Sie nicht lange damit, einen Satz wieder und wieder zu lesen, weil Sie ein bestimmtes Wort nicht verstehen. Denken Sie über die allgemeine Aussage des Satzes nach und stellen Sie eine Vermutung an, welche Bedeutung das Wort haben könnte.

TIPPS Die folgenden Regeln können Ihnen dabei helfen, Text A zu lesen.

1 Oft können Sie die Bedeutung eines Wortes aus den umliegenden Wörtern erschließen.
   → Unemployment **crept** from 10.9% last year to 12% this year …
   Die ansteigenden Zahlen lassen erkennen, dass das Verb „ansteigen" bedeutet. Aufgrund der langen Zeitspanne könnte man sogar eine langsame Bewegung, die *creep* (kriechen) beschreibt, vermuten.

2 Sie können einen Teil des Wortes identifizieren. Betrachten Sie das Präfix (erster Teil eines zusammengesetzten Wortes) oder das Suffix (letzter Teil eines zusammengesetzten Wortes) und überlegen Sie, ob Sie es verstehen.
   → job**less** → **counter**productive
   Im ersten Beispiel heißt „-los" *less* . *counter* bedeutet „kontra" oder „gegen".

3 Sie können ein Wort als Bestandteil einer Wendung identifizieren.
   → … bringing **budget deficits** below 3%.
   Da das Wort *budget* zu diesem Ausdruck gehört, wissen Sie, dass es um Geld gehen muss, auch wenn Sie das Wort *deficit* nicht kennen (*budget deficits* = Haushaltsdefizite).

4 Das Wort oder die Wendung könnte im Text erklärt sein. Wenn ein Ausdruck ungewöhnlich, aber wichtig für die übergeordnete Bedeutung ist, steht die Erklärung häufig im Text.
   → **Austerity policies** have been introduced in many countries to save money …
   Der Zweck von *austerity policies* (Sparpolitik) wird genannt.

5 Sie wissen wahrscheinlich, ob das Wort ein Substantiv, Verb, Adjektiv oder Adverb ist. Dieses Wissen kann Ihnen helfen, die übergeordnete Bedeutung des Satzes zu verstehen.
   → The European commission has made plans to **boost** training and apprenticeships for young people …
   Boost ist ein Verb. Der Satzzusammenhang macht deutlich, dass es „anschieben" oder „bewegen" heißen muss. Die genaue Bedeutung ist nicht wichtig, aber der Sinn des Wortes wird deutlich.

6 Wenn ein Wort mit einem Großbuchstaben beginnt, bezeichnet es sehr wahrscheinlich einen Eigennamen. Manchmal wird die Person oder Institution etc. näher erklärt.
   → … according to **Eurostat**, the European statistics office.
   Wissen Sie, wer oder was *Eurostat* ist? Wenn das nicht der Fall ist, können Sie die Erklärung direkt im gleichen Satz finden.

Exam skills and strategies

Lesen Sie nun die Wörter im Zusammenhang. Die Zahl hinter dem hervorgehobenen Wort gibt die angewendete Regel (1–6) an.

A

Apprenticeships on the rise to combat unemployment

The European Commission has made plans to **boost**[5] training and apprenticeships for young people across Europe. This decision was reached after the **jobless**[2] rate in Europe reached new and unacceptable levels in February.

Unemployment **crept**[1] from 10.9% last year to 12% this year, according to **Eurostat**[6], the European statistics office. Approximately 26.3 million young people are out of work across the EU. **Austerity policies**[4] have been introduced in many countries to save money and help the economy by bringing budget **deficits**[3] below 3%. Unfortunately, these policies have been **counterproductive**[2], and have had a negative effect on economic growth and employment.

Lesen Sie nun den Rest des Artikels. Wenden Sie die Regeln auf die hervorgehobenen Wörter (a–f) an. Eine der Regeln kann nicht angewendet werden.

B

Natalia Aivazova[a], from the Peterson Institute for International Economics, stated that one reason many economies are still struggling with **sluggish**[b] growth and high unemployment is that young people do not have the skills that employers are looking for. Implementing apprenticeship programmes could help to solve this problem.

Brussels has started a **"Youth Guarantee" programme**[c], in which all EU member states give young people the possibility to get work within four months of leaving school or college, or to get more education. This **ensures**[d] that all young people have either employment, or an apprenticeship or **traineeship**[e].

Natalia Aivazova reported that Germany, Austria, and Switzerland, three countries with low youth unemployment and high levels of apprenticeship education, offer valuable **insights**[f] into the training of young people.

(230 words)

Decide whether these statements about the complete text are true, false, or are not found in the text. Give reasons for your answer.

a Since February last year, unemployment levels have risen by 5%.
b Unemployment rates in the UK rose in February 2013.
c Attempts to save money have had a negative effect on youth employment.
d Natalia Aivazova blames unskilled young people for slowing down economic growth.
e Many young people leave school or college and go abroad in search of work.
f Brussels has put a limit on the number of apprenticeships available to young people.
g The youth guarantee programme is open to school-leavers who have been unemployed for more than a year.
h Aivazova believes that many countries could learn from Germany, Switzerland and Austria.

▸ *Lösungen, S. 290*

A recent survey on care of the elderly found that approximately 414,000 over-65s live in residential care (old people's homes / nursing homes). Almost the same number of over-65s (414,780) receive community-based care and support at home. Of the people aged 65+ who receive adult social care and support services, 55% said their quality of life was "good", 35% said it was "all right" and 10% described their quality of life as "bad".
Research@ageuk.org.uk

Marie Stopes International is the UK's leading provider of sexual and reproductive health care services. Our nationwide network of sexual health clinics see over 100,000 men and women each year who come to us for information, advice and professional care.

3 Supporting families

1 Choose the most appropriate caption for the pictures and texts 1–9 above.

  a   Unwanted pregnancy? Talk things over with a counsellor
  b   Combining family with a career
  c   Divorce – when families break apart
  d   Equal chances for same-sex couples
  e   The next generation
  f   What shall we do with Granny?
  g   The dysfunctional family
  h   The traditional family
  i   Adopting across cultures

dysfunctional [dɪsˈfʌŋkʃənl]
Not working properly or normally.

2 Brainstorm other useful words and phrases that can be used to talk about the pictures. Then choose one of the pictures and describe it in detail to a partner. Say what the people in the picture might be thinking.

› Bilder beschreiben und analysieren, S. 210

She/He might be wondering whether …

They probably are …

It looks as if …

According to a 2013 poll, 14.8% of UK mothers did not have a job to return to after taking maternity leave, and 11% of women had been replaced by their maternity leave cover. Of the 40% of women who returned to work, almost half (45.53%) felt that the job they were given when they returned to work was less interesting than the job they had before they took leave.   www.slatergordon.co.uk

 Which of the pictures illustrate types of families or situations you are familiar with? Tell your partner.

What's to come

In this unit, you will …
- consider different family models.
- discuss the problems and patterns of dysfunctional families.
- describe a case involving an unwanted pregnancy and consider criteria for adoption.

At the end of the unit, you will write and produce a scene from a scripted reality show that focuses on the family.

Before you begin, think about where your support might be effective, i.e. what difficulties you might deal with. What professional skills might you need to use while supporting families?

A Meet the family

S You have been accepted as a trainee at a family support centre in London. The organization helps children, adults and their families cope with difficult situations. As part of your training, the senior social worker asks you to look into different types of families and some of the problems they face.

1 **Reading: defining the family**

On your first day at the family support centre, the senior social worker shows you and two other trainees a folder with the different types of families they are dealing with at the moment.

A Work with two partners and match the English expressions for six types of family set-ups below to the labels given to them by social workers.

extended family • intercultural family • migrant family • nuclear family • single-parent family • stepfamily

| a family that has moved to a new country **1** | grandparents, parents and children **2** | one parent with a child or children **3** | parents and children **4** | parents from different cultural backgrounds **5** | (step)parents and (step) children **6** |

B Still working in your group of three, choose two labels each and scan the texts below to find the description of "your" types of family. Then read your two texts and be prepared to share your information with your partners.

a
Until the middle of the 20th century, if you had asked western Europeans to describe a family, they would probably have described a mother, a father and their children. The husband was the "breadwinner" who went out to earn the money. His wife stayed at home and was a full-time housewife and mother. In the 1950s, this type of family was the one that the media often presented in adverts. This type of family still exists today but it has become less common than it used to be.

b
This type of family hasn't changed much over time. Wherever they live, the family members prefer to hold on to traditional set-ups that they have brought with them from their homeland, e.g. a patriarchal household in which the women stay at home and the men go out to do business. In some cases, the children marry within their own culture; sometimes the marriages are arranged. On the other hand, some of these families are fully "integrated" and look and behave exactly the same as "native" families in the new country.

c
Until the early 1960s, this type of family was usually the result of the death of one parent. Today, these families are more likely to be the result of separation or divorce. In the majority of cases, the mother looks after the child or children, with the father having access on certain days. Some parents split the caring down the middle, and the child or children live part of the week with one parent and the rest of the week with the other.

d
It is less common than it used to be, but you still see this type of family today: a man or a woman – or both – living with one of their children and their child's family. If the grandparent is still fit, he or she can be a real help to a working mum. Sometimes, however, the older person is in need of care. You'll often find that the daughter or daughter-in-law is the main carer.

e
As far as this type of family is concerned, any couple with different cultural backgrounds should ideally take time to sort out any problems to do with their own cultural differences before they start a family. If they can get it right, their children could grow up in a culturally-rich environment, experiencing the best of both parents' worlds. They might learn both parents' languages and get to know both parents' countries.

f
This family, in which at least one parent brings a child from a previous relationship, is a common set-up today as a result of the rise in divorce. Making the set-up work can be difficult, especially when parents from different cultural backgrounds take their children into a new relationship. When it does work, close bonds can develop between family members. The experience of growing up in such a family can be very beneficial to a child.

Unit 3   Supporting families

C Work together to complete the table below using keywords from your texts.

Type of family	Family members	How this type of family comes into being	How this type of family has changed over the years
…	…	…	…

D CHALLENGE! Choose one of the types of families and point out the potential problems that might arise among the family members.

2 Discussion: talking about change

Exchange information about the situation in your town, school or circle of friends. How have things changed over the last ten years? What kind of families were there ten years ago? What kind of families are there now?

There used to be fewer …

Ten years ago, it was unusual to see … .

Lately, there have been more …

Describing change

Things **have changed** over the years.
Since the beginning of the millennium, families **have grown** …
- We use the present perfect to connect the past with the present. › *Present perfect, p. 214*

In the 1950s, women usually **stayed** at home. Grandparents **used to live** with the younger members of the family, but now …
- We use the simple past to talk about a state or habit in the past. With *used to* + infinitive we can contrast a past habit with what we do now. › *Simple past, p. 213*

3 Watching a video: "Just a family"

A The senior social worker now asks you to watch a video about an American family. At the start of the video, Heather Greenwood introduces some members of her family. Watch the introduction with the sound off and make notes about Heather's family. Then watch, listen and check.

B Watch the video until the end. Describe the family. Talk about positive and negative experiences.

 If you would like guidance, turn to file G4 on page 173.   › *Mit Sehverstehensaufgaben umgehen, S. 207*

4 Writing: the changing family

The senior social worker has asked you to report on what you have learned about families. Write a text describing how families have changed over the years. Describe the potential problems modern families could have and why. Point out how these changes influence the types of problems social workers have to deal with.   › *Eine Stellungnahme schreiben, S. 208*

 If you would like guidance, turn to file G7 on page 174.

B Problems and patterns

> **S** You are halfway through your training period at the family support centre. The senior social worker would like you and the other trainees to give a talk on dysfunctional families.

1 Reading: What is a dysfunctional family?

The senior social worker asks you to consider what makes a family dysfunctional and gives you some tasks to do in small groups.

A Decide if the statements are true or false, and find proof for your decision in the text below.

1. A dysfunctional family is not a healthy family.
2. A crisis often turns a healthy family into a dysfunctional family.
3. Many dysfunctional families start to behave better after the stress is over.
4. Children who grow up in a dysfunctional family could take their problems with them when they have a family of their own.
5. Every dysfunctional family behaves in the same way.

> When we describe a family as being "dysfunctional", we mean that something continually happens in the family which stops the family functioning in a healthy way.
> Almost every family is faced with stressful events at some time, e.g. a serious illness or a death in the family, but healthy families usually get back to normal after the crisis has passed. In dysfunctional families, problems are always there and are never dealt with in a healthy way. Negative patterns of behaviour are repeated on a regular basis and are often handed down from generation to generation.
> There are many types of dysfunctional families. Some parents neglect their children. Other parents control their children's lives and never allow them any independence. In some families, children are the victims of sexual and/or physical abuse.
> (130 words)

B Copy the Venn diagram and sort these common behaviour patterns of dysfunctional families into the correct sections.

> adultery • alcoholism • bullying • lying •
> manipulative behaviour • mental abuse •
> physical abuse / battering • playing truant •
> promiscuity • sexual abuse •
> stealing from parents • substance abuse

parents — both — children

Die Figuren Bart und Homer Simpson auf dem Walk of Fame in LA.

C What soap operas or series do you know? Describe some of the families who appear in them.

- What are the relationships like between parents and children, and between siblings?
- What behaviour patterns do the family members often/sometimes/never show?
- Say how the families might be described as dysfunctional.

If you do not know these kinds of TV shows, ask other people to describe them.

> **Talking about behaviour**
>
> Healthy families **usually** get back to normal after a crisis.
> Characters on TV soaps **frequently** commit adultery.
> Bart Simpson **often** plays truant; his sister **never** does.
>
> - We use adverbs of frequency to say how often something happens, from *never* (0 times) to *always* (100%). ▶ Adverbs of frequency, p. 223

Unit 3 Supporting families

2 Listening: describing the dysfunctional family
> *Mit Hörverstehensaufgaben umgehen, S. 207*

You next listen to a podcast that could be useful for your research.

In this week's podcast from the Social Pulse team, Fran talks to Jim Allan about working with dysfunctional families. Jim is a senior social worker, working in a London family support centre.

A Before you listen, explain what these phrases from the interview mean.

GUIDANCE *If you would like guidance, turn to file G5 on page 173.*

1. to cope with the situation alone
2. afraid to go to a women's refuge or seek assistance
3. to break out of the pattern
4. lack of empathy
5. marginalized
6. denial
7. to stand by and do nothing

1/4

B Now listen and check your answers with what is said in the interview.

C What else have you learned about dysfunctional families? Answer these questions.

1. Why does everyone in a dysfunctional family accept bad behaviour as normal?
2. Why does an abused child often have to cope with his/her situation alone?
3. What kind of help does Jim offer to the families he works with?
4. How can someone who was brought up in a dysfunctional family break out of the pattern?

3 Discussing two cases

The senior social worker now gives you two summaries of cases that the centre has dealt with and asks you to explain what is happening.

Getting help

Many types of institutions offer help to families in trouble. Here are just a few:
- family pastoral care *Familienseelsorge*
- women's refuge *Frauenhaus*
- youth welfare services *Jugendhilfe*
- welfare department *Sozialamt*
- family doctor *Hausarzt/-ärztin*
- district nurse *Pflegekraft in der ambulanten Pflege*

A Work with a partner and read the case notes in your file. Look up any words you don't know and make notes. Then use the information you have learned about dysfunctional families to describe and explain the case to your partner.

Partner A: file 1, page 152
Partner B: file 8, page 155

I think the mother should go ...

B Where would you recommend that the families get assistance?

C **CHALLENGE!** Talk about a case currently featured in the news. Describe the situation and say how you would support the family in question.

If a child is afraid, he/she might call ...

4 Presentation: supporting dysfunctional families

> *Präsentieren, S. 209*

Now it is time to give your talk on dysfunctional families and offer suggestions on how to support them. Focus on dysfunctional families in general or describe a particular family you know. If you like, you can talk about a family you have seen on TV.

35

C Making decisions

> You are nearing the end of your training at the family support centre. The senior social worker asks you to describe one of your cases: a pregnant teenager who has decided to give her baby up for adoption. In a team, you will assess prospective adoptive couples who would like to adopt the baby.

1 Reading and summarizing case notes

A Read the case notes below and do these tasks with a partner.

1. Describe the areas of conflict and dysfunctional behaviour in Molly's family.
2. Identify the patterns you see running through the family.
3. Explain Molly's reasons for putting the baby up for adoption.
4. Describe how things are proceeding.

Case # 358	Pregnant teenager

Molly P. is 15 years old. She is pregnant. She lives with her mother, stepfather and two half-brothers. The family has changed neighbourhoods frequently to avoid paying rent, and Molly "thinks" she attended six different primary schools. In November, the family moved into the Brixton area and Molly started to attend the Holy Cross Secondary School.

Molly was referred to us by the school social worker who had a chat with Molly when she noticed changes to Molly's figure. Molly is not sure who the father of the baby is. The only person who knows about her pregnancy is her 16-year-old best friend.

Since moving to Brixton, Molly has stayed for a few days with her friend because there was trouble at home. Examples she gave included her stepfather's aggressive behaviour when drinking, verbal abuse from her mother and one brother's hostility.

The family has been known to the family support team for two years. Molly's mother was also a single, teenage mother. She decided to keep her child and she continued to live with her own (single) mother. Molly was brought up well by her grandmother and insists that she was never neglected. When Molly was eight years old, she and her mother moved in with her current stepfather. The couple have two common children, both boys. According to Molly, her two half-brothers "are treated like gods".

Molly is realistic about her situation and does not want to bring up her child in her current circumstances. Apart from the fact that she is now in her 26th week of pregnancy and cannot legally have a termination, Molly is from a Roman Catholic family. She has decided to give her child up for adoption as she would like to see it grow up in a nice family and be well looked after. She is attending an antenatal clinic regularly, the pregnancy is developing normally and she should be able to give birth without any problems.

We are liaising with the adoption agency and are assessing potential adoptive couples.

B You want to make sure you understand some key vocabulary. Match these German words with their equivalents from the case notes and the info box.

1. *schwanger; Schwangerschaft; vorgeburtlich*
2. *Schwangerschaftsabbruch legal vornehmen lassen; Abtreibung*
3. *entbinden; (ein Kind) großziehen*
4. *ein Kind zur Adoption freigeben; potenzielle Adoptivpaare*
5. *(eine Klientin / einen Klienten) überweisen; mit jdm zusammenarbeiten*

Termination of pregnancy

Medical professionals tend to use the term "termination" when talking about induced *(eingeleitet)* abortions because it sounds less traumatic to the patient. It is also more precise, as the term "abortion" also refers to the spontaneous miscarriage of a foetus.

C Summarize the case for the senior social worker.
Partner A, you are the trainee. Use phrases from the box on page 37.
Partner B, you are the senior social worker. Ask questions to get more information and to check the facts.

Unit 3   Supporting families

Describing a case

The client
- The client's name is …
- He/She is … years old.
- He/She lives …

The family background
- The client's family is …
- He/She was looked after by his/her …
- When he/she was … years old, …

Client's assessment of the situation
- The client is (not) able to understand his/her situation.
- He/She would (not) like to …

The current situation
- We are looking into …
- We have spoken to … and are currently …

> *Describing a case, p.198*

---

2 **Discussion: assessing adoptive parents** > *An Diskussionen teilnehmen, S. 210*

You are on a team assessing possible adoptive parents for Molly's baby. Follow the steps below.

A Think: In groups of six, brainstorm family situations and other criteria which should be taken into account when assessing adoptive parents, such as whether both parents work, etc. Discuss which of the aspects might negatively affect the potential adopters' application.

B Pair: Divide into three pairs. With your partner, read the notes on the candidates in your file.

Partners A and B: file 4, page 153
Partners C and D: file 11, page 156
Partners E and F: file 6, page 154

C Share: Work again in your team of six. Describe "your" set of parents and point out the agency's recommendations. Decide in your team which (if any) of the candidates might be suitable. Explain your decisions to the class.

Tom and Julie Laurence, with children
Kevin and Gale Jameson
Evan and Helen Fletcher

---

3 **Writing: termination or adoption?** > *Elne Stellungnahme schreiben, S. 208*

During your time with the family support team, you have counselled many couples on the pros and cons of termination and adoption and supported them in their choice. Before you leave the team, the senior social worker asks you to write a short text for the trainee file.

GUIDANCE *If you would like guidance, turn to file G9 on page 175.*

D Practice and projects

1 Describing change

A Put the verb in brackets into the correct form.

1. The definition of "family" (change) over the decades.
2. Intercultural families (always be) common in London.
3. Many years ago, most mothers (not go out) to work; instead they (stay) at home and (take) care of the house and children.
4. Divorce rates (rise) over the years, which (mean) an increase in single-parent families and stepfamilies.
5. Over the last ten years, more and more gay couples (adopt) children.
6. Until recently, single-parent families (not get) enough help from the social services.

> *Present perfect, p. 214; Simple past, p. 213*

B Make sentences with *used to* and *didn't use to* about couples and families fifty years ago.

1. bigger families
2. marry more than once
3. take leave after childbirth
4. share household duties
5. take care of elderly parents at home

2 Saying how often things happen

Decide where to put the adverbs of frequency in the following sentences.

1. The Browns are a dysfunctional family. They are fighting. (always)
2. Mr Brown comes home drunk and beats his wife. (often)
3. The family eats together (never) and the children look hungry. (always)
4. In the old days, single mothers left home to give birth to their babies in secret. (sometimes)
5. The grandmothers brought up the babies as their own children. (frequently)
6. Single mothers have more choices nowadays. (usually)

> *Word order, p. 223*

3 Completing case notes

Complete the case notes with words and phrases from the box.

> appointment • care home • children in danger • community service • drugs • liaising • organization • pregnant • social services • terminate

Janice W. is 14 years old. She is three months ⬤¹. She was born in Glasgow, but is currently living in a home for ⬤² in Lennoxtown.

Janice was referred to our ⬤³ by the home. She has attended one antenatal appointment at the local hospital. A follow-up ⬤⁴ has been made.

Janice's family is known to the Glasgow ⬤⁵. Her mother is on ⬤⁶ and an older brother is currently doing 90 days' ⬤⁷. Janice says that the father of the baby is a 15-year-old boy who also lives in the ⬤⁸. Janice says that she is not "with" him any longer. He does not know that she is pregnant.

Janice does not want to ⬤⁹ the pregnancy and would like to keep the baby when it is born. We are ⬤¹⁰ with a home for teenage mothers in Glasgow.

Unit 3   Supporting families

Producing a scene from a scripted reality show

Your task is to work in groups and develop a scene from a scripted (or semi-scripted) reality show in which a carer or counsellor is helping a family cope with difficulties.

Step 1 Talk about which reality shows on TV focus on the family. What support are families given? Who supports them? How are conflicts shown? Make a mind map.   > *Mindmaps erstellen, S. 207*

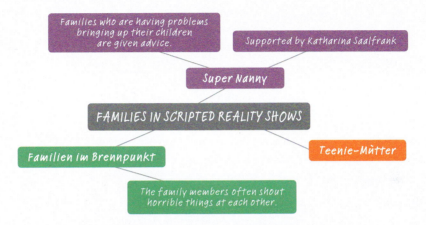

Step 2 Choose one of the shows and brainstorm ideas for an episode. Make notes.

Step 3 Use your notes to produce a list of characters. One of the characters should be a carer or counsellor.

Step 4 Now, write your story as a report. Explain the situation, say who is involved and say how the characters are being supported.

Step 5 Imagine an important scene showing how the carer or counsellor supports the family. Rewrite that part of your report as a TV script.

Step 6 Present your show to the class and act out the scene you have chosen.

Checking progress

Browse through the previous pages in the unit, looking at headings and pictures.
What have you learned? What can you do now that you have learned these things?
- ✓ I can describe different types of family set-ups.   (Part A)
- ✓ I can recognize some of the problems and patterns that can occur in dysfunctional families.   (Part B)
- ✓ I can describe a case and summarize information for an adoption application.   (Part C)
- ✓ I can present a fictional case and show how a carer or counsellor might support a family.   (Part D)

Write down two more statements of your own.

How has this unit helped you understand different types of families you may work with one day? How have you used your own life experience while working through this unit?

Exam skills and strategies

Textproduktion: Umgang mit Operatoren

Wichtig für:
- Textproduktionsaufgaben, die Operatoren enthalten

In einer Prüfung kann es vorkommen, dass Sie einen Text lesen und dazu Textproduktionsaufgaben bearbeiten sollen, die Arbeitsanweisungen, sog. „Operatoren", enthalten. Es ist wichtig, sich mit diesen Begriffen vertraut zu machen und zu wissen, was bei den einzelnen Operatoren verlangt wird. Operatoren sind in drei „Anforderungsbereiche" unterteilt: I – Inhalt, II – Analyse und III – Interpretation.

> *Liste der Operatoren, S. 203*

BEISPIEL-AUFGABE Read the text on p. 41 and complete the tasks a–d.
a **State** the author's main idea in your own words.
b **Outline** the aspects of diversity that are mentioned in this text.
c **Analyse** the author's use of informal language to engage readers.
d **Discuss** possible reasons that TV programmes are made about non-stereotypical families.

TIPPS

1 Überfliegen Sie den Text, damit Sie einen Eindruck vom Inhalt bekommen. Lesen Sie dann die Textproduktionsaufgaben. Behalten Sie diese im Hinterkopf und lesen Sie den Text gründlich. Durchsuchen Sie danach den Text auf Informationen, die für die erste Aufgabe relevant sind.

> *Schwierige Texte lesen, S. 16*

2 Die Operatoren „state" und „outline" in Aufgaben a und b gehören zum Anforderungsbereich I und untersuchen, wie gut Sie den Inhalt des Textes verstehen und wie genau und klar Sie diesen wiedergeben können. Es ist jedoch erforderlich, dass Sie Ihre eigenen Worte verwenden.
→ a *The main idea of the text is that families have always been diverse, and television programmes have always reflected this.*

3 Der Operator „outline" in Aufgabe b erfordert eine Beschreibung einiger Fakten des Textes. Um die Fakten zu organisieren, empfiehlt es sich, Ihre Ideen vor dem Schreiben zu ordnen und sich eine Struktur für den Text zu überlegen.

> *Mindmaps und Gliederungen erstellen, S. 76*

4 Der Operator „analyse" in Aufgabe c gehört zum Anforderungsbereich II. Hierbei müssen Sie untersuchen, wie der Autor / die Autorin den Text aufgebaut hat, um einen bestimmten Zweck zu erreichen.
Der Zweck eines Textes könnte sein, zu informieren, überzeugen, beschreiben, Anweisungen zu erteilen oder ein Thema zu erörtern. Wenn Sie einen Text analysieren, sollten Sie die verwendeten Mittel und deren Wirkung verknüpfen und die einzelnen Aspekte mit Beispielen aus dem Text stützen.
→ c *The author uses informal language to talk directly to the reader. For example, when he asks questions like "What is a `normal family´?" at the start of the text. Informal phrases like "Let's look at …" and "Let's skip ahead to …" also speak directly to the reader and function as invitations to keep reading.*

5 Operatoren aus den Anforderungsbereichen I und II verlangen sachliche Antworten. Ihre persönliche Meinung über den Text sollten Sie nicht einbringen.
→ ~~I was surprised~~ *It is surprising that television families were non-stereotypical even in the 1950s.*

Exam skills and strategies

6 Der Operator „discuss" in Aufgabe d gehört zum Anforderungsbereich III. Hier müssen Sie „zwischen den Zeilen lesen" und sowohl die explizite als auch die implizite Bedeutung oder Absicht erklären. Oft kann es auch vorkommen, dass Sie Vor- und Nachteile aufzeigen und eine persönliche Beurteilung geben müssen.

> Einen Aufsatz oder eine Stellungnahme schreiben, S. 88

→ d *TV production companies need to make money from their product. Therefore, they make programmes that people want to watch. Clearly, TV shows about unusual families are more interesting to viewers. Another reason may be that ...*

Television as the mirror of family life

What is a "normal family"? Many people would say a normal family is a mother, father, two children, possibly a pet, that all live together in a house in the suburbs. But ... were families ever really like this? Television programmes often mirror real life. Let's look at different TV families from popular American television programmes and see how many of them really reflect this stereotype.

Right back at the start of commercial television in the 1950s, the most popular American TV show was *I Love Lucy*. This featured Lucille Ball and her real-life husband, Desi Arnaz, who was from Cuba, and six years younger than her. This inter-cultural, older-woman-younger-man couple were childless when the series began. Eventually, the TV couple had a child, because Lucille Ball became pregnant in real life – at the age of 40. In general, the family was very different to the stereotypical family of this era.

Let's skip ahead to the 1970s. At this time, the most popular family on TV was the *Brady Bunch* family. It was the story of a single man with three boys who met a single woman with three girls. The couple married, and all of them lived together happily. The writer of the show read that around 20–30% of marriages had at least one child from a previous marriage, and wanted to represent that on television.

The 1980s gave TV audiences *The Cosby Show*, which was about a wealthy, upper-middle class family. Both parents had successful careers, but always had time for their five children. The Cosbys were the epitome of a perfect family. There was just one unexpected aspect – the family was African-American. They were successful, well-educated, and black.

One of the few famous stereotypical families in TV history is *The Simpsons*. They fulfil every cliché about a traditional family. The parents and children live in a house in the suburbs with their pets. The mother stays at home, and the father works. And they have provided TV audiences with numerous examples of family dysfunction.

The most famous American family currently on TV are the Pritchetts from *Modern Family*. Mitchell and Claire's parents are divorced. Their father is now married to a much younger woman from Columbia. They live with her son from her first marriage, and their common child. Although Claire is traditionally married with children, Mitchell lives with his same-sex partner, Cameron, and their adopted Vietnamese daughter.

So, the most famous TV families from the 1950s until now have not been homogeneous, nuclear or perfect. They've been culturally diverse, patchwork, and problematic. Family diversity is nothing new, and has been represented on television since the first shows were broadcast.

(451 words)

a **Describe** the stereotypical family the author says is *not* shown on television.
b **Examine** the author's use of descriptive language to illustrate the contrast between the stereotypical families and the families represented in the series.
c **Discuss** a television family you know but which is *not* mentioned in the text, and whether or not it is really representative of modern family life.

> Lösungen, S. 290

4 Learning to listen

1 Talk about the picture above. Describe the people you see and say who or what might be threatening them. Point out what might happen to them.

The child might be …

Sometimes elderly people …

2 Say where someone who feels threatened might find help. Use the posters on the opposite page for ideas.

3 Listen to the song and describe Luka's situation. What does Luka expect from the neighbours?

Perhaps Luka is a …

Luka might …

If the neighbours …, then Luka …

1/5

My name is Luka
I live on the second floor
I live upstairs from you
Yes, I think you've seen me before
If you hear something late at night
Some kind of trouble, some kind of fight

Just don't ask me what it was …

I think it's 'cause I'm clumsy
I try not to talk too loud
Maybe it's because I'm crazy
I try not to act too proud
They only hit until you cry
After that you don't ask why

You just don't argue anymore …

Yes I think I'm okay
I walked into the door again
If you ask, that's what I'll say
And it's not your business anyway
I guess I'd like to be alone
With nothing broken, nothing thrown

Just don't ask me how I am …

(Suzanne Vega, 'Luka', Solitude Standing, 1987)

What's to come

In this unit, you will …
- learn how to recognize the unspoken signs of domestic abuse.
- learn about school violence and victimization.
- practise active listening in a telephone counselling session.

At the end of the unit, you will write and act out a helpline dialogue.

Before you begin, name the skills you need to be able to listen carefully and understand what a client really wants to tell you.

A Listening between the lines

> Developing sensitivity to signs and signals is an important part of caring for people. You are attending a three-day seminar for trainee counsellors who have to deal with violence and crime. On day one, the focus is on domestic abuse.

1 Reading: understanding unspoken signs

The trainer has distributed a handout describing the unspoken signs of domestic abuse, i.e. abuse between partners in a relationship.

A With a partner, read the text and use a–h to complete the gaps on the handout below.

  a depressed, anxious or suicidal.
  b with their partner to report where they are and what they're doing.
  c clothes or accessories which might hide bruises or scars (e.g. wearing sunglasses indoors).
  d in public without their partner.
  e everything their partner says and does.
  f access to money, credit cards or the car.
  g work or social occasions, without giving an explanation.
  h major personality changes (e.g. an active person becomes passive and withdrawn).

Counsellor Training Seminar, DAY 1

Understanding unspoken signs of abuse

It can happen to anyone, whether rich or poor, educated or uneducated. The problem is often overlooked, excused or denied. No one knows with certainty what goes on behind closed doors, but there are some clear signs and symptoms of emotional abuse and domestic violence that you should be aware of.

General warning signs
Someone who is being abused could:
- seem afraid or anxious to please their partner.
- often check in ● 1
- go along with ● 2

Warning signs of physical violence
Someone who is a victim of domestic violence may:
- have frequent injuries, and say they were caused by accidents.
- wear ● 3
- frequently miss ● 4

Warning signs of isolation
Someone who is being restricted by their abuser might:
- be kept away from family and friends.
- have limited ● 5
- rarely appear ● 6

Psychological warning signs
Someone who is being emotionally abused could:
- have very low self-esteem, even if they used to be confident.
- be ● 7
- exhibit ● 8

B How can you spot an abuser? Use the correct form of the words from the box to complete the sentences and to make up your own.

Abusers often seem / appear / look …
When they are alone with their victims, they act …
When they are with other people, they often behave / react …

> aggressive • angry • anxious • bad • calm •
> confident • excited • friendly • kind •
> normal • sorry • unhappy

Talking about how people look and behave

When other people are around, an abuser often appears to be **normal**. Abusers treat their victims **badly**.

- We use adjectives to say how something or somebody is, looks, etc.
- We use adverbs to say how something happens or is done.
> Adjectives and adverbs, p. 222

44

Unit 4 Learning to listen

2 Listening: the cycle of violence in domestic abuse

The trainer is going to talk about the stages in the cycle of violence from the point of view of the abuser. Before he starts, he gives you another handout with some incomplete slides from his presentation and asks you to complete them.

Asking for and giving opinions

- I think that … . What about you?
- I don't agree. How do you feel about …?
- Yes, you're probably right.
- What do you think of …?
- I'm not sure. How about … instead?

> Discussions, p. 196

1/6

A Work with a partner and look at the six slides. Decide where the words below should go on the slides. Then listen and check.

fantasizing about abuse • feel sorry • making excuses • "normal behaviour" • physical abuse • setting a trap

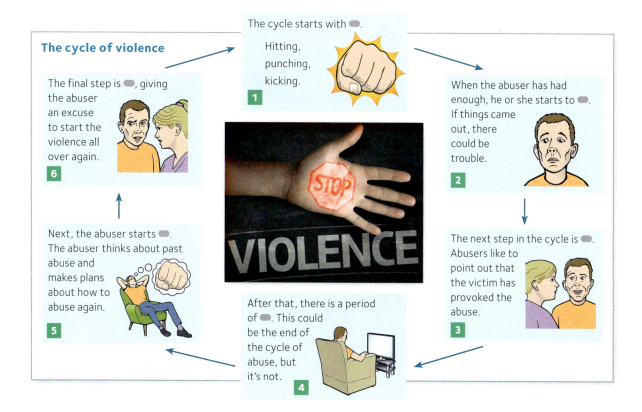

The cycle of violence

The cycle starts with ●.

1 Hitting, punching, kicking.

2 When the abuser has had enough, he or she starts to ●. If things came out, there could be trouble.

3 The next step in the cycle is ●. Abusers like to point out that the victim has provoked the abuse.

4 After that, there is a period of ●. This could be the end of the cycle of abuse, but it's not.

5 Next, the abuser starts ●. The abuser thinks about past abuse and makes plans about how to abuse again.

6 The final step is ●, giving the abuser an excuse to start the violence all over again.

B Work in small groups. Listen to the trainer again and make notes on the points below, then discuss the cycle of violence together, adding your own ideas.

1 the reasons why the abuser feels sorry
2 the usefulness of blaming the victim
3 how physical violence is like taking drugs
4 the purpose of the trap

---

3 Writing: domestic abuse

Write a short summary in German of the main points you have learned in the seminar so far.

 GUIDANCE *If you would like guidance, turn to file G31 on page 183.*

45

B School violence and victimization

> S It is day two of the seminar and the focus is on violence and victimization in schools.

1 Reading: violence and victimization in schools

The trainer starts the session by asking you to read about the four main forms of violence and victimization in schools. Get into four groups, distribute the topics below and read your text.

Text A: traditional bullying (file 7, page 154)

Text C: sexual harassment and violence (file 12, page 156)

Text B: cyberbullying (file 3, page 152)

Text D: violence associated with gangs, weapons and fighting (file 17, page 159)

A On your own, skim your text and make a note of three words or expressions which you think are useful for discussing violence in schools. Then pool the useful words and expressions with the others in your group and make sure everybody knows what they mean.

B Read your text again and summarize the contents. Make sure your group agrees on the main points.

C Now work with three people, one from each of the other groups, and draw up and complete a table with three headings:

types of violence or victimization • forms it takes • facts and figures

2 Listening: finding causes

A school psychologist has just given a talk about the causes of school violence and victimization at the seminar. She is now ready to take questions.

A Before you listen, write down three possible causes of school violence and victimization. Then compare your ideas with a partner's and make a list.

1/7

B Now listen. Which of the items on your list does the school psychologist mention?

C What words and phrases did the speakers use to say the following? Find the English equivalents, then say how they relate to the topic.

1 Gruppenzwang
2 sich (in eine Gruppe) einfügen
3 erniedrigende Situationen
4 jdn verspotten
5 kichern
6 unmännlich
7 auf jdm herumhacken
8 Streber/in
9 Vorurteile

Unit 4   Learning to listen

3 Talking: recognizing signs
> An Diskussionen teilnehmen, S. 210

Read these statements from parents whose children were victimized at school. What were the causes? What were the signs that something was wrong?

> Fiona was a star pupil. She was liked by everyone, especially her teachers. She was in the school choir and was enjoying training to be a cheerleader. Then, suddenly, her marks dropped and she stopped all her extra-curricular activities.
>
> My daughter gets migraines. She says she is too ill to go to school. We are not from around here, and I know the teacher doesn't like her or any of the other kids from our country.
>
> Paul is smaller than all the other boys in his class and is often bullied. He developed neurodermatitis and scratched himself till his arms bled. Now the boys make comments about the scratches, and the bullying has become worse.
>
> The cyberbullying began with a dispute over a boy my daughter had dated for a while. She stopped going out with the boy, but the bullying didn't stop. She developed an eating disorder. Now she only weighs 36 kilos.
>
> The gang leader gave my son a knife and told him he had to prove that he was not gay. He was supposed to stab the teacher. Instead, he simply stopped going to school. We only found out about it when we had a letter from the school saying that he was playing truant.

4 Discussion: establishing a violence-free environment

The trainer has asked you to brainstorm solutions for keeping violence out of schools.

A Work in groups and come up with some possible solutions. Pool your results with other groups and make a list on the board.

> stamp out neighbourhood gangs
> try to get parents to go to parent-teacher evenings

B Talk in your group about your solutions and the expected results.

If you stamp out neighbourhood gangs, then …

If parents go to parent-teacher evenings, they …

Talking about possible solutions and expected results

If you **check** students for weapons when they come to school, there **will be** fewer injuries.
- We can use type 1 *if*-sentences to talk about possible actions or situations and the results you can expect from them.
> If-sentences, p. 220

5 Giving a talk: school violence and victimization
> Mindmaps erstellen, S. 207; Präsentieren, S. 209

The trainer asks you to give a talk about school violence and victimization.

A Work in groups. Use information from this day of the seminar to produce a mind map. Include forms of violence and victimization, the causes and the signs that someone might be a victim.

B Use your mind map to prepare and then give your talk. Finish your talk by making some suggestions about what might be done to prevent the problems.

C I'm listening

> On the third day of the seminar, you are going to focus on listening to and reacting to victims of violence who need help. The medium for dealing with this is the telephone helpline.

1 Discussion: making referrals

The trainer begins the session today by explaining the need to respect a caller's anonymity. However, there are times when a counsellor must make a decision to call in one of the emergency services or suggest that the caller contact another professional. The trainer asks you to brainstorm situations in which you would find it necessary to a) immediately get help for the caller and b) give the caller details of who to contact.

A You and your group have come up with the list below. Sort the situations into the categories **a** or **b**. Say what service(s) you would contact or advise the caller to contact.

The caller
1 is a woman who has been raped.
2 is a child who says that she and her baby brother have been alone for two days.
3 is an alcoholic and says he would like to stop drinking.
4 is a teenager who is the victim of cyberbullying.
5 tells you that she has swallowed a whole bottle of sleeping pills.
6 would like to get off drugs.

B Brainstorm more situations where clients need to be referred to other services. Say what services you would contact or suggest to the caller.

Making referrals

- I would recommend that the person call …
- I'd suggest that the client get in touch with …
- I think he/she should call …
- I would contact …

the police • a counsellor • youth protection services • a doctor • his/her therapist • his/her general practitioner

> Making referrals, p. 198

2 Listening: a helpline call

Encouraging clients to talk can help them get in touch with their feelings. The trainer plays a recording which was made especially for the seminar so you can see how active listening works.

1/8

A Listen to the call and describe the situation. Identify the problem and the suggestion the counsellor makes.

B Listen again and pay attention to the counsellor's language. Choose guidance or challenge and follow the instructions in your file.

GUIDANCE If you would like guidance, turn to file G8 on page 174.
CHALLENGE! If you would prefer a challenge, turn to file C2 on page 184.

Unit 4 Learning to listen

3 Reading: skills for active listening

The trainer asks you to read a text about active listening and gives you some tasks to make sure you understand the main points.

A Answer these questions using information from the handout.

1 What is active listening?
2 How do you listen actively?
3 Why should you listen actively?
4 How can you show a client that you are interested?
5 How will your feedback help the client?

B Which of the techniques in the list of tips did the counsellor on the recording in exercise 2 do? Explain how he did them or what he said.

Counsellor Training Seminar, DAY 3

Skills for active listening when working with clients

Have you ever told somebody a story and got no reaction? The person you were talking to was present, but you knew that he/she was not actually listening to you. How did you feel? If your story was not vitally important, you may have gone away from the encounter feeling disappointed at the listener's lack of interest. But what if you wanted to talk about a problem and hoped that the listener could help you solve it? What if your problem was a matter of life and death? As counsellors, we are often told about serious issues. We need to listen actively to our clients, whether face-to-face or over the phone.

Active listening

Active listening means giving your full attention to the speaker, concentrating fully on what is being said and paying attention to how the message is being given.

It is important to show the client that you are listening. If you don't do this, they may think that what they are talking about is uninteresting to you, the listener. By using verbal and non-verbal messages you can reassure the client that you are indeed interested. Your "feedback" helps make the client feel more at ease and enables them to communicate more easily, openly and honestly.

Active listening is a skill every counsellor has to learn. It can be difficult, but, with practice, you will master it.

TIPS

- Show you are listening and that you understand by using appropriate words and making sounds like "uh-huh", "mmm, mmm", "yes", "OK".
- Repeat some of the client's words to encourage them to say more.
- Repeat what the client says in your own words.
- Use silence and be patient. Give the client time to explore their thoughts and feelings and to work up to what they want to say. Don't feel you have to jump in with questions or comments every time there are a few seconds of silence.
- Judge when to use questions to help the client to open up and tell you more.
- If you are in a face-to-face situation, non-threatening, open body language will make the client feel comfortable. Nodding your head will indicate that you are listening.
- Always remain neutral and non-judgemental. Never take sides or offer your personal opinion. Remember, only the client can really be sure what's best for them.

---

4 Role-play: helpline calls

Your trainer ends the session by having you practise active listening techniques using role-plays.

A Work with a partner. You and your partner are going to take turns to play the roles of a counsellor and a caller. When you take the part of the counsellor, use skills for active listening to encourage the caller to talk.

Partner A: file 9, page 155   **Partner B:** file 5, page 153

B ⬛CHALLENGE!⬛ Record your version of a successful counselling session and share it with the class.

Active listening

- What's the problem?
- Shall we talk about it?
- I understand.
- Take your time.
- So, you feel as if …?
- If I understand you correctly, …
- Is it true that …?

> *Active listening, p. 196*

49

D Practice and projects

1 Completing a report

Complete the report with words and phrases from the box.

> abusing • abusive • apologizes • apology • back to normal •
> cycle of violence • excuse • excuses

Client A is married to a woman who has a son from a previous marriage. Client A has come for counselling as he is ●¹ to his partner. He hits her in the face and on the back of the head. When he has finished ●² her, he ●³ for his behaviour. During counselling, he has admitted that he is afraid that his partner will go to the police.

Not long after the ●⁴, Client A starts to make ●⁵ for his behaviour. He says that his partner takes her son to visit his father so that she can have an affair with her ex-husband.

Once he has said this, life gets ●⁶ for a few weeks but, soon, the ●⁷ continues. Client A dreams about hitting his partner again and he thinks up another ●⁸ for doing so.

2 Adjectives and adverbs

Choose the correct word to complete the sentences.

1. The client grew up in a (violent/violently) household.
2. His father behaved (aggressive/aggressively).
3. Counselling is helping him get (deep/deeply) in touch with his own feelings.
4. The client feels (bad/badly) about his behaviour towards his children.
5. He feels that the counselling sessions are doing him (good/well).
6. His father was always (sad/sadly) after he had been abusive.

> Adjectives and adverbs, p. 222

3 A jumbled helpline call

Unjumble this helpline call between a counsellor (CO) and a young caller (CA).
Start like this: c – h – b …

a **CO** Do you know of anything that might have made your mum depressed?
b **CO** Have you tried talking to her?
c **CO** How can I help you?
d **CO** I'm glad that you called. I hope things will get better soon.
e **CO** I see, she won't talk to you. Is there anyone in the family your mum could talk to?
f **CO** You know, even when people argue with each other, they are sometimes more unhappy when they're apart. What about talking to the family doctor about your mum? There are organizations like Marriage Guidance where your mum and dad could go for counselling.
g **CA** No. There's only me and mum.
h **CA** My mother is depressed and I am very worried about her.
i **CA** Yes. I'll talk to the doctor. Maybe she can get them to go to Marriage Guidance. Thank you for your help.
j **CA** My dad moved out a few months ago, but I don't think that's the problem. Mum wanted him to leave. She and dad were arguing a lot.
k **CA** She won't talk to me. She always tells me she's OK.

Unit 4　Learning to listen

Solutions to problems

Make type I *if*-sentences using the words below.

1　be fewer adult programmes on daytime TV / young children not be exposed to so much violence
2　children have more respect for other people / their parents set a better example
3　knives be allowed in schools / there be more violence
4　teachers have more authority / they be able to check their students' phones
5　students be taught about different ethnic groups / they learn to be more tolerant
6　schools employ security personnel / gangs stay away

> *If-sentences, p. 220*

Writing and acting out a helpline dialogue

You are going to write a dialogue for a telephone helpline session, then act it out. After that, you are going to write a report on the call. Work in a small group to do all the steps below.

Step 1　You and your group are trainee counsellors working on a helpline. Think of reasons why someone would call. Decide together on your scenario and write it down.

Step 2　Put yourselves in the shoes of the caller. How would he/she talk about his/her problem? Say whole sentences out loud and write them down as they are spoken. Your speech should sound as natural as possible.

Step 3　Think about how a counsellor might respond to what the caller says. Make notes.

Step 4　Use the notes to write a dialogue for a telephone helpline conversation.

Step 5　When your script is ready, read it through and see how it sounds. Choose two people to act it out and decide if you need to rewrite anything before you perform it in front of the class.

Step 6　When you have finished, write a report on the call.

> *Describing a case, p. 198*

Checking progress

Browse through the previous pages in the unit, looking at headings and pictures. What have you learned? What can you do now that you have learned these things?
- ✔ I can interpret the unspoken signs of abuse correctly.　(Part A)
- ✔ I can describe issues related to violence and victimization in schools and suggest possible ways to resolve them.　(Part B)
- ✔ I can understand the concept of active listening and put it into practice in a counselling session.　(Part C)
- ✔ I can write and act out a telephone helpline dialogue.　(Part D)

Write down two more statements of your own.

How much has this unit helped you become an attentive listener? How has it helped you develop your observation and interpersonal skills?

51

Exam skills and strategies

Mit Hör-/Sehverstehensaufgaben umgehen

Wichtig für:
- Hör-/Sehverstehensaufgaben

Üblicherweise werden Hör-/Sehverstehensaufgaben oder Videos zweimal abgespielt. Der erste Durchgang ist dazu bestimmt, eine allgemeine Vorstellung vom Inhalt zu bekommen oder die Kernaussage zu verstehen. Beim zweiten Hören/Sehen sollten Sie sich mehr auf bestimmte Details konzentrieren.

BEISPIELAUFGABE

Sie hören einen Text über die Selbstmordraten bei Männern in Großbritannien. Die Aufnahme wird zweimal vorgespielt. Lesen Sie die Fragen und hören Sie aufmerksam zu. Beantworten Sie danach die Fragen.

1/9

1. Um wie viel höher ist die Selbstmordrate bei Männern (verglichen mit der Selbstmordrate bei Frauen) in Großbritannien?
2. Welche Gruppe von Männern ist am meisten gefährdet?
3. Was hält Jane Powell von Calm für die Gründe, warum Männer keine Hilfe bekommen, wenn sie Selbstmordgedanken haben?
4. Welcher Teil Großbritanniens hat die höchste Selbstmordrate bei Männern?
5. Was wird als Reaktion auf diese Zahlen erwartet?

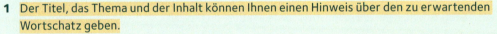

TIPPS

Vor dem ersten Hören:

1. Der Titel, das Thema und der Inhalt können Ihnen einen Hinweis über den zu erwartenden Wortschatz geben.
   → *Thema:* Suicide rates in men in the UK
   Möglicher Wortschatz: suicide, society, gender, reasons, mental health, prevention

2. Lesen Sie die Aufgabe sorgfältig und halten Sie nach Schlüsselwörtern Ausschau. Achten Sie darauf, dass Sie verstanden haben, welche Informationen Sie benötigen. Denken Sie dazu über die Fragen nach, die Ihnen gestellt werden. Schauen Sie sich die hervorgehobenen Wörter in den Fragen an. Was wissen Sie bereits über diese Themen? Worüber könnten die Personen sprechen?
   → 1 **Um wie viel höher** ist die **Selbstmordrate** bei **Männern** (verglichen mit der Selbstmordrate bei Frauen) in Großbritannien?
   Es werden viele Zahlen zu Beginn des Textes genannt. Sie möchten die Rate, also eine bestimmte Zahlenangabe, heraushören. Hören Sie auch auf Wörter, die einen Vergleich anzeigen, zum Beispiel „higher than".
   2 **Welche Gruppe von Männern** ist am meisten **gefährdet**?
   Hören Sie beim Wort „risk" genau hin. Achten Sie rund um dieses Wort auch auf Anhaltspunkte für einen bestimmten Personentyp, z. B. Sozialstatus oder Alter.
   3 Was hält Jane Powell von Calm für die **Gründe**, warum Männer **keine Hilfe bekommen**, wenn sie Selbstmordgedanken haben?
   Konzentrieren Sie sich beim Hören auf Wörter, die auf fehlende Hilfe deuten, beispielsweise „problem". Der Tonfall des Sprechers könnte ebenfalls einen Hinweis liefern.

52

Exam skills and strategies

4 **Welcher Teil Großbritanniens** hat die höchste Selbstmordrate bei Männern?
Versuchen Sie, einen Ortsnamen oder einen ungefähren Standort herauszuhören.

5 Was wird als **Reaktion** auf diese **Zahlen erwartet**?
Achten Sie beim Hören auf eine mögliche oder wahrscheinliche Auswirkung, die aus der genannten Statistik hervorgeht. Sie sollten das Wort „cause" oder „result" hören.

Während des ersten Hörens:

1 Denken Sie daran, dass es nicht notwendig ist, jedes einzelne Wort zu verstehen. Versuchen Sie, die Wörter, die Sie nicht verstehen, zu ignorieren. Nutzen Sie Ihr Allgemeinwissen, um die Bedeutung zu erschließen.   ▸ *Mit unbekannten Wörtern umgehen, S. 28*

2 Richten Sie Ihre Aufmerksamkeit auf Fakten und Schlüsselwörter. Machen Sie sich Notizen, um Ihr Gedächtnis zu entlasten.

Men 40–45
NE of England

3 Schreiben Sie beim Hören mit. Tragen Sie Ihre Antworten danach in den Antwortbogen ein.

Vor dem zweiten Hören:

Lesen Sie die Fragen noch einmal. Konnten Sie alle Fragen beantworten? Wenn ja, überprüfen Sie Ihre Antworten. Wenn nicht, ermitteln Sie, auf welche Informationen Sie beim erneuten Hören achten müssen.

Videos verstehen

Wenden Sie die gleichen Fertigkeiten beim Schauen eines Videos an wie beim Hören einer Aufnahme. Der Vorteil eines Videos ist allerdings, dass Ihnen zusätzlich die Bilder helfen. Körpersprache, Mimik, Gestik und Schauplatz können Ihnen Hinweise auf die Handlung geben. Lesen Sie jeden Text, der auf dem Bildschirm erscheint, um so viele nicht-hörbare Informationen wie möglich zu erhalten.

Während des zweiten Hörens:

Beantworten Sie die Fragen detaillierter und ergänzen Sie fehlende Informationen.

1 Sie sehen ein Video mit dem Titel „Bullying: Prevention and Tips". Das Video wird zweimal gezeigt. Entscheiden Sie, ob die Aussagen a–e richtig oder falsch sind und begründen Sie Ihre Entscheidung auf Deutsch. Beantworten Sie danach die untenstehenden Fragen f–h auf Deutsch.

a In den USA ist eins von drei Kindern Opfer von Mobbing in Schulen.
b Mobbing wiederholt sich ständig und gibt dem Täter ein Gefühl von Macht.
c Social media, wie z. B. Facebook, hat dazu beigetragen, Mobbing in Schulen entgegenzuwirken.
d Der üblichste Schauplatz für Mobbing ist der Schulhof.
e Lehrer wissen meist von Mobbing-Fällen, tun aber nichts dagegen.
f Aus welchen Gründen wird jemand zum Mobber?
g Wie sieht das Profil eines typischen Opfers aus?
h Welcher Rat wird gegeben, wie man mit Mobbing umgehen soll?

2 Jim Constantin works in a community outreach centre. He has received three voicemail messages. Listen to the information and complete the form on the right. You will hear the messages two times.   ▸ *Lösungen, S. 291*

Message for: Jim Constantin
Name of caller: …
Date and time of call: …
Message: …

53

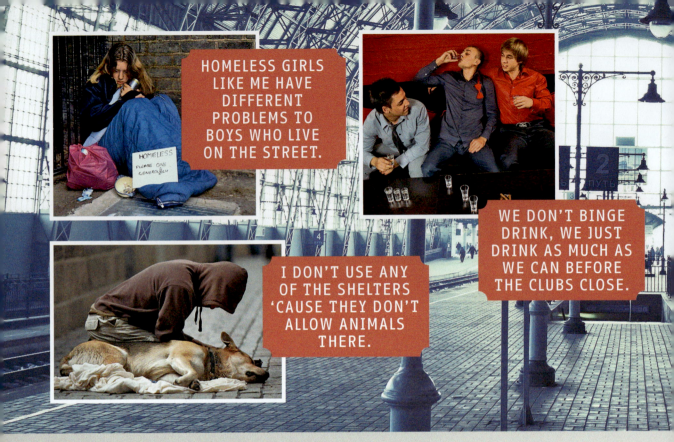

5 Reaching out to at-risk teens

1 Study the images and texts. Choose one or two items and describe them. What do you find interesting, surprising or shocking?

2 Choose one of the questions below and discuss it in groups. Share your ideas with the rest of the class.

- Can you imagine being any of the people shown in the pictures? Why (not)?
- What are the causes of drug abuse and binge drinking? What could the consequences be?
- Why do you think some people choose to leave or are forced to leave their family home?
- Why are some asylum seekers homeless?
- What is the equivalent of "The Big Issue" in your area? Who sells it and why?

I don't know. Perhaps …   Probably …   I think there are some / aren't any …   I believe …

Routes into Homelessness

- Forced to leave family home — 45.8%
- Chose to leave family home — 20.3%
- Left care facility — 10.2%
- Left own home — 10.2%
- Asylum seekers or refugees — 13.5%

nach: mentalhealth.org.uk

DRUG DEATHS DECREASE IN PARTS OF EUROPE

This year, the number of drug deaths among teens recorded in Germany is the lowest since 1989. Throughout the country, 944 people died as a result of drug-taking – 42 fewer than last year. Crystal meth, which is manufactured mainly in

3 What kind of help is available to street kids and to other homeless people in your community? What about to people with alcohol or drug problems? What kind of help is missing?

What's to come

In this unit, you will …
- learn about reasons for homelessness and hear some personal stories.
- find out about programmes to help homeless teenagers and put together a "street kit".
- explore issues concerning drug use and decriminalization.

At the end of the unit, you will do internet research and give a presentation.

Before you begin, think about what skills you need to be able to work effectively with troubled and homeless teenagers.

A Teams for teens

> It is your first day at work at an Outreach centre in Cardiff. Outreach UK is an organization which helps and advises teenagers in trouble, both those living at home and those living on the street.

1 Listening: greetings and small talk

Colin Young, the Senior Social Worker at Outreach, is greeting some new trainees. Unfortunately, you are late! When you finally arrive, he has already welcomed the two other trainees.

1/11

A Listen to the conversation and find out the names of the trainees, where they live and how they got to work.

B Listen again and make a note of the language the speakers use for greetings, introductions and small talk.

Outreach centre, Cardiff

Trainee Social Workers

Making small talk

Making small talk is one important way of making a good, friendly impression when you meet someone for the first time. You can talk about the weather, how you got to the meeting and where you live.

2 Role-play: introducing yourself

Work in groups of four. Take it in turns to play different members of the Outreach team and introduce yourselves, then make small talk.

Introductions and greetings

- Hi, I'm … / my name is … . I'm the …
- Nice to meet you.
- Nice to meet you, too. / You too.
- Hello. How are you?
- Very well, thanks. And you?   ➤ *Introductions, p. 190*

3 Listening: Outreach's mission and a personal success story

1/12

Colin gives a short talk about Outreach and introduces a client.

A Listen to the first part of Colin's talk and take notes to complete the gaps below.

Outreach centre, Cardiff
- Typical client problems: [1]
- Mission: [2]
- Four main activities: [3]
- Number of participants in the education programme: [4]

Success rates – percentage of clients who have made progress in these areas:
mental health: 82.8%   alcohol abuse: [7]
anger management: [5]   drug abuse: [8]
self-harm: [6]   offending: 71.1%

1/13

B Listen to Tony's story, then do the tasks below.

1. Explain the circumstances that led to Tony's homelessness.
2. Explain when and why Tony started to smoke and drink.
3. Describe how Tony was introduced to Outreach. Say what the result was.
4. Describe Tony's situation now.

C Colin and Tony used the following expressions in their talks. Can you explain what they mean?

1. to be entitled to sth
2. to get to grips with sth
3. to chuck sb out
4. to vandalize
5. to go right off the rails
6. to sleep rough

GUIDANCE *If you would like guidance, turn to file G6 on page 173.*

4 Speaking: telling someone's story

Work with a partner. Use the notes in your files to tell the story of two more Outreach clients. Discuss similarities and differences between all three cases.

Partner A: file 13, page 157   **Partner B:** file 34, page 167

5 Mediation: street kids in Germany

> Mediation, p. 211

You have found an article in a German magazine that might be interesting for the team. Make notes about the main points in English, then summarize the text.

GUIDANCE *If you would like guidance, turn to file G18 on page 178.*

Straßenkinder

Wohnungslosigkeit trifft immer mehr Jugendliche und junge Erwachsene. Die Jugendlichen, die sich in Straßenszenen aufhalten, werden oft als „Straßenkinder" bezeichnet. Gemeinsam ist ihnen, dass meist massive Störungen und gravierende Probleme im Elternhaus sie dazu gebracht oder gezwungen haben, die Familie zu verlassen. Sexueller Missbrauch, körperliche und psychische Gewalt, Kontrolle und starke Einschränkungen oder völlige Vernachlässigung sind typische Erfahrungen. Manche sind aus Familien, andere aus Heimen oder Psychiatrien ausgerissen, wieder andere aus dem Elternhaus „hinausgeworfen" worden.

Auf der Straße leben ist nicht einfach
Viele der Jugendlichen und jungen Erwachsenen sagen, die Straße sei besser als alles, was sie vorher erlebt haben. Dennoch stellt Wohnungslosigkeit für die Betroffenen eine Notlage dar.

Oft ist die ohnehin schon knappe Sozialhilfe durch Forderungen von Gläubigern stark verringert. Daher sind viele auf Betteln oder sogar Diebstähle angewiesen, um über die Runden zu kommen. Und dies führt wiederum zu Kriminalisierung. Wer auf der Straße lebt und nicht in eine Übernachtungseinrichtung gehen will oder kann, muss draußen schlafen oder bei Bekannten unterkommen. Insbesondere für Mädchen gehört die Angst vor Überfällen bzw. die sexuelle Gegenleistung für einen Schlafplatz bei Bekannten zum Alltag. Wer draußen schläft, setzt sich massiven gesundheitlichen Gefahren aus. Körperpflege und Hygiene sind generell nur eingeschränkt möglich, auch das macht anfällig für Krankheiten. Auf der Straße gibt es keine Rückzugsmöglichkeiten. Mehr als Schlafsack und Rucksack zu haben, bedeutet Ballast. Zum Alltag gehören Polizeikontrollen, Hausverbote und/oder Platzverbote und infolgedessen Kriminalisierung.

B Programmes and activities

> **S** Outreach, Cardiff uses its website to keep the public and its sponsors informed. The latest online newsletter describes the difficulties of reaching homeless teenagers and announces a new programme aimed at helping young homeless people come off drugs and alcohol for good.

1 Reading: supporting homeless teenagers

> *Schwierige Texte lesen, S. 202*

A Read the newsletter article and complete this chart about the problems and challenges the Outreach team has to face and the strategies they are using.

Challenges and problems	Strategies
persuading teenagers to talk	…

B Trust, respect, dignity: define the three terms in your own words, and say why they are important when working with homeless teens.

TRUST, RESPECT, DIGNITY

A new programme and a project for Cardiff's homeless teenagers
The Outreach bus is well known in Cardiff wherever young homeless people have made their shelters.

Trust
One of our main challenges is persuading homeless teenagers to trust us. Some of the young people we are trying to reach have chosen to live rough because they have had disagreements with their parents. As a result, they are unwilling to talk to us in case we send them back home. Moreover, many of them have had negative experiences with social services, so they are suspicious of us. It takes a lot of persuasion to get people to talk to us and trust us. We gain their trust by making it clear to the teenagers that we won't force any help on them if they don't want it.

Respect
Once we've made contact, a specific social worker looks after his or her own particular homeless youths. Everyone we talk to has a name and a face for us – we don't just view them as case numbers. By recognizing that our clients are individuals with their own specific problems, needs and hopes for the future, we treat our clients with the respect they deserve.

Dignity
One of the biggest challenges for homeless teenagers is retaining their dignity. Thus, one of the purposes of our bus is to give homeless teens a place to meet privately if they want to open up and talk to us. A qualified nurse travels with us every time the bus goes out, so anyone with a medical problem can be examined in privacy and given medication if needed. We are also in the process of putting together individual "street kits" of hygiene and medical items that will be distributed to homeless teenagers to help them cope with their circumstances.

Get clean, stay clean – a programme we hope will help
To help homeless teens get healthy and off drugs and alcohol, Outreach works hand-in-hand with medical services and rehabilitation clinics. Unfortunately, many teenagers fall back into old habits once they leave the clinic or rehab and return to the streets. In order to tackle this problem, Outreach is setting up a new programme: "Get clean, stay clean". With this programme, we hope to help those teenagers who have made up their minds to get off drugs to stay off drugs for the rest of their lives.

(385 words)

Unit 5   Reaching out to at-risk teens

2 Talking about current activities and schedules

It's Monday morning and there is a lot going on at the Outreach centre. Read the schedule and say what the staff do every Monday, what they are doing now and what they are doing later.

	Mary	Patsy	Colin	Ian	Jennifer	Ahmed
Monday morning	visit sheltered accommodation	on duty in media centre	speak to police psychologist	write up case notes	on bus duty	counsel client
Monday afternoon	drug counselling session	prison visits	AA group	group therapy session	"street kit" project	on bus duty

What does Mary do on Monday afternoons?

What is Ian doing at the moment?

Where is Ahmed going in the afternoon?

Talking about current activities and regular schedules

The therapy session **takes place** on Monday.
- We use the simple present to talk about things that happen on a regular basis. ▸ *Simple present, p. 212*

What **is** Colin **doing** at the moment?
- We use the present progressive to talk about what is happening now.
  ▸ *Present progressive, p. 212*

When **is** the AA group **meeting** this week?
- We also use the present progressive to say what you have already arranged to do. ▸ *The future, p. 216*

3 Watching a video: "Young and homeless"

You are helping out in the Outreach media centre. Patsy asks you to review a video which has just arrived.
Watch the video and make notes. Then write a short summary for the media centre's catalogue.

4:32

▸ *Mit Hör- und Sehverstehensaufgaben umgehen, S. 207*

4 Writing: asking for contributions

Your final task of the day is to work on the street kits that will be distributed to homeless teens. With a partner, follow the steps below.

1 Brainstorm a list of items that homeless teens might need for hygiene, health and simply to make life more pleasant. The items should easily fit in a small rucksack.

2 Decide which companies might contribute items. Write an email to one of the companies, explaining who you are and where you work, what your organization does and what you're planning at the moment. Describe the kits and ask for contributions of items to go into them. Don't forget to mention that the firm's name will be displayed on your website.

Asking for contributions

- I am writing on behalf of (*name of organization*) where I'm a/an (*job title*).
- We are putting together kits for …
- Our aim is to …
- As a well-known manufacturer of (*product*), we are sure you would like to contribute …
- We are looking specifically for (*items*).

▸ *Writing emails, p. 188*

59

C Drug facts and figures

> You and the other trainees have been assigned to Mary, a case worker who specializes in counselling street kids who have problems with substance abuse. Today, she is filling you in on some background.

1 Describing a graph: drug use

Mary shows you a graph which depicts the use of drugs by age group and year.

A Read the sentences and look at the lines on the graph which represent the data for ages 16–19 and 20–24. Choose the word or phrase that Mary probably uses to describe the trends.

1. As you can see, both of these age groups are at the *bottom* / *top* of the scale in drug use.
2. If we look at the year 1999, we see that drug use amongst 16 to 19-year-olds is at its *highest* / *lowest* level.
3. Consumption amongst 20 to 24-year-olds reaches an all-time *high* / *low* of 32 per cent in 2001, then it *drops* / *rises* to just above 30 per cent around the beginning of 2003.
4. Drug use amongst the 16 to 19-year-old age group *drops* / *rises* to 28 per cent in 2001 and *decreases* / *increases* only slightly in 2002 before *plunging* / *soaring* to around 20 per cent in 2008.

1/14

B Now listen to Mary and check your answers. According to Mary, how might legalization or decriminalization of drugs affect the numbers of drug users?

C Mary asks you to describe the trends for the other age groups. In a group of three, use the graph below and phrases from exercise 1A to prepare your presentations.

Partner A: Complete the analysis of age groups 16–19 and 20–24 that Mary started.
Partner B: Compare and contrast the age groups 25–29, 30–34 and 35–44.
Partner C: Describe the complete graph and interpret your findings.

> Schaubilder beschreiben und analysieren, S. 210; Describing trends, p. 137

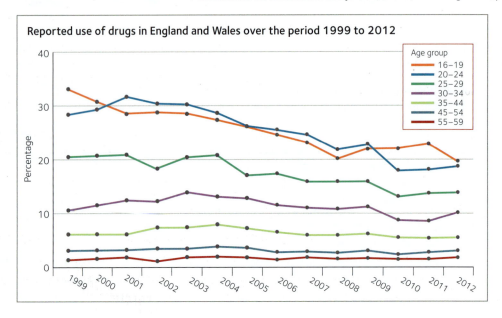

60

Unit 5   Reaching out to at-risk teens

2 Reading: decriminalizing drugs

> *Schwierige Texte lesen, S. 202*

You are interested in the arguments for and against the decriminalization or legalization of drugs and have found an article online.

A Decide if the following statements are correct or incorrect according to the text below.

1 People who are caught with drugs in Portugal are immediately sent to jail.
2 If drug users do not accept treatment, they are sent to jail.
3 People who buy and sell drugs are usually offered treatment.
4 The number of young drug users has fallen since decriminalization has been introduced.
5 The British government does not wish to follow the Portuguese example.
6 The writer of the article agrees with the British government's point of view.

B Comment on the statement in the text: "Since decriminalization was introduced [in Portugal], HIV infections among drug users have fallen, drug-related deaths have declined and there has been a decrease in trafficking."

PORTUGAL DRUG DECRIMINALIZATION 'A RESOUNDING SUCCESS': WILL BRITAIN RESPOND? NO.

Until 2001, Portugal had some of the worst drug problems in Europe. The turnaround since decriminalization has been dramatic, especially as we see that the drop in drug use in Portugal has come against a background of increasing drug use across the rest of the EU.

Europe's most liberal drug policy has been a huge success. A study has found that in the five years after decriminalization, Portugal's drug problems have improved in every way.

Portuguese policy is that possession of small amounts of any drug is not a criminal offence; if you are found in possession, you can be put before a panel made up of a psychologist, a social worker and a legal adviser, who will decide appropriate treatment. You are free to refuse that treatment, and a jail sentence is not an option. Drug trafficking is still illegal and punishable by jail.

A look at the current figures shows that drug use among Portugal's 13 to 15-year-olds fell from 14.1 per cent in 2001 to 10.6 per cent in 2006. Among 16 to 18-year-olds, it has dropped from 27.6 per cent to 21.6 per cent.

These positive results come after years of steadily increasing drug use among the young. For example, between 1995 and 2001, use in the 16–18 bracket leapt up from 14.1 per cent to its 2001 high. Apart from that, since decriminalization was introduced, HIV infections among drug users have fallen, drug-related deaths have declined, and there has been a decrease in trafficking. A huge amount of money has also been saved by offering treatment instead of prison sentences.

No one believes that decriminalization would work in Britain, and the Portuguese experience is unlikely to change UK policy. A Home Office spokesperson says, "Our priorities are clear; we want to reduce drug use, crack down on drug-related crime and disorder and help addicts come off drugs for good. However, the government does not believe that decriminalization is the right approach."

The Portuguese experience suggests that decriminalization is exactly the right approach for reducing drug use and crime. As the British approach has been shown to achieve nothing, it looks like it may be time to change that approach.   (363 words)

from *The Telegraph*, 28.09.10, abridged

---

3 Debate: the pros and cons of legalizing drugs

> *An Diskussionen teilnehmen, S. 210*

In two groups, hold a debate on the legalization of drugs. One group is pro-legalization, the other group is anti-legalization.

1 Prepare a short presentation of your arguments.
2 Hold the debate.
3 Decide which team had the best arguments.

61

D Practice and projects

1 Introducing yourself and others

A Complete the sentences with the correct form of the verbs in brackets.

Good morning. My name (be)[1] Gwen. I (be)[2] from Wales. I (be born)[3] in Cardiff, but I (live)[4] in Hamburg now. I (do)[5] a two-year course at vocational school. At the moment, I (work)[6] in a youth club. This (be)[7] my friend Monica. She (do)[8] her nursing training at the moment. And (you know)[9] Uwe and Anna? They (visit)[10] me from Berlin but (go back)[11] home tomorrow.

B Introduce yourself and another person to a friend.

2 Completing a story

Use words and phrases from the box to complete the story of one of the Outreach street kids.

> abused • addicted • beg • homeless shelter • sheltered accommodation •
> shoplifting • steal • therapy • training • voluntarily

"I left home ⬤[1]. I'd been physically ⬤[2] by my father for years. I had no job and no money for rent or food but I didn't care. The main thing was that I was free of my dad. For the first couple of nights, I slept in a park, but then it got cold so I went to a ⬤[3]. I had to ⬤[4] for the money to pay for it. I hadn't been on the streets long when I started using drugs. I became ⬤[5] very quickly and had to ⬤[6] to feed my habit. I started ⬤[7] – mostly food – but sometimes I also stole things I could sell. I was caught, of course, but the shopkeeper was kind and, instead of handing me over to the police, he called Outreach. These people are great. They got me into ⬤[8]. I've been clean for eight months now. I have a room in a ⬤[9] flat and a place on a ⬤[10] programme. I'm learning to be a motor mechanic."

3 Describing a line graph

> Describing trends, p. 137

You have been asked to write an article about Outreach's street kits for "The Big Issue". Describe the graph below for your article. Make up reasons for the increases and decreases.

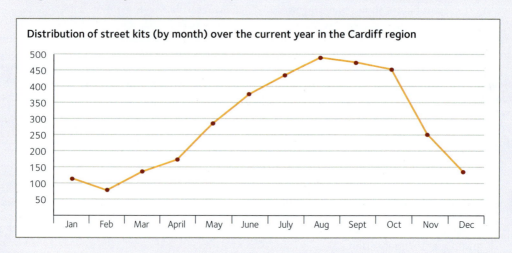

Distribution of street kits (by month) over the current year in the Cardiff region

62

Unit 5   Reaching out to at-risk teens

4 Talking about current activities and regular schedules

Talk about people at Outreach. Use the prompts below to say what they usually do and what they are (not) doing at the moment. Say what they have planned to do later in the day.

1. Colin (run) the AA meeting at the moment.
2. What (the trainees do) later? They (sit in) on the drug counselling session.
3. Jennifer and Patsy always (enjoy) basketball training with the girls.
4. Mary (write) a report about the visit to the shelter, so don't bother her.
5. Why (Ian not take part) in the meeting this afternoon? – He (visit) a client in hospital.
6. Ahmed usually (work) at home one morning a week. He (come) in to the office later.

> *Simple present, p. 212; Present progressive, p. 212; The future, p. 216*

Presenting facts and figures: homeless teens in your area

Work in a team to prepare a presentation related to homeless teenagers in your area. You may focus on reasons for homelessness, or on a specific problem related to homeless teenagers. Before you start, decide how your team is going to share the tasks below. Will you all do each step together, or would you prefer to allocate the tasks?

Step 1 Do internet research to find out about homelessness among teenagers in your area. If you come across relevant graphs, decide which one(s) you would like to use in your presentation.

Step 2 Make notes in English about what you would like to say. Refer to the phrase bank (page 195) to help you prepare your talk.

Step 3 Upload your graph(s) and any other visuals onto slides.

Step 4 Make copies of your graph(s) and other visuals so you can give your audience a handout.

Step 5 Give the presentation and answer any questions from the audience.   > *Präsentieren, S. 209*

Step 6 After the presentation, ask the other teams to give feedback on the language you used in your talk.

Checking progress

Browse through the previous pages in the unit, looking at headings, pictures and graphs. What have you learned? What can you do now that you have learned these things?
- ✔ I can mediate a German article in written English.   (Part A)
- ✔ I can write an email asking for contributions.   (Part B)
- ✔ I can describe a graph and put forward arguments in a debate.   (Part C)
- ✔ I can do research and give a presentation on homeless teenagers.   (Part D)

Write down two more statements of your own.

How far has this unit helped you towards working with troubled clients? How has it helped you develop social competences?

Exam skills and strategies

Einen Text zusammenfassen

Die Kompetenz, einen Text zusammenzufassen, ist wichtig, um einen Text vollständig zu verstehen, und um einen Text auf seine wesentlichsten Informationen zu kürzen.

Wichtig für:
- Schreiben einer Stellungnahme
- Leseverstehen
- Mediation
- materialgestützten Aufsatz
- rollenbasierte Stellungnahme

BEISPIEL-AUFGABE Lesen Sie den Text „Number of street kids rising in Germany" und schreiben Sie eine kurze Zusammenfassung auf Englisch.

Number of street kids rising in Germany

According to the online news portal Expatica, there are more than 7,000 kids living on the streets of Germany and more than a third of those are living in the nation's capital. Poverty, troubled family backgrounds, violence, drugs and alcohol are just some of the reasons that the German street kid scene is growing.

The charity Terre des Hommes reports that life is getting tougher for these young people, especially because of increasing violence. In the past, the average age of Berlin's street kids was 18. Now it's down to 16, with some among them only 14. Without family or friends, some street kids end up addicted to drugs.

They mostly come from broken homes or poor family backgrounds. After they arrive in the city, they have no idea where they should go to seek help.

Various organizations have been set up to help deal with this problem. The biggest aid organization in Berlin is the Karuna Association, which helps up to 800 homeless teenagers annually find work and shelter. Some youngsters get "one-euro jobs", and later, those without school-leaving certificates are encouraged to study for them. After that, they are helped to find apprenticeships.

Other organizations include Off Road Kids, which is active in Berlin, Hamburg, Dortmund and Cologne, and Klik in Berlin. These offer advice and guidance for street kids.

The question is, will these organizations be able to help the kids before it is too late? (248 words)

TIPPS

1 Lesen Sie den Text gründlich. Behalten Sie während des Lesens die Kernideen im Kopf – schauen Sie sich dafür die hervorgehobenen Abschnitte an.

▶ Schwierige Texte lesen, S. 16

2 Lesen Sie und machen Sie sich Notizen. Um sicherzugehen, welche Informationen wichtig sind, formulieren und beantworten Sie W-Fragen.

→ Who? *Young people who are living on the streets and organizations who try to help them*
→ What? *Youth homelessness getting worse – organizations trying to help*
→ Where? *Germany, especially Berlin and other big cities*
→ When? *Nowadays*
→ Why? *Poverty, bad family background, violence, drugs and alcohol are all reasons that kids end up on the streets. Kids need help urgently.*

3 Nun können Sie beginnen, Ihre Zusammenfassung anhand Ihrer Notizen zu schreiben. Beachten Sie dabei folgende Grundsätze:
- Beschreiben Sie in einem oder zwei einleitenden Sätzen, um was es geht.
  → *This article is about young people who live rough on the streets of big cities in Germany, and the organizations that try to help them.*

64

Exam skills and strategies

- Wenn Sie die Zusammenfassung schreiben, lassen Sie alles weg, was nicht von Bedeutung ist. Das sind unter anderem Beispiele, Auflistungen, Namen, Zitate und Statistiken.
  → *The text states that young people come to big cities* ~~like Berlin, Hamburg, Dortmund and Cologne~~ *and become involved with drugs and violence.*

- Äußern Sie nicht Ihre Meinung.
  → ~~I agree with the text that~~ **According to the author**, *many young people who arrive in the city have no idea where to get the help they need.*

- Gebrauchen Sie Ihre eigenen Worte.
  → ~~The biggest aid organization in Berlin is the Karuna Association.~~
  The Karuna Association is the largest organization in Berlin.

- Wenn Sie jemanden aus dem Text zitieren möchten, schreiben Sie das Zitat um, indem Sie indirekte Rede verwenden.
  → ~~"The question is, will these organizations be able to help the kids before it is too late?"~~
  Finally, the author asks whether the organizations would be able to help the kids before it was too late.

> Reported speech, p. 217

4 Überprüfen Sie Ihre Zusammenfassung auf Fehler, und stellen Sie sicher, dass Sie alle relevanten Aspekte des Textes mit einbezogen haben.
  → *This article is about young people who live rough on the streets of big cities in Germany, and the organizations who try to help them. The text states that young people come to Berlin and become involved with drugs and violence. Often, they have no idea where to get the help they need. This is why various organizations have been set up to help deal with this problem. According to the author, the Karuna Association is the largest organization in Berlin. Finally, the author asks whether the organizations would be able to help the kids before it was too late.*

1 Read the following text and write a summary of it.

> Lösungen, S. 291

Teens living rough

Eighteen year old Sascha stands at a subway station every day, playing his guitar, trying to earn a few euros so he has shelter for the night. "When I make enough money to get a night in a hostel, it's great, because I get food and a shower too," says Sascha. "A lot of the time I sleep on a park bench."

Paying for a bed is just one of the problems faced by Sascha and the other 2,000 young people sleeping rough in Berlin. Many turn to drugs as a way of dealing with their situation. Many face increasing violence. There are many health risks. Some kids get Hepatitis or HIV from using dirty needles. If they get injured in a fight, they can have major problems with their bones. If they are sleeping outdoors, they can get illnesses because they are run down from lack of sleep. Often, they get infections because they can't wash properly.

But help is at hand. Teams of social workers from Off Road Kids are going onto the streets to find young people and help them find places in shelters and hostels.

Their mission is to educate these kids on the importance of looking after themselves. The kids need to know about the importance of hygiene. They are encouraged to use condoms. Although the aim is to stay away from drugs, if that isn't possible, they are told to use clean needles and not to share them. These basics stop the spread of diseases and prevent a lot of unnecessary deaths every year.

(263 words)

65

"What? I can't get promoted just because of my skin colour? Are we back in the 1960s?!"

"It's the way he looks at me. It freaks me out."

supervision sexual harassment
harassment
mediation stress
alcoholism burnout
counselling
conflict
racial discrimination
face-to-face discussion

6 Solving problems at work

1

A Skim the word cloud. What three topics do you think the unit is going to cover?

I think one topic will be …

Yes, and it looks like the unit will also cover …

B Match four of the words to the speech bubbles.

C Use your ideas from exercise 1A to produce three headings, then sort the words from the word cloud under the headings.

2 Describe and analyse the cartoon. What does it say about resolving conflicts?

The cartoon shows …

The cartoon has the effect of …

I think the cartoonist wants to say …

> Cartoons beschreiben und analysieren, S. 210

legal advice
intimidation
depression
inner resignation

"Things just kept piling up until I reached the point where I didn't know how to deal with them any longer."

"I'm just so physically and mentally tired – I can't even get up in the mornings anymore."

"A mediator hasn't worked, so I brought in everyone's moms."

3 Have you ever experienced or witnessed a conflict during a work placement or summer job? If so, how was the situation resolved? Tell a partner.

What's to come

In this unit, you will …
- advise a client on how to deal with harassment.
- mediate between a client and his supervisor and write a record of the meeting.
- write a comment on how to deal sensitively with workers faced with restructuring.

At the end of the unit, you will create guidelines to help managers and team leaders prevent problems among staff.

Before you begin, think about what you have learned at college about dealing with problems. What resources from your core course can you draw on?

A Case 1: harassment

> **S** You have just begun a work placement at Management Counselling, a company which offers mediation in the workplace. Today, you are assisting Claudia Weber, who has been called in by an electronics firm. The first session is with Vera Lebedeva, a 45-year-old electronics engineer who recently came to Germany from Russia to live with her German partner. Vera has complained to HR about being harassed by male colleagues.

1 Mediation: understanding what harassment is
> Mediation, S. 211

Claudia Weber would like you to prepare yourself for the session, which is to be held in English. Claudia gives you the information below and asks you to familiarize yourself with the terms in English.

Match words and phrases in the text to the English translations below, then summarize the document in English.

1. intimidation
2. jokes about sexual orientation
3. offensive remarks
4. picking on someone
5. sexually suggestive emails
6. sexual gestures
7. sexual harassment
8. staring in a sexually suggestive manner
9. telling sexual or lewd jokes
10. touching in an inappropriate manner

Konfliktmanagement § 35: Beispiele für Belästigung

Einige Beispiele sexueller Belästigung
Anstößige Bemerkungen zum Aussehen, zur Kleidung, zu Körperteilen
Witze über die sexuelle Ausrichtung
Das Anstarren auf geschlechtlich betonte Weise
Unangemessene Körperberührung
Das Erzählen von sexuellen oder anzüglichen Witzen
Erotikbetonte Bilder am Arbeitsplatz; sexuelle Gebärden

Die Versendung, Weiterleitung oder Anforderung aufreizender oder zweideutiger Briefe, Schriftstücke, E-Mails oder Abbildungen

Beispiele für andere Arten von Belästigung
Einschüchterung
Das Herumhacken auf jdm.
Negative Bemerkungen über das Alter von Kolleginnen und Kollegen, die 40 Jahre oder älter sind.

---

2 Listening: scenes from a session
> Mit Hörverstehensaufgaben umgehen, S. 207

1/15

A Listen to the first part of the session and answer the following questions.

1. How does Claudia introduce herself?
2. How does she introduce you? What is your function at the session?
3. What does Claudia say and do to make Vera feel comfortable?

B Listen to the second part of the session and take notes to complete Vera's description of the harassment.

GUIDANCE If you would like guidance, turn to file G13 on page 177.

XYZ Electronics

Vera Lebedeva
R & D

334001012

Unit 6   Solving problems at work

C Use the information from the document in exercise 1 to describe the situation as Vera perceives it. Which examples of sexual harassment does she report?

1/16

D Listen to the conclusion of the session. Take notes so that you can do the following tasks.

1. Describe what Vera did when she opened the email. Say how the men behaved.
2. Outline the options Claudia offers Vera.
3. Explain Vera's decision. Point out her reasons for the decision.

E CHALLENGE! Listen "between the lines" to the complete session. What observations of your own can you make about the situation?

3   Mediation and role-play: dealing with harassment

Vera has decided to wait and see how things develop. Claudia gives you the German text below and asks you to use it to give Vera some advice.

A First make sure you know what the highlighted words mean in English. (Use your dictionary if necessary.) Then make notes in English for your meeting with Vera.

Konfliktmanagement, § 36: Mobbing

Ratschläge für angemessenes Verhalten bei Mobbing

Sprechen Sie den Kollegen, von dem Sie sich gemobbt fühlen, auf sein Verhalten an – am besten unter vier Augen. Fordern Sie ihn auf, dieses Verhalten zu beenden – aber sprechen Sie dabei keine Drohungen aus. Allerdings funktioniert ein solches Gespräch nur, wenn sich die Situation nicht schon zu weit zugespitzt hat.

Lassen Sie sich durch Kritik oder Nörgelei nicht einschüchtern. Nehmen Sie keine Verteidigungshaltung ein.

Schreiben Sie Vorfälle, die Ihnen als Mobbingversuche erscheinen, mit Datum, Beteiligten und eventuellen Zeugen genau auf. Pflegen Sie, wo immer das möglich ist, gute Kontakte zu Ihren Kollegen. Nehmen Sie weiterhin aktiv am betrieblichen Alltagsleben teil.

Schreiben Sie auf nachprüfbare Weise Ihre laufenden Arbeitsleistungen auf, um gegen mögliche Vorwürfe gewappnet zu sein. Protokollieren Sie auch, falls Ihnen unzumutbare Arbeiten zugewiesen werden.

Überdenken Sie Ihre bisherigen Verhaltensweisen im Betrieb: Könnte es sein, dass Sie durch unangemessenes Verhalten auch selbst zur Mobbing-Situation beigetragen haben?

B Now work with a partner. One of you takes on Vera's role while the other gives her advice.

Giving advice

- It's a good idea to …
- If you can, you should …
- Try not to …
- Perhaps you could think about …
- It might not be a bad idea to …
- Have you ever considered talking …?
- Why don't you try speaking …?

› *Giving advice, p. 196*

69

B Case 2: assessment

> **S** The second session today is to be held with Glen Carter, a 36-year-old employee who works in IT Support. The company doctor believes that Glen is suffering from stress, and the session today is to decide how to support him. Glen is from the USA. He has asked for the session to be conducted in English.

1 Reading: analysing a stress checklist

Glen has completed a two-page stress checklist. Claudia would like you to go through the pages with her before the session.

A Work with a partner. After you have read the section "Before you start … " together, Partner A stay on this page and study how Glen has evaluated the statements. Partner B turn to file 15 on page 158 and read Glen's comments. Now compare information and discuss any patterns you see.

Stress Checklist page 1
Before you start … This checklist will help us find out if your stress level is too high. It will also help you to recognize some of the conditions that cause you to feel stressed.
Evaluate the statements below as they relate to your experience: from 0 = Never to 5 = Always.
When you have completed the checklist, please use page 2 for comments.

Statement		Evaluation
1	I have too much responsibility.	0
2	My work situation is unclear; there are too many people to satisfy.	5
3	There is a great deal of time pressure at work.	3
4	I have trouble focusing on a given task.	0
5	I have difficulty communicating with my spouse, children, family, boss or co-workers.	5
6	I handle most things alone with little support from family, friends or co-workers.	5
7	I do not have enough say in decisions that affect me.	5
8	I regularly have headaches; I have muscle tension in my shoulders, neck or back.	5
9	I have stomach pains, indigestion or other digestive problems.	4
10	I regularly take aspirin, indigestion medication, sleeping pills or tranquilizers.	5
11	I drink a great deal of coffee or other caffeinated beverages.	4
12	I drink alcohol every day/regularly.	0

B Add up the numbers and compare the result with the table in file 30 on page 165. Discuss the advice given and decide what recommendations might be suitable.

2 Listening: the challenging client

Glen arrives 15 minutes late for his appointment and takes a while to settle down.

1/17

A Listen to an excerpt from the first part of the session and do the tasks below.

1 Point out how Glen feels about counselling.
2 Describe how Claudia responds to Glen's feelings.
3 Explain what Claudia would like to do.

XYZ Electronics

Glen Carter
IT Support

334001009

70

Unit 6   Solving problems at work

B Listen to the conclusion of the session and find out:
1 why Glen is not motivated.
2 how he would like things to change at work.
3 how he might achieve his aims.

3 Reporting what someone says

Glen had made some more notes about what his boss and colleagues said. Use the dialogue extracts below to report what was said.
Start like this: *Glen told his boss that he wanted … . He asked his boss if …*

1 Glen: "I want to take on more responsibility. Can I take on another project?"
Boss: "No, I think it's better if you just take it easy and focus on your current tasks."
2 Glen: "I studied at the Massachusetts Institute of Technology and graduated at the top of my class."
Boss: "I know that. But what year was that?"
3 Colleague A (at the water cooler): "Do you know what is wrong with Glen? He always eats alone at his desk and looks so unhappy."
Colleague B: "I don't know. I think he's angry that he didn't get the promotion. I'll ask him to join us at the canteen, but he'll probably just say something nasty to me."

Reporting what someone says

Glen: "I wrote down what my colleagues said."
Glen **told** Claudia that he **had written down** what his colleagues **had said**.

- We usually report what someone has said with reporting verbs (e.g. *tell sb*, *say*, *ask if*) in the simple past. In this case, the verb(s) in the original sentence move(s) back in time.

> *Reported speech, p. 217*

---

4 Role-play and writing: the follow-up appointment

Claudia has arranged a follow-up meeting with the aim of mediating between Glen and his supervisor. She has asked you to sit in on the meeting and take notes.

A Work in groups of four.
Partner A: You are Glen (file 2, page 152).
Partner B: You are Claudia (file 22, page 161).
Partner C: You are Glen's supervisor (file 40, page 170).
Partner D: You are the trainee. Your task is to take notes which can be used to write a record of the meeting. While the others are preparing their roles, write the names of the participants in your notebook, leaving enough space beside each name to make notes.

Writing a record of a meeting

As a professional in the field of caring, you may be asked to produce a record of a meeting for a client's file. This record will include specific details so that everyone who is involved with the client knows what has been discussed and agreed. It is important to record everything carefully and accurately, and include the date, time and place of the meeting, who was present (with their job titles if appropriate) and any decisions which have been made.

Useful phrases
- X explained/suggested/recommended that …
- It was decided/agreed that …
- Y is to talk to / meet with …

> *Writing a record of a meeting, p. 197*

B Still in your group, read the trainee's notes together and add anything else from the meeting which you think is important. Write the record of the meeting together.

C Case 3: closure

> A US multinational company is restructuring its European offices. Tomorrow you will accompany Claudia to one of the offices that has been affected and will meet some of the employees. In preparation, you read some entries from a forum.

1 Reading: effects of downsizing

http://BusinessOnline.com/forum

Is your company being restructured? Has your job been affected? Tell your story.

ALVIN   I've just been told that I'm being laid off at the end of the month. The HR manager explained very fully about why the cuts were necessary and described how badly the market was doing in our sector. She explained how my severance package would be calculated. All the time I was in her office, I kept waiting for her to say: "Thanks for the 22 years of your life that you've invested in the company." She didn't.

CLARA   In my firm, it was all done very quickly. On the Monday morning, a notice was pinned up on the bulletin board to inform the staff that there would be some lay-offs, and staff who were affected would be invited to a meeting later in the week. At 4.45 p.m. on the Wednesday, a circular email was sent out to 127 people, announcing a 5 p.m. meeting. For the first 15 minutes of the meeting, one of the bosses explained current trends, the future of the company and how these lay-offs would benefit the company before he finally broke the news: "You will all be leaving in two weeks' time".

DEAN   I gave my life to my work. I worked overtime to meet delivery dates. I worked on concepts and plans during my holiday. Where am I now? After 28 years as a company man, I am now back to square one: 52 years old and standing in line at the job centre with kids just out of university. I've heard that my old company is already hiring new staff – university graduates. No experience, but, hey, they're cheap and they're keen to show how smart they are. I'd be happy to take my experience and know-how to any of our rivals, but I'm too expensive.

EVELYN   When my company downsized last year, social factors were used to decide who would be fired and who would be kept on. I'm a single parent with two school-aged children so I had enough points and could stay on. In the downsizing process, my department was axed, so the company was forced to offer me another position. I was retrained as a teleworker and work from home. The work is OK, but I miss my colleagues and the atmosphere in the office, so I am thinking about looking for another job.

JOHN   The company I worked for behaved insensitively, too. My boss was great, though. She told me to finish up what I was working on and use the rest of my time and the office resources to look for new jobs. I'm well qualified and I would have found a job in my sector easily. In the end, though, I decided to go freelance. That was six years ago, and my business is now doing so well that I have to outsource some of my work.   (520 words)

A Scan the text to find:
1. five words or expressions that have to do with being made unemployed.
2. the term for the conditions offered to employees when their work contracts are ended.
3. three words to describe alternative ways of working or getting work done.

B Use the following points to talk about the cases.
1. Describe the "insensitive" behaviour experienced by Alvin and Clara.
2. Analyse Dean's point of view: "After 28 years as a company man, I am now back to square one: 52 years old and standing in line at the job centre with kids just out of university."
3. Explain why Evelyn is doing telework; say how she feels about it and what she intends to do.
4. Describe the positive experience John had just after he had been told he was being laid off; say what he did and describe how things are now.

72

Unit 6   Solving problems at work

2 Discussion: Who said what?

Claudia asked you to take notes during the talks with employees at the company.

A First, complete the original quotes with the missing verbs.

> have been given • have been laid off •
> have been made • is being outsourced •
> was respected • will all be given

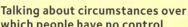

Talking about circumstances over which people have no control

Work **is being outsourced**.
Many people **have been laid off** by their companies.

- We use the passive when we do not know the subject of the sentence or it is not important.
- We use *by* in a passive sentence to say who does the action. ▸ *The passive, p. 219*

1 My entire staff ⬤ starting next month. At least they ⬤ a good severance package.
2 These cuts ⬤ in order to keep the company running and to provide workplaces for local people abroad.
3 For me this is great news. I ⬤ the chance to do my own thing and am looking forward to starting my own business.
4 I always thought I ⬤ by my superiors and colleagues, but clearly I was mistaken.
5 So many good employees ⬤ so far. The news hasn't been easy to give, nor to receive.

B Now match the quotes to the people who said them. What other types of comments would you expect these people to make?

> CEO • employee • future freelancer •
> HR manager • senior manager

3 Discussion: socially sensitive restructuring

Claudia emails you a list of tools that firms can use to restructure in a socially sensitive manner.

A There is a problem and the tools have become jumbled. Match 1–7 with a–g.

1 counselling in order to work through
2 skills assessment to assess the benefits
3 training to prepare an employee for
4 mobility assistance to help an employee
5 alternative work schedules and/or ways
6 severance packages as compensation for
7 survivor round tables to provide the

a of working e.g. part-time, flexitime, teleworking
b feelings of grief and find closure
c who has to move away to find work
d loss of earnings
e of retraining people
f opportunity for those still employed to talk openly about the change
g a move to another department

B Sort the tools into the categories **a** and **b** below. (Some will be in both.) Which tools would have been useful for helping the people who posted on the forum?

a support for employees who will be kept on under different conditions
b support for employees who have lost their jobs

4 Writing: how (not to) restructure

▸ *Elne Stellungnahme schreiben, S. 208*

Take on a point of view of your choice, e.g. as a mediator or an employee, and comment on how staff are affected by restructuring and downsizing. Give examples.

D Practice and projects

1 Problems at work

A Add words from each box to form collocations you can use to talk about clients who have problems at work. You can use some of the words in more than one collocation.

1 digestive	7 sexual	conditions	pains
2 face-to-face	8 sexually suggestive	discrimination	pressure
3 follow-up	9 stress	discussion	problems
4 muscle	10 stomach	level	remarks
5 offensive	11 time	manner	session
6 racial	12 working	orientation	tension

B Which collocations can be used to talk about:

a counselling/giving advice?   c medical problems?
b harassment?   d work?

2 Reporting what people said

Change the direct speech into reported speech.

1 "I've had enough of this company. I'm leaving," Vera said.
2 "Ms Lebedeva does not speak German well. This causes some problems," the supervisor said.
3 "We would like to apologize if we have hurt Vera's feelings. We really thought she would see it as a joke," one of her colleagues said.
4 "I'm one of the best in my field," Glen said.
5 "I'm willing to give him another chance, but he has to adopt a more positive attitude," the boss said.
6 "We are trying to include Glen in some of our after-work activities," one of his colleagues said.
7 "The economic situation at the moment is not good," a spokesperson for the company said.
8 "We have given our workers excellent severance packages," the CEO said.   ▶ *Reported speech, p. 217*

3 Talking about being laid off

Complete the forum entry with words from the box.

> downsize • laid off • lay-offs • meeting • overworked • rumours •
> sector • severance package • trends

Before we heard the news from management, my colleagues and I read about the proposed ⬤¹ in "Business Online". The news didn't come as a big surprise. There had been ⬤² that the company had problems. Once the news was out, management called a ⬤³. The CEO began by saying that the company had been forced to ⬤⁴ because of market conditions in our ⬤⁵. He went on to say that the company had been keeping a close eye on ⬤⁶ for several months and had tried all they could to avoid it but, sorry, some people would have to go. I got a good ⬤⁷ and I got another job quite quickly. I met some of my old colleagues last week and they complained about being ⬤⁸. I'm happy with my new job, and glad I was ⬤⁹.

74

Unit 6   Solving problems at work

Changing active to passive

Change these active sentences into passive sentences. Remember to use *by* when necessary.

1 Some male colleagues harassed Vera.
2 Vera's supervisor has advised her to have counselling.
3 The doctor told Glen about the effects of stress.
4 They will assess Glen's case next week.
5 The company employs a lot of highly-qualified workers.
6 They have laid off 200 people.
7 The boss gave the staff reasons for the lay-offs.
8 Most of the workers have accepted the severance pay that the company offered.   › *The passive, p. 219*

Guidelines: preventing problems among staff

You are going to create guidelines for preventing problems among staff and publish the document.

Step 1 In a group, discuss situations which you have come across in this unit or in real life in which employees have felt dissatisfied with their treatment at work, by colleagues or by management. Write down your findings on small cards and pin them up on posters under the following headings:

- dissatisfaction with company changes
- dissatisfaction with behaviour of colleagues

Step 2 With a partner, formulate six useful suggestions for dealing with the problems mentioned in the lists above. Make sure you express positive ideas. Share your suggestions with another pair and choose the six best. Write them on separate cards and pin them up near the posters from Step 1.

Step 3 Divide the class into five groups. Each group works on one aspect of the guidelines:

| feedback and evaluation | communication and openness | respect | supervision and dealing with problems | team building |

In your group, use suggestions from Step 2 to formulate as many ideas as you can for preventing problems among staff.

Step 4 Peer-review the work of one of the other groups. Make any necessary changes to your work.

Step 5 When you are ready, put together the suggestions in the order you think they should appear. Write a short introduction, then publish the guidelines in the form you have agreed on.

Checking progress

Browse through the previous pages in the unit, looking at headings and pictures.
What have you learned? What can you do now that you have learned these things?
✔ I can give advice to help people deal with problems at work.   (Parts A, B and C)
✔ I can write a record of a meeting.   (Part B)
✔ I can develop guidelines which can be used to prevent problems among staff.   (Part D)

Write down two more statements of your own.

To what extent has this unit given you an insight into problems that can arise at work?

75

Exam skills and strategies

Mindmaps und Gliederungen erstellen

Wichtig für:
- materialgestützten Aufsatz
- Schreiben einer Stellungnahme

Bevor Sie Texte jeglicher Art verfassen, sollten Sie Inhalt und Struktur Ihres Textes vorbereiten. Mindmaps eignen sich, um schnell viele Ideen niederzuschreiben (Brainstorming) und diese gleichzeitig zu strukturieren. Mithilfe einer Grobgliederung teilen Sie das, was Sie schreiben möchten, in mehrere Sinnabschnitte auf. Die einzelnen Gliederungspunkte helfen, einen Text inhaltlich zu strukturieren und somit übersichtlicher zu machen.

BEISPIEL-AUFGABE Write at least 200 words on how an employer can create a good work environment. Name typical problems and possible solutions.

TIPPS

1 Schreiben Sie das Thema in die Mitte eines Blatt Papiers.

2 Notieren Sie die wichtigsten Gedanken zu diesem Thema ringsherum und verbinden Sie diese jeweils mit dem Hauptthema durch zweigartige Linien. Die Begriffe dieser Verästelungen können die Grundlage für die einzelnen Paragraphen Ihres Textes darstellen.

3 Fügen Sie jedem Unterbegriff weitere Wörter und Gedanken hinzu. Das ist das Gerüst, das Sie benötigen, um Ihre Ideen auszuarbeiten.

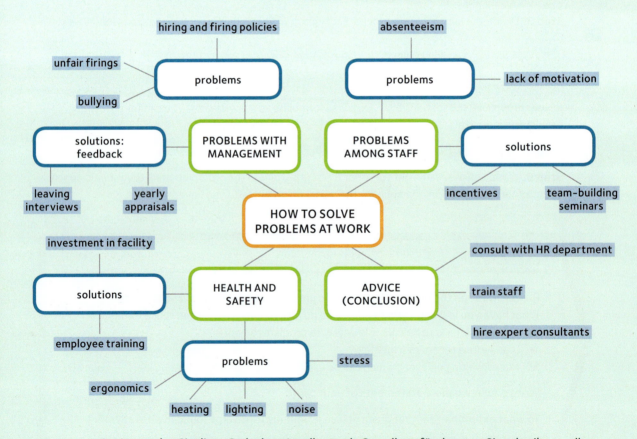

4 Verwenden Sie diese Gedanken-Landkarte als Grundlage für das, was Sie schreiben wollen.

Exam skills and strategies

1 Zur Vorbereitung auf das Schreiben eines Aufsatzes über arbeitsrechtliche Bestimmungen wurde die folgende Mindmap begonnen. Vervollständigen Sie diese mithilfe der Wendungen aus dem Kasten.

> *holiday entitlement* • *equal pay for men and women* • *weekly hours* • *overtime* • *maternity and paternity leave* • *women re-joining the workforce after giving birth* • *minimum wages* • *incentives* • *family-friendly working hours*

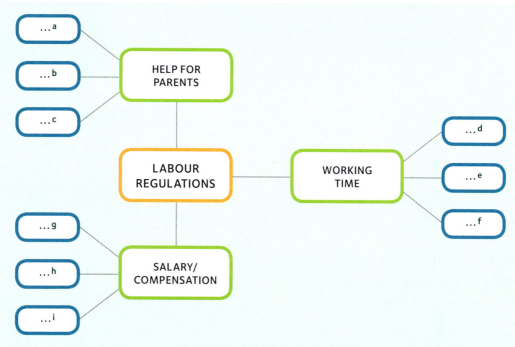

2 Comment on this statement: "Although telecommuting is becoming a popular way of working, many managers think that their employees work better when they are surrounded by their team." First, complete the outline below with statements from the box. Then write your comment.

Introduction
▬¹

Paragraph 1: Working at home is attractive for employees.
a ▬²
b ▬³
c ▬⁴

Paragraph 2: Many telecommuters work more effectively than people in offices.
a ▬⁵
b ▬⁶
c ▬⁷

Conclusion

The time they save by not travelling can be spent on their work. • *People who have children have an easier time organizing their home lives.* • *I disagree with this statement.* • *They have no stress from travelling to and from work, and a lot of time is saved.* • *There are not as many distractions, because they don't get interrupted by colleagues.* • *Telecommuting saves time for the worker, and saves money for the company (win-win situation).* • *Employees enjoy having the communications technology at home.*

3 Describe the role of the human resources department of a typical company. (Make a mind map or outline before you write your text.)

› *Lösungen, S. 291*

77

From the UN Convention on the Rights of Persons with Disabilities, 2006

Article 3 – General principles

a   Respect for inherent dignity, individual autonomy including the freedom to make one's own choices, and independence of persons;
b   Non-discrimination;
c   Full and effective participation and inclusion in society;
d   Respect for difference and acceptance of persons with disabilities as part of human diversity and humanity;
e   Equality of opportunity;
f   Accessibility;
g   Equality between men and women;
h   Respect for the evolving capacities of children with disabilities and respect for the right of children with disabilities to preserve their identities.

7 Working with clients with special needs

1
A Look at the photos. What kind of disabilities do they show?

B What other types of disabilities do you know? Collect words together and start a mind map.

2   Scan the texts for numbers and dates and explain what they mean.

3
A Think about schools in your area. How many (if any) of them practise inclusion? How do they integrate pupils who are physically or mentally challenged?

B What employment possibilities are there for disabled people in your area?

C When did you last help someone with a disability? What sort of help did you give? Tell a partner and describe the positive effects it had. What did you learn from the experience?

D In what way can society respond to and meet the requirements of citizens with special needs?

ITALY: INCLUSION WORKS, BUT WHERE ARE THE JOBS?

Since the year 1997, there have been no special schools in Italy, and 99% of differently-abled pupils attend mainstream schools. Inclusion is a fact of life, but problems arise when people leave school. The country which shows most advances in schooling has the fewest numbers of job places for the differently-abled.

WORK OPPORTUNITIES FOR THE DISABLED

According to the latest World Report on Disability (WRD), more than 1 billion people in the world have some form of disability. This corresponds to about 15% of the world's population. Globally, between 110–190 million people have very significant physical or mental difficulties.

The report states that disabled people of employment age are more likely to be unemployed than non-disabled people. In OECD* countries, the employment rate of people with disabilities (44%) is slightly over half that for people without disabilities (75%). Despite anti-discrimination laws, many people with disabilities have difficulties finding employment.

* Organization for Economic Cooperation and Development

FULL INCLUSION FOR ALL BERLIN SCHOOLS BY THE START OF THE NEXT DECADE?

At the moment, almost 50% of children with special needs are being taught in mainstream schools in Berlin. Today, the government announced that it aims to have full inclusion by the year 2020. While most people welcome the proposal, there is some concern that putting the scheme into action might be difficult. "Many schools are not prepared to cope with people with mobility difficulties. We also need more well-trained, motivated staff," said

---

What's to come

In this unit, you will …
- investigate the inclusion of differently-abled children in the classroom.
- look into employment opportunities for the disabled.
- join an international group on a visit to a sheltered workshop.

At the end of the unit, you will develop and present a concept for a workshop or day centre facility for differently-abled clients.

Before you begin, walk through your village, town or city and make a note of situations which might make life difficult for someone who is differently-abled. How would you cope with these difficulties if you were disabled?

A Why this school?

> **S** You would like to work as a paediatric assistant. Inclusion is a topic that interests you, so you look online to see what kind of information you can find there on the subject.

1 Reading: for and against inclusion

The first thing you find is a forum where people have posted comments.

A Read the posts and say which of the writers is for and which of the writers is against inclusion.

Alan My son has trisomy 21 (Down's syndrome). He's been at a mainstream school all his life. Now, the secondary school he attends says his development will suffer if he continues in mainstream education. I can't understand this as he's doing so well. Academic expectations are higher in a mainstream school, and my son has achieved much more as a result.

Barbara Sorry. The idea of inclusion is very nice for differently-abled children, what about the able children? There are children with developmental problems in my son's class. He's a very bright child, but is not getting the attention he deserves as his teachers spend far too much time assisting the less able children. I realize that differently-abled children have a right to an education, but every time I see them, I think "Why this school?"

Carmen I completely agree with Alan's point of view. My daughter, who has cerebral palsy, attends a regular primary school. I believe that inclusion is not only the best thing for children with special needs, it is also good for society. My daughter's school friends are helping her to grow up normally. She goes to their parties and they come to us for parties and sleepovers. It is great for both the abled and the disabled to live in a community which adapts to people with special needs.

Don I'd like to add something to Barbara's statement. Day after day, we hear there is no money for education. So why is a specialist teacher being brought into our local school? Is it fair to other children that schools are allocating resources to training teachers to look after differently-abled children?

Eve As a teacher, I know that many schools include differently-abled children very well, but at the school where I work, we do not have the time or the ability to adapt lessons to suit the needs of the differently-abled child. Resources are limited, and teachers have not been trained to cater for children with special needs.   (332 words)

B You want to make sure you understand what the people have written so you look up some words in a bilingual dictionary. Find the English equivalents in the posts.

1 *Regelschule • Sekundarschule • Sonderschule • Grundschule*
2 *Leistungserwartungen • Aufmerksamkeit • Recht auf Bildung*
3 *Ressourcen zuteilen • Bedürfnissen gerecht zu werden*

C Read the posts again and note down the arguments for and against inclusion.

D **CHALLENGE!** If you would like a challenge, turn to file C3 on page 184.

---

2 Reading: a Texas waiter does the right thing

In another forum you visit, you find a link to the article on the next page.

A After you have read the article, correct the false statements below.

1 Michael Garcia, who used to work as a waiter, became famous when he opened a school.
2 The Castillo family, which includes a deaf child called Milo, is well known to Michael Garcia.
3 Garcia laughed when a young couple that was sitting next to the Castillos made fun of Milo.
4 The Rise School, which practises inclusion, would not accept Garcia's gift of money.
5 Ashley Kress, who works at the school, is worried that Garcia will lose his job.

Unit 7   Working with clients with special needs

> **TEXAS WAITER DEFENDS DOWN SYNDROME BOY AND FUNDS SCHOLARSHIP**
>
> At the beginning of the month, Michael Garcia was an unknown waiter at Laurenzo's restaurant in Houston, Texas. By the end of the month, Garcia was a national hero who was on his way to becoming a school benefactor.
> Garcia has welcomed and served the Castillo family for years. Milo, the five-year-old son, has Down syndrome. A few weeks ago, when another family made rude comments about Milo, 45-year-old Garcia refused to serve them.
> Ever since the story broke on national news, Garcia has received letters, extra high tips, gifts and donations from people thanking him for standing up for the boy. Last Thursday, he presented the money he had received to the boy's school, the Rise School of Houston. The preschool offers a special programme for children born with Down syndrome and other disabilities.
> Ashley Kress, who is the development director of the Rise School, says: "Michael Garcia had no personal motive for acting the way he did. He could have lost his job by refusing to serve the other customers, but he didn't care. He stood up for Milo. Maybe other people can learn from him."
>
> (187 words)

B Recreate some extracts from the article by adding the extra information in brackets to the sentences. Look at the grammar box for help.

1. Garcia will use his free time to raise awareness about children with special needs. (He still works as a waiter.)
2. The Rise School is a preschool. (It caters for children with and without disabilities.)
3. It was founded by parents. (They believe in inclusion.)
4. The National Down Syndrome Society published the news about Garcia on its website. (The society is funded by donations.)

> **Adding extra information**
>
> The restaurant **which/that** is mentioned in the article has become a tourist attraction.
> We all know some people **who/that** have negative feelings about inclusion.
>
> - We often join sentences by putting *who*, *which* or *that* in place of *he*, *she*, *it* or *they*.
> ▷ *Relative clauses, p. 224*

3   Watching a video: "Graduation day at the Rise School"

You find this video about the Rise School on the internet.

4:45

A Watch the video with the sound off. What do you think the voice-over is saying? Collect vocabulary and phrases on the board, then listen and check.

B Working in groups, watch the clip again and take notes in order to do the following tasks.

1. Describe the pupils who go the Rise School.
2. Point out the mission of the school and say how the school achieves its aims.
3. Describe the contribution of the Texas Medical Center.
4. Explain why the Rise School is particularly important for Ashley Kress and the other parents.

4   Writing: inclusion – both sides of the story

▷ *Eine Stellungnahme schreiben, S. 208*

Use information from these pages to write a comment on the issue of inclusion of differently-abled children in mainstream schools. Include the points of view of all parties concerned.

GUIDANCE   *If you would like guidance, turn to file G11 on page 176.*

81

B The right to work

> **S** You have applied for a position in a social enterprise in York, England. One of the focuses of the enterprise is finding employment for less severely impaired clients. In preparation for your interview, you read the information below.

A	B	C	D	E	F	G	H	I

equal opportunity *n.* Absence of discrimination (in the workplace), based on race, age, gender, sexual orientation, national origin, religion, or mental or physical disability.

Which word?

In the UK, the expression "disabled people" is generally preferred to "people with disabilities". The term "disabled people" is widely used by international organizations, such as Disabled Peoples' International (DPI). You will also hear "people with impairments" (e.g. "people with visual impairments"), and most people would rather be referred to as "a person with a disability" than as "a handicapped person".

EMPLOYMENT OPPORTUNITIES FOR DISABLED PEOPLE

Worldwide, the number of people with disabilities is growing rapidly due to ageing populations and the increase in the number of chronic conditions. Statistics suggest that disability disproportionately affects vulnerable populations (women, older people and the poor). Speaking at a conference on employment opportunities for disabled people, Maeve Binder, spokesperson for the campaigning organization Integration Works!, said "Despite the stereotypical view of a disabled person as a wheelchair user, there are many different types of disability, and the range of difficulty caused by them goes from mild to severe with all the gradations in between. We would like to see more special training for adults who are never considered for employment simply because they have a disability." Ms Binder went on to say that some people object to describing certain conditions as disabilities. "Take deafness and autism, for example," she said. "It is more appropriate to consider these conditions as developmental differences that have been unfairly stigmatized by society."

Defining disabilities and impairments

Intellectual disability
This term refers to a group of disorders characterized by a limited mental capacity. Social interaction and activities such as managing money, schedules and routines are often difficult. Intellectual disability originates before the age of 18 and may result from physical causes, such as autism or cerebral palsy. Non-physical causes, like lack of stimulation and lack of responsiveness in adults towards the developing child, might also lead to intellectual disability.

Physical disability
This describes the total inability to use one or more parts of the body completely because of a physical condition, illness, injury, etc. Examples of physical disabilities are motor neuron disease, multiple sclerosis, cerebral palsy, paraplegia, quadriplegia, amputated limbs, total deafness, total blindness.

Physical impairment
Any problem which limits the physical function of limbs or motor ability is a physical impairment. If someone's ability to see, speak or hear has been damaged but not destroyed completely, they are described as having an impairment, e.g. vision impairment (sometimes called "visual impairment"), speech impairment (sometimes called "a speech impediment") or hearing impairment. Mild hearing loss may sometimes not be considered a disability.

Invisible disabilities
Several chronic disorders, such as diabetes, asthma, inflammatory bowel disease or epilepsy, are counted as invisible disabilities, as opposed to disabilities which are clearly visible, such as those requiring the use of a wheelchair.

Unit 7　Working with clients with special needs

1　Reading: disabilities – definitions and rights

> *Schwierige Texte lesen, S. 202*

A Find the following words and phrases in the texts on page 82.

1. two phrases that mean "the same chances of employment for everyone"
2. two general terms to describe "people who are differently-abled"
3. two phrases used to illustrate developments which might influence the number of people with disabilities
4. two terms for physical causes that may lead to intellectual disability
5. two phrases that describe non-physical causes which may lead to intellectual disability
6. one phrase that means "a long-lasting condition that is difficult to cure"

B Do the following tasks with a partner.

1. Explain the difference between an impairment and a disability.
2. Point out to what extent the chronic conditions mentioned in the texts are disabling.

C Return to the mind map you produced when you started on this unit. Use information from the texts on the previous page to add words connected to disabled people. Expand your mind map with other words you know. Use a German/English dictionary if you like.

GUIDANCE　*If you would like guidance, turn to file G12 on page 176.*

2　Listening: assisting disabled people looking for work

You find a podcast that could contain useful information for your interview.

In our podcast today, Mark from the Social Pulse team talks to Angela Rankin about helping disabled people to enter the workplace. Angela is a Disability Employment Adviser (DEA) who works in a Job Centre.

A Before you listen, read the list of topics covered in the interview and describe the logo on the right. In which part of the interview might Angela talk about it?

- what a DEA does
- disability-friendly employers
- matching disabilities to jobs
- prejudices against hiring the disabled
- a success story

2/2

B Make a table with the list of topics above, then listen to the interview and take notes. Write down anything you find interesting. Don't forget to check your ideas about the logo.

C Work with a partner. Pool your notes from exercise 2B and summarize the interview.

3　Presentation: employment opportunities for the disabled

> *Präsentieren, S. 209*

As part of the application process, you are invited to an assessment centre. Your task is to give a presentation on employment opportunities for disabled people. Use what you have learned while working through this section to prepare and give your presentation.

> *Presentations, p. 195*

83

C   A visit to a sheltered workshop

> **S** You have started work at the social enterprise in York. Your boss is interested in expanding to include a workshop which employs differently-abled people. She asks you to visit a sheltered workshop in Germany and shows you the invitation below.

Open day for professional care workers 25 October
The Eider Werkstätten GmbH runs sheltered accommodation, workshops and day care facilities for adults with disabilities. Self-esteem, independence and empowerment are our aims for our employees. You can see these aims being put into action at our open day.

1   Reading and mediation: preparing for the visit
> *Mediation, S. 211*

A First, look at the invitation. What do the terms "self-esteem", "independence" and "empowerment" mean? Why do you think these are important aims for adults with disabilities? How do you think the workshop can help the employees achieve these aims?

B Your boss has given you a list of questions. Look at this printout of the organization's "About us" page below and find the answers.

1 What kind of organization is Eider Werkstätten?
2 Who works there?
3 What sort of jobs do the differently-abled employees do?
4 Why is there such a variety of jobs?

PROFIL

Wer sind wir?
In der Eider Werkstätten GmbH arbeiten Kolleginnen und Kollegen mit und ohne Behinderung zusammen, die sich mit vielfältigen Problemen auseinandersetzen, die ihre gemeinsame Arbeit aufwirft.

Was wollen wir?
Wir gestalten im Rahmen der Eingliederungshilfe den Alltag von Produktion und die Produktion von Alltag. Der ideologische Gegensatz von individueller Förderung und betrieblicher Produktivität wird durch die Praxis von Kollegialität und Leistung aufgehoben.

Im Arbeitsbereich arbeiten ca. 12 Kolleginnen und Kollegen mit dem Gruppenleiter / der Gruppenleiterin in einer Produktionsgruppe zusammen. Als Werkstatt für Menschen mit Behinderung bieten wir ein breites Angebot an verschiedenen Arbeitsplätzen in unterschiedlichen handwerklichen und industriellen Bereichen an (u. a. Metallbearbeitung, Autopflege, Gartenbau, Montage, usw.), um den Interessen, Neigungen und Fähigkeiten jeden Mitarbeiters mit Behinderung gerecht zu werden. Darüber hinaus ist jeder Bereich in Tätigkeiten mit unterschiedlichen Schwierigkeitsgraden gegliedert. Nicht alle unsere Angestellten stellen neue Produkte her; manche packen lediglich z. B. Süßigkeiten um, deren Verpackung während des Transports beschädigt worden ist und befüllen neue Tüten mit der richtigen Menge. Dies ermöglicht jeder Kollegin und jedem Kollegen, an dem Arbeitsplatz zu arbeiten, der seinem Leistungsvermögen entspricht.

C Your boss needs this information for her files. Summarize the text for her in English.

GUIDANCE *If you would like guidance, turn to file G25 on page 181.*

---

2   Listening: a tour of the workshop

2/3

You have arrived at the workshop in Germany. The senior supervisor, Jana Dalk, welcomes you and the other visitors at reception and takes you on a tour of the building.

A Look at the floor plan on the next page and listen to the tour. Take notes on what each room is used for.

84

Unit 7 Working with clients with special needs

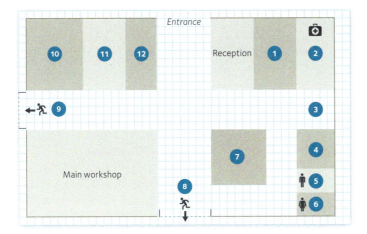

B Work in groups and do the tasks below.

1. Describe how the building has been designed. Explain why.
2. What kind of feeling does one of the visitors describe? Explain what provokes this feeling.
3. Explain what the glass cube is normally used for and how the visitors will use it later.
4. Give an example of how the company encourages empowerment.
5. Describe the kind of work the employees do.

3 Listening: on the job

2/4

During your visit to the workshop, Olli, an assistant carer and one of the team leaders in the workshop, talks about his work.

A Listen and make notes on the following points.

1. what room Olli and his team are working in and the job they are doing
2. the team's favourite goods
3. Olli's experience working with disabled people before he joined the company
4. what Olli likes about the work and his motivation for working
5. what is important for the employees at the workshop

B **CHALLENGE!** If you would like a challenge, turn to file C4 on page 184.

4 Giving an oral report: the Eider Werkstätten GmbH

Your boss asks you to tell her about the workshop so that she can decide if she should start one in York. Describe the workshop using the floor plan. Point out what the work gives the employees, e.g. self-esteem. Say what your enterprise in York can learn from your visit.

GUIDANCE *If you would like guidance, turn to file G16 on page 178.*

Showing someone around

- This is where the employees …
- This area is used for …
- The kitchen is opposite / next to / on the right/left of …
- Over there, in the corner, is the …
  > *Showing somebody around, p. 191*

85

D Practice and projects

1 Talking about integration in schools

A Make as many collocations as you can by matching words from the two boxes. Who has the most collocations in the class?

academic	mainstream		abilities	needs
bright	regular		care	problems
developmental	secondary		children	school
differently-abled	special		expectations	teacher

B Complete the text using collocations from above.

Working as a special ―¹ with children who have developmental ―² can be very fulfilling. Differently-abled ―³ who attend a mainstream ―⁴ may have a few academic ―⁵. However, their presence in the classroom encourages classmates to develop feelings of responsibility towards people with disabilities. One teacher says: "Children do not always need to have great academic ―⁶ to be able to shine in a classroom. There are as many bright ―⁷ in the special ―⁸ where I work as there are in any regular ―⁹."

2 Adding extra information

Combine the two sentences with *who*, *which* or *that*.

1 I know somebody. She teaches in a special school.
2 The school promotes inclusion. My daughter attends that school.
3 Michael is a waiter. He works in Lorenzo's.
4 People gave Michael tips and donations. They also deserve praise.
5 Happy Eating is a restaurant chain. It employs disabled people.
6 The girl was diagnosed with autism. She works in an IT firm.
7 The people work in the sheltered workshop. They have a lot of self-esteem.
8 The sweets are for the Christmas market. The employees are putting them into nets.

> Relative clauses, p. 224

3 Disabled people in the UK

Complete the text with words and phrases from the box.

disabled • impairment • non-disabled • stable • unfair treatment • working-age

According to a long-running survey being conducted by the government, there are over eleven million people in the UK living with a long-term illness, ―¹ or disability today. Around 6% of children are ―², compared to 16% of ―³ adults and 45% of adults over the age of 65.
In 2012, 46.3% of working-age disabled people were in employment compared to 76.4% of ―⁴ people. This 30.1% gap, which represents over 2 million people, has remained ―⁵ over the last two years despite the economic climate. Disabled employees are more likely to experience personal problems at work than non-disabled people. In 2008, 19% of disabled people reported ―⁶ at work compared to 13% of non-disabled people.

Unit 7   Working with clients with special needs

Showing someone around

Choose the most suitable word from the brackets to complete the sentences.

1   Let's start here, (before / into / outside) reception.
2   Our meeting room is to the (near / opposite / right) of reception.
3   The corridor (next / over / to) there leads to one of the fire exits.
4   There is another fire exit (left / opposite / up) the lift.
5   The senior social worker's office is (at / in / over) another part of the building.
6   This is my office, and (nearby / next / opposite) door to me is the medical room.
7   The kitchen is (back / behind / close) the medical room.
8   The men's and women's toilets are (at / on / up) this floor, too.

Developing and presenting a concept for a facility for clients with special needs

Working in a small group, you are going to discuss options for activities for differently-abled clients and then develop a concept for an after-school programme or a sheltered workshop for 12 differently-abled clients.

Step 1 Choose your target group from among the clients you have learned about while working through this unit.

Step 2 Write a mission statement (i.e. a summary of your organization's aims and values). How do you want to help your clients and society?

Step 3 Brainstorm ideas about activities you might offer.

Step 4 Think carefully about your target group and discuss whether the activities are appropriate. Discard any activities that might cause the clients difficulties.

Step 5 Make a list of the remaining activities and decide how much assistance the clients in your target group are likely to require. Decide how many assistants might be necessary to keep the after-school programme or workshop running smoothly.

Step 6 Present your concept to the class and ask for feedback.

Checking progress

Browse through the previous pages in the unit, looking at headings and pictures.
What have you learned? What can you do now that you have learned these things?
   ✔ I can read and understand opinions about the issue of inclusion.   (Part A)
   ✔ I can give a presentation on employment opportunities for disabled people.   (Part B)
   ✔ I can describe a facility and report on the benefits.   (Part C)
   ✔ I can develop and present a concept for a facility for clients with special needs.   (Part D)

Write down two more statements of your own.

How much has this unit given you an insight into working with clients with special needs? Which, if any, of the target groups could you imagine working with?

Exam skills and strategies

Einen Aufsatz oder eine Stellungnahme schreiben

Wichtig für:
- Schreiben eines Aufsatzes oder einer Stellungnahme
- materialgestützten Aufsatz
- rollenbasierte Stellungnahme

Textproduktionsaufgaben fordern Sie heraus, nicht nur grammatikalisch korrektes, sondern auch gut strukturiertes und verständliches Englisch zu gebrauchen. Bei den meisten Aufgaben zur Textproduktion sollen Sie objektiv über ein Thema schreiben, ohne Ihre Meinung zu äußern. Wenn eine Aufgabe jedoch Operatoren wie „*comment*" oder „*discuss*" enthält, ist Ihre eigene Meinung, eine Beurteilung oder eine Erörterung erforderlich.

▸ *Textproduktion: Umgang mit Operatoren, S. 40 / S. 202*

BEISPIELAUFGABE Write an essay / a comment on this statement: "The costs of hiring people with disabilities outweigh the benefits."

TIPPS Bevor Sie beginnen:

1. Lesen Sie sich die Aufgabe mehrmals durch und vergewissern Sie sich, was gefordert ist.
   - Um einen Aufsatz zu schreiben, müssen Sie Argumente finden, die diese Aussage sowohl stützen als auch bestreiten.
   - Wenn Sie eine Stellungnahme schreiben, müssen Sie Ihre eigene Meinung äußern und diese auch untermauern.

2. Brainstorming: Schreiben Sie alle Gedanken auf, die Ihnen in den Sinn kommen, wenn Sie über das Thema nachdenken, und ordnen Sie diese in einer Struktur an. Grobgliederungen und Mindmaps eignen sich dafür sehr gut.

   > My opinion: I disagree strongly – the social benefits of diversity outweigh the costs.
   > Argument 1: The costs of inclusion are not very big – maybe some new equipment, or some training.
   > Argument 2: Benefit to company: tax breaks
   > Argument 3: Benefit to company: good PR

▸ *Mindmaps und Gliederungen erstellen, S. 76 / S. 207*

Den Aufsatz oder die Stellungnahme schreiben:

3. Schreiben Sie einen Einleitungssatz, der das Thema/Problem und die darauf zurückzuführende Situation darstellt. Beschreiben Sie dann das Thema mit anderen Worten und äußern Sie Ihre Meinung. Geben Sie Ihren Lesern/-innen abschließend einen Überblick der Argumente, die Sie anführen wollen.
   → *Some employers are still reluctant to hire disabled workers. They argue that the costs of doing so will be too high. (Stellungnahme:) This excuse is unreasonable and I will argue against it. I will also name some benefits that come with employing disabled workers.*

4. Schreiben Sie nun den Hauptteil Ihres Aufsatzes. Behandeln Sie jedes Argument in einem eigenen Abschnitt. Stützen Sie Ihre Argumente mit Fakten und Beispielen. Stellen Sie sicher, dass Ihre Argumente logisch und leicht nachvollziehbar sind. Verwenden Sie Wörter und Wendungen, die die Struktur Ihres Textes klarer machen.

Exam skills and strategies

→ (Stellungnahme:) *First, let's look at* the "expense" excuse. Is it really very expensive to modify a workplace for a disabled person's needs? Not unless the company is so poor it cannot, **for instance**, afford a small amount of training, or some equipment – like a handrail. **In other words**, if any adjustments need to be made, the cost of these will probably be minimal. **Therefore**, concerns about the cost are not a good argument against hiring a disabled person, as any costs will be very small, and there might not even be any additional expenses.

Next, let's look at the tax breaks available to the company when they have a disabled member of staff …

Writing clearly

listing arguments
first, second, third, etc.
next, further, furthermore, in addition

giving examples
for example, for instance, to illustrate my point

comparing and contrasting viewpoints and arguments
on the one hand / on the other hand, likewise, similarly, although, however, nevertheless, on the contrary, and yet

showing results and consequences
as a result, consequently, for this reason, so, then, therefore, otherwise

summarizing
in conclusion, in other words, on the whole

5 Schreiben Sie in der Schlussfolgerung eine Zusammenfassung dessen, was Sie bereits geschrieben haben. Führen Sie hier keine neuen Argumente ein. Unterstreichen Sie Ihren Standpunkt kurz und knapp in einem Schlusssatz. Dieser sollte in einer Stellungnahme Ihre eigene Meinung widerspiegeln.

→ **In conclusion**, employers who are willing to challenge prejudice benefit in many ways. They receive tax breaks and good publicity. By performing a service to society, the company enhances its public image. The workplace benefits from diversity. (Stellungnahme:) *This is why I believe all employers should include positive discrimination as part of their employment policy.*

Das Geschriebene bearbeiten:

6 Überprüfen Sie Ihren Entwurf auf Rechtschreib- und Grammatikfehler hin. Achten Sie besonders auf mögliche Fehler bei der Wortstellung.
→ (Stellungnahme:) ~~Much persons~~ **Many people** think ~~so,~~ that disabled people ~~don't can~~ **can't** take responsibility for themselves. This is down to a lack of information~~s~~.

7 Vorsicht vor „falschen Freunden" – das sind englische Wörter, die deutschen Wörtern ähnlich sind, aber etwas anderes bedeuten.
→ (Stellungnahme:) I ~~mean~~ **think** that consumers should ~~become~~ **get** the chance to respond to any job ~~announcement~~ **advertisement**.

8 Überlegen Sie, ob Sie Ihren Text verbessern können, indem Sie abwechslungsreicheres Vokabular verwenden.

Writing with varied vocabulary

- Instead of the word *say*, use *mention, remark, state, express, claim*.
- Instead of *good*, use *decent, favourable, great, outstanding, superb, excellent*.
- Instead of *not good*, use *poor, dreadful, terrible, unpleasant, disgusting*.
- Instead of *very*, use *really, quite, extremely, highly, remarkably*.

 Many adults with cognitive disabilities like the social contact and support they get in a sheltered workshop but some say they would like to work in ordinary jobs. Plan and write an essay on the following topic: "What advantages and disadvantages would employees with cognitive disabilities find working in ordinary jobs? What are the advantages to business and society?"

› *Lösungen, S. 292*

89

The **MEDIA** bombards us with hundreds of **ADVERTS** every day, filled with beautiful **SKINNY** models telling us how we **SHOULD LOOK**. This **OBSESSION** with beauty and **WEIGHT** can lead even the most "normal" person to develop problems with **BODY IMAGE**. The facts speak for themselves …

THE MEDIA'S INFLUENCE ON GIRLS | MEN'S BODY HANG-UPS

50% of advertisements aimed at girls speak about PHYSICAL ATTRACTIVENESS.

69% of girls in one US study said that magazine models influence their idea of the PERFECT BODY.

47% of girls in 5th–12th grade felt magazine pictures influenced them to want TO LOSE WEIGHT.

29% are ACTUALLY clinically overweight.

nach: raderprograms.com

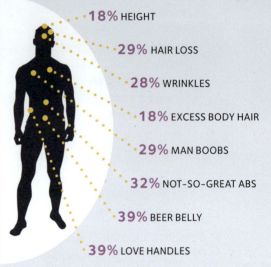

- 18% HEIGHT
- 29% HAIR LOSS
- 28% WRINKLES
- 18% EXCESS BODY HAIR
- 29% MAN BOOBS
- 32% NOT-SO-GREAT ABS
- 39% BEER BELLY
- 39% LOVE HANDLES

nach: JWT Intelligence Survey

8 Staying healthy, keeping fit

1 A What topics come to mind when you look at the infographic? What do you find interesting or surprising?

- It's interesting that …
- I find it hard to believe that …
- I'm (not) surprised that …
- I can/can't imagine that …

B Work in pairs and describe one set of statistics and one image to your partner.

› Statistiken beschreiben und analysieren, S. 210
› Bilder und Cartoons beschreiben und analysieren, S. 210

2 Collect words and phrases used to talk about staying healthy and keeping fit on the board.

3 How do you personally stay healthy and fit? Share your tips with your class or group.

POOR BODY IMAGE = RISK FACTOR FOR EATING DISORDERS | # WAY OUT

DID YOU KNOW? | ## HEALTHY EATING/KEEPING FIT!

Nearly 20 million women will suffer from an eating disorder at some point in their life.

National Eating Disorders Association (NEDA)

Females between ages 15–24 with anorexia are 12 times more likely to die from the illness than all other causes of death.

OBESITY WORLDWIDE

65% of the world's population live in countries where they are more likely to die of obesity than malnutrition.

OBESITY RATES*

 31.8%

 24.9%

 21.3%

* % of adult population

nach: World Health Organization (WHO)

How many times a week do Germans do sport?

- daily — 1.1%
- 4–6 times a week — 10.6%
- 2–3 times a week — 26.9%
- once a week — 15.7%
- not at all — 39.7%

What stops people doing sport?*	
no/little time	51%
can't be bothered / too lazy	18%
job	14%
no money	8%
family	4%
no response	25%
*408 people surveyed; more than one answer possible	

nach: INJOY Studie

What's to come

In this unit, you will …
- help some pre-teens aged 9–12 at an international after-school club consider their eating habits and plan a healthy meal.
- discuss eating disorders with a group of older teenagers.
- analyse the media's role in pressurizing people into wanting "the perfect body".

At the end of the unit, you will design and present your ideas for an advertising campaign to promote health and fitness.

Before you begin, think about how the pages that follow might be useful to you in a personal as well as in a professional way. Make notes on where you might find chances to improve your own health and fitness.

A You are what you eat

> **S** You are working as a trainee in an international after-school club. Today, you are talking to pre-teens aged 9–12 about food and nutrition.

1 Talking about food

You use the illustration on the right to talk to the kids about eating a balanced diet.

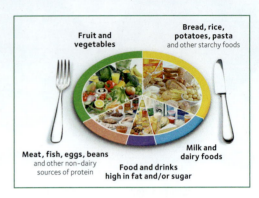

A Study the plate and say what percentage of each of the food groups we should eat to stay healthy.

B Draw an empty plate and copy the headings from the image. Brainstorm types of food and drink and write them in the correct place on the plate.

CHALLENGE! *If you would prefer a challenge, turn to file C5 on page 184.*

2 Discussion: the types of food kids eat

After you have spoken about balanced diets, the children tell you about the food they eat.

A Match the types of food the children mention (1–7) to the descriptions (a–g).

1 "My parents only ever bring home **ready meals**. They've never learned to cook."
2 "My stepmum and dad are both working, so we eat a lot of **convenience food** in our house."
3 "My mum never buys **factory-farmed** chicken or beef. She says that type of meat is full of chemicals."
4 "When I visit my dad, we always have **fast food**."
5 "My grandad says there's nothing that beats a good, **home-cooked** meal."
6 "We can't get **free-range** eggs in our local supermarket."
7 "I get the shopping with my sister. She only ever buys **processed food**."

a a way of farming in which animals are kept in natural conditions where they can move around
b food that is prepared from scratch, using fresh ingredients, in a private kitchen
c food which can be cooked quickly in a microwave oven
d food which has been treated in order to make it last longer
e frozen or canned food that you can prepare quickly and easily
f hot food served very quickly in restaurants and often taken away to be eaten
g livestock kept in small spaces and fed special food so that they will produce more eggs, meat or milk

B Use the food plate to give the children advice on healthier types of food.

If you and your parents took some cooking lessons, you could start making home-cooked meals.

> **Talking about making changes**
>
> If you **ate** fewer burgers, you **would lose** weight.
> Your skin **would look** better if you **drank** more water.
>
> • We use type 2 *if*-sentences to describe what the future would be like if the present were different. ▶ *If-sentences, p. 220*

92

Unit 8   Staying healthy, keeping fit

3 Interaction: planning a healthy meal

The children would like to cook a meal from scratch. You choose a suitable recipe and organize the cooking equipment you will need.

Work in groups of three. Use information in the files below to reconstruct a recipe you can use with the children.

Partner A: file 18, page 159   **Partner B:** file 23, page 162   **Partner C:** file 19, page 160

---

4 Mediation: What's in the picture?

One of the kids has brought in a photo from a German magazine.

A Look at the chicken nuggets in the picture. What parts of the chicken do you think are used to make them?

B Read the description in file 20 on page 160 and summarize the German text in simple English for the kids.

---

5 Listening: an interview with a nutritionist

› *Mit Hörverstehensaufgaben umgehen, S. 207*

You find a podcast on a similar topic.

In this week's podcast, Fran talks to Andrew Ferrie, a nutritionist who analyses fast food products.

A Before you listen, read the description of the podcast and speculate about the contents.

B Read the tasks below, then listen and take notes to help you do them.

1. List all the unnatural ingredients in a chicken burger.
2. Define the word "derivative" and give examples.
3. Explain what TBHQ and PDMS are.
4. Explain what Andrew means by: "Nothing is wasted".
5. Point out what can be found in factory-farmed meat.
6. Discuss what Fran means when she asks: "What are the costs to our health?"

GUIDANCE   *If you would like guidance, turn to file G17 on page 178.*

---

6 Writing: the impact of fast food

› *Eine Stellungnahme schreiben, S. 208*

Considering the information given in this section, discuss the impact of fast food on people's health and life. Take the point of view of a parent, an educator or an employee in the food industry.

B Dying to be slim

> Today, you and some of the teenagers at the after-school club are talking about body image. One of the girls shows you a magazine article that she would like to talk about.

1 Reading: the end result of anorexia ▸ *Schwierige Texte lesen, S. 202*

A Look at the picture and describe it to a partner. Then read the headline. What do you think the article is about?

FRENCH MODEL FINALLY LOSES HER BATTLE AGAINST STARVATION

Isabelle Caro, the French model who became a symbol of the fight against anorexia, has died at the age of 28. In 2007, Caro was photographed naked for a controversial advertising campaign to promote awareness of anorexia.

The poster campaign caused anger among some campaigners who feared that her skeletal image might inspire young women rather than warn them. Isabelle Caro herself, however, disagreed with the criticism, saying she believed most young girls would be disgusted by the photo on the poster. "I want it to shock. It's really a warning that anorexia is a serious illness. It is an unvarnished photo, without make-up. It is everything but beauty, the complete opposite. The message is clear – I have psoriasis, I am pigeon-chested, I look like an elderly person. Anorexia causes death."

The Italian photographer, Oliviero Toscani, who shot the hard-hitting campaign, put forward a similar argument. "Looking at my ad, girls with anorexia must say to themselves that they have to stop dieting," he said.

The posters, which were originally displayed around Milan on the eve of Fashion Week, immediately sent shock waves through the industry. The posters were banned by the Italian advertising watchdog, but the images went viral and fuelled the debates about anorexia and bulimia.

In 2009, during an interview on American TV, Caro said her weight had risen to 39 kilograms. When she was asked if some anorexia sufferers might misunderstand the message of the ad she said, "I hope not. My tailbone is like an open wound, I will never have long hair again. I've lost several teeth. My skin is dry. My breasts have fallen. No young girl wants to look like a skeleton. No one would want to look like that. I don't think there's any question about it."

During the interview Caro also spoke about how she had started modelling during her last year of high school and had been immediately told she had to lose 10 kilograms. Despite her frail physique, Caro said she had never once been told by a modelling agency to put on weight.

"People are just used to seeing skinny people at the modelling agencies and in the media," she said.

Isabelle Caro in the talk show "Barbareschi Sciok" on 05.03.2010, with the poster behind her. When the photo for the poster was taken, Caro weighed less than 28 kilos. She was 1.65 metres tall.

Commenting on the interview, a spokesperson for the NEDA (National Eating Disorders Association) said, "The most common behaviour that leads to eating disorders is dieting."

Caro died on 17 November, 2010 in a French hospital. The exact cause of death is not known, but she had been in hospital for two weeks being treated for an acute respiratory problem.

Caro was a role model for many young women and, after her death, some pro-anorexia internet forums posted messages glorifying her problems. One blog placed a picture of Caro alongside the words "die young, stay pretty".

(474 words)

Unit 8   Staying healthy, keeping fit

B Decide if these statements are true or false, and correct the false statements.

1. The French model, Isabelle Caro, died at the age of 28 in 2007.
2. A photo of Caro was used on a poster for a campaign to promote awareness of anorexia.
3. All the campaigners were certain that the poster would help win the fight against anorexia.
4. Caro found the photo on the poster beautiful.
5. In an interview, Caro described how she had to lose weight in order to get modelling jobs.
6. After her death, Isabelle Caro became a role model for some young women.

C Translate the German words below using expressions from the text.

1. skelettartig
2. ernst zu nehmende Krankheit
3. Schuppenflechte
4. eine Hühnerbrust haben
5. Steißbein
6. eine offene Wunde
7. gebrechlicher Körperbau
8. Atembeschwerden

2 Discussion: it's a matter of opinion …

A Discuss how Isabelle Caro's eating disorder might have been triggered. Who or what might have provoked her illness? Describe some of the ways the illness changed her body.

B "Die young, stay pretty" Analyse this quote from one of the blogs which glorified Isabelle Caro. What would you say to young people to warn against such messages?

Body Mass Index

Body Mass Index (BMI) is the relationship between weight and height. Consisting of a simple mathematical formula, BMI gives an objective view of healthy weight. The equation is:

$$BMI = \frac{body\ weight\ (kg)}{(height\ (m))^2}$$

3 Reading and research: getting help

In order to help the teenagers understand more about anorexia and eating disorders in general, you show them some information about Germany.

Eating disorders and where to get help
In Germany, a total of 7,498 children and adolescents aged 11 to 17 years recently answered a questionnaire aimed at identifying cases of suspected eating disorders. In total, 21.9% of the participants showed symptoms of eating disorders. With 28.9%, girls were more frequently affected than boys (15.2%). Children and adolescents with low socio-economic status (SES) were, with 27.6%, almost twice as often affected than those with high SES (15.6%). Migrants have an approximately 50% higher rate compared to non-migrants.

A Read the information and discuss the statistics. Compare and contrast girls and boys; talk about the influence of socio-economic status and family background.

B Search the internet for professional organizations offering support for sufferers of eating disorders and their families in your area. Describe your findings in a short comment.

GUIDANCE   If you would like guidance, turn to file G19 on page 179.

C The influence of the media

> After looking at the article about anorexia, you are interested in how media and advertising influences people in their health and fitness choices. You decide to have the teenagers do a survey of what is on offer.

1 Reading: dreams for sale

A You start with the internet where your search has thrown up a list of seven health and fitness sites. In groups, analyse the list and sort the sites into those aimed at a) men, b) women, c) either sex. Decide together what each site promises.

1. 60-day plan for the perfect body
2. Get in shape fast (just like celebrities do)
3. 15-minute workouts for the ideal figure
4. Your dream bikini figure in time for the summer
5. Slimmer, sleeker, sexier
6. Reach higher levels of strength and fitness
7. Get lean, build muscle, boost strength

B Read the home page of one of the sites in the list and find the following information.

1. what unhealthy people would like to do
2. what people want from a fitness programme
3. how participants can achieve their goals of getting fit and staying fit
4. what is included in the programme
5. why the Get Fit Stay Fit programme (supposedly) works

GET FIT STAY FIT – THE IDEAL PROGRAMME FOR YOU

If you hate what you see when you look in the mirror, then you are probably ready for the Get Fit Stay Fit programme.

If you're feeling slow and sluggish, our Get Fit Stay Fit programme will make you feel better.

If you tried other programmes but gave up after a few days, then they weren't the right ones for you. Our Get Fit Stay Fit programme will keep you motivated.

Look at all those beautifully fit, toned and active people you see on TV and in the spotlight. Do you want to know how to look like them? Do you want to know the most effective, efficient and the longest-lasting way to improve yourself and achieve the perfect body?

If you want to get fit, build the body of your dreams and improve your health, our Get Fit Stay Fit programme has to be your choice.

Getting fit and staying fit is more than working out every day and watching what you eat. Getting fit and staying fit is also about developing

a positive attitude and adopting a healthy lifestyle.

Unlike other programmes, the Get Fit Stay Fit programme covers everything you need.

You don't have to keep an exercise log. Our exercise plans do that for you.

You don't have to count calories or take vitamin supplements. Our healthy meals plans do that for you.

The Get Fit Stay Fit programme starts slowly and builds up to a daily routine which you can easily fit into your busy day.

Click below to see a schedule aimed at helping you achieve your goals. This schedule produces the greatest, best and longest-lasting results. It can be easily integrated into your daily life so that sticking to it doesn't become difficult and you remain motivated.

Are you ready to start your transformation? Click below …   (306 words)

C In groups, talk about what the programme promises. Would you join this programme? Why? / Why not?

96

Unit 8   Staying healthy, keeping fit

2   Research and discussion: messages in magazines

> An Diskussionen teilnehmen, S. 210

Together with the teenagers, you decide to investigate how the magazines they read present the human body in photos, articles and advertisements.

Look at some typical magazines for this target group, either in print or online. Then work in groups and follow the steps below.

1 Study the images of male and female models and describe how they look.
2 Scan the titles of the articles. How many of the titles are about a) dieting, b) exercise, c) self-esteem?
3 Look at the advertisements. What promises do they make?
4 Decide what messages the images, articles and adverts put across. Describe your thoughts about these messages to the class.

3   Watching a video: "Boot camps boom in Australian outdoors"

You would like to remind the teenagers that exercise is generally good for you and have found an interesting video.

A Before you start watching, brainstorm ideas in the class about what you know about boot camps.

B Next look at the image and the title and guess what you will see. Try to predict which of the words in the box you might hear. Then watch and check.

drills • entertainment • exercises • gym • interval • motivating • push-ups • refreshments • relaxing • sprints • squats • swimming • training sessions • workouts

C Before you watch the video again, choose guidance or challenge.

GUIDANCE   If you would like guidance, turn to file G24 on page 181.
CHALLENGE!   If you would prefer a challenge, turn to file C6 on page 185.

D What do you think about the scenes from the boot camp you have just watched? Would you like to give it a try? Explain why or why not. If you have ever worked out in a group, how motivating was it?

4   Writing: a letter to the editor or an enquiry

Work with a partner and choose one of the following options.

Option 1 Draft a letter to the editor of a magazine expressing your own opinion on the way young people are influenced by current representations of "the perfect body".

Option 2 Write an enquiry to the organizers of the boot camp. Ask for information about costs, dates, etc. Apply to join it.

> Correspondence, pp. 186–189

97

D Practice and projects

1 Mind mapping: living a healthy life

> *Mindmaps erstellen, S. 207*

Make a mind map showing how we can live a healthy life. Collect words from the whole unit and add more as you work through your course. Here are some ideas to start you off.

2 Odd one out

Say which word or phrase does not fit in the sets of words and phrases below. Explain why.

1 factory-farmed • free-range • home-cooked
2 balanced diet • fast food • fresh ingredients
3 anorexia • bulimia • a respiratory problem
4 body mass index • eating disorders • height and weight
5 active • slow • sluggish
6 exercise plan • fitness programme • weight-reducing products

3 Analysing a cartoon

> *Cartoons beschreiben und analysieren, S. 210*

Describe the cartoon and link its message to Part A.

4 Talking about health and fitness

Complete these if type II *if*-sentences with the correct form of the verbs in brackets.

1 If you (take) more exercise, you (feel) much better.
2 If I (lose) weight, I (fit) into my favourite jeans.
3 You (be) healthier if you (follow) the recommendations on the food plate.
4 If the fitness club (not cost) so much, I (go) there more often.
5 (you enjoy) exercising more if you (do) it in a group?
6 What (you say) to your friend if she (have) an eating disorder?
7 If I (be) a vegetarian, I (eat) mostly salad and fruit.
8 I (enjoy) the Australian boot camp if I (go) there.

> *If-sentences, p. 220*

Unit 8   Staying healthy, keeping fit

Designing an advertising campaign to promote health and fitness

Your task is to work in small groups and develop and design an advertising campaign to promote health and fitness.

Step 1 Decide which group or groups of people you would like to target and how you can best reach them. Choose the advertising medium or media which is most suitable from the box.

billboard • internet ad • newspaper or magazine advert • poster • radio spot • TV commercial

You can also use this checklist to make notes.

Campaign title:	
Purpose:	
Target group:	– sex
	– age
	– socio-economic status
	– other features/aspects
Market:	– region / country / EU
Medium/Media:	– one or several

The AIDA model of advertising

Attention Adverts need to have an immediate impact, so get people's attention quickly by surprising them or by asking an engaging question such as "Have you ever …?" or "What would you do if …?"

Interest Once you have their attention, you have to arouse their interest, for example by demonstrating the benefits of your campaign.

Desire The next step is to make people desire what you are offering. You can do this by showing them how good other people look and feel when they are fit and healthy.

Action Encourage action by giving examples of things they can do. Make it easy for them to adopt a healthy lifestyle or at least to get more information.

Step 2 Gather information, decide what information is useful and how you might use it in the campaign.

Step 3 Design your campaign. What information would you like to focus on? Where will you put the other content?

Step 4 If you have not yet done so, read the information about the AIDA model of advertising before you begin to design your campaign ad(s). Depending on the medium you have chosen, you might need illustrations or a catchy tune, so do some research on the internet. Write a detailed description or make a sketch of your ad(s).

Step 5 Present your campaign to the class.

> Präsentieren, S. 209

Checking progress

Browse through the previous pages in the unit, looking at headings and pictures. What have you learned? What can you do now that you have learned these things?
- ✓ I can talk about a healthy diet and issues related to nutrition. (Part A)
- ✓ I can do internet research on eating disorders and look for suitable treatments. (Part B)
- ✓ I can analyse the influence of the media on people's behaviour. (Part C)
- ✓ I can plan and design a health and fitness campaign and present it to the class. (Part D)

Write down two more statements of your own.

It is said that sometimes a helper needs help and, by being helped, the helper becomes a better helper. How has this unit helped you? How will it help you become a better helper?

Exam skills and strategies

Präsentieren

Die Kompetenz, eine wirkungsvolle Präsentation vor einem Publikum zu halten, ist in fast jedem Lebensstadium von Bedeutung, angefangen von der Schule bis hin zum Arbeitsleben. Nicht nur der Inhalt ist wichtig, sondern auch, wie klar und verständlich dieser vorgetragen wird.

> **Wichtig für:**
> - Präsentieren
> - mündliche Prüfung
> - Analyse und Kommentieren einer visuellen Vorlage

BEISPIEL-AUFGABE

Halten Sie eine Präsentation über das Thema „Have fun while getting fit".

TIPPS

1 **Bereiten Sie Ihr Thema sorgfältig vor und stellen Sie sicher, dass die Webseiten, die Sie wählen, glaubwürdige Quellen darstellen.**
Überlegen Sie sich angemessene Begriffe, nach denen Sie suchen können, damit Sie nicht bloß im Netz surfen. Verlassen Sie sich nicht auf die ersten Informationen, die Sie finden.

Wenn eine URL auf .org, .edu oder .gov endet, ist sie wahrscheinlich eine glaubwürdige Quelle. Prüfen Sie auch den „*About us*"-Link und finden Sie heraus, wer für den Inhalt verantwortlich ist.

2 **Schreiben Sie Ihre Notizen, die Sie für Ihre Präsentation verwenden, auf Englisch.**
Kopieren Sie nicht ganze Informationsabschnitte aus dem Internet oder aus Büchern. Ganz gleich, ob Sie sich bei Ihrer Präsentation mit Karteikarten behelfen oder frei sprechen, sollten Sie Ihre eigenen Worte verwenden.

> *Fitness – things to think about re:*
> *– age / weight / general health*
> *– What is realistic?*
> *– What sort of sport / fitness training is fun?*

3 **Prüfen Sie die Korrektheit Ihrer Notizen in Bezug auf Informationsgehalt und Sprache.**
Am wichtigsten ist es, dass Sie alle Wörter richtig aussprechen können. Wenn Sie sich nicht sicher sind, hören Sie sich Beispiele in einem Online-Wörterbuch wie Leo oder Pons an, oder suchen Sie nach Videos, die diesen Begriff enthalten.

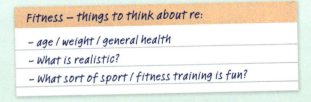

Video: Trainer explains callisthenics

4 **Machen Sie Ihre Präsentation für Ihre Zuhörer/innen einprägsam mithilfe von angemessenem Anschauungsmaterial.**
- Wenn Sie ein Flipchart oder Whiteboard benutzen: Überlegen Sie, wie dieses am Ende der Präsentation aussehen soll, und denken Sie daran, sauber und ordentlich zu schreiben.

- Wenn Sie Ihre Präsentation in PowerPoint erstellen: Überfrachten Sie die Folien nicht mit zu vielen Informationen. Die Aufmerksamkeit sollte auf Ihnen liegen, nicht auf den Folien.

> **Fitness and Fun?**
> **Oh yes!**
> - Zumba, Salsa, Disco Dancing
> - Skateboarding, dirt biking, rollerblading
> - Karate, Aikido, Capoeira

✅

Fitness and fun don't have to be mutually exclusive. Basically, you have to find a form of exercise that's right for you. There are lots of alternatives. Think about these:
- Did you ever consider dancing as a form of exercise?
- What do you think of getting outdoors and going mental in the fresh air with your friends?
- How about some fun forms of martial arts?

In fact, there are even some forms of exercise that you might not even think of as exercise, because they are just so much fun. For example, dancing is a great form of aerobic exercise. So are street activities, like skateboarding. Getting out into the fresh air might sound boring – until you're out there! Then it's really fun and interesting. And everyone wants to be The Karate Kid, so why not try a form of martial arts?

❌

- Auch Gegenstände können effektives Anschauungsmaterial sein. Besorgen Sie für Ihre Präsentation, wenn möglich, reale Gegenstände, wie z. B. Souvenirs, Flyer etc.

5 Machen Sie Ihre Präsentation lebendig und interessant.

Probieren Sie eine Live-Vorführung aus, führen Sie etwas auf, oder erzählen Sie eine Geschichte, einen Witz oder eine persönliche Anekdote.

→ *As for me, the last thing I want to do in my free time is get sweaty with a group of total strangers in a gym. However, I really love animals, so I found a place not far from where I live where you can go horseback riding.*

Überhäufen Sie Ihre Zuhörer/innen nicht mit Zahlen und Daten.

Verwenden Sie so wenige wie möglich, und entlasten Sie Ihr Publikum, indem Sie sie in schriftlicher Form zeigen.

Interagieren Sie mit Ihrem Publikum.

Halten Sie Blickkontakt und stellen Sie ab und zu Fragen.

→ *Think about something you loved doing as a child. Did you like climbing on the monkey bars in the playground, or chasing your friends in the park? Why not do something like that now?*

6 Üben Sie so oft wie möglich.

Üben Sie, ruhig zu stehen, ohne dabei zu zappeln oder sich unnötig zu bewegen. Bleiben Sie auf der Stelle. Üben Sie das, was Sie vortragen möchten, möglichst oft, um einen Blackout zu vermeiden. Proben Sie Ihre Präsentation zunächst vor einem Spiegel, dann vor einem imaginären Publikum und schließlich vor Freunden. Sie können gar nicht oft genug üben!

> **Giving a presentation**
>
> **Introducing yourself and your topic**
> - Good morning/afternoon. My name is …
> - Today I am going to talk about …
> - The subject of my talk is …
> - My topic today is …
> - If you have any questions, please don't hesitate to interrupt me.
> - I'd like to ask you to please save your questions for the end of the presentation.
>
> **Beginning your first point**
> - I'd like to begin by saying something about …
> - I want to start by explaining …
>
> **Guiding your audience through your presentation**
> - There are a number of points I'd like to make.
> - I'll start with …. Then I'll talk about …
>
> - Firstly …. Secondly … / First of all …./ And finally, …
> - And now, moving on to …
> - The next topic I'd like to focus on is …
> - Now I'd like to discuss …
> - Now we'll move on to …
> - Let's look at …
> - Why is this important? Because …
> - The significance of this is …
>
> **Ending your presentation**
> - Let's summarize briefly what we've looked at.
> - Let me remind you of some of the issues we've covered.
> - In conclusion, …
> - I would like to finish by saying …
> - Thank you very much for you attention.
> - If you have any questions, I'm happy to answer them now.

1 Halten Sie nun die Präsentation über das Thema „Have fun while getting fit".

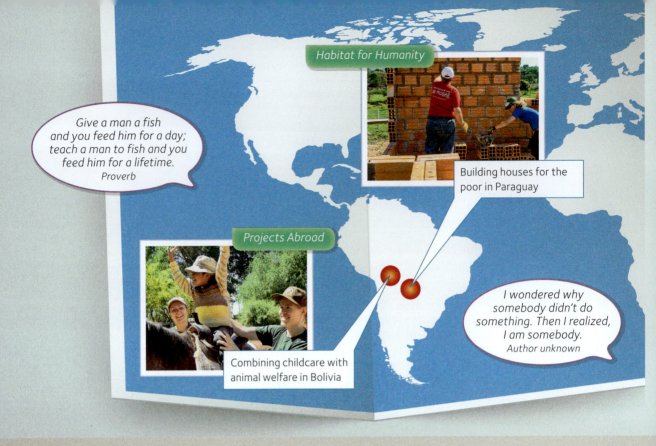

9 Volunteering abroad

1 **A** Choose one of the pictures and describe it to a partner.

B Compare and contrast two or three of the photos. What other activities do you think the volunteer organizations mentioned above are involved in?

> Bilder beschreiben und analysieren, S. 210

2 Choose one of the statements in the speech bubbles and explain what it might mean in the context of volunteering abroad.

3 **Think:** What experience (or not) do you have of volunteering?
Pair: Tell your partner, then discuss how volunteers benefit (or not) from the experience.
Share: In class, discuss the possible benefits of volunteer projects for the communities where the projects take place. What might be the disadvantages?

Last year I worked on a project in …

For me, the experience was …

I think that overall the communities …

Using your talents to help disadvantaged children in Moldova

Paediatric rounds at MSF's inflatable hospital in Tacloban. Many children are suffering severe psychological distress as a result of typhoon Haiyan.

Projects Abroad

Outward Bound

Médecins Sans Frontières

Working with youths to clean up the Singapore coast

The reality is that doing good unto others actually does more good for you.
Richelle E. Goodrich

If you think you are too small to be effective, you have never been in bed with a mosquito.
Betty Reese

Help someone, you earn a friend. Help someone too much, you make an enemy.
Erol Ozan

 4 What competences, skills and attitudes does a volunteer need? How can volunteers prepare themselves to deal with problems?

What's to come

In this unit, you will …
- read about "voluntourism" and find out about opportunities to take part in volunteer projects abroad.
- volunteer to work in an experiential learning organization.
- deal with an emergency.

At the end of the unit, you will plan an outdoor adventure excursion and present it both in writing and orally.

Before you begin, think about how educators can purposefully engage with different types of people in volunteer projects.

103

A Learning for life

> **S** You would like to gain experience as a volunteer. You check the internet for suitable programmes and projects and find some interesting information.

1 Reading: voluntourism

> *Schwierige Texte lesen, S. 202*

A Read the introduction to the text, then choose the best definition of the word "voluntourism".

1 A new type of inexpensive holiday package being promoted by the tourist industry
2 Charities which offer free sightseeing trips to students who work for them
3 Doing good while experiencing new places and challenges in places you might otherwise have never had the opportunity to visit

B Now read the rest of the text and do the following tasks. Use your own words as much as possible for tasks 3–5.

1 Name two different types of organizations that work with volunteers.
2 Outline the areas of work in which volunteers can assist.
3 Point out and discuss the problems that might arise in communities that are being assisted.
4 Evaluate the recommendations suggested by the study.
5 Examine this quotation from the text: "Many voluntourism programmes cater more to the needs of the volunteer than to the project."

VOLUNTOURISM

Young and adventurous? Want to see the world? How about volunteering? During the 1990s, the travel industry began to offer short-stay volunteer trips to young people taking gap years. Travellers visit underdeveloped or developing countries in order to assist non-governmental organizations (NGOs) or non-profit organizations as volunteers.

Typical voluntourism activities focus on community development (e.g. building projects, digging wells), education (e.g. teaching English), environmental projects (e.g. reforestation) and social welfare (e.g. caring for orphans).

Many people volunteer to increase their international awareness and to help them understand poverty and its effects. Others believe that the trip will change the way they think when they return home. Some just wish to help people.

All in all, voluntourism sounds like a worthwhile thing. But is it?

A recent study has found that many programmes cater more to the needs of the volunteer than to the project. Volunteers are often privileged travellers who have a different socio-economic status to the people they are assisting. They arrive in a country with little or no understanding of the history, culture or way of life of the community they have chosen to help. From the start, there is a distinct division of roles with the volunteer playing the part of the benevolent giver and the members of the community cast as the grateful receivers of charity. Stereotypes and preconceptions are reinforced, and the "us" and "them" divide remains.

While it is true that many relief programmes would never be established without the money brought in by the "voluntourists", these programmes can sometimes exploit the communities they are intended to help. Some projects can even make problems more severe. Root causes of the problems are often not tackled, and little thought is given to sustainability. Sustainability is especially important when projects are started off by volunteer organizations, but then left in the hands of the local population.

The study concluded with a list of recommendations:
- Instead of focusing on the symptoms of poverty, organizations should focus on the causes of the problems.
- It's important to invest time and energy in promoting mutual respect and understanding between different societies.
- Organizations should make sure there is enough funding and support for the project to be completed after they leave.
- Prospective volunteers should be made aware of their own (direct or indirect) role in global poverty so as to encourage them to get involved in a more realistic way.
- Organizations should be accredited and should offer accreditation opportunities to young volunteers.

Before you sign up for that holiday with a difference, why not check out the database of European Voluntary Service accredited organizations. By volunteering for an accredited organization, you really will make a difference.

(451 words)

Unit 9   Volunteering abroad

C Find synonyms for the words and phrases below.

1. the state of being extremely poor
2. separation of functions that people have in a project
3. a kind person who donates their time and energy to a project
4. poor people who accept help
5. ability to last a long time
6. equal feelings of admiration
7. potential

D Summarize the text.

> Einen Text zusammenfassen, S. 208

GUIDANCE If you would like guidance, turn to file G21 on page 180.

2 Research: checking a website for information

You decide to look into the European Voluntary Service to find out more.

Work in groups. Choose one of the following links from the website and make notes in your group. Then sit with people from the two other groups and exchange information.

- European Voluntary Service: what is it really?
- Why EVS?
- Volunteering in Europe

3 Watching a video: "Youth in Action – EVS for refugees"

6

You next watch a video about an EVS project in Poland that won a "Youth in Action" award.

A Describe what Youth in Action does. Say what the young people who participate in projects learn.

B Watch the video again and take notes so that you can answer these questions.

1. Who makes up the target group of Czerwony Bór?
2. What makes integration with local people difficult?
3. What do volunteers do?
4. How might the discussions between refugees and volunteers improve things for refugees?
5. How do young Europeans benefit from the volunteer programmes?

4 Writing: the pros and cons of volunteering

Use information from these pages to describe and discuss the pros and cons of volunteering activities for individuals and for society.

> Eine Stellungnahme schreiben, S. 208

105

B Getting down to work

> You have decided to volunteer as an assistant at an international experiential learning organization. You find the following information online.

1 Reading: the Outdoor Experience Centre

A Skim the text and answer the following questions.

1. Where is the organization located?
2. What three issues does the organization focus on?
3. Where do the volunteers work?

---

http://www.OEC_OutdoorExperienceCentre/Romania

Outdoor Experience Centre Romania

Theme 1	Youth leisure
Theme 2	Education through sport and outdoor activities
Inclusion	Cultural differences, economic difficulties, geographical difficulties

Our volunteers have the opportunity to learn many different things with us. You will be actively involved in duties in our office and in our Outdoor Experience Centre.

1) In the office. Here, you will assist staff in preparing and organizing international projects. Office work includes working on the website, taking telephone calls, working with Word and Excel, making flyers and posters and mailing them to international participants, and writing grant proposals. You will also participate in the weekly staff meeting.

Duties include:
- assisting the centre manager with administrative duties.
- working in the medical room.
- preparing and cleaning equipment.

2) The Outdoor Experience Centre. Here, you will assist our instructors in activities like mountain biking, hiking, white-water rafting and cross-country skiing.

While working as a volunteer, you will learn the skills you need to become an accredited trainer, including outdoor skills as well as techniques for effective facilitating and debriefing. You will attend local staff training sessions and have the chance to attain the qualifications you need in order to become an accredited instructor. The accreditation is recognized on an international level.

(188 words)

B Find words and expressions in the text which match the German words below.

1. *Freizeit*
2. *Schulerlebnispädagogik*
3. *Zuschussanträge*
4. *Verwaltungsaufgaben*
5. *anerkannt*
6. *Fertigkeiten im Freien*
7. *Vermitteln*
8. *Nachbesprechen*

C Now read the text carefully and do the following tasks.

1. Point out the volunteers' duties while working in the office.
2. Describe what goes on in the Outdoor Experience Centre and explain what the volunteers do there.
3. Discuss how volunteering at this site might help the candidates later in life.

106

Unit 9   Volunteering abroad

2 Listening: taking a message

> Mit Hörverstehensaufgaben umgehen, S. 207

You have been accepted as a volunteer at the Outdoor Experience Centre and are working in the office alongside Kate Flynn, the office manager. She receives a phone call from the head of a Finnish vocational school who would like some information.

2/6

A Listen to the phone call and make a note of:

1. the caller's name.
2. the name of the person he should speak to.
3. the caller's phone number.
4. details of what he would like to know.

B Listen again and make a note of what Kate says to:

1. indicate how she will deal with the caller's request.
2. ask for the caller's name.
3. check the caller's name.
4. indicate that the caller should wait.
5. confirm that the caller is still on the line.
6. explain that someone is not available.
7. make a suggestion.
8. ask for contact details.
9. confirm details.
10. close the call.

GUIDANCE If you would like guidance, turn to file G22 on page 180.

2/7

C Now listen to the next three calls and take messages.

3 Role-play: making and changing appointments

Now it is your turn to staff the phones. Work with a partner and take and make some calls.

Partner A: file 14, page 157
Partner B: file 26, page 163

> Telephoning, p. 192

Changing appointments

- I'm afraid I've had to change my plans.
- I'm going to have to cancel the appointment.
- How about Friday afternoon instead?
- Would that suit you?

> Telephoning, p. 192

4 Writing: a report on your time as a volunteer

Kate has asked you to write a short report of what you have done and learned as a volunteer. The report will be added to the volunteers' training file.

GUIDANCE If you would like guidance, turn to file G20 on page 179.

A Work with a partner. You have been involved in all of the activities described in the advert on the opposite page. Brainstorm ideas about competences, skills and attitudes you acquired while working as a volunteer. Make notes on which tasks and activities helped you do the following:

- deal with problems.
- practise your interpersonal skills.
- develop your leadership skills.
- add to your knowledge of technical and safety skills.

B With your partner, write your report.

107

C Dealing with an emergency

> Today, you are on duty for the first time in the medical room at the Outdoor Experience Centre. When you started work this morning, you did not think that you would have to deal with an emergency.

1 Brainstorming: being prepared

Emil, the medical officer in charge, gives you a list of excursions the centre offers and asks you to speculate about what might go wrong on trips like these.

Think: Try to imagine difficult situations and problems that might arise.
Pair: Choose one of the activities from each section of the list and consider how you can avoid problems.
Share: As a class, pool your ideas and make a poster about safety during outdoor activities.

OUR ACTIVITIES INCLUDE

All year round:
abseiling • white-water rafting • orienteering • rock climbing
Summer activites:
canyoning • diving in underground lakes • navigating a swamp • treetop wandering
Winter activites:
cross-country skiing • tobogganing • underground adventure in disused coal mines

2 Packing a first-aid kit

Next, Emil asks you to pack a first-aid kit for an excursion. With a partner, sort the items below under the following headings: wound care, medication and extras.

1 antibiotic ointment
2 antihistamine
3 assortment of bandages
4 aspirin
5 emergency shock blanket
6 hypothermia blanket
7 iodine
8 roll of adhesive tape
9 roll of gauze
10 safety pins
11 small scissors
12 tweezers

3 Listening and discussion: being prepared for all eventualities

Emil notices that some items are missing from the kit and explains why they must be included.

A Before you listen, think about what the items below are used for. Match the sentence halves.

1 Paracetamol
2 An EpiPen® needle
3 Hydrocortisone cream
4 Latex gloves
5 A SAM splint

a relieves the symptoms of bites, stings and rashes.
b can save the life of someone having an allergic reaction.
c helps stabilize breaks and sprains.
d relieves pain and reduces fever.
e prevent wound infection.

B Listen to Emil describing the items and check your answers. Explain why the items are important.

C Work in a small group. Choose one of the activities below and assemble a suitable first-aid kit.

1 a day trip to the seaside with a group of young children in the middle of summer
2 a short trek in the mountains with a group of fit seniors
3 a night-time Halloween event with a group of disabled teenagers

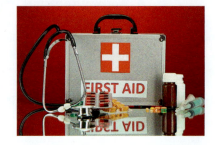

108

Unit 9   Volunteering abroad

4   **Role-play: emergency!**

At the end of the day, you and a supervisor accompany a group from a Finnish vocational school on a cross-country skiing tour. One student, Virpi Hakala, hits a rock and injures her leg. You help your supervisor administer first aid and make Virpi comfortable while waiting for an ambulance.

Work in a group of four. Do all of the tasks together and take turns playing the different roles.

A At the hospital, the admissions nurse wants to know what happened and what first-aid measures were taken. Look at the nurse's questions and create a dialogue between you and the nurse. Be prepared to act it out.

Can you describe what happened?

Was the patient wearing a helmet?

What had she been doing before the accident?

Did she lose consciousness at any time?

Have you given her any medication?

> **Describing past actions and events**
>
> We **were skiing** in the forest when it suddenly **started** snowing.
> - We use the past progressive and simple past together to describe how an action that was already in progress was interrupted by a second action or event.
>   > *Past progressive, p. 213; Simple past, p. 213*
>
> Virpi **had lost** consciousness before I got to her. Before the accident happened, she **had been skiing** at a normal pace.
> - We use the past perfect (progressive) to talk about events that happened (or were happening) before other events in the past.
>   > *Past perfect, p. 214; Past perfect progressive, p. 215*
>
> I **have learned** first aid so I knew what to do.
> - We use the present perfect to talk about past events which have an effect on the present.
>   > *Present perfect, p. 214*

GUIDANCE   *If you would like guidance, turn to file G23 on page 180.*

B The admissions nurse asks you help Virpi complete some forms. Use information in the role cards to prepare and then act out the dialogue.

Partners A and B: "You" (file 25, page 163)
Partners C and D: Virpi (file 27, page 164)

C The doctor, who speaks a bit of German but no English, assesses Virpi's injuries and explains what will happen next. Listen to the doctor and mediate for Virpi in English.

5   **Writing: a report of the accident**

Emil has to submit a report to the Finnish school. He asks you to write a short summary of the accident and the outcome in English. Summarize the information from your role-play and make up the rest of the story. What happened after the doctor spoke to you?

109

D Practice and projects

1 Volunteering

Complete the text with the words in the box.

> accredited • experience • NGOs • orphans • poverty • protection • relief •
> root • sustainability • volunteers • voluntourism • wishing

⬤¹ and non-profit organizations are always looking for ⬤² to work on their programmes. There are many opportunities. You may be asked to join a building project, teach English, work in a wildlife ⬤³ programme or care for ⬤⁴.

When asked why they volunteer, people give various reasons. Understanding ⬤⁵ and its effects is one; simply ⬤⁶ to help people is another reason; gaining ⬤⁷ and learning key skills yet another. Although many ⬤⁸ programmes would never get off the ground without ⬤⁹, it is not always a good thing. The ⬤¹⁰ causes of the problems are often ignored and ⬤¹¹ is sometimes lacking. Volunteers are advised to enrol with an ⬤¹² organization.

2 Using the telephone

Use words from the box to complete the telephone phrases.

> are • breaking • change • connect • hear • help • hold •
> make • pass • put • speak • spell

1 I'd like to ⬤ to someone in administration, please.
2 Just ⬤ on one minute and I'll try to ⬤ you.
3 ⬤ you still there? I'll ⬤ you through.
4 I'll ⬤ on your message.
5 How can I ⬤ you?
6 I'd like to ⬤ an appointment, please.
7 Can you ⬤ your name, please?
8 I'm sorry, but I have to ⬤ my appointment.
9 You're ⬤ up. I can hardly ⬤ you.

3 Talking about what happened earlier

Complete the sentences using the correct form of the verbs in brackets.

1 The organization (run out) of money long before they (leave) the country.
2 The people (suffer) for weeks before the relief organization (arrive).
3 I (just decide) to volunteer when I (see) the advert for assistants in Romania.
4 We (hike) for an hour when it (start) to rain.
5 Where (you be)? The patient (lie) here for two hours.
6 When we (reach) the hospital, the patient (already recover).
7 The volunteer (work) here for six months so she (take charge) immediately after the accident.
8 I (go) to the emergency room last week because I (hurt) my arm.

> ❯ *The past tenses, pp. 213–215; Present perfect, p. 214*

Unit 9   Volunteering abroad

Describing the uses for items in a first-aid kit

Without looking back at the unit, say which items from a first-aid kit you would use to deal with the situations below.

1. clean a wound and reduce risk of infection (two items)
2. deal with a serious allergic reaction
3. prevent a patient cooling down while they are lying still
4. reduce inflammation when someone has a sprain
5. reduce pain where aspirin is not a good choice (i.e. when the patient is bleeding)
6. soothe rashes and bug bites
7. stabilize an injured limb

Planning and presenting an outdoor adventure excursion

You are Outward Bound instructors and want to plan an excursion for a group of international students. Work in groups. The project is in two parts. Do all of the steps below in your group.

Planning the excursion

Step 1   Decide what age group the excursion is aimed at and brainstorm ideas about suitable activities you would like to offer.

Step 2   Write a description of the programme to put online. Include information on logistics, e.g. length of the trip, accommodation, instructors (accredited?) and activities, e.g. what type and why (confidence-building, problem-solving, etc.).

Step 3   Prepare first-aid kits and make a list of other equipment you will need to take along, e.g. helmets, ropes, climbing gear.

Presenting the excursion

Step 4   Present your excursion to the rest of the class. Remember that the organization you work for is in competition with other organizations. Try to persuade your audience that your excursion is the best. Answer questions and ask for feedback.

› Präsentieren, S. 209

Checking progress

Browse through the previous pages in the unit, looking at headings and pictures.
What have you learned? What can you do now that you have learned these things?
- ✔ I can think critically about the pros and cons of volunteering.   (Part A)
- ✔ I can take messages and make appointments on the phone.   (Part B)
- ✔ I can talk about first aid and how to deal with a medical emergency.   (Part C)
- ✔ I can plan an excursion and give a persuasive presentation.   (Part D)

Write down two more statements of your own.

Reflect on how this unit has helped you increase your knowledge, develop your skills and clarify your attitudes towards working with people.

Exam skills and strategies

Bilder und Cartoons beschreiben und analysieren

Wichtig für:
- materialgestützten Aufsatz
- Analysieren und Kommentieren einer visuellen Vorlage
- rollenbasierte Stellungnahme

Wenn Sie ein Bild oder einen Cartoon beschreiben, sollten Sie sich auf die Hauptaussage konzentrieren und sich nicht in Details verlieren. Vermeiden Sie, „um die Ecke zu denken", sondern bleiben Sie im Rahmen des Themas.

BEISPIELAUFGABE Beschreiben Sie und analysieren Sie den Cartoon. Vergleichen Sie ihn mit dem Text.

TIPPS

1 **Beschreiben Sie das Bild: Schauen Sie sich alle Aspekte der Abbildung an, gehen Sie jedoch nur auf die Elemente ein, die für die Aussage wichtig sind.**
Geben Sie an, welches Objekt Sie beschreiben, indem Sie genau bestimmen, wo es sich im Bild befindet.
→ *In the foreground there is a tourist with a large backpack. Behind him, there is a sign that says "World Heritage site".*
→ ~~*In the background there are some circular buildings.*~~

Verwenden Sie die Verlaufsform *present progressive*, um den Inhalt der Abbildung darzustellen.
→ *The backpacker is walking through an ornate gateway. He is reading a brochure entitled "Low impact tourism".*
→ ~~*The backpacker walks … He reads …*~~

Achtung: *be, seem, look, show* und *describe* werden i. d. R. nicht in der Verlaufsform verwendet.
→ *The tourist doesn't seem to be paying attention to where he is going. It looks as if he is completely absorbed in what he is reading.*
→ ~~*He isn't seeming … It is looking …*~~

2 **Interpretieren Sie das Bild: Wenn Sie der Meinung sind, dass die Darstellung nicht viel aussagt, erwähnen Sie dies in Ihrer Interpretation. Bezeichnen Sie die Abbildung als mehrdeutig oder unklar.**
→ *The message of this cartoon is unclear. Either the cartoonist wants to say that all tourists are careless, or …*
→ *The tourist represents irresponsible tourists in general.*

> **Describing the picture**
> - The cartoon shows …
> - The picture seems to show …
> - The scene depicts …
> - In the foreground/background/centre there is …
> - On the left/right there is …
> - The person seems to be (hold**ing** something / writ**ing** / walk**ing** away)
> - It seems as if the person is (hold**ing** something / writ**ing** / walk**ing** away)

> **Interpreting the picture**
> - The picture/cartoon deals with …
> - The cartoon is intended to create …
> - The (person in the centre) represents/shows/ symbolizes …
> - This shows/reveals/indicates …
> - The impression of … is created.
> - The point of the cartoon is / seems to be …

112

Exam skills and strategies

3 Stellen Sie dar, welche Auswirkung das Bild auf Sie hat: Fassen Sie die Hauptaussage zusammen und geben Sie Ihre eigene Meinung wieder.

→ *The cartoon makes me consider the impact I have when I go on holiday, because even tourists with good intentions can have a negative impact.*

→ *In my opinion, this cartoon makes a fair point, but the message is too obvious.*

Commenting on the picture

- I think … / In my opinion …
- The cartoon makes a fair point.
- The cartoon convinces / doesn't convince me.
- I agree with the cartoonist, but …
- The cartoonist is partly right.
- The cartoonist exaggerates a little / a lot.
- It forces you to think about …
- It has the effect of …

4 Falls ein unabhängiger Text dazu einbezogen werden kann, vergleichen Sie die Abbildung mit dem Inhalt des Textes: Sagen Sie, ob das Bild die Aussage des Textes unterstützt oder ihr widerspricht.

From Easter Island to Venice, locals are demanding that tourists stay away from world heritage sites. Communities worldwide are defending themselves against the damage caused by tourism. As more destinations suffer from "backpacker fatigue", it is thought that some of the great wonders of the world could be closed off to the public in the future.

Comparing the picture with the text

- Although the picture shows … , the text says …
- In the text we found out that …
- The cartoon/picture supports the information in the text in the following way.
- The cartoon/picture gives a completely different opinion about the information in the text.

→ *The cartoon supports the information in the text. The cartoon depicts the phrase "backpacker fatigue" in the text.*

→ *The picture illustrates the information in the text by showing the destruction that backpackers can cause.*

1 Describe and analyse the cartoon below. Write at least 150 words.

2 Compare the cartoon with the text.

"My experience volunteering in India was the most incredible year of my life. The organization started training me online even before I left home. Working at the orphanage was challenging. I had to work long hours and was often very tired, but people were always willing to help me and answer my questions."

› Lösungen, S. 292

113

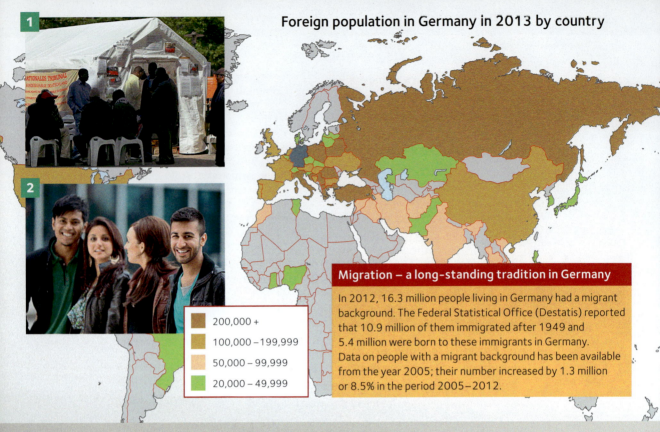

Foreign population in Germany in 2013 by country

- 200,000 +
- 100,000 – 199,999
- 50,000 – 99,999
- 20,000 – 49,999

Migration – a long-standing tradition in Germany

In 2012, 16.3 million people living in Germany had a migrant background. The Federal Statistical Office (Destatis) reported that 10.9 million of them immigrated after 1949 and 5.4 million were born to these immigrants in Germany. Data on people with a migrant background has been available from the year 2005; their number increased by 1.3 million or 8.5% in the period 2005–2012.

10 Helping people cope with change

1
A Describe the map. Analyse what it tells us about migration in Germany.

B Describe the charts. Discuss reasons for and consequences of the information shown there.

> *Schaubilder und Statistiken beschreiben und analysieren, S. 210*

2 Compare and contrast two of the photos. Think about why the people shown might want to live in Germany and what they might have left behind. Describe how the people in the photos might feel and what they might be thinking.

The people in photo … might be thinking …

The people in photo … appear to be …

> *Bilder beschreiben und analysieren, S. 210*

114

3  **4**

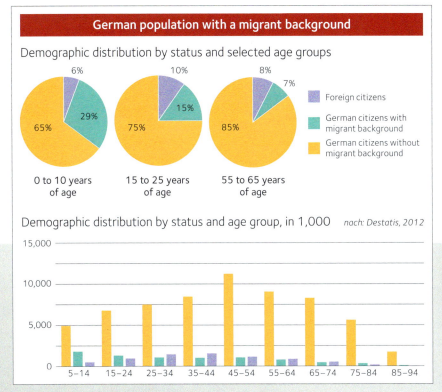

I am not against migration. It is simply pragmatic to restrict migration, while at the same time encouraging integration and fighting discrimination. I support the idea of the free movement of goods, people, money and jobs in Europe.

Ayaan Hirsi Ali, Somali-born author

It was my father who taught us that an immigrant must work twice as hard as anybody else, that he must never give up.

Zinedine Zidane, Algerian footballer of Kabyle-Berber descent, whose parents migrated to Paris in 1953

I have been a foreigner all my life, first as a daughter of diplomats, then as a political refugee and now as an immigrant in the US. I have had to leave everything behind and start anew several times, and I have lost most of my extended family.

Isabel Allende, Chilean author

 Choose one of the quotes above. How does the speaker feel about migration? Use examples to expand on what he or she says.

What's to come

In this unit, you will …
- consider the integration of young migrants in Germany.
- look into the role of cultural competence in the field of caring.
- help recruit volunteers for a home for asylum seekers.

At the end of the unit, you will research and present one facet of working with migrants.

Before you begin, think about what you know about migrants in your area and how familiar you are with people from different cultures. What skills do you have that might help you to work with migrants?

A Settling down in a new country

> You are a trainee at a local agency in Germany that does some work at a centre for newly arrived immigrants. As part of your training, you attend regular, international workshops on integration. The first item on the workshop agenda is dealing with the problems children face.

1 Reading: schooling for young immigrants
> *Schwierige Texte lesen, S. 202*

The trainer asks you to prepare for the workshop by reading the following article.

A Read the text and say where these sentences go.

a A 78% increase in migrants from Greece is one of many examples.
b Germany is the second "new start" for many immigrants.
c His teacher says he is more or less fully integrated.
d "Living in Germany will give me better chances for work too," she adds.
e The challenge for the education system is huge.
f This is where volunteers from Teach First Deutschland come in.

INCREASE IN NUMBER OF MIGRANTS MEANS EXTRA WORK FOR SCHOOLS

The boom in immigrants to Germany from countries that have been hit by the euro crisis has resulted in an increase in the number of children and young people entering German schools without being able to speak the language. [1] *One way to cope with these overwhelming numbers is to offer special classes.*

In the first six months of 2012, there was a sharp rise in immigration from euro crisis countries compared to the previous year. [2] Since the most recent enlargement of the EU, migrants from Bulgaria and Romania have also come to Germany in large numbers. Alongside the highly skilled workers, academics and professionals looking for employment, there are also many working-class families. The children of these families, no matter what their background, are putting a huge burden on the education system.

Nearly all recently arrived pupils start school with no German. While some learn quickly and can soon be integrated into regular classes, others need months to learn the language. The problem is made worse by the rate at which their numbers are growing. Many schools do not have enough qualified staff to teach German as a second language, nor do they have the budget to contract new teachers on a freelance basis. [3] The non-profit organization supports schools in Baden-Württemberg, Berlin, Hamburg, Hessen, North Rhine-Westphalia and Thuringia. With the help of volunteers, pupils can get extra hours of specialized German language instruction.

In a classroom in Berlin, a young student named Ricardo explains that his parents were successful estate agents in Madrid, but when the euro crisis hit and property sales dropped dramatically, the family decided to move to Germany. Ricardo is a fast learner and aims to go to technical college. [4] "I feel happy in Germany but I don't expect to live here forever," he says. "My main goal is to return to Madrid and use my German qualifications to get work there."

An interesting trend in German schools is the number of students who have spent time living with their families as immigrants in other countries. [5] Turkish pupils who have grown up in Bulgaria, and Algerian children born in France are two examples.

Elena, a Greek teenager who grew up in Portugal, moved to Stuttgart four months ago. "I was lost when I came here first but now that I can speak German and have made some friends it's more like home," she says. [6]

(412 words)

116

B Find expressions in the text that have the same meaning as the German expressions below.

1 *steigende Einwandererzahlen*
2 *eine starke Zunahme der Einwanderung*
3 *Erweiterung der EU*
4 *sehr gut ausgebildete Arbeitskräfte*
5 *unabhängig ihrer Verhältnisse*
6 *eine starke Belastung*
7 *vor kurzem angekommene Schüler/innen*
8 *steigende Wachstumsrate*

C Outline the information presented in the text.

---

2 Listening: coping with problems

The trainer plays you a recording of four pupils describing how they felt when they first came to Germany.

2/10

A Listen and take notes. What were the problems and how did Adam, Lee, Rosa and Nikita cope with them?

B The strategies below were taken from an online manual for pupils who are unhappy at school. Use the correct form of the verbs in the box to complete the sentences. Then decide which strategies you might have recommended to each of the four pupils.

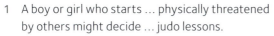

change • do (×2) • feel • go • ignore • take (×2) • talk • work

1 A boy or girl who starts … physically threatened by others might decide … judo lessons.
2 A child who hates … homework might like … on it with some friends.
3 Some students enjoy … things over with other students from the same cultural background.
4 It is best if you can manage … people who tease you.
5 If a pupil refuses … to school because of bullying, we suggest … to another school.
6 Some pupils plan … revenge on people who have hurt them. Luckily, most pupils decide not … this.

Talking about strategies

Cem **likes playing** chess so he **decided to join** a club.
He **hopes to make** some new friends.
I **suggest talking** to an adult about your problems.

- In a sentence with more than one verb, the main verb can be followed by the *to*-infinitive or the *-ing* form (gerund). There are no rules on why certain verbs require a particular form. All you can do is learn them.

> *Gerund/Infinitive, p. 221*

C Think of other strategies, then prepare and act out a dialogue in which a pupil explains his/her problem and a counsellor suggests possible ways of dealing with it.

---

3 Writing: towards successful integration

Discuss the problems young immigrants might face when they come to Germany. Present a list of strategies for helping them integrate successfully that you could offer them as a professional in social and health care.

B Working with elderly migrants

> The next part of the workshop focuses on working with elderly migrants. The trainer gives you some tasks to do.

1 Reading and writing: reports from the field

First, the trainer asks you to read what some care professionals say about working with older clients from other cultures.

A Read the cards and sort what the people say under the following headings:

- cultural knowledge • cultural skills • cultural encounters

1
I work in a community centre. We have regular "getting to know you" events in which people from different cultures can mix. A lot of the older people tell their stories and talk about where they lived as children. We also have musical evenings and folk dancing evenings. The ladies prepare the food for these evenings. The events are part of an integration programme and aimed at the local community, and I've learned a lot from them, too.

2
People have different beliefs about God and religion. Some people believe you die and go to heaven. Other people say that you come back to Earth as something else after you die. In some countries, talking about death is a taboo subject, the mourners cry and the funeral is often sad. In other countries they celebrate a person's death in a happy way. Other people do not want to have a funeral as we know it. It doesn't matter what we think, we have to respect our clients' wishes and the wishes of their families.

3
We deal with a lot of migrants in the hospital I work in. In some cultures men and women are strictly separated. They attend different schools, sit in different parts of their place of worship or eat apart from each other. Some of our clients are very strict about who can touch them. The men will only accept a male carer, and female carers look after women. Some of the patients have dementia. Even though many of the migrants have lived here for years and can speak the language, they slowly start to lose it until only their mother tongue remains. It's fortunate that we have a multilingual staff.

B Think: Which of the three topics above interests you most?
Pair: Find a partner who has chosen the same topic as you. Pool your ideas and write a card like the ones above.
Share: Read out your card in groups or in class. Say what you think of the ideas. How far will they help you in becoming a culturally competent caring professional?

2 Reading and discussion: Who are the older migrants?

Before you can work with older migrants, the trainer would like you to talk about the background of many of the older clients.

A Work in pairs and discuss the photos. Where are the people from? When did they probably migrate to Germany? Why did they come here?

B You and your partner are going to read two different texts to find out if your ideas above are correct. Once you have read your texts, you will exchange information with your partner.

Partner A: file 29, page 165   **Partner B:** file 31, page 166

C After you have exchanged information with your partner, get into groups with other pairs. Who are the older migrants? What options might there be for care professionals working with them or their children?

---

3 Listening: developing cultural competence
> *Mit Hörverständnisaufgaben umgehen, S. 207*

The next part of the workshop involves an interview with Liam Kelly, a lecturer at a vocational college. Liam has been invited to talk about cultural competence in the field of caring.

A Before listening, make sure you know the meanings of the words below. Give synonyms or definitions, and use a dictionary if necessary.

1. ethnic
2. diverse
3. encounters
4. to differ
5. prejudice
6. to impose sth on sb
7. agnostic
8. atheist

GUIDANCE *If you would like guidance, turn to file G26 on page 182.*

2/11

B Now listen to the interview and answer the questions.

1. What is cultural competence?
2. What is its place in the caring business?
3. What might the expression "diverse cultural and ethnic backgrounds" mean?
4. What is cultural knowledge and how might someone acquire it?
5. How does a carer become sensitive to the way of life of other cultures?
6. What are cultural skills?
7. What are cultural encounters?
8. What are Liam's two pieces of advice?

C Work in groups. Use your answers to the questions above to start a mind map on cultural competence in care work. Brainstorm more ideas and add them to the mind map.
> *Mindmaps erstellen, S. 207*

---

4 Role-play: an interview with a carer
> *An Diskussionen teilnehmen, S. 210*

The final task of the workshop is to prepare and carry out an interview.

Work in groups of four and use the information in your files to prepare and then act out the interview.

Partners A and B: file 36, page 168   **Partners C and D:** file 10, page 155

C Supporting asylum seekers

> **S** As part of your training with the German agency, you are doing practical work in a home for asylum seekers.

1 Brainstorming: ideas about asylum seekers

A As a class, write a list of countries and nationalities of people seeking asylum in Germany. For each nationality, brainstorm reasons that might make someone leave their country. Think about who the asylum seekers are, e.g. old/young, qualified/unqualified.

human rights violations
refugees *traumatized*
victims of war
religious *safety* *political*
victims of ethnic cleansing
torture

B Now focus on the thoughts that local people have about asylum seekers. Are the thoughts positive or negative? Supportive or harmful? True or false? Where do the ideas come from?

C Talk in groups. What kind of care assistance might asylum seekers need?

2 Mediation: looking for a volunteer mentor

> *Mediation, p. 211*

The senior social worker at the home for asylum seekers would like to attract multilingual volunteers. She asks for your help in developing an advertisement in English for the home's website. She gives you the German version of the advertisement.

A Work with a partner. Read the job advertisement and discuss which parts of it you need to convey.

B Use a dictionary to find the correct translation of any words you do not know.

C Write the job description in English. Remember, this is not a translation exercise.

Angebot Mentorenprojekt (ehrenamtlich)

Seit 1986 hilft unsere Einrichtung traumatisierten Flüchtlingen und Opfern von extremen Menschenrechtsverletzungen. Wir sind eine politisch und religiös unabhängige nichtstaatliche Menschenrechtsorganisation. Unser Ziel ist es, Opfern von Folter, Krieg und anderen schweren Menschenrechtsverletzungen sowie ihren Familienangehörigen einen Raum des Schutzes und psychotherapeutische Hilfe wie auch soziale Begleitung anzubieten.

Möchten Sie einem Menschen beratend, unterstützend und ermutigend zur Seite stehen? Möchten Sie ihm bei der Orientierung in der Stadt, bei der Wohnungssuche, im Umgang mit Behörden und Bürokratie, bei Bildungs-, Ausbildungs- und Arbeitsangelegenheiten, beim Aufbau zwischenmenschlicher Kontakte und beim Umgang mit anderskulturellen Lebensgewohnheiten helfen?

Haben Sie Kenntnisse der englischen, arabischen oder einer osteuropäischen Sprache? Dann werden Sie bei uns gebraucht!

Zeitlicher Rahmen: 1× pro Woche, 2–3 Stunden nach Absprache

vorbereitende Einzelgespräche • kostenfreie Informationsbroschüre • Beratung bei allen aufkommenden Fragen • Leitfaden zur Vorbereitung auf Ihre zukünftige Tätigkeit • Internetforum für alle Ehrenamtlichen

Bitte setzen Sie sich telefonisch mit uns in Verbindung unter folgender Nummer:

Unit 10   Helping people cope with change

3   Listening: voicemail messages

2/12

A few days after the English advert appears, there are four messages from potential volunteers.

Listen to the messages and take notes.

Name of caller:	…	Experience (if any):	…
Nationality:	…	Contact details:	…
Languages:	…		

4   Speaking: voicemail messages

The senior social worker has asked you to call two of the people back to arrange a meeting. As neither is at home, you have to leave a message both times.

Work with a partner. Follow the steps below to prepare and then leave your messages.

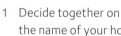
Bitte Olena Melnyk und Daniel Mills zurückrufen und jeweils einen Termin vereinbaren.

Telephoning

Spelling names
"Müller. That's M–U with an umlaut–double L–E–R."
"Pabst. That's papa–alpha–bravo–sierra–tango."
> *International spelling alphabet, p. 193*

Saying phone numbers
0176 33816745. "That's oh–one–seven–six, double three–eight–one, six–seven–four–five."
NOT: "thirty-three, eighty-one …"

Leaving a message
- My name is …
- I'm calling on behalf of … about your application to …
- We were pleased … and would like to …
- If that date and time is not possible, …
- If you are still interested in …, perhaps you would …
- The number is …
- Thank you. > *Telephoning, p. 192*

1 Decide together on the name of your home for asylum seekers and make up a phone number.
2 Think about a good way to start the call (stating your name, job title, why you are calling) and make sure you know how to end the call politely.
3 Now turn to one of the files below, read the social worker's notes and leave the message.
   Partner A: You are calling Olena Melnyk (file 35, p. 167).
   Partner B: You are calling Daniel Mills (file 24, p. 162).
4 Evaluate your partner's message. Was it clear and effective?

5   Role-play: interviewing prospective volunteers

The senior social worker has asked you to sit in on an interview with two prospective volunteers who cannot speak German. Use the information in your file to prepare and then do the role-plays.

Partners A and B: file 28, page 164   **Partners C and D:** file 38, page 168

6   Writing: benefits of living abroad

> *Eine Stellungnahme schreiben, S. 208*

Comment on the following statement: Every student who wants to work in the field of caring should have to work in another country for at least six months.

121

D Practice and projects

1 Talking about working with young migrants

Combine words from the two boxes to make collocations you can use to complete the text.

> German • integration • large •
> recently-arrived • regular • skilled •
> specialized • technical

> classes • college • diploma •
> instruction • language • numbers •
> programme • pupils • workers

Germany is becoming the home of ―¹ of young migrants. These young people will become some of Germany's ―² of the future but first they have to go to school. Before they can attend ―³, many of the ―⁴ have to learn the language. Some of them join an ―⁵ and can go to a school where they will be given ―⁶. Many of today's young immigrants will study at university or ―⁷ and gain qualifications. Some of them hope that a ―⁸ will help them find employment when they return home.

2 Caring for the elderly in multicultural Germany

Complete the job advertisement with the correct word from the brackets.

> **We are** a multicultural day centre for the elderly. We are looking for a (cultural / culturally)¹ competent assistant to work with clients from all kinds of cultural and (ethnic / ethnicity)² backgrounds.
>
> **You are** aware that (cultural / culturally)³ differences exist and you are (sensitive / sensible)⁴ to the values, religious beliefs and (practices/practises)⁵ of other people.
> You are able to assess a client's (personal / personnel)⁶ set of values and religious beliefs in order to take care of each client (individual / individually)⁷.
> You may have interacted with people from as many (cultural / culturally)⁸ diverse backgrounds as possible and have absorbed (much / many)⁹ of the different attitudes and problem-solving (strategy / strategies)¹⁰ of people from other countries.
> If you remember that every client is an individual and if you have an (open / openly)¹¹ and objective attitude and would enjoy working in a friendly and (careful / caring)¹² environment, please click here to apply.

3 Gerund or infinitive?

Complete the sentences with the most suitable form of the verb in brackets.

1. Many asylum seekers decide (come) to Germany to find a new life.
2. Why do you dislike (live) here? – I hate (share) a room with other people.
3. The girl seems (be) happy here.
4. Do you enjoy (work) with people from other cultures?
5. The boy avoided (answer) questions until the volunteer was there.
6. The young migrants learn (speak) German quite quickly.
7. Few of the young migrants expect (live) their whole life in Germany.
8. What do you suggest (do) after school?

> *Gerund / Infinitive, p. 221*

Unit 10   Helping people cope with change

4 Leaving a voicemail message

Complete the voicemail message with words and phrases from the box.

application • behalf of • call • look • looking • volunteer • volunteering

Good morning, my name is Ben Grant. I'm calling on ⬤¹ the Care and More Agency about your ⬤² to join our team as a ⬤³. If you are still ⬤⁴ to play a role and are interested in ⬤⁵ perhaps you would give me a ⬤⁶. My number is 0758 764809.
I ⬤⁷ forward to hearing from you.

Making a poster: options for working with migrants in your area

You are going to make a poster showing local options for caring professionals who would like to work with migrants.

Step 1 Walk through your neighbourhood or town and look for places which might offer possibilities to migrants. These could be community centres or multicultural cafés. Find out if there are any homes for asylum seekers in your area. In some cities, you will find information in *Stadtteilmanagement* offices.

Step 2 Choose one or two of the places and get information about what happens there. (You will have to do this in German.) Find out about the clientele and the roles carers play there. If it is appropriate, you might like to get this information by talking to someone in charge. Send an email enquiry first, explaining who you are and why you would like to visit the place and talk to somebody face-to-face.

Step 3 Once you have done your research, gather all your information and decide what you are going to present in English on your poster. Think about texts, photos, illustrations and graphs.

Step 4 Design and produce your poster. Hang all the posters on the classroom wall and do a gallery walk. Take notes, decide on one option and perhaps even take action by contacting the organization.

Checking progress

Browse through the previous pages in the unit, looking at headings and pictures. What have you learned? What can you do now that you have learned these things?
- ✔ I can help young migrants cope with some of the problems they face in Germany.   (Part A)
- ✔ I can understand the concept of culturally competent care for elderly migrants.   (Part B)
- ✔ I can assist in a home for asylum seekers.   (Part C)
- ✔ I can give a presentation on options for working with migrants in my area.   (Part D)

Write down two more statements of your own.

How much has this unit given you an insight into working with migrants? What has the unit taught you about culturally competent care?

Exam skills and strategies

An Diskussionen teilnehmen

Wichtig für:
- Interaktion

Ganz gleich, ob Sie an einer Gruppendiskussion, Debatte oder einem Rollenspiel teilnehmen, ist es wichtig, sich aktiv zu beteiligen und auf die anderen Teilnehmer/innen zu reagieren. Es ist eine gute Möglichkeit, frei zu sprechen, aber denken Sie daran, beim Thema zu bleiben.

BEISPIEL-AUFGABE Discuss this statement with your partner or in small groups: "Germans must realize that immigrants are their country's only hope for a successful future."

TIPPS

1 Bereiten Sie sich inhaltlich vor, indem Sie sich einzelne Aspekte des Themas noch einmal ins Gedächtnis rufen und Schlüsselbegriffe auf Englisch notieren.

> Why is immigration important to Germany?
> - Low birth rate in Germany – ageing population
> - Wealthy country – can afford to take new people
> - Can give refugees the chance of a new life
> - Benefits of cultural diversity on society
>
> What about negative factors of immigration?
> - Do people ever really accept immigrants?
> - Cost of integration programs

2 Legen Sie sich, falls genügend Zeit ist, ein paar Fragen/Antworten zum Thema zurecht.

> Can you think of any examples of good or bad integration from real life?
> Imagine you left Germany. How would you integrate into another culture?

3 Denken Sie nach, bevor Sie anfangen zu sprechen, aber versuchen Sie, spontan zu sein. Sie können sich nicht auf alles vorbereiten! Wenn Sie also mit unerwarteten Fragen konfrontiert werden, klinken Sie sich einfach in das Gespräch ein.
  → My spontaneous reaction to your question is …
  → I've thought about this, and my opinion is …

4 Äußern Sie Ihre Meinung und begründen Sie das, was Sie sagen.
  → Personally, I think/believe/feel that …, because …   → The reason is …
  → I'm convinced that …   → … and that's why I think that …

5 Fragen Sie andere nach ihrer Meinung und ob sie Ihnen zustimmen oder nicht.
  → What do you think about …?   → Would you agree that … is right/wrong/better/worse?
  → What's your opinion on …?   → Don't you agree?

6 Stimmen Sie anderen zu und seien Sie anderer Meinung.
  → I absolutely agree with what you said.   → I'm not sure I agree with you.
  → That's exactly how I see it.   → Do you really think so?
  → I'm afraid I can't go along with you on that.   → You must be joking!

7 Prüfen Sie, ob Sie verstanden wurden und ob Sie die anderen verstanden haben.
  → Do you see what I mean?   → So, am I right in thinking that …
  → Does that make sense?   → Unless I've got it wrong, the general idea is …

Exam skills and strategies

8   Haben Sie keine Hemmungen, jemanden zu unterbrechen.
    → I'm sorry to interrupt, but …   → Can I stop you there for a moment?
    → Excuse me for cutting in.   → Hold on a second.

9   Versuchen Sie, schüchterne oder ruhige Teilnehmer/innen in das Gespräch mit einzubeziehen.
    → What do you think about that?   → What's your opinion, [name of the person]?

10 Verwenden Sie genügend Ausdrücke, um Interesse, Überraschung oder andere emotionale Reaktionen auszudrücken. Das macht die Diskussion lebhafter.
    → I see. / Right. / OK then.   → Really? / Is that true? / Unbelievable!
    → Oh dear! / You're joking!

11 Bleiben Sie beim Thema und schweifen Sie nicht ab.

12 Gehen Sie auf Ihre/n Gesprächspartner/in ein und halten Sie Blickkontakt.

1 **Paired discussion:** Discuss the difficulties faced by people migrating to Germany from Spain, Greece and Italy. Why do they make the decision to move in the first place? Do you think they have the intention of staying temporarily or permanently? If they intend to go back to their own country one day, should they try to integrate into German society?

2 **Group discussion:** First, read the quotations.

"These days, it feels to me like you make a devil's pact when you walk into this country. You hand over your passport at the check-in, you get stamped, you want to make a little money, get yourself started … but you mean to go back! Who would want to stay? Cold, wet, miserable; terrible food, dreadful newspapers … In a place where you are never welcomed, only tolerated. Just tolerated. Like you are an animal finally house-trained."
   Zadie Smith, British writer, from her book White Teeth

"Every immigrant who comes here should be required within five years to learn English or leave the country."
   Theodore Roosevelt, former US President

In groups, using your knowledge of the subject, discuss how tolerance of migrants can become more widespread. What should each side do, or not do, to strengthen this relationship?

3 **Role-play:** In a group of four, role-play the following situation.

Partners A and B are social workers who help migrants integrate into German society.
   ▸ Turn to file 32 on page 166.

Partners C and D are siblings from Greece, and have been living in Germany for a short time.
   ▸ Turn to file 37 on page 168.

125

nach: InformationIsBeautiful.net

Afterglow

I'd like the memory of me to be
a happy one.
I'd like to leave an afterglow of
smiles when life is done.
I'd like to leave an echo whispering
softly down the ways,
Of happy times and laughing times
and bright and sunny days.
I'd like the tears of those who
grieve, to dry before the sun
Of happy memories that I leave
when life is done.

Unknown

11 Giving support at times of loss

1

A **Think:** Write down five ideas you have about death and dying.
Pair: Compare your list with a partner's.
Share: Interview other members of the class. Find out what they think about death and dying.

B Now look at the word cloud. How many words there came up in your discussions?
Still in your group, make sure you understand all the terms, using a dictionary if necessary.
Can you think of related words to extend the cloud?

2

A Look at the purple circles on the mind map, showing the main categories for the causes of death in the previous century. Which categories would you put the following under?

- Diarrhoea 226m
- Drugs 125m
- Stroke 410m
- Digestive illness 147m
- Famine 101m
- Skin cancer 5m

B Study the mind map carefully and look up any words you don't know. Compare some of the figures for specific causes of death. What do you find interesting or surprising?

126

Funeral Blues

Stop all the clocks, cut off the telephone,
Prevent the dog from barking with a juicy bone,
Silence the pianos and with muffled drum
Bring out the coffin, let the mourners come.

Let aeroplanes circle moaning overhead
Scribbling on the sky the message He Is Dead,
Put crepe bows round the white necks of the public doves,
Let the traffic policemen wear black cotton gloves.

He was my North, my South, my East and West,
My working week and my Sunday rest,
My noon, my midnight, my talk, my song;
I thought that love would last for ever: I was wrong.

The stars are not wanted now: put out every one;
Pack up the moon and dismantle the sun;
Pour away the ocean and sweep up the wood.
For nothing now can ever come to any good.

W. H. Auden (1938)

sorrow
sadness   death   condolences
suffering   **bereavement**   sympathy
memories   loss   remembrance
mortality   mourning   eulogy   grief

3 Analyse the poems and their relevance to the topic of losing someone. Compare their messages.

What's to come

In this unit, you will …
- consider working with the bereaved and decide whether or not the work is for you.
- assist an elderly man and talk about his case with a close relative.
- assist a foreigner who is dealing with a death in Germany.

At the end of the unit, you will give a presentation on celebrations of life.

Before you begin, think about what makes for quality of life at the end of life. How might you as a caring professional assist someone who is nearing death? How might you support them and their family?

A When a child dies

> You are living in London and thinking about volunteering at a local children's hospice. Prospective volunteers are asked to read some information on the hospice's website.

1 Reading: working with bereaved families › Einen Text zusammenfassen, S. 208

A Skim the text and say what it is about.

Clinical Care Volunteers

A hospice is a home providing care for the sick or terminally ill. You are considering working with the families of children who have died. You might be unsure about what the job involves. You might also be unsure if you are the right person for the job. These FAQs aim to give you some insights into the work.

What is bereavement work?

Parents of a child who has died and any surviving siblings need assurance, information and someone who listens without judgement. They also need the opportunity for laughter, love and friendship. Simple and humble acts of kindness are important.

Volunteers can help in many ways, for example by:
- keeping the bereaved family involved with their local community
- making sure the school is ready to help children return to school after the death of a sibling
- coordinating support for the family, e.g. organizing childcare so that the parents can have time alone
- giving the parents the opportunity to talk and grieve about the child who has died
- putting parents in contact with other parents who have experienced the death of a child
- advising parents about support groups for themselves and their children
- helping parents to know what to expect during the period of grief

Do volunteers work as therapists?

No, they do not. Therapy is a specialist field which is carried out by qualified grief counsellors. There are, however, a number of therapeutic tasks a volunteer can help with, including:
- assisting the family to write a biography of the child
- honouring and remembering the child, on his/her birthday
- enabling other family members and friends to remember the child

Who will I be working with?

Clinical care volunteers assist the care team with practical support for bereaved families, both inside and outside of the hospice. When you provide additional support, the care team can focus on the service that we provide to our children and their families. You will be working alongside nurses, social workers, psychological social workers, pastoral care workers and teachers.

Who can volunteer?

There is no such thing as a "typical volunteer". We welcome people from all walks of life, and benefit greatly from drawing on their personal skills and life experiences. Even if it is only a few hours a week or an hour a day, there is always a role to suit most people.

Volunteering might be the right thing for you if you are: ✔ sensitive ✔ open ✔ tolerant

We are always happy to take on trainee social workers and health care workers.   (419 words)

B Read the text carefully and summarize the job in one paragraph.

C Find words and expressions in the text which are used to describe:

1 families of a child who has recently died.   3 qualities needed in volunteers.
2 the great sadness felt by these families.   4 professionals who are involved with these families.

GUIDANCE *If you would like guidance, turn to file G15 on page 177.*
CHALLENGE! *If you would prefer a challenge, turn to file C7 on page 185.*

Unit 11   Giving support at times of loss

2   Listening: assisting parents after the death of a child

A link on the hospice's website leads you to a podcast.

2/13

In today's Social Pulse podcast, Mark is talking to Aysun Keskin, a volunteer at a children's hospice, about her role in assisting bereaved families.

A Listen and make a note of Aysun's answers to the questions below.

1 When does bereavement work start?
2 Can parents prepare for their child's death?
3 How does grieving before the death help some parents cope better with the mourning process?
4 What is the carer's role?
5 What are some of the difficulties in working with parents whose child has just died?
6 What should someone who is thinking about working at a children's hospice consider?

B Look at these quotes from the interview. Use your own words to explain what Aysun meant.

1 "Parents who can come to terms with the closeness of death and the probability of loss are ready and better prepared when it finally happens."
2 "For parents with a child who has died, the road can be long, hard and often lonely."
3 "They [The parents] may feel the ground has been ripped out from under their feet."

---

3   Role-play: an interview at the children's hospice

You have decided to volunteer and have been invited to an interview with the social worker in the hospice interdisciplinary team (IDT).

Work with a partner. You are going to role-play the main part of the interview using information from these pages. Read your role cards carefully and do all the tasks.

Partner A: file 33, page 167   **Partner B:** file 16, page 158

> GUIDANCE   *If you would like guidance, turn together to file G27 on page 129.*

---

4   Reflection: clarifying your thoughts

You have been offered a place as a volunteer at the hospice. Before you decide if you are going to accept, you carefully consider whether or not the job is for you. Think about everything you have learned while working through these pages. Make notes, then write a diary entry saying what you have decided and why.

---

5   Writing: working at a hospice   ▸ *Einen Aufsatz schreiben, S. 208*

Search on the internet and use information from these pages to find out more about working at a hospice. Describe the benefits of a hospice for the terminally ill and their families.

B "What should we do with Grandad?"

> Your stay in London is over and you are now training in a nursing home in Germany. One of the new arrivals is a 78-year-old British man who has been transferred to your facility after a spell in hospital. Mr Watson has been living in Germany for almost 60 years. As your boss knows that your English is excellent, he asks you to accompany him when he speaks to the client's grandson who is visiting at the moment.

1 Listening: the background to the case

> Mit Hörverstehensaufgaben umgehen, S. 207

You decide to find out more about the case and to speak to Mr Watson.

A Before you visit Mr Watson in his room, your boss asks you to read his medical record and make notes in English. Use a dictionary to translate the medical terms.

Name:	William Watson	Notaufnahme:	19.07.20..
Geburtsdatum:	29.11.19..	Diagnose:	Hirnschlag mit halbseitiger Lähmung links
Beruf:	Koch (i. R.) (Militär)	Anamnese:	mögliche TIA*, Diabetes 2, Bluthochdruck, AMD**

Kontaktperson:
(vorübergehend) Michael Watson (Enkel)

* TIA transitorische ischämische Attacke
** AMD altersabhängige Makuladegeneration

2/14

B Next, you ask Mr Watson to describe his stroke. Listen to his description of what happened and take notes. What is one of his main concerns?

GUIDANCE If you would like guidance, turn to file G28 on page 182 before you listen.

2 Reading and discussion: ailments and diseases of the elderly

Before your appointment with Mr Watson's grandson Michael, you read some information on the internet.

Read the text and discuss the questions below in small groups.

1. Which of the ageing-related illnesses have you heard of?
2. Which do you know from personal experience, i.e. from members of your family? Describe the symptoms.

AILMENTS AND DISEASES ASSOCIATED WITH AGEING

Some ailments and diseases are complications arising from growing older and are sometimes referred to as "diseases of the elderly". Examples of ailments and diseases associated with ageing include visual impairment (such as cataracts and age-related macular degeneration), hearing impairment, atherosclerosis and cardiovascular disease, cancer, arthritis, osteoporosis, type 2 diabetes, hypertension, dementia and Alzheimer's disease. Of the approximately 150,000 people who die each day around the world, roughly two thirds – 100,000 per day – die of ageing-related causes. In industrialized nations, this figure is much higher, reaching 90%.
The incidence of developing these ailments and diseases increases rapidly with ageing.

(100 words)

Unit 11   Giving support at times of loss

3 Role-play: answering a relative's questions

Michael Watson has arranged to meet with your boss, the chief administrator of the nursing home, and then with the medical staff. He has some questions about his grandfather's condition.

A Look at some of the questions Michael might ask. How might your boss and the medical staff answer? Match 1–5 with a–e.

1. Has my grandfather had this kind of stroke before?
2. Can he take anything for it?
3. How effective are the meds he's taking?
4. Could you tell me how his mind is? Is he thinking clearly?
5. How long does he have to stay here?

a. He's sometimes confused, but confusion is typical among stroke patients.
b. It is recommended that he stays at least a week.
c. The medication is thought to have good results.
d. He appears to have had one or two mini-strokes before this one.
e. He's being given several types of medication.

B Now get into groups of four and use the instructions in your files to role-play the two meetings.

Partners A and B: file 21, page 161
Partners C and D: file 41, page 170

Giving an objective report

You grandfather **is thought** to have called the ambulance himself.
The medicine **is said** to work well.
It is recommended that he rests for a few days.

- We use the passive to express ourselves in an objective way. The passive forms above are often used by people in the medical profession when talking to patients and their families.

> *Other passive forms, p. 220*

Asking delicate questions

- Could you tell me / explain …?
- Do you happen to remember when …?
- Would you mind telling me how …?
- …, if you don't mind me asking.

4 Dictation and writing: a letter to a son

2/15

> *Umgang mit Operatoren, S. 202*

After Michael and his wife have gone back to Britain, William Watson decides that he would like to make contact with his son, Bill. Because of his eye problems, he dictates a letter to you and asks you to send it to his son.

A Listen once without writing, then listen again and take the dictation. Read the letter and add punctuation where necessary.

B Now do the following tasks.

1. Explain when Mr Watson saw Bill last and describe the family's life before Bill and his mother left.
2. Compare a father's involvement in children's upbringing then and now.
3. Point out what Mr Watson thinks of his son's skills as a parent.
4. Analyse the tone of the letter with respect to Mr Watson's reflection on his past.
5. Outline Mr Watson's situation after his wife and Bill left him.
6. Explain what Mr Watson would like Bill to do.
7. Speculate about how you think Bill will react to Mr Watson's letter. Taking into account Bill's attitude towards his father and the state his father is in, draft Bill's letter in response.

131

C Death in Germany

> **S** Mr Watson has died. Michael and his wife had been called to his bedside, and now you and your boss are going to talk them through the next steps.

 ### Reading: burial vs cremation – the environmental aspects

Michael gives you a printout of an article that he found among his grandfather's possessions. His grandfather appears to have made some notes and highlighted some of the facts.

A Look at Mr Watson's notes and the parts of the text that he highlighted. Help Michael decide if his grandfather had wanted to be buried or cremated.

Ethical living
Should I ... be buried or cremated?

Leo Hickman's guide to a good death   *The Guardian*, Tuesday 18 October 2005

It's better to burn out than fade away. Kurt Cobain clearly thought so, quoting this famous Neil Young lyric in his suicide note, but then he obviously wasn't referring to the issue of ==greenhouse gas emissions== when it comes to the somewhat thorny cremation vs burial debate. For most environmentalists, it's actually ==better to fade away than burn out==. Much better, in death, to ==compost down as nature intended==. *— that's a lot!*

A cremator uses about 285 kilowatt-hours of gas and 15kWh of electricity on average per ==cremation== – roughly ==the same domestic energy demands as a single person for an entire month==. Aside from the considerable amount of greenhouse gas emissions this creates, cremation is also responsible for 16% of the UK's mercury pollution (via our dental fillings). The industry has been told that all 650 crematoria must halve mercury emissions by 2012, but, ironically, one way to do this is to cremate at a higher temperature, thereby leading to more emissions. *— that's an issue too of course*

Then there are the ==materials used to make a coffin==. Wooden coffins are often made from solid oak or pine, though 89% are made from veneered chipboard, which is bonded with a ==formaldehyde resin== which ==enters the atmosphere when it is burnt==. These materials also enter the ground if burial is the preferred option, as do ==embalming chemicals – also formaldehyde-based== – which can, over time, ==enter the watercourse==. *And that's another thing*

==Burial at sea== might seem ==a logical eco option==, but the authorities generally frown on us choosing to become ==fishfood==: just 50 or so non-navy sea burials are granted each year for the UK's three licensed locations. ==Woodland burials== are becoming an increasingly popular option, as is the use of fully biodegradable coffins. There are now about 200 woodland burial sites in the UK which offer families an alternative to cemeteries or crematoria. Managed either privately or by a local authority, these burial sites are left unmarked or are ==marked by the planting of a tree or wild flowers==. Any coffin used must be made from a fully biodegradable material such as cardboard or wicker, or a cloth can be used instead. *no fish food!!! Is that allowed in Germany?*

While many find much comfort in this naturally-minded option, there is a question about just ==how sustainable it can be to offer everyone who can afford it their own piece of woodland==. One of the reasons cremation superseded burials in the UK was because available space had greatly diminished over the decades. The post-war drive to get more people to consider cremation included the slogan "Save the land for the living".

Eco alternatives to burial and cremation are still being sought. Just last week, a Swedish town announced it was set to try freeze-drying its dead into brittle, compostable remains using liquid nitrogen. Solar-powered crematoria have been proposed to help save the millions of tonnes of wood burnt each year cremating India's dead. But while we wait to learn whether these are viable options, it seems that being buried in ==a modest, fully biodegradable coffin== remains the option that ==is least harmful to the environment==. *that will do for me*

(502 words)

132

Unit 11   Giving support at times of loss

B Work with a partner. Scan the text and make two lists of words or phrases that are useful for a) discussing the disposal of human remains and b) talking about the environment. Make sure you understand all the words, then compare your lists with another pair's.

C Copy this table and complete it with information from the text.

Disposing of remains		
Methods	Positive aspects	Negative aspects
…	…	…

2 Mediation: dealing with a death in Germany
> Mediation, S. 211

The supervisor would like you to help him explain some of the formalities and bureaucracy associated with a death in Germany to Michael and his wife.
Work in groups of four and follow the steps below.

Partners A and B: You are going to explain what to do immediately after death has occurred and what must be done within 36 hours of the death. Turn to file 42 on page 171 and read the instructions.
Partners C and D: You are going to give advice on how to make funeral arrangements. Turn to file 39 on page 169 and read the instructions.

3 Watching a video: "High-tech headstones"
> Mit Hör-/Sehverstehensaufgaben umgehen, S. 207

7

You discover a video on one way of remembering and celebrating a life.

A Watch the video and take notes. What do you think of the idea of high-tech headstones? Discuss the pros and cons in groups.

B Use your notes to write a short print advertisement describing the headstones.

GUIDANCE *If you would like guidance, turn to file G29 on page 183.*

C You mention the idea to Michael and his wife and they are intrigued. They ask you to help them put together some information to celebrate William Watson's life. What kind of material would you suggest? Make a list.

4 Writing: pros and cons of regulations
> Eine Stellungnahme schreiben, S. 208

Michael thanks you for your assistance and remarks on the number of rules and regulations regarding the disposal of remains in Germany. As you may have to deal with family members from different cultural backgrounds in the future, you decide to find out more. Do internet research and use your findings to write a comment on the pros and cons of rules and regulations relating to the disposal of remains, from the point of view of both the state and the bereaved.

133

D Practice and projects

1 Working with the bereaved

Match the English phrases to the German expressions.

1	helping the families of the terminally ill	a	*Trauerarbeit leisten*
2	doing bereavement work	b	*mit Therapie unterstützend einwirken*
3	supporting surviving siblings	c	*überlebende Geschwister unterstützen*
4	doing humble acts of kindness	d	*den Familien von Todkranken helfen*
5	coordinating support	e	*eine Biografie des Kindes schreiben*
6	referring to support groups	f	*Unterstützung koordinieren*
7	assisting with therapeutic tasks	g	*dem Kind Ehre erweisen und ihm gedenken*
8	writing a biography of the child	h	*praktische Unterstützung anbieten*
9	honouring and remembering the child	i	*auf Hilfsvereinigungen verweisen*
10	giving practical support	j	*einfache Handlungen der Freundlichkeit bekunden*

2 Ageing-related ailments and diseases

Use words and phrases from the box to complete the text.

> *admitting • Alzheimer's disease • cataracts • complications •*
> *growing • heart • longer • medical*

Because of ⬤¹ advancements, people in the western world are living ⬤². As a result, our hospitals are ⬤³ more and more people suffering from the ailments and diseases associated with ⬤⁴ old. Some of the ⬤⁵ arising from growing older are problems with the eyes, for example ⬤⁶, deafness, cardiovascular problems (ailments associated with the ⬤⁷), cancers of all types and cognitive problems like dementia and ⬤⁸.

3 Giving an objective report

Reformulate these sentences using the passive voice and the prompts in brackets. Sometimes two sentence structures are possible.

Examples: The man was over 100 years old when he died. (think)
   The man was thought to be over 100 years old when he died.
   It is thought that the man was over 100 years old when he died.

1 The medicine will work very quickly. (expect)
2 The patient will die tomorrow. (expect)
3 The nursing home offers excellent care. (say)
4 The patient was unconscious for several hours. (believe)
5 The operation will go well. (expect)
6 The patient will be able to go home soon. (think)
7 The patient fell down the stairs. (believe)
8 The patient burned his hand while cooking. (think)
9 The carers who work here are very highly trained. (say)
10 The home was left a lot of money by a patient who died. (believe)

> *Other passive forms, p. 220*

Unit 11   Giving support at times of loss

4   Making a mind map
> *Mindmaps erstellen, S. 207*

Think: Look back over the unit and choose the topic that interests you most: working with bereaved families, ageing related diseases or dealing with death in Germany.

Pair: Work with a partner who has chosen the same topic as you and collect thematically relevant vocabulary to make a mind map.

Share: Pool your ideas with others who have chosen the same topic. Then, as a class, put all three topics together into one mind map entitled "Giving support at times of loss".

Research and presentation: celebrations of life

You are going to work in groups to research funeral customs in the multicultural world we live in. When you have gathered your information, you will give a presentation comparing and contrasting different funeral customs.

Step 1 Brainstorm ideas about "typical" funeral customs in Germany. Think about things like burial vs cremation. Say who takes care of the arrangements, etc. Expand on your answers by talking to an older member of your family or by searching the internet. Make notes and collect material that might be useful for your presentation.

Step 2 Do research to discover how many different nationalities or religious cultures make up your town or city. You can do this by visiting your town hall or looking on the internet. You can also refer to the multicultural setting within your class.

Step 3 Choose two or three of the nationalities or religious cultures that interest you. Do research to find out how people from the cultures you have chosen organize funerals. Compare and contrast these funerals with each other and with "typical" German funerals.

Step 4 Illustrate in what way you can professionally assist the surviving family members before and after the funeral.

Step 5 Prepare and then give your presentation.
> *Präsentieren, S. 209*

Checking progress

Browse through the previous pages in the unit, looking at headings and pictures.
What have you learned? What can you do now that you have learned these things?
- ✔ I can understand what it means to work with the bereaved.   (Part A)
- ✔ I can deal with elderly people and their relatives in a sensitive manner.   (Part B)
- ✔ I can help with administrative issues surrounding a death in Germany.   (Part C)
- ✔ I can give a presentation on funeral customs in different cultures.   (Part D)

Write down two more statements of your own.

How much has this unit given you an insight into working with bereaved families and the families of elderly people or children who are ill? What has the unit taught you about working as a caring professional in a multicultural society?

Exam skills and strategies

Schaubilder und Statistiken beschreiben und analysieren

Wichtig für:
- Analyse und Kommentieren einer visuellen Vorlage
- materialgestützten Aufsatz
- Präsentationen

In einer Prüfung kann es vorkommen, dass Sie statistische Daten beschreiben sollen, die in einer Grafik, einem Diagramm oder einer Tabelle dargestellt sind. Am besten bereiten Sie sich darauf vor, indem Sie lernen, wie Sie Ihre Beschreibung/Analyse strukturieren, und sich signifikante Wörter bzw. Phrasen zur Beschreibung und Erläuterung statistischer Daten verinnerlichen.

BEISPIEL-AUFGABE

Describe and analyse the following information collected by a funeral home.

A Client survey: Do you believe in life after death?

	Religious	Non-religious
Yes	85%	30%
No	5%	21%
Not sure	10%	49%

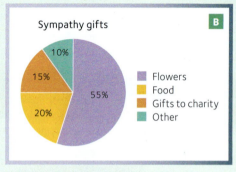

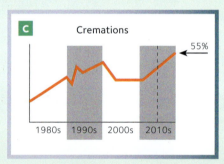

BOCKS FUNERAL HOME
est. 1980

TIPPS

1 Beschreiben Sie zunächst, worum es in der Statistik geht.
   → a *This table indicates what percentage of customers believe in life after death.*
   → b *This pie chart compares how often each type of sympathy gift is given.*
   → c *This line graph shows the share of customers who have chosen cremation over burial since the 1980s.*

2 Fassen Sie dann kurz die Entwicklung oder die Entwicklungstendenz zusammen.
   → a ***Nearly** a third of non-religious customers said they believed in life after death, **about** 20% said they didn't believe in it, and **roughly** half said they weren't sure.*

   Expressing approximation
   roughly, nearly, approximately, around, about, just under/over, well under/over

   Wenn es mehrere Informationen gibt, vergleichen Sie diese.
   → b *The **most common** gift is flowers. Food was **more common** than charitable gifts. The **least common** gifts are grouped together as "other".*

> Comparison of adjectives and adverbs, S. 223

Exam skills and strategies

→ c Cremations **increased steadily** in the 1980s and 90s, with only a **slight fluctuation**. In the 2000s there was a **significant drop**, and for some time the rate **stayed at** the same level. Since then, cremations have **soared** and they are projected to keep doing so in the future.

> **Describing trends**
> - Use words like *rise, increase, surge, soar,* and *improve* for upward movement.
> - Use *decline, decrease, dip, drop, fall, plummet* and *slump* for downward movement.
> - *Fluctuate/fluctuation* expresses frequent change.
> - *Remain stable / constant, stay at / maintain / keep the same level*, and *stabilize* all indicate no change.
> - Adverbs and adjectives give variation to how much or how quickly something moves: *considerable/-ly, gradual/-ly, moderate/-ly, quick/-ly, rapid/-ly, sharp/-ly, significant/-ly, slight/-ly, slow/-ly, steep/-ly, substantial/-ly, sudden/-ly*

3 Schreiben Sie zum Schluss eine kurze Schlussfolgerung der Informationen. Äußern Sie nicht Ihre Meinung.

→ a The difference between the beliefs of the religious and non-religious customers is very big. The majority of people as a whole are at least considering the possibility of life after death.

→ b ~~As I expected~~, More than half of all people give flowers when someone dies.

→ c The general trend is that more and more people are getting cremated.

1 Complete the text about the line diagram with words from the box.

- considerable fluctuation
- dipped
- gradual increase
- rising
- slowly decreased
- generally considerably higher
- remained stable
- dropped suddenly
- peaked
- rise sharply

Russian Life Expectancy *Sources: demoskope.ru and gks.ru*

This line graph shows the life expectancy in Russia since the 1950s. Life expectancy for females in Russia is ⊙^a than for males. For both male and female Russians, there was a ⊙^b between 1950 and 1965, then the male life expectancy ⊙^c while the female life expectancy ⊙^d. There was ⊙^e between 1980 and 2005: Life expectancy ⊙^f for both sexes in the early 1990s, then began to ⊙^g until it ⊙^h again in 1998, and ⊙ⁱ again in the early 2000s. Since then, life expectancy has been ⊙^j slowly.

2 Describe and analyse the diagram in 150 words.

> Lösungen, S. 293

CAUSES OF DEATH IN THE EUROPEAN UNION, BY AGE GROUP

Source: Eurostat

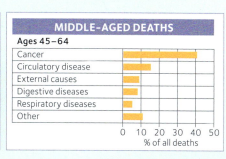

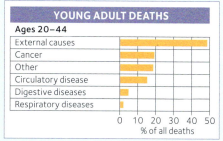

137

Hospitals
- 2,083 hospitals in Germany
- 300,417 people employed in the nursing services
- 503,000 beds
  nach: Statistisches Bundesamt

Nursing aid
- There are 2,000 care and service providers in Germany.
- Over 6 million people are prescribed some kind of nursing aid each year.
- Over €10 billion is spent in the homecare sector every year of which €6.8 million is spent by private households.
  nach: Salenus

TODAY

Residential care homes
- 11,000 part-residential care homes in Germany
- 799,000 places
- 709,000 people in need of care
- 574,000 people employed
  nach: Statistisches Bundesamt

People with disabilities
- 8.6 million people with disabilities in Germany of whom 7.1 million are severely disabled
- 29% of all severely disabled people are over 75 years old.
  nach: Statistisches Bundesamt

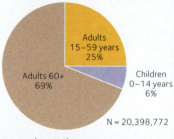

Distribution of people worldwide in need of palliative care by age group

Adults 60+ 69%
Adults 15–59 years 25%
Children 0–14 years 6%
N = 20,398,772
nach: www.thewpca.org

12 Looking ahead

1 **Think:** What advances in social and health care have happened in the last five years? Write down a few ideas.
Pair: Compare your ideas with a partner, then discuss what changes might happen in the next five years.
Share: Compare and contrast your information for "today" and "tomorrow". Discuss in class how you as professional carers might be affected by these developments.

2 Analyse the statistics above. What does the information tell us about our society today and in the future?
> *Schaubilder und Statistiken beschreiben und analysieren, S. 210*

3 Compare and contrast two of the photos. What do you think the people in the photos are saying or thinking?

> I love you, Dad.

> Can I get you anything else?

> You'll get good care here.

138

Robots are friendly helpers

Japan's Institute of Physical and Chemical Research

The first successful artificial heart

Medical tourism continues to increase in popularity due to the many benefits that are associated with receiving medical treatment abroad. Destinations for medical tourists from western Europe include eastern Poland, the Czech Republic and the UK. Medical tourists from eastern Europe, Russia and the United Arab Emirates can be found in most of the western European countries.

TOMORROW

Asia is the goal for many Europeans who are looking for care in old age

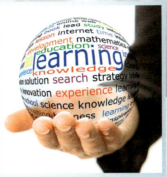

Bionic hand allows the wearer to "feel" things

Learning for the future

People with good levels of education are still likely to be best placed in the social and health care workplace. However, education should be more about how you learn, rather than for knowledge itself. If you need to retrain and learn new skills, it will be easier if you have a good general education and are in the habit of learning.

4 How much have you learned for the future? What have you learned? What do you intend to learn? Consider how you, working in the field of social and health care, can cope with possible developments.

What's to come

In this unit, you will …
- visit a social and health care fair and listen to a lecture about a global health threat.
- learn about a "smart environment" where people with Alzheimer's and dementia can live safely.
- look into global developments and options for caring professionals.

At the end of the unit, you will develop an infographic presenting the caring profession in the year 2025.

Before you begin, think about your personal wishes for the future. What would you like to be doing in 2025?

A Developments in the health sector

> **S** You and a group of trainees are planning to visit the "We Care Social & Health Care" Trade Fair. You prepare yourselves for the visit by looking at the fair programme online.

1

Reading: investment in professional care

One of the aims of the exhibitors at the fair is to attract professional visitors to their stands.

A Read the descriptions of some of the exhibitors and find one who:

1. aims to help an older demographic group to remain independent.
2. is a global organization.
3. is concerned with international public health.
4. sells equipment and aids for a specific target group.
5. offers advice about practical arrangements and information on laws related to home care.
6. will let prospective customers try out some of their products.

B Find words and phrases in the text which can be used to talk about:

1. aids and equipment for disabled people (4 words and phrases).
2. staying independent in old age (4).
3. collecting data (3).
4. how everyone in the world should work together to take care of health issues (1).
5. how everyone in the world should have the same chances to be healthy (1).

---

www.WeCareSocial&HealthCare.com/tradevisitors

WELCOME TO "WE CARE SOCIAL & HEALTH CARE"!

| HOME | GENERAL INFORMATION | EXHIBITOR INFORMATION | VISITOR INFORMATION | PROGRAMME | IMPRESSIONS |

CAPABILITY presents the latest equipment for disabled people. We will show you all the latest technical innovations that are coming on the market soon. We have everything from assistance for daily use in the care sector to long-term aids like prosthetics and wheelchairs. We are sure you will be interested in our products which help people with disabilities to live as independently as possible. Free trial of many of our appliances.
Check out our list of demonstrations.

SelfReliant Seniors
We focus on the needs of the elderly, particularly those who are keen to be self-reliant and retain their independence for as long as possible.
Our aim is to provide the latest information on health, wellness and mobility in old age.
We also advise on security and safety, and can help plan and make adjustments to the home.
Visitors to our stand can take away comprehensive information related to home care.
Click here for further information.

WHO is the directing and coordinating authority for health within the United Nations system.
It is responsible for providing leadership on global health matters, shaping the health research agenda, setting norms and standards, collating evidence-based policy options, providing technical support to countries and monitoring and assessing health trends.
In the 21st century, health is a shared responsibility, involving equitable access to essential care and collective defence against transnational threats.
Click here to find our list of lectures to be given during the fair.

(237 words)

Unit 12 Looking ahead

2 Listening: the global challenge
> Mit Hörverstehensaufgaben umgehen, S. 207

You decide to go to one of the WHO lectures: "Pandemics: the global challenge".

A Listen to the lecture and take notes on the following points.

1 the differences between an outbreak, an epidemic and a pandemic
2 some past pandemics
3 antivirals, vaccines and antibiotics
4 major areas for health care investment

B With a partner, explain these words used in the lecture.

diminishing • threat • localized • full-blown • mortality rate • eradicated • second line of defence

C Summarize the main points of the talk in one paragraph.

The next few decades are going to be critical for humanity. In this lecture, speaker Geoffrey Hsu describes some ways in which we may tackle global pandemics in the future.

3 Talking: predicting the future

Use the notes below to predict how things will be in the next ten years.

polio and AIDS / be eradicated
somebody / discover cure for cancer
pandemic / destroy population of major cities
people / control wheelchairs with their minds
medication / available to reverse Alzheimer's
people / keep working until at least 75

Polio is going to be completely eradicated soon. There are already very few cases.

I don't think anybody will discover a cure for cancer in the next ten years.

Making predictions and describing plans

There **will be** a rise in the number of pandemics over the next ten years.

- We use the *will* future to say what we think, guess or calculate will happen in the future.

The next decades **are going to be** critical for humanity.
I'm going to talk about antivirals later.

- We use the future with *going to* to predict the future when we have firm evidence now that something is going to happen. We also use it to describe intentions or plans.
> The future, p. 215

4 Writing: an enquiry or an unsolicited job application
> Correspondence, pp. 186–189

Choose one of these options.

Option 1 Write an enquiry to Capability or SelfReliant Seniors. Ask for information about their products or services.
> Writing enquiries, p. 199

Option 2 Write an unsolicited application to the WHO. Explain who you are and ask if there are any places available for someone with your qualifications.

 If you would like guidance for either option, turn to file G30 on page 183.

141

B Technological advances

> **S** The head of the care provider where you are doing your practical training has asked you to take a look at the stand run by the Alzheimer's Society. He would like you to pick up some information.

1 **Reading: the smart home**   > *Schwierige Texte lesen, S. 202*

A Read the text. How might the smart home help people suffering from Alzheimer's or dementia as well as their families and caregivers?

Helping the elderly live independently at home

Due to a globally ageing population, disability resulting from chronic disease is on the rise. In particular, the number of people diagnosed with dementia is expected to double worldwide by 2030 and triple by 2050.

Even though they recognize that their cognitive abilities are declining, many dementia sufferers want to continue living independently in the community for as long as they can. At Washington State University (WSU), computer scientists are working on a system that could enhance the quality of life of older adults who want to stay in their homes longer despite mental and physical limitations.

Professors Diane Cook, an expert in artificial intelligence, and Maureen Schmitter-Edgecombe, who has done research on memory and ageing, are working together to develop a "smart environment" – an apartment equipped with technology aimed at assisting people to remain independent longer.

The scientists have set up some test apartments with sensors to monitor motion and collect data about the daily activities of the people living in them. The sensors, small white boxes about one inch by two inches (2.54 × 5.08 cm), have been installed in each room. Some of them track the use of appliances and water; others give a warning if a cooker has been left on. Sensors placed in beds and chairs can provide an early warning if the resident does not return by a predetermined time.

A computer in the apartment is equipped with software that recognizes and analyses information from the various sensors and provides feedback, either immediately or in the form of reports, to both the residents and caregivers. With these reports, the computer could, for instance, tell caregivers, either while they are visiting the home or remotely, what the resident is or has been doing.

"Our aim is not to make people dependent on technology," says Schmitter-Edgecombe. "But, if they are having difficulties, then the technology can assist them."

The research team has been given about $3 million in grants to create the "smart environment" to help older people remain independent longer.

Cook estimates that it will be about five years before the "smart environment" is available for sale to the general public. She estimates that currently it would cost about $5,000 to retrofit a home.

Nora Gibson directs a non-profit organization for the elderly in Seattle as well as a chapter of the Alzheimer's Association. She wonders how comfortable elderly people will feel with a house full of computerized sensors.

"Some older adults may be suspicious," she says, "but when I talk to people who are used to our technological world, they find the idea great. They've seen how technology supports them."

Gibson has volunteered one of her adult day health centres for real trials. She is also pleased to report that WSU is not alone in recognizing the demand.   (465 words)

B Do these tasks. > Umgang mit Operatoren, S. 202

1. State the reasons for developing a "smart environment".
2. Describe and explain the test environment.
3. Find evidence to show that the idea of a smart environment is being taken seriously.
4. Comment on the statement: "Our aim is not to make people dependent on technology".

C Find the English equivalents of these German words in the text.

1. *geistige Fähigkeiten*
2. *die Lebensqualität verbessern*
3. *überwachen*
4. *Haushaltsgeräte*
5. *vorher festgelegt*
6. *aus der Ferne*
7. *nachrüsten*
8. *misstrauisch*

2 Taking a tour: the smart home

Work with a partner. Study the plan of the smart home and take turns to describe where the sensors are placed and what the sensors do.

Start like this: *There is a motion sensor on the cooker in the kitchen. If the cooker is left on, the sensor sends a signal to the data manager in the bedroom, which …*

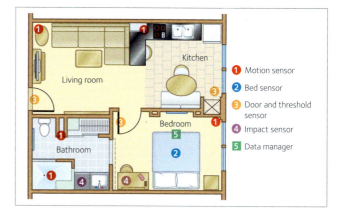

3 Mediation: the smart environment > Mediation, S. 211

A neighbour, whose mother has been diagnosed with dementia but wants to keep living in her own home, is interested in WSU's research into the smart home. He asks you to explain the most interesting parts of the text in German.

GUIDANCE *If you would like guidance, turn to file G14 on page 177.*

4 Writing: advantages and disadvantages of a smart environment

Your boss asks you to write a comment on the advantages and disadvantages of a smart environment for the service's website.

Before you start, analyse these statistics and relate them to the importance of this technology.

Germany dementia statistics

- Dementia affects 1,200,000 people at the moment (70% women, 30% men).
- Experts estimate that by the year 2030, 2,500,000 people will be affected by dementia.
- Every year 200,000 new cases of dementia are diagnosed.
- Between the ages of 65 and 69, every 20th person is affected by dementia; between the ages of 80 and 90, every third person. *nach: www.deutsche-alzheimer.de/*

C Where are we heading?

> One of the information stands at the fair is run by Careers in Caring. The organization, which is funded by the EU, is hoping to interest people in working in the field of caring.

1 Discussion: How does our future look? > *An Diskussionen teilnehmen, S. 210*

Careers in Caring has interactive screens at the front of their stand. You click onto the first page.

A Read the information below and think about what it means to the world.

B Get into groups and discuss the implications. How might the statistics affect your life as a caring professional in 2025?

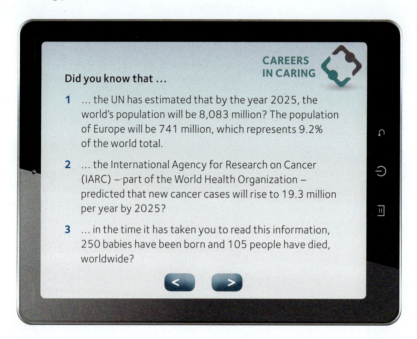

CAREERS IN CARING

Did you know that …

1 … the UN has estimated that by the year 2025, the world's population will be 8,083 million? The population of Europe will be 741 million, which represents 9.2% of the world total.

2 … the International Agency for Research on Cancer (IARC) – part of the World Health Organization – predicted that new cancer cases will rise to 19.3 million per year by 2025?

3 … in the time it has taken you to read this information, 250 babies have been born and 105 people have died, worldwide?

2 Reading: the future for professional carers

The next screens you look at relate to job opportunities.

A Describe the photos. Which fields do you think the people are working in?

Unit 12 Looking ahead

B Read the text to check your answers. Then work in groups and rank the ten jobs mentioned or described below from 1 (most likely) to 10 (least likely) to be a job in the future.

The future for social and health care professionals

According to predictions made by employment experts, it is likely that our jobs and the way we work will be very different by the year 2025.

Job titles such as "body part maker" and "holistic carer" could be appearing in recruitment ads all over the world.

At a conference on "Working Tomorrow", experts from all over the globe are meeting next week to discuss the future for employees in the social and health care fields. Here is a taste of some of the exciting talks in store.

1 Training for the future – Ivan Berg, futurologist

As computers get more intelligent, they will be able to do many tasks that we associate with caring professionals today. To create a balance between technology and humans, caring professionals will need to develop their human skills like leadership, motivation and compassion. People are going to have to focus on these skills to survive in the workforce. Their best bet is to train for work that computers and robots can't do, such as caring for children, looking after the terminally ill and counselling the bereaved.

2 Jobs for health professionals in the future – Hella Klein, medical researcher

Continuing advances in health care will lead to an older population which will need different remedies and treatments. I can see a place for "wellness" consultants who will specialize in personalized, holistic care for elderly patients. More and more physiotherapists and occupational therapists will be needed.

3 Going further than the guide dog – Bella Fry, caring animal trainer

Guide dogs that support the blind have been around for many decades. Over the years, we have trained other animal companions to work with humans in need of care. Some examples are dogs who can remind their owners to take their medicine, and monkeys who can bring objects to patients with limited mobility. This talk will focus on working with caring animals in the social and health care sectors in the future.

Other talks will focus on future careers such as:

- Child designer: designing offspring that fit parental requirements
- Personal medical apothecary: providing a tailor-made range of alternative therapies

(352 words)

Writing: caring professions in 2025

Choose one or two of the options below.

Option 1 Use information from these pages and internet research to write a blog entry entitled "What will the caring profession look like in 2025?"

Option 2 Write a letter to the editor of a magazine for social and health care professionals expressing your views on developments in the field.

Option 3 Analyse and comment on the quote below from the speaker in the talk about the profession of "child designer". What are the ethical implications?
"Experts predict that 30 years from now, you'll be able to design the child you want. It is ethically questionable, but you could do it."

145

D Practice and projects

1 Talking about social and health care

Make as many collocations as you can by matching words from the two boxes. Who in the class has the most collocations?

care	health
demographic	home
disabled	professional
elderly	public
global	social

care	people
group	research
health	sector
issues	trends

2 Describing the smart home

Work with a partner. Without looking back at the text, try to remember what you learned about smart environments and the smart home. Then use the prompts below to help you make sentences.

A Why smart environments are needed

1. globally ageing population / disability / chronic disease / on the rise
2. numbers diagnosed with dementia / double globally / 2030 / triple / 2050
3. dementia sufferers / continue / independently / in community / as long as they can
4. older adults / stay / their homes / despite / mental / physical
5. smart environment / apartment / equipped / technology / people / remain independent

B How the smart home works

1. apartments / sensors / monitor motion / collect data / daily activities / people living in them
2. sensors / installed / each room / track / use / appliances / water
3. warning / cooker / left on
4. sensors / beds and chairs / warning / resident / not return / pre-determined time
5. computer / software / recognizes and analyses / information / provides feedback

3 Our future, our jobs

Complete the text with words from the box.

> bereaved • care • clients • companions • computers • demographic •
> holistic • humans • occupational therapists • professionals • robots • terminally

According to a recent study, the future for employees in the social and health ●¹ sectors is going to be very exciting. Because of ●² developments, more professionals will be needed to look after older ●³. Physiotherapists and ●⁴ will be busy, and ●⁵ care for elderly patients is likely to become popular. Animal ●⁶ to work with all humans in need of care are being trained right now, though some of them might be replaced by ●⁷ over the coming years. By 2025, ●⁸ will be doing many tasks that caring ●⁹ do today. They won't be able to do everything, though, and ●¹⁰ will still care for children, look after the ●¹¹ ill and counsel the ●¹².

146

Unit 12 Looking ahead

 4 **Talking about plans and predictions**

Use the most suitable form of the verb in brackets to talk about the future.

1 The speaker at tonight's workshop (talk) about Alzheimer's and dementia.
2 According to the announcement, she (start) by discussing symptoms and diagnosis.
3 What do you think the future (look) like in your field?
4 Do you think there (be) enough work for everyone in the future?
5 The government has calculated that we (need) more professional carers by 2025.
6 It's clear that there (be) more people who require care by 2025.

> *The future, p. 215*

 Mapping the future: an infographic about the social and health care sectors in the year 2025

You are going to work in groups and design and produce an infographic poster about the topic above.

Step 1 Before you start, read the information box on the right and look (again) at all the infographics that appear in Social Pulse. Discuss how they get their messages across quickly. Analyse the components.

Step 2 Search the internet for data and visual elements which are related to your subject.

Step 3 When you have found enough material, take a big piece of paper and plan where each part should go. Using a pencil, sketch your images, add your statistics, etc. and see how it looks.

Infographics

Information graphics or infographics are visual representations of complex information condensed into a form that is easily understood by the reader. In order to convey the maximum amount of data in the least amount of space, you should use strong images, a clean design and the most appropriate charts and other visuals for the information you wish to get across.

Step 4 Ask yourselves the following questions: Do we have a good balance of text, figures and images? Is there enough material? Does our message (what people need to know) stand out clearly? Change, adjust and improve things as necessary.

Step 5 When you are satisfied, produce your poster and hang it on the wall. Do a gallery walk and comment on the posters.

Checking progress ... and looking ahead

Browse through the previous pages in the unit, looking at headings and pictures. What have you learned? What can you do now that you have learned these things?
- ✓ I can understand global developments related to my profession.   (Part A)
- ✓ I can describe how technical developments might assist clients.   (Part B)
- ✓ I can write about the future of social and health care for professionals. (Part C)
- ✓ I can plan and design an infographic about my profession in the future.   (Part D)

Write down two more statements of your own.

What are your long-term aims? Write down five steps on the way to achieving your aims. Tell a partner which step you are going to take first. Take that step now!

Exam skills and strategies

Mediation

Mediation bedeutet „Vermittlung". In einer Mediationsaufgabe übermittelt man die Informationen aus fremdsprachlichen Quellen an jemanden, der die Fremdsprache nicht beherrscht. Sprachmittlung ist in der alltäglichen und beruflichen Kommunikation von großer Bedeutung. Bei einer Übersetzung muss man sich möglichst getreu nach dem Original richten; bei einer Mediation dagegen geht es lediglich darum, die wesentlichen Informationen im Originaltext zu verstehen und in die andere Sprache sinngemäß und adressantenbezogen zu übertragen. Form und Inhalt Ihrer Zusammenfassung hängen von folgenden Faktoren ab, die in der Aufgabenstellung vorgegeben werden:
- Adressat (Mitschüler/innen, Kunden einer Firma usw.)
- Medium (Info-Broschüre, E-Mail usw.)
- Ort (Schule, Arbeitsplatz, Jugendgruppe usw.)
- Zweck (Infos/Ratschläge/Argumente zu einem spezifischen Thema aufbereiten)

> **Wichtig für:**
> - schriftliche (und mündliche) Mediation/Sprachmittlung
> - rollenbasierte Stellungnahme
> - materialgestützten Aufsatz

BEISPIEL-AUFGABE

Situation: Sie arbeiten in einer Reha-Klinik für junge Menschen, die seit kurzem eine Behinderung haben und lernen, mit ihrer Behinderung umzugehen. Ein großes Problem in dieser Gruppe sind Angst vor der Zukunft und Sorgen über den Verlust ihrer Unabhängigkeit. Viele Ihrer Kollegen kommen aus anderen Ländern und sprechen Englisch.

Aufgabe: Ihr Chef bittet Sie, den Artikel „Roboter hilft Behinderten beim Arbeiten" zu lesen und einen Aushang für Ihre Kollegen auf Englisch zu schreiben. Erklären Sie im Detail, was der Roboter „Friend" ist, und wie er Menschen mit Behinderung helfen kann.

Roboter hilft Behinderten beim Arbeiten

Querschnittsgelähmte haben auf dem Arbeitsmarkt kaum Chancen. Lena Kredel hat nach elf Jahren endlich wieder einen Job gefunden – dank des Roboters „Friend".

Bremen. Lena Kredel sitzt seit mehr als 20 Jahren im Rollstuhl. Anfangs konnte sie noch ihre Arme bewegen, doch inzwischen sind auch diese gelähmt. Kredel ist ständig auf Hilfe angewiesen. Ein Glas Wasser trinken, sich kratzen oder die Tür öffnen – all das kann sie alleine nicht mehr. Trotzdem arbeitet sie seit einiger Zeit wieder. Möglich macht das ein Assistenzroboter.

„Friend" haben die Forscher der Universität Bremen ihren Prototypen getauft: ein wuchtiger Elektro-Rollstuhl ausgerüstet mit Computer, Roboterarm und Kameraauge. Mit seiner Hilfe wird Kredel bald Bücher in der Universitätsbibliothek katalogisieren können – und zwar ohne, dass andere Menschen sie dabei unterstützen. „Das ist schon eine wahnsinnige Selbstständigkeit für mich", sagt die zierliche Frau.

Zum Steuern braucht Kredel nur ihren Kopf. Mit ihrem Kinn bedient sie einen Joystick, um auf dem Computerbildschirm die gewünschten Funktionen

Die Roboterarm-Rollstuhl-Kombination „Friend" für schwer körperlich behinderte Menschen: Mit einem „Kinn-Joystick" wird dabei die Steuerung des stählernen Armes bedient.

auszuwählen. Mit ihrer Stirn löst sie an einer Hal-
terung den Mausklick aus. „Das System macht alles
alleine, aber die Nutzerin behält die Kontrolle", er-
läutert Projektleiter Torsten Heyer vom Institut für
Automatisierungstechnik.

Zurzeit arbeiten Heyer und seine Kollegen noch
daran, die Software zu verbessern. Außerdem entwickeln sie gerade ein Lesegerät, das mit Unter-
druck die Seiten von Büchern ansaugt und dann
mit einem Hebel umblättert. Kredel sitzt in ihrem
Rollstuhl in einer Ecke des Labors und beobachtet
die Wissenschaftler bei der Arbeit. Im Sommer wird
das System wahrscheinlich soweit sein, dass sie damit in der Bibliothek starten kann.   (286 Wörter)

TIPPS

1 <mark>Lesen Sie den Text schnell durch, um sich einen Überblick zu verschaffen. Lesen Sie bei kleineren Verständnisproblemen einfach weiter – wahrscheinlich ergibt sich der Sinn schwieriger
Stellen aus dem Kontext.</mark>

2 <mark>Lesen Sie die Aufgabenstellung genau durch – sie gibt Auskunft über den Zweck der Zusam-
menfassung, den Adressaten, das Ausgangs- bzw. Zielmedium sowie darüber, welche Infor-
mationen aus dem Text benötigt werden.</mark>
→ Zweck: Um Ihre Kollegen über eine neue Technologie zu informieren
→ Adressat: Ihre Kollegen
→ Ausgangsmedium: Zeitschriftenartikel
→ Zielmedium: Aushang
→ Benötigte Informationen: Erklärung, was der „Friend" ist, und wie er Menschen mit
   Behinderung helfen kann

3 <mark>Gehen Sie den Text jetzt Absatz für Absatz durch und unterstreichen Sie die wesentlichen Sätze
und Satzteile (dieser Schritt wurde für Sie im Text bereits erledigt).</mark>
Folgende Textstellen können bei einer Mediationsaufgabe als unwesentlich betrachtet werden:
Wiederholungen (oft eingeleitet durch *in other words*, *to put it another way*), Anekdoten und
Exkurse (oft eingeleitet durch *by the way*, *incidentally*) und unnötige Statistiken.

4 <mark>Fassen Sie die unterstrichenen Teile zusammen (auf Englisch bei Mediation D–E und auf
Deutsch bei Mediation E–D). Übersetzen Sie nicht Wort für Wort. Beachten Sie dabei
folgende Punkte:</mark>
● Vergewissern Sie sich, dass Ihr Text adressaten- und mediumgerecht ist, z. B. muss eine E-Mail
   an einen Freund deutlich informeller als ein Bericht für Ihren Chef sein.
   → ~~Dear Sir or Madam,~~ *Dear colleagues,*
● Gebrauchen Sie so weit wie möglich Ihre eigenen Worte. Verwenden Sie ein Wörterbuch,
   um Synonyme oder Antonyme für Wörter aus dem Originaltext zu finden und diese so
   umschreiben zu können.
● Nehmen Sie keine Stellung zum Text. Dies gehört in der Regel nicht zur Aufgabenstellung.
● Berücksichtigen Sie, dass eventuell bestimmte kulturelle Aspekte aus dem Originaltext in Ihrer
   Zusammenfassung erklärt werden müssen.
● Mit Beispielen und Zitaten müssen Sie etwas vorsichtiger umgehen. Manchmal werden Zitate
   nur angeführt, um eine Ausführung zu veranschaulichen; in journalistischen Texten sind jedoch
   gelegentlich Kernaussagen des Textes in Zitaten enthalten. Auf jeden Fall sollte ein Zitat auf
   seine Kernaussage reduziert und in indirekte Rede umgewandelt werden. In manchen Zieltexten ist es unangebracht, den Originaltext zu zitieren.
   → ~~Kredel cannot drink a glass of water, scratch herself, or open the door.~~
   As you know, our patients are unable to do many things.

Exam skills and strategies

→ ~~"It is incredible independence for me."~~
One user said it was incredible independence for her.
→ ~~"The system does everything alone, but the user stays in control."~~
The project leader said that the system did everything alone, but the user stayed in control.

> *Reported speech, p. 217*

5 Gehen Sie alle Textteile, die Sie unterstrichen haben, nochmals durch. Vergewissern Sie sich, dass Sie sie alle in Ihrem Text berücksichtigt haben.

6 Prüfen Sie: Ist der Aufbau klar? Sind die Sätze vollständig? Ist die Rechtschreibung korrekt?

> *Lösungen, S. 293*

Sie sind Teil eines Teams von Pflegefachkräften, die an einem Kulturaustausch mit Arbeitsplatzwechsel in fünf Ländern über einen Zeitraum von drei Jahren teilnehmen. Ihr Team besteht aus zehn Pflegemitarbeitern/-innen aus zehn verschiedenen Ländern. Ihr Ziel ist es, sowohl etwas über kulturelle Unterschiede zu erfahren als auch den anderen Teilnehmern/-innen Ihren eigenen kulturellen Hintergrund näherzubringen. Barbara Blasedale leitet das Programm. Sie hat eine E-Mail an alle Teilnehmer/innen auf Englisch geschrieben. Ihr österreichischer Kollege, Herr Mösel, spricht nicht fließend Englisch. Schreiben Sie eine Mail, in der Sie …

- ihn informieren, dass Sie ihm die E-Mail von Frau Blasedale weiterleiten.
- ihm erklären, von wem und woher die E-Mail kommt.
- ihn über die wichtigsten Punkte im Text informieren.

> *Lösungen, S. 293*

EMAIL

Dear cultural exchange team

Firstly, congratulations on becoming part of the programme. We had over 200 applications, and only ten places to fill. You were chosen to take part because we think you will do a great job.

Some of what I'm going to write may seem obvious, but it is worth keeping in mind. When you go abroad, remember that you are effectively an ambassador for your country. Many of the people you are dealing with will never have met someone from your country before, and any opinions they have already will be confirmed or destroyed by you.

Cultural differences are easier to deal with in theory than in reality. You will be confronted with situations that might seem ridiculous or difficult. When you come across something that is totally different to what you are used to, try to approach it with an open mind. Accept that it is different without judging it to be good or bad.

Avoid making generalisations wherever possible. Don't start sentences with the words "People from your country …" or "You guys …". There is a very fine line between opinion and prejudice. Also, someone's background is made up of many influences. It is possible that what an individual does is not representative of their entire nation.

Finally, as far as possible, support and encourage one another. The next two years are going to be very rewarding and fulfilling, but they are not going to be easy. You are all in the same boat. A large part of your everyday work will be helping each other, as well as the people in your care.

If any conflicts or fundamental problems raise their heads, please contact me or another member of the management as soon as possible. I wish you all the best of luck.

Yours faithfully

Barbara Blasedale
Team Leader

(300 words)

APPENDIX

Partner files	152
Guidance and challenge files	172
Business correspondence	186
Phrase bank	190
Skills file	202
Grammar summary	212
Basic word list	228
Unit word list	234
A–Z word list	268
Exam skills and strategies – answer key	290
Irregular verbs	294
Quellenverzeichnis	295

PARTNER FILES

FILE 1 — Unit 3, Part B, Exercise 3A, p. 35

Partner A

Jason L. (aged 12) often comes to school with bruises or a black eye. He claims he was clumsy or that he fell off his skateboard but he is lying to cover up for his father, who has been physically abusing him. When the social worker calls on the family, she notices that Jason's mother had a black eye. She said that this was because she had fallen down the stairs. Jason's mother says that her son often causes trouble at home, as he is rude to his father. She has been known to social services since her childhood when she was taken into care after her father beat her.

FILE 2 — Unit 6, Part B, Exercise 4, p. 71

Partner A

Glen Carter

Your aim is to get your supervisor to recognize your skills.

Preparation: Re-read your stress checklist and make notes. Read the transcript of the previous meeting and make notes on that, too. Remember, you feel that you are being treated unfairly by your supervisor and your colleagues and they are not keeping their promises.

Here are a few things that have been said about you:

HR Manager
You're the best candidate for the job. I can imagine that you will soon be head of the department!

You will go far, Glen. You are one of my best students. — Your professor at MIT

FILE 3 — Unit 4, Part B, Exercise 1, p. 46

Text B

Cyberbullying

A survey across 25 European countries investigated cyberbullying. Over 25,000 internet users between the ages of 9 and 16 were interviewed, together with one parent of each interviewee. Six per cent of the interviewees reported that they had been sent nasty or hurtful messages online, and three per cent admitted that they themselves had sent such messages to others. One form of cyberbullying is "sexting", i.e. posting naked photos of a victim online. The worrying aspect of this practice is that the photo had often originally been posted by the victim him- or herself. A number of children and teenagers who are known to have been victims of cyberbullying have attempted or committed suicide. Studies suggest that the suicides do not result directly from cyberbullying, though for young people with problems, being a victim of cyberbullying can only add to their troubles.

Partner files

| FILE 4 | Unit 3, Part C, Exercise 2B, p. 37 |

Partners A and B

1   Read and discuss the information below about the prospective parents you have been asked to assess.

> **Julie and Tom Laurence**
> Mr and Mrs Laurence are in their late 30s. The couple has two children, aged 7 and 10. Both children are healthy and well looked after. Julie Laurence is a full-time wife and mother. Tom Laurence works in an office. Both Julie and Tom are smokers.
>
> **Passive smoking**
> Many children who are put up for adoption have been neglected and have health problems. Some of them have asthma. Passive smoking is a risk for every child.
>
> **Recommendations**
> - The agency should explain the risks of exposing children to passive smoking.
> - Mr and Mrs Laurence's views on smoking and any decisions they make on smoking should be taken into account in their application.
> - Mr and Mrs Laurence could be referred to a "quit smoking" programme. The agency medical adviser may be able to advise.

2   Describe the Laurences to the other members of the team. Point out any negative aspects in their application and explain the agency's recommendations.

| FILE 5 | Unit 4, Part C, Exercise 4A, p. 49 |

Partner B

You and your partner are going to take turns playing the role of a counsellor and the role of a caller.

1   Your first role is as the **counsellor**. Listen to Partner A's problem. Remember to use skills for active listening to help the caller to talk.

So, you feel as if …   *I understand.*   *Take your time.*

2   When you play the role of the **caller** during the second call, describe the situation below to the counsellor and ask for advice.

> You are the parent of a teenage girl who is overweight. One day last week, your daughter came home from school with her clothes torn. She told you that she had been involved in a fight with some other girls at school. These girls are bullying your daughter and calling her names. You suggested that you both go to the head teacher and complain so that the teacher would stop the bullying. Your daughter, however, believes this would only make things worse. Instead, your daughter has gone on a diet. She has not eaten for three days, and you are worried about her.

153

PARTNER FILES

FILE 6 — Unit 3, Part C, Exercise 2B, p. 37

Partners E and F

1. Read and discuss the information below about the prospective parents you have been asked to assess.

Helen and Evan Fletcher
Mr and Mrs Fletcher are in their late 20s. Both work for social services. The couple have decided not to have children of their own as Mrs Fletcher has an auto-immune disease[1] which may be passed on genetically.

Offences
Mr Fletcher was convicted for vandalism and stealing cars when he was a teenager. He did community service[2] at the time. He has no other convictions. Mr Fletcher told the agency himself about these offences.

Recommendations
- The agency feels that Mr Fletcher's criminal record[3] should not make a difference to the couple's application to adopt.
- Mrs Fletcher should give us copies of her medical records.
- A medical check-up should be carried out on Mrs Fletcher by the agency medical adviser.

[1] auto-immune disease *Autoimmunkrankheit*
[2] community service *gemeinnützige Arbeit*
[3] (to have a) criminal record *vorbestraft sein*

---

2. Describe the Fletchers to the other members of the team. Point out any negative aspects in their application and explain the agency's recommendations.

FILE 7 — Unit 4, Part B, Exercise 1, p. 46

Text A

Traditional bullying

All of the studies agree that bullying is not a one-off incident, but a repeating pattern of victimizing behaviour. The most common form of bullying is verbal, calling people names or saying things to put pressure on someone who doesn't fit in. If verbal bullying is not stopped, things can escalate and physical violence can take place.
The findings of most of the studies indicate that boys are more likely to engage in physical bullying, while girls most often use words to harass their peers.
A Scandinavian study, however, suggests that many girls are now using physical violence. In Sweden, for example, 15 per cent of girls aged 11–15 report that they have been the victims of physical bullying.

Partner files

| FILE 8 | Unit 3, Part B, Exercise 3A, p. 35 |

Partner B

Sylvia M. is the mother of three young children: a ten-year-old daughter, Alice, and twins aged four. Her husband, who was a bank manager, was killed during a robbery in the bank. Since the death of her husband, Sylvia M. has been unable to cope. She has become dependent on sleeping pills and neglects the children, her home and herself. Alice has been looking after the twins. During the current school term, Alice has played truant for a total of 46 days.

| FILE 9 | Unit 4, Part C, Exercise 4A, p. 49 |

Partner A

You and your partner are going to take turns playing the role of a counsellor and the role of a caller.

1 Your first role is as the **caller**. Describe the situation below to the counsellor and ask for advice.

Your flatmate is being physically abused by her boyfriend. When you first got to know your flatmate, she liked to go out with you and other friends to clubs and parties. Since she met her boyfriend, she says she is tired and doesn't want to go out in the evenings. Once or twice, when you noticed bruises on her arms, your friend said she'd had a fall. The last time she came home with a bruise, she said that her boyfriend was jealous. You have heard that your flatmate's boyfriend has been in trouble with the police for fighting. You are worried about your friend.

2 When you play the role of the **counsellor** during the second call, listen to Partner B's problem. Remember to use skills for active listening to help the caller to talk.

So, you feel as if …   *I understand.*   *Take your time.*

| FILE 10 | Unit 10, Part B, Exercise 4, p. 119 |

Partners C and D

You are the carers. You will take turns to answer the interviewers' questions.

1 Read the transcript of the interview with Liam Kelly together and identify the answers he gave to the questions that he was asked. Decide together how you as carers can use and possibly adapt these answers. Make notes.
2 Brainstorm ideas for other questions that might be asked. Remember, you are carers being asked about how you do your work, so you should focus on practical aspects like taking care that every client's religious practices are respected. Add your ideas to your notes above.
3 Practise your interview with Partners A and B then perform all or part of your interview in front of the class.

155

PARTNER FILES

FILE 11   Unit 3, Part C, Exercise 2B, p. 37

Partners C and D

1 Read and discuss the information below about the prospective parents you have been asked to assess.

Gale and Kevin Jameson
Mr and Mrs Jameson are in their mid-30s. The couple have no children. Mrs Jameson has been receiving fertility treatment[1] for the last four years. As they have had no results so far, the couple are now considering adoption. Mrs Jameson still hopes to give birth to her own child and would like to continue fertility treatment for the next few years.

Infertility[2]
Experience suggests that infertile[2] couples need time to accept their situation before they are ready for adoption. If a couple continues with fertility treatment, and it is successful, their response to the adopted child might change.

Recommendations
- The agency should explain the problems attached to continuing with fertility treatment.
- Mr and Mrs Jameson should be offered counselling on why their approach is not in the interests of the (adopted) baby and should be asked to consider the consequences if a child is born after a baby is placed with them.
- They should complete the fertility treatment and, if it is still not successful, apply for adoption again.

[1] fertility treatment *Fruchtbarkeitsbehandlung*
[2] infertility / infertile *Unfruchtbarkeit / unfruchtbar*

2 Describe the Jamesons to the other members of the team. Point out any negative aspects in their application and explain the agency's recommendations.

FILE 12   Unit 4, Part B, Exercise 1, p. 46

Text C

Sexual harassment and violence

Precise data on sexual harassment and violence in and around schools is difficult to collect. Not every incident is reported as some victims are ashamed or afraid that they or their families might be stigmatized. Others fear that their story will not be believed, while others are frightened that their abuser will punish them for talking.
Studies indicate, however, that sexual violence is relatively common in schools. In Germany, 6.2 per cent of students (of both sexes) reported that they had been sexually abused, either physically or verbally.
In Canada one in four girls surveyed said they had experienced sexual harassment in school. In some cases, the aggressor was another pupil; in other cases, school staff had taken advantage of their position of power to abuse their pupils.

Partner files

| FILE 13 | Unit 5, Part A, Exercise 4, p. 57 |

Partner A

Use the notes from the case file below to tell your partner about Christina, one of Outreach's clients.

Client name: Christina
Sex: female
Age: 17

Background: born in Scotland; alcoholic mother died when Christina was 13 years old; sent to live with aunt in Cardiff.

Ran away from aunt several times; put into care home.
Left care home at 16, lived on the street, drinking and taking drugs.
Stole alcohol from shops and earned money as a prostitute.
Picked up several times by the police, put on probation and given a "last chance" by a judge. Came to Outreach via probation officer.

Now in shared flat with two other girls. Training to be a hairdresser.
Comes into Outreach now and again for a cup of tea and a chat.

| FILE 14 | Unit 9, Part B, Exercise 3, p. 107 |

Partner A

Before you start each call, read through the instructions carefully and make notes.

Call 1: You are looking after the phones for Kate while she is at a meeting. Follow the instructions below, adding relevant details where necessary. Remember to ask the caller to repeat or spell anything that is unclear.

- Take the call and greet the caller.
- Ask what you can do for the caller.
- Tell him/her that the colleague they should talk to is not available at the moment.
- Ask if you can have the caller's contact details so that the colleague can phone back.
- Confirm the caller's details and say that you will pass them on.
- Thank the caller for phoning and say goodbye.

Call 2: You are the caller. Use the information below to make a phone call. Add your own ideas regarding the details. Just for fun, you can make up a difficult name which you have to spell.

- Give your name and say where you are calling from.
- You would like to cancel an appointment you have made with Frank Schultz.
- Give a reason why the date and time suggested are not suitable.
- Agree on a new date and time.
- Thank the person who took your call and say goodbye.

PARTNER FILES

FILE 15   Unit 6, Part B, Exercise 1A, p. 70

Partner B

Read Glen's comments on page 2 of the stress checklist and exchange information with your partner, who has page 1. Discuss any patterns you see.

> He appears to dislike …

> Over and over again, he suggests that …

Stress Checklist   Glen Carter   page 2

Statement	
1	I don't have enough responsibility, as I've frequently said!
2	My colleagues let me deal with all the difficult calls. I have asked my supervisor to have us take turns, but so far nothing has happened.
3	Only for me. My colleagues are allowed to take more breaks.
4	I am extremely focused!
5	I don't have a spouse, children or family. My boss and my co-workers ignore me.
6	See above.
7	My desk is in the worst position in the office. Nobody asked me if I wanted to sit next to the water cooler.
8	I get headaches and muscle tension because my colleagues always meet and chat at the water cooler and that disturbs my concentration and makes me tense.
9	The doctor thinks this is because I eat sandwiches at my desk at lunchtime. I prefer sandwiches to the canteen. The office is nice and quiet when the others are at lunch.
10	See 8 and 9.
11	I'm a computer geek, for heaven's sake!
12	It's up to me how much I drink.

FILE 16   Unit 11, Part A, Exercise 3, p. 129

Partner B

You are the social worker. Follow these steps to prepare for the interview.

1 Prepare for the interview by thinking about the questions you would like to ask the candidate, for example: What would you do when a child in the hospice dies? What support would you offer the family?
2 Make sure you understand the vocabulary that is associated with working with the bereaved.
3 At some point in the interview, you should ask the candidate about the qualities and skills he/she has that will make him/her a good candidate for the job of working with the bereaved. Note down the qualities and skills you are looking for.
4 When you have prepared, indicate to your partner that you are ready to start the interview.

Partner files

| FILE 17 | Unit 4, Part B, Exercise 1, p. 46 |

Text D

Violence associated with gangs, weapons and fighting

Studies into physical violence in schools have shown that fighting or physical violence can be a reaction to a one-off occurrence, e.g. an attack by one boy on another who has "stolen" his girlfriend, or it may happen as a result of a build-up of anger, frustration or humiliation which has nothing directly to do with the victim or victims. This is often the case in school shootings.

The fear and insecurity that fighting and physical assault provoke among victims and people who witness such attacks is made worse by the availability of weapons, usually knives but sometimes guns. Weapons are also often associated with gang violence. Gang violence in schools appears most often in areas where violence is common and where weapons, gangs and drugs are part of the local culture.

| FILE 18 | Unit 8, Part A, Exercise 3, p. 93 |

Partner A

With Partners B and C, follow the steps below to reconstruct a recipe for making pizza.

1 The ingredients

You are responsible for preparing the base of the pizza. Which of the ingredients below will you need? (You need five altogether.) Which will your partners need for the sauce and toppings? Work with your partners to distribute the ingredients.

- 50 g grated parmesan
- 1 level teaspoonful salt
- 15 g fresh yeast
- a handful of chopped basil
- some black olives

- a small piece of butter
- 100 g mozzarella cut into cubes
- 1 clove of garlic, crushed
- 400 g tin of chopped tomatoes
- a handful of cherry tomatoes, halved

- about 150 ml water
- 1 tablespoon tomato paste
- some fresh basil leaves
- 225 g flour

2 The instructions

The recipe has nine steps in all, but only three of them are below (and not in the correct order). Work with your partners to put all nine steps (a–i) into the correct order. Which steps are you responsible for?

a After the dough for the base has risen, knead it again then divide it into two balls.

b Bake for 8–10 minutes until crisp, then repeat the final step for the remaining pizza. Serve with a little more olive oil and additional basil leaves.

c Finally, smooth half of the sauce over one of the dough bases with the back of a spoon. Scatter half of the tomatoes, the olives and basil leaves over the sauce and sprinkle half of the cheese mixture over the toppings. Put one pizza, still on its baking paper, on top of the preheated baking tray.

PARTNER FILES

FILE 19 — Unit 8, Part A, Exercise 3, p. 93

Partner C

With Partners A and B, follow the steps below to reconstruct a recipe for making pizza.

1 The ingredients

You are responsible for preparing the toppings for the pizza. Which of the ingredients below will you need? (You need five altogether.) Which will your partners need for the base and sauce? Work with your partners to distribute the ingredients.

- 50 g grated parmesan
- 1 level teaspoonful salt
- 15 g fresh yeast
- a handful of chopped basil
- some black olives
- a small piece of butter
- 100 g mozzarella cut into cubes
- 1 clove of garlic, crushed
- 400 g tin of chopped tomatoes
- a handful of cherry tomatoes, halved
- about 150 ml water
- 1 tablespoon tomato paste
- some fresh basil leaves
- 225 g flour

2 The instructions

The recipe has nine steps in all, but only three of them are below (and in the wrong order). Work with your partners to put all nine steps (a–i) into the correct order. Which steps are you responsible for?

g Drain the tinned tomatoes and mix them with the tomato paste, chopped basil and crushed garlic. Leave the mixture to stand at room temperature while you shape the base.

h Cut each pizza into eight slices and serve with a fresh garden salad.

i Turn the dough onto a lightly floured surface and knead for 5 minutes until it is smooth. Put the kneaded dough back into the bowl, cover the bowl with a clean cloth and leave it in a warm place to rise.

FILE 20 — Unit 8, Part A, Exercise 4B, p. 93

Summarize this German description of the photo on page 93 into simple English. The translations below will help you.

Chicken Nuggets – lecker oder eklig?

Wissenschaftler haben festgestellt, dass über 50% der üblichen Chicken Nuggets, die in Fastfood-Ketten verkauft werden, aus Separatorenfleisch[1], das durch maschinelles Entbeinen von Hühnern gewonnen wird, bestehen. Wenn die teuren Fleischstücke[2] vom Hühnchen entfernt sind, werden die übrig gelassenen Knochen durch ein Hochdrucksieb[3], das das Fleisch zu 100% sauber abschabt, durchgedrückt. Diese Paste, die wie Erdbeereis oder Paprika-Frischkäse aussieht, ist das Ergebnis. Die Paste, die auch von den Kadavern[4] der Truthähne, Schweine und Rinder gewonnen wird, ist nicht nur ein Hauptbestandteil von Chicken Nuggets, sondern auch von Hot Dogs, Peperoniwurst, Salami, etc. Die Industrie nennt diese Methode „Advanced Meat Recovery".

[1] mechanically separated chicken meat
[2] cuts of meat
[3] carcasses
[4] high-pressure sieve

160

Partner files

FILE 21   Unit 11, Part B, Exercise 3B, p. 131

Partners A and B

Part 1: You and your partner are the chief administrator and the trainee in the nursing home. (Decide who is who.) You have an appointment to meet with William Watson's grandson, Michael Watson, and his wife, Elisabeth. Relatives usually have a lot of questions and they are often worried about their loved ones, so one of the carer's main tasks is to reassure relatives that everything possible is being done for the patient.

- Prepare for your meeting with Michael and his wife by reading over the notes you have made in preparation for the appointment. Think about what Michael will probably ask, e.g. what medical problems his grandfather has.
- During the meeting, be polite and sympathetic but stay firmly in your role as a member of the nursing home staff. When Michael asks: "What should we do with grandad?" refer him to the doctor.

Part 2: Now you and your partner are Michael and his wife Elisabeth. (Decide who is who.) You have spoken to the administrator and the trainee and are now speaking to the medical staff. You are satisfied with the treatment William Watson has been given, but you now wish to know what comes next.

- Explain that you are the only ones in the family who have contact with Michael's grandfather.
- Say that Michael's grandparents split up when his father was a child.
- Explain that you were getting ready to visit him in Germany when you got the news that he had been admitted to hospital.
- Say that your father(-in-law) and his mother (William's wife) are worried, and that they would like to know how things will develop.

FILE 22   Unit 6, Part B, Exercise 4, p. 71

Partner B

Claudia Weber

Your task is to mediate between an employee, who is suffering from stress, and his supervisor. Your aim is to find the best solution for your client.

Preparation: Re-read the skills for active listening on page 49. Read the transcript of the previous meeting and make notes. Remember, Glen Carter feels that he is being treated unfairly by his supervisor and his colleagues.

Here are a few things that you have heard during your visits to the company:

Glen's colleague Mae: *Glen works really hard. Sometimes I think he does too much.*

Glen's colleague Klaus: *Glen is a very careful worker. He doesn't make mistakes.*

161

PARTNER FILES

FILE 23 Unit 8, Part A, Exercise 3, p. 93

Partner B

With Partners A and C, follow the steps below to reconstruct a recipe for making pizza.

1 The ingredients

You are responsible for preparing the sauce for the pizza. Which of the ingredients below will you need? (You need four altogether.) Which will your partners need for the base and toppings? Work with your partners to distribute the ingredients.

- 50 g grated parmesan
- 1 level teaspoonful salt
- 15 g fresh yeast
- a handful of chopped basil
- some black olives
- a small piece of butter
- 100 g mozzarella cut into cubes
- 1 clove of garlic, crushed
- 400 g tin of chopped tomatoes
- a handful of cherry tomatoes, halved
- about 150 ml water
- 1 tablespoon tomato paste
- some fresh basil leaves
- 225 g flour

2 The instructions

The recipe has nine steps in all, but only three of them are below (and in the wrong order). Work with your partners to put all nine steps (a–i) into the correct order. Which steps are you responsible for?

d First, prepare the base. Blend the yeast with the water. Then, mix the flour and salt together and rub in the butter. After that, pour the yeast and water mixture into the flour and mix well to make a soft dough.
e Before you put the sauce and toppings on the base of the first pizza, place a large baking tray on the top shelf of the oven and preheat the oven to 220 °C.
f On a floured surface, use a rolling pin to roll out the dough into two large discs, each about 25cm across. The dough needs to be very thin as it will rise in the oven. Lift the discs onto two floured sheets of baking paper.

FILE 24 Unit 10, Part C, Exercise 4, p. 121

Partner B

Follow the senior social worker's instructions to call Daniel Mills and leave a message in English.

> *Bitte Daniel Mills anrufen*
> *– fragen Sie ihn, ob er Interesse hat, zweimal pro Woche Computerkenntnisse zu vermitteln*
> *– wenn ja, bitten Sie ihn, für ein Interview entweder am Montag um 10.30 Uhr oder 15.30 Uhr zu kommen*
> *– erklären Sie ihm, dass wir gerne hätten, dass er möglichst bald beginnt, falls er geeignet ist*
> *– er würde eine Gruppe von sechs jungen Männern aus verschiedenen Ländern unterrichten*

Partner files

FILE 25 — Unit 9, Part C, Exercise 4B, p. 109

Partners A and B

1   Work with your partner and put the parts of the form below into a logical order. Copy the form onto a piece of paper, leaving room to fill in Virpi's information. What other information will the hospital need to know? Add it to the form.

Date of admission:

Name:
Address:

Symptoms:
Principal diagnosis, i.e. the condition which best accounts for the patient's admission to hospital:

Telephone:
Mobile phone:

Date of Birth:
Sex:

Other conditions present:

Next of kin:
Contact details:

Regular medication:

Allergies:

2   Take it in turns to explain the form to Virpi. Ask her for the information on the form and help her to complete it.

FILE 26 — Unit 9, Part B, Exercise 3, p. 107

Partner B

Before you start each call, read through the instructions carefully and make notes.

Call 1: You are the caller. Use the information below to make a phone call. Add your own ideas regarding the details. Just for fun, you can make up a difficult name which you have to spell.

- Give your name and say where you are calling from.
- You would like to speak to someone about volunteering.
- Give details of who you are and say why you are interested in volunteering.
- If the person is not available, ask if you should call again.
- Thank the person who took your call and say goodbye.

Call 2: You are looking after the phones for Kate while she is at a meeting. Follow the instructions below, adding relevant details where necessary. Remember to ask the caller to repeat or spell anything that is unclear.

- Take the call and greet the caller.
- Ask what you can do for the caller.
- Offer the caller a new appointment.
- If the day and time are not convenient for the caller, offer an alternative.
- Confirm the new arrangements.
- Thank the caller for phoning and say goodbye.

163

PARTNER FILES

FILE 27   Unit 9, Part C, Exercise 4B, p. 109

Partners C and D

You are Virpi. The volunteer assistant who has accompanied you to hospital is going to help you complete an admissions form.

1. You have already thought of some of the things the assistant will want to know. Talk about what other information you might have to give. Think about personal details, any medication you take, any accidents you have had before. Think, too, about how you feel at the moment.

- *Akneeta Hakala (mother)*
- *I wish I did not have such a terrible headache.*
- *Right now, I feel as if I've been kicked by a horse.*
- *Contraceptive pill*
- *Aleksanterinkatu 21, 00100 Helsinki*
- *Riding accident, aged 10, broken arm*
- *Allergic to tree pollen, penicillin*

2. Take it in turns to answer the questions the volunteer assistant asks. Spell any words or names that are difficult.

FILE 28   Unit 10, Part C, Exercise 5, p. 121

Partners A and B

You are going to interview two potential volunteers together in one interview. Neither of the candidates can speak German very well, so the interview will be in English.

Partner A: You are the senior social worker.
Partner B: You are playing yourself in the role of the volunteer.

1. Preparation for the interview

    Prepare yourselves for the interview by making a list of questions you would like to ask the prospective volunteers. Think about what the interviewees might like to know from you, e.g. nationalities of the asylum seekers, types of activities volunteers do with them.

2. The interview

    Partner A begins by introducing him/herself and Partner B.
    Explain that Partner B is already a volunteer and say that the interviewees might like to ask him/her questions later in the interview.
    Make some small talk, e.g. ask if the interviewees found the home all right, then start the interview by asking the interviewees to introduce themselves and say a few words about why they are interested in volunteering in a home for asylum seekers.

Partner files

| FILE 29 | Unit 10, Part B, Exercise 2B, p. 119 |

Partner A

You are going to tell your partner about "Gastarbeiter" in West Germany.

1 First, read the text below. Use your dictionary to find out the meaning of any words you don't know.

How did "Gastarbeiter" come to be in West Germany?
During the 1950s, Germany experienced a so-called "Wirtschaftswunder" (economic miracle) and needed workers. The government signed bilateral agreements allowing recruitment of "Gastarbeiter" to work in the industrial sector in jobs that required few qualifications. The construction of the Berlin Wall in August 1961 reduced the large-scale flow of East German immigration, and so a second wave of recruitment started in the 1960s.

Where did "Gastarbeiter" come from?
The first "Gastarbeiter" came from Italy in 1955. After that, workers came from Greece, Spain, Turkey, Morocco, Portugal, Tunisia and Yugoslavia.

What was the main benefit for the home countries of the "Gastarbeiter"?
The Federal Republic saw employment of "Gastarbeiter" as a form of developmental aid. It was hoped that the "Gastarbeiter" would learn useful skills in Germany, which could help them develop their home countries after returning home.

Where are the "Gastarbeiter" now?
Some of them returned to their home countries but many of them brought their wives and family members to Germany and became a fixed part of the German population.

2 Your partner has been reading about "Vertragsarbeiter" in the former GDR (German Democratic Republic). Find out the following things from your partner.

1 How did "Vertragsarbeiter" come to be in East Germany?
2 Where did "Vertragsarbeiter" come from?
3 How did the GDR government benefit from employing "Vertragsarbeiter"?
4 Where are the "Vertragsarbeiter" now?

| FILE 30 | Unit 6, Part B, Exercise 1B, p. 70 |

Stress Checklist	
Overall score	**Stress level and advice**
25 or under	Good – Stress level is low.
26–35	Average – Lowering stress level would be beneficial.
36-45	Bad – Employee should think seriously about changes in life to reduce stress.
46 or above	Dangerous – Having this amount of stress can lead to serious illnesses. Employee needs assistance in lowering stress levels as soon as possible.

165

PARTNER FILES

FILE 31 — Unit 10, Part B, Exercise 2B, p. 119

Partner B

You are going to tell your partner about "Vertragsarbeiter" in East Germany.

1 First, read the text below.

> **How did "Vertragsarbeiter" come to be in East Germany?**
> After the division of Germany into East and West in 1949, there was a shortage of labour in East Germany. When the Berlin Wall was built in 1961, the labour shortage got even worse, and the GDR (German Democratic Republic) began to recruit workers from other countries.
>
> **Where did "Vertragsarbeiter" come from?**
> In 1965 the GDR signed its first "guest worker" contract with Poland, followed by other Eastern Bloc countries. Later, workers from Mozambique, Vietnam, North Korea, Angola and Cuba began to work in the GDR.
>
> **How did the GDR government benefit from employing "Vertragsarbeiter"?**
> The GDR used its "Vertragsarbeiter" programme to build international solidarity among fellow communist countries.
>
> **Where are the "Vertragsarbeiter" now?**
> Following the fall of the Berlin Wall in November 1989 and German reunification in 1990, the population of guest workers still remaining in the former East Germany faced deportation, premature discontinuation of residence and work permits as well as open discrimination in the workplace. Of the 100,000 guest workers remaining in East Germany after reunification, about 75% left because of an increase in xenophobia in former East German states.

2 Your partner has been reading about "Gastarbeiter" in West Germany. Find out the following things from your partner.

1. How did "Gastarbeiter" come to be in West Germany?
2. Where did "Gastarbeiter" come from?
3. How did the home countries of "Gastarbeiter" benefit?
4. Where are the "Gastarbeiter" now?

FILE 32 — Unit 10, Exam skills and strategies, Exercise 3, p. 125

Partners A and B

Find out how Partners C and D have adjusted to life in Germany. Ask about their work, language course, social network, and any problems they might have encountered. Make notes on these subjects and give some recommendations about how they could integrate further into German society.

Partner files

FILE 33   Unit 11, Part A, Exercise 3, p. 129

Partner A

You will play yourself. Follow these steps to prepare for the interview.

1 Prepare for the interview with the social worker by thinking about the questions the interviewer might ask.
2 Make sure you understand the vocabulary that is associated with working with the bereaved.
3 Think about your qualities and skills. What makes you a good candidate for a voluntary job working with the bereaved? Make a short list of the qualities and skills you should have.
4 When you have prepared, indicate to your partner that you are ready to start the interview.

FILE 34   Unit 5, Part A, exercise 4, p. 57

Partner B

Use the notes from the case file below to tell your partner about Sean, one of Outreach's clients.

> **Client name:** Sean (pronounced Shawn)
> **Sex:** male
> **Age:** 19
>
> **Background:** came from Ireland looking for work three years ago. Worked illegally on a building site; was not paid any wages so could not pay his rent.
>
> Began to sleep rough but when winter came, got ill and ended up in hospital.
>
> When he came out of hospital, began to drink heavily and got into fights. During one fight, he stabbed another boy, who nearly died; put into a young offender institution for 18 months.
>
> Now in council apartment, reporting to probation officer once a week. Working in factory and attending vocational school two days a week where he is studying mechatronics.

FILE 35   Unit 10, Part C, Exercise 4, p. 121

Partner A

Follow the senior social worker's instructions to call Olena Melnyk and leave a message in English.

> *Bitte Olena Melnyk anrufen*
> *– erklären/sagen Sie ihr, dass wir erfreut über ihren Anruf waren*
> *– fragen Sie sie, ob sie Zeit hat, morgen um 16.30 Uhr für ein Interview vorbeizukommen*
> *– falls nicht, wäre es auch am Dienstagnachmittag nächste Woche möglich*
> *– erzählen Sie ihr, dass wir einige ukrainische Familien hier haben*

167

PARTNER FILES

FILE 36 Unit 10, Part B, Exercise 4, p. 119

Partners A and B

You are the interviewers. You will take turns to interview the two carers.

1 Read the transcript of the interview with Liam Kelly together and identify the questions that he was asked. Decide together which of the questions you should focus on in your interview with the carers. Write them down.
2 Brainstorm ideas for other questions that would suit your interview with the carers. Then use all your ideas to come up with five to seven questions to ask the carers.
3 Practise your interview with partners C and D then perform all or part of your interview in front of the class.

FILE 37 Unit 10, Exam skills and strategies, Exercise 3, p. 125

Partner C

You work as a doctor in a hospital, where you speak mostly English. You have not yet found a German language course and you don't speak very much German at all. You miss your family in Greece very much and would like them to move to Germany, too. Make up any other details you need to answer the social workers' questions, and make notes on their recommendations for you.

Partner D

You work in the kitchen of a Greek restaurant, where all the other employees are Greek. You don't serve customers because you don't speak German yet. You haven't yet found a language course. You've been sleeping on your sibling's (Partner C's) couch because you haven't been able to find a flat of your own. Make up any other details you need to answer the social workers' questions, and make notes on their recommendations for you.

FILE 38 Unit 10, Part C, Exercise 5, p. 121

Partners C and D

You have both been invited to an interview by the senior social worker and will be interviewed together. The interview is going to be conducted in English.

1 Preparation for the interview

   Prepare yourselves for the interview by deciding who you are and where you are from. Think about your reasons for volunteering for the job. Make a list of questions you would like to ask the interviewers, e.g. nationalities of the asylum seekers, how you would support them.

2 The interview

   Partner A will begin by introducing him/herself and Partner B, and will make some small talk, e.g. talking about the weather. Then the interview will start.

Partner files

| FILE 39 | Unit 11, Part C, Exercise 2, p. 133 |

Partners C and D

You are going to take turns to mediate the information below to Michael Watson and his wife Elisabeth (i.e. partners A and B).

1 Read the information together and make sure you know all the words in English. Talk over anything you do not understand. (Use a dictionary or ask your teacher if necessary.)
2 When you are ready, explain to the family that there are several formalities to be dealt with after a death. Then go through the checklist, describing what has to be done. Use your own words as often as possible.

3 Bis zur Trauerfeier und Beerdigung/Bestattung

A Vorbereitungen I

- Bestattungsform bestimmen (Bestattungsarten: z. B. Erd- & Feuerbestattung, Seebestattung, usw.)
- Friedhof und Grab auswählen. Grabnutzungsrechte erwerben bzw. verlängern
- Termin für Bestattung mit dem Friedhofsträger/der Grabstättenverwaltung festlegen
- Genehmigung des Krematoriums einholen (nur bei Feuerbestattungen)
- Terminabsprache und Trauergespräch mit dem/der Pfarrer/in oder Trauerredner/in

B Vorbereitungen II

- Aufsetzen einer Todesanzeige und Versenden der Trauerkarten
- Grabschmuck für Trauerhalle und Grab bei Gärtnerei bestellen (Blumen, Kränze, Trauerschleifen)
- Gaststätte/Café für Leichenschmaus bzw. Totenmahl oder Beerdigungskaffee reservieren

4 Nach der Trauerfeier / Beisetzung

- Laufende Zahlungen beenden & Verträge, Mitgliedschaften, Miete, Abos, Strom, Telefon kündigen
- Abmelden bei Versicherungen, Rentenkasse, Krankenkasse, Firma, Behörden, Ämter, usw.
- Akte mit wichtigen Dokumenten anlegen (z. B. Sterbeurkunde, Grabnutzung & Pflege, Abrechnungen)

Quelle: http://www.todesfall-checkliste.de/todesfall-checklisten/

PARTNER FILES

FILE 40   Unit 6, Part B, Exercise 4A, p. 71

Partner C

Glen Carter's supervisor

Your aim is to get your department running smoothly. You would like to have Glen Carter transferred to another department.

Preparation: Make notes on the following points.

- There is a high level of demotivation in the department due to Mr Carter.
- He is constantly negative, he is often off sick.
- Work does not get done on time because Mr Carter is continually complaining.
- Here is an exchange you and he had a few days ago.

During the discussion, stay polite but remain firm.

FILE 41   Unit 11, Part B, Exercise 3B, p. 131

Partners C and D

Part 1: You and your partner are Michael Watson and his wife Elisabeth. (Decide who is who.) You are concerned about Michael's grandfather and have asked to speak to the person in charge of the nursing home.

- Your main concern is to get information about Michael's grandfather. You need to know what's happening now.
- Ask questions about his state of health, e.g. what other medical problems he has apart from the stroke.
- Try to find out how his health is likely to develop, e.g. ask if he is likely to have another stroke or if he has dementia or Alzheimer's.
- When you feel you have learned enough, ask: "What should we do with grandad?"

Part 2: Now you and your partner are a doctor and nurse in the nursing home. (Decide who is who.) You know from experience that relatives have a lot of questions and that they are often worried about their loved ones.

- Listen to Michael and his wife carefully and respond appropriately.
- Assure them that everything possible is being done for Michael's grandfather, e.g. he is resting, will have more tests, be prescribed the proper medicine, etc.
- Be polite and sympathetic but stay firmly in your role as a member of a medical team.

Partner files

FILE 42 — Unit 11, Part C, Exercise 2, p. 133

Partners A and B

You are going to take turns to mediate the information below to Michael Watson and his wife Elisabeth (i.e. partners C and D).

1 Read the information together and make sure you know all the words in English. Discuss anything you do not understand. (Use a dictionary or ask your teacher if necessary.)

2 When you are ready, explain that there are several formalities to be dealt with after a death. Then go through the checklist, describing what has to be done. Use your own words as often as possible.

1 Unmittelbar nach Eintreten des Todes

- Arzt/Ärztin verständigen, um den Tod offiziell feststellen zu lassen (Totenschein wird ausgestellt)
- Wichtige Unterlagen suchen (Personalausweis, Geburtsurkunde, Heiratsurkunde, usw.)
- Verträge und Verfügungen des/der Verstorbenen suchen und entsprechend handeln (z. B. Testament, Vorsorgevertrag mit Bestattungsinstitut, Organspende, Willenserklärung zur Feuerbestattung, usw.)

2 Innerhalb von 36 Stunden nach dem Todesfall

A Beerdigungsvorbereitungen
- Bestattungsart wählen
- Verwandte und Bekannte kontaktieren
- Bestatter auswählen
- Bestattungsvertrag & Leistungsumfang klären – welche Aufgaben werden selbst übernommen?
- Auswahl / Bestimmung des Sarges, der Urne, der Totenbekleidung, Umfang der Trauerfeier, usw.
- Abholung des/der Verstorbenen und Überführung des Leichnams in die Leichenhalle

B Amtsgeschäfte

- Sterbefall beim Standesamt melden und Sterbeurkunde ausstellen lassen
- Erbschein beim Nachlassgericht beantragen
- Weitere Benachrichtigungen:
  - Krankenkasse melden; Lebens- und Unfallversicherung informieren;
  - Pfarramt benachrichtigen, falls kirchlicher Beistand erwünscht ist;
  - Arbeitgeber/in des/der Verstorbenen verständigen.

Quelle: http://www.todesfall-checkliste.de/todesfall-checklisten/

GUIDANCE AND CHALLENGE FILES

FILE G1   Unit 1, Part B, Exercise 2, p. 11   **GUIDANCE**

Follow the steps below to help you compare and contrast the three organizations.

1. Re-read the texts and answer the questions below.
   - What are the names of the organizations?
   - When was each organization set up?
   - Where/How can people get in touch with the three organizations?

2. Use your answers to exercise 1C to make notes on the following:
   - Who is each organization aiming to help or assist (the target group)?
   - What kind of activities and help does each organization offer?

3. Use your answers and notes from Steps 1 and 2 above and the phrase below to write a short text.

   > The … is an organization dealing with …
   > In contrast, the …
   > One of the organizations is in … while the others are in …
   > All three organizations aim to …
   > On the one hand, … . On the other hand, …

FILE G2   Unit 1, Part C, Exercise 3B, p. 13   **GUIDANCE**

Follow the steps below to help you write your responses.

1. Answer the questions below.
   - Would you like to talk about your problems to an older person?
   - If you were stressed at work, would you like to talk to someone about it?
   - Is it important that people like you?

2. Compare your answers with what Jose, Angie and Mary said, and make notes.
   - Who is most like you?
   - Who is not like you at all?

3. Use your answers and notes from Steps 1 and 2 above and the phrases below to write one or two short responses.

   > My attitude to supervision is …
   > I agree/disagree completely with (*name*).
   > As far as I am concerned, …
   > In contrast to (*name*), I believe that …
   > Supervision is …

172

Guidance and challenge files

| **FILE G3** | **Unit 2, Part C, Exercise 3B, p. 25** | **GUIDANCE** |

Here are some of the things that were said in the interview. Sort them into a list of dos and don'ts for face-to-face interviews.

1 make sure that you're dressed well
2 always arrive at an interview in good time
3 try to relax before the interview begins
4 look as if you're in a panic
5 walk into the room as confidently as possible
6 shake hands and make eye contact
7 be shy
8 talk about politics or problems family problems
9 look directly at the interviewer or interviewers
10 keep focused on the job
11 show your interest in the company and the job
12 just walk out the door when the interview is over

| **FILE G4** | **Unit 3, Part A, Exercise 3B, p. 33** | **GUIDANCE** |

Read through the tasks below, then watch the video and take notes. Use your notes to do at least three of the tasks.

1 Describe Ed and Dolores. Say why they decided to adopt biracial children.
2 Describe the experiences the parents went through when the children were small. How do these experiences compare with Heather's experiences?
3 Describe Heather's biological parents and explain why Heather feels sad.
4 Point out how Heather benefited from learning more about her biological parents.
5 Explain who Silas is and say what he believes about mixed-race families.
6 Describe how Heather's husband feels about his children. How does he think his family has helped others?

| **FILE G5** | **Unit 3, Part B, Exercise 2, p. 35** | **GUIDANCE** |

Match the phrases from the interview 1–7 to the explanations a–g.

1 to cope with the situation alone
2 afraid to go to a women's refuge or seek assistance
3 to break out of the pattern
4 lack of empathy
5 marginalized
6 denial
7 to stand by and do nothing

a an example of denial
b to decide not to carry over one's experience into one's own adult relationships
c to get on with things without any help from anyone else
d pushed to one side and ignored
e the inability to understand another person's feelings
f the refusal to accept that something painful or unpleasant is true
g too scared to leave and get help

| **FILE G6** | **Unit 5, Part A, Exercise 3C, p. 57** | **GUIDANCE** |

Match the expressions (1–6) that Colin and Tony used in the talks to the definitions (a–f).

1 to be entitled to sth
2 to get to grips with sth
3 to chuck sb out
4 to vandalize
5 to go right off the rails
6 to sleep rough

a to throw sb out of the house
b to cope with sth, e.g. a problem
c to destroy property deliberately and for no good reason
d to spend the night outside, usually in uncomfortable conditions
e to start behaving in a way that is unacceptable to society
f to have a right to have or do sth

173

GUIDANCE AND CHALLENGE FILES

FILE G7 — Unit 3, Part B, Exercise 4, p. 33 — GUIDANCE

Complete the sentence below with words from the box. Then use the sentences to write your text.

> *breadwinner* • *cultures* • *discrimination* • *divorce* • *dysfunctional* • *grandparents* •
> *nuclear* • *patriarchal* • *racism* • *same-sex* • *smaller* • *tolerance*

1. Nowadays families are usually much … than they used to be, and there are fewer cases of … and other relatives living with younger members of the family.
2. The … family is no longer the only family set-up considered respectable. In many cases, the woman is now the "…" and families are less … .
3. Despite this, women still face … when trying to balance a career with family life.
4. Adoption processes are less discriminatory than they used to be and it is easier for … couples to adopt.
5. It is also more common to adopt across … . Unfortunately, … can still be a problem for such families.
6. Social workers might have to deal with more … families in the future, as there has been an increase in … rates and the number of single-parent families.
7. However, on the positive side, there also seems to be more … of difference in modern families than in previous generations.

FILE G8 — Unit 4, Part C, Exercise 2B, p. 48 — GUIDANCE

Find somebody else who has chosen "guidance", then follow the steps below.

1. Listen to the call again and, with your partner, complete the sentences with words and phrases from the box to reconstruct what the counsellor says.

> *behave* • *behaving* • *close* • *counselling* • *counsellor* • *get better soon* •
> *lost* • *never have the chance* • *part of the problem* • *self-help group* •
> *talking* • *worried* • *you called*

1. I can understand that you're … .
2. Have you tried … to your son?
3. Is there anything you know of that might have caused your son to … like this?
4. When did your son start … like this?
5. Was he … to his grandmother?
6. Perhaps that's … . Your son has … his grandmother.
7. He knows that he'll … to have that closeness again.
8. Do you think you could talk to your family doctor about …?
9. There is a youth grief … at the local hospital, or a school … might be of help.
10. I'm glad that … . I hope your son will … .

2. Sort the completed sentences into the categories below.

   a making suggestions
   b showing empathy
   c asking for more information

174

Guidance and challenge files

| FILE G9 | Unit 3, Part C, Exercise 3, p. 37 | GUIDANCE |

Follow the steps below to write your text.

1 Copy this table and complete it with the sentences below.

Termination		Adoption	
pros	cons	pros	cons
…	…	…	…

a   Gives couples who can't have children of their own the chance to be parents.
b   Many people are against this for religious reasons.
c   May be a good option for mothers who feel they would not be able to cope with a baby.
d   Not all adoptive families will be able to offer the child a 'perfect' upbringing.
e   Some women find the experience traumatic.
f   The baby has a chance of going to a good family and having a happy life.
g   The biological mother might find it difficult to let the baby go and could suffer for a long time afterwards.
h   The mother might be a young girl and feel unable to tell people about the pregnancy.
i   The pregnancy might be the result of sexual abuse. Keeping the baby could cause mental health issues.
j   When they find out about their situation, many of these children are told that they were "chosen" by their parents. This gives the child a feeling of being special.

2 Use words and phrases from above to complete the text below.

Termination or adoption: pros and cons

A termination may be an option in some cases, for example, in the case of a young girl ●¹, when a mother feels ●² or when the mother's life ●³. Similarly, a termination may be an option for a pregnancy which has come about as the result of ●⁴, as in this case, keeping the baby could ●⁵. In some cases, these kinds of issues might also surface after a termination has been performed as some women ●⁶. Finally, many people are against termination for ●⁷.

Adoption may be a difficult choice for a mother, as ●⁸ and ●⁹. However, it may be a good option for mothers who feel ●¹⁰. While not all adoptive families will be able to ●¹¹, the baby has the chance of ●¹². Many adoptive parents tell the children ●¹³. This makes the children feel ●¹⁴. Last but not least, adoption helps ●¹⁵.

If you need some more help, then you can also use these phrases to complete the gaps 1–15.

- cause mental health issues
- couples who can't have children of their own
- find the experience traumatic
- having a happy life
- is at risk
- offer the child a "perfect" upbringing
- religious reasons
- sexual abuse
- she may find it difficult to let the baby go
- special
- suffer for a long time afterwards
- they were "chosen"
- unable to cope with a baby
- unable to give up the baby
- who has been abused

175

GUIDANCE AND CHALLENGE FILES

FILE G10 Unit 2, Part A, Exercise 3C, p. 21 — **GUIDANCE**

Follow the steps below to make your notes.

1 Read the first paragraph of the completed web page "How to write your CV" and answer the questions below.
 - What is a CV?
 - How can you guide a reader through your CV?
 - What must you always do when you write your CV?

2 Copy the headings from the text into a table like the one below, leaving space on the right for your own notes.

Headings	Notes
Personal details	…
Profile	…
…	…

3 Carefully read the tips beside each of the headings in the text and complete the table with your details.

FILE G11 Unit 7, Part A, Exercise 4, p. 81 — **GUIDANCE**

Work with a partner and follow the instructions below.

1 Read the advice about writing a comment on page 208 so that you know exactly what to do.
2 Now read through all the material on pages 80 and 81 to get an overview of the information you have to work with.
3 Decide together how you are going to organize this information into notes. Would you like to make a mind map or a list? If you and your partner are hands-on learners, sticky notes or cards might be an option so that you can move the points around and try out different ways to structure your comment. You decide.
4 Once you have decided on the structure for your comment, write it down. This is your writing plan.
5 Follow your plan and use your notes to write your comment.
6 When you have finished, give your comment to another pair to read. Ask them to check if you have given your opinion clearly, justified your opinion and used examples to illustrate it.

FILE G12 Unit 7, Part B, Exercise 1C, p. 83 — **GUIDANCE**

Here are pieces of the mind map to get you started. Copy them into your notebook and add words from the texts on page 82 or any other words you know.

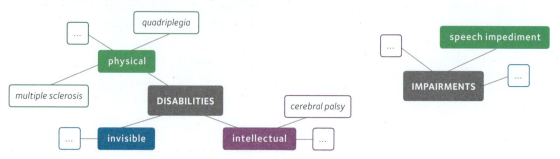

176

Guidance and challenge files

FILE G13   Unit 6, Part A, Exercise 2B, p. 68   **GUIDANCE**

Complete the gapped sentences with words and phrases from the box. Then listen and check.

bad jokes • difficult • disgusting • figure • frightened • hell • hung up • image • love • sexual harassment • sexy • talked

The men I work with are making my life ⬤¹.
They ⬤² about my clothes and my ⬤³.
They made ⬤⁴ about women who ⬤⁵ each other.
I was really ⬤⁶.
They made my life ⬤⁷.
They ⬤⁸ a ⬤⁹ calendar.
They sent me an ⬤¹⁰ in an email.
It was a ⬤¹¹ photograph.
I could ask questions to prove there has been ⬤¹².

FILE G14   Unit 12, Part B, Exercise 3, p. 143   **GUIDANCE**

A Work with a partner. The neighbour whose mother has dementia has given you a list of questions. Use them to decide which parts of the text you should use for your mediation.

1 Meine Mutter möchte so lange wie möglich unabhängig bleiben. Wie kann ihr die „intelligente Umgebung" dabei helfen?
2 Wer entwickelt die Technologie?
3 Wie wird die Technologie getestet?
4 Wie lange wird es brauchen, bis die Technologie für den allgemeinen Gebrauch verfügbar ist?
5 Wie viel würde es mich kosten, wenn ich die Wohnung meiner Mutter nachrüsten lassen würde?
6 Was halten ältere Menschen von der neuen Technologie?

B Follow the structure below to prepare your mediation.

1 Die intelligente Umgebung könnte …
2 Die Technologie wird derzeit von … entwickelt.
3 Zurzeit würde es … kosten.
4 Einige ältere Personen könnten … sein. Andere, die im Umgang mit Technologien erfahrener sind, könnten … empfinden.

FILE G15   Unit 11, Part A, Exercise 1C, p. 128   **GUIDANCE**

Match these words from the text with the categories 1–4.

openness   pastoral care workers
grief   psychological social workers
nurses   care team   sensitivity
grief counsellors   teachers   tolerance
the bereaved   social workers

1 families of a child who has recently died
2 the great sadness felt by these families
3 qualities needed in volunteers
4 professionals who are involved with these families

177

GUIDANCE AND CHALLENGE FILES

FILE G16 Unit 7, Part C, Exercise 4, p. 85 **GUIDANCE**

Here are some questions the boss asked you. Use your answers to the questions to structure your oral report.

1. Who works there?
2. What are the aims of the company?
3. How does the company achieve its aims?
4. What goes on in the company?
5. How is it set up? Can you talk me through the floor plan?
6. Where can the employees relax?
7. What is the general feeling among the employees, both abled and differently-abled?
8. What are the benefits that the employees get from working in this environment?
9. How much (if at all) are disabled employees involved in decision-making?

FILE G17 Unit 8, Part A, Exercise 5B, p. 93 **GUIDANCE**

1. List all the unnatural ingredients that go into a chicken burger. Choose from the list below.

   AMR meat • bones • growth hormones • pesticides • pharmaceuticals • sugars • vaccines

2. Complete the definition of the word "derivative". What two examples are mentioned in the interview?
   A derivative is something that …
   The two examples of derivatives mentioned in the interview are: … and …
3. Describe what TBHQ and PDMS are. Which one is a petroleum derivative and which one is a silicone?
4. Explain what Andrew means by: "Nothing is wasted". Note down the parts of the carcasses that are used in the AMR process.
5. Point out what can be found in factory-farmed meat. Focus on things like medical treatment and food that the livestock has been given.
6. Discuss what Fran means when she asks: "What are the costs to our health?" Mention the unhealthy things Andrew has described in the interview.

FILE G18 Unit 5, Part A, Exercise 5, p. 57 **GUIDANCE**

Complete these sentences to produce your English summary.

The article is about …
What these young people have in common is …
Some of them come from …
Many of these young people believe that …
However, their situation is …
Some of the problems are …
Girls in particular are …
Other difficulties like illness, hygiene …

178

Guidance and challenge files

FILE G19 — Unit 8, Part B, Exercise 3B, p. 95 — GUIDANCE

1 In preparation for your internet search, copy the start of the mind map below into your notebook or onto your computer.

2 Do a search for "what are eating disorders?" Useful sites:
  - The National Institute of Mental Health (NIMH)
  - The National Eating Disorders Association (NEDA)
  - The Eating Disorder Foundation

  Gather information about different types of eating disorders and add them to your mind map.

3 A search for "wo finde ich Hilfe bei Essstörungen?" will lead you to links to therapists, clinics and advice in your area. Look closely at the sites. Which ones look the most professional? Which of them is supported by a well-known association or by a hospital?

  If you are having difficulties deciding, ask your teacher for advice.

FILE G20 — Unit 9, Part B, Exercise 4, p. 107 — GUIDANCE

Find a partner who has also chosen guidance and follow the steps below to do the writing task.

1 Match the headings (1–6) to the "can dos" (a–f).

1 Professional knowledge, skills and attitudes
2 Instructional knowledge and skills
3 Leadership knowledge and skills
4 Environmental knowledge, skills and attitudes
5 Technical and safety skills
6 Interpersonal skills and attitudes

I can …
a demonstrate professional rescue practices and set a good example of safety while in charge of a group.
b understand current trends and issues in outdoor activities.
c take responsibility for decisions and solve problems quickly using my own judgement, based on experience.
d plan and teach outdoor activities in a fun and informative way.
e practise environmental care and use my ecological awareness to lead courses in a low-impact way.
f lead a course in a way that is inclusive of all participants (no matter what gender, race, ethnicity, ability, sexual orientation or other identities they have).

2 Use your notes to write a short report of your time as a volunteer at the Societatea pentru Tineret. Describe what you have learned using your answers from step 1 above.

179

GUIDANCE AND CHALLENGE FILES

FILE G21 Unit 9, Part A, Exercise 1D, p. 105 **GUIDANCE**

Complete the sentences below to produce a short summary of the article. Use your own words as often as possible.

- Started in the 1990s by tour companies, voluntourism is aimed at ⬤[1].
- Four typical voluntourism activities are ⬤[2].
- People volunteer for several reasons, including ⬤[3].
- According to a study, voluntourism is not necessarily a good thing because, ⬤[4].
- Some programmes can ⬤[5].
- The study recommended five ways to improve volunteering abroad. These are: ⬤[6].
- Anyone who would like to make a difference by volunteering abroad should ⬤[7] because ⬤[8].

FILE G22 Unit 9, Part B, Exercise 2B, p. 107 **GUIDANCE**

Match a–j to the functions 1–10 below to show what Kate says to:

1. indicate how she will deal with the caller's request
2. ask for the caller's name
3. check the caller's name
4. indicate that the caller should wait
5. confirm that the caller is still on the line
6. explain that someone is not available
7. make a suggestion
8. ask for contact details
9. confirm details
10. close the call

a. Are you still there?
b. Can I ask who's calling, please?
c. Can I have your phone number, please?
d. Can I take a message?
e. Could you repeat your name, please?
f. I'll just read that back to you.
g. I'll pass on your message. Mr Schultz will phone you as soon as he can. Thank you for your call.
h. I'll put you through to Frank Schulz.
i. I'm afraid Mr Schultz isn't in his office at the moment.
j. Just hold on one moment and I'll try to connect you.

FILE G23 Unit 9, Part C, Exercise 4B, p. 109 **GUIDANCE**

Follow the steps below to prepare your dialogue.

1. Look at the nurse's questions (1–7). Then complete the answers (a–g) with the correct form of the verbs in brackets and match them to the questions.

1. What time did the accident happen?
2. Can you describe what happened?
3. Was she wearing a helmet?
4. What had she been doing before the accident?
5. Did she lose consciousness at any time?
6. What did you do for the patient?
7. Have you given her any medication?

a. Yes, she (lose) consciousness for about five minutes.
b. Yes, she (be). We always (wear) ski helmets on these trips.
c. The accident (happen) at 9.30 p.m.
d. No. I (not give) her any medication.
e. Ms Hakala (ski) at a normal pace when she (hit) a rock and (injure) her leg.
f. After I (assess) her injuries, I (make) her comfortable and (keep) her calm until the ambulance (arrive).
g. She (ski) normally with the others before she (fall).

2. Now add other questions and answers to make a realistic dialogue.

180

Guidance and challenge files

FILE G24	Unit 8, Part C, Exercise 3C, p. 97	GUIDANCE

First scan the sentences below. Then watch the video again and find the missing words or phrases.

1. Boots camps like this have become Australia's latest … . Over the last five years …
2. People don't always want to be stuck in a … .
3. About a third of … train … at boot-camp style sessins each week. For them, sharing the … with a group is a powerful … .
4. I initially started doing it because … with what I was doing.
5. You get encouraged by … to sort of …, you know.
6. Trainers say that boot camps and … can help people each week.
7. There's several mornings when I think to myself, I'm … again.
8. But the satisfaction, I guess, and the feeling after …, there's nothing more … .
9. Australia is one of the … earth.
10. Now the country's … have become a front line in … against bulging …

Now use the completed sentences to help you summarize the video.

FILE G25	Unit 7, Part C, Exercise 1C, p. 84	GUIDANCE

Your boss asks you to summarize the text in English for her files. Before you begin, read the text carefully and look up any words you don't know in your dictionary. When you write your summary, focus on the information which has been highlighted below. Rewrite these sentences in English first, then use your sentences as the main points of the summary.

Wer sind wir?
In der Eider Werkstätten GmbH arbeiten Kolleginnen und Kollegen mit und ohne Behinderung zusammen, die sich mit vielfältigen Problemen auseinandersetzen, die ihre gemeinsame Arbeit aufwirft.

Was wollen wir?
Wir gestalten im Rahmen der Eingliederungshilfe den Alltag von Produktion und die Produktion von Alltag. Der ideologische Gegensatz von individueller Förderung und betrieblicher Produktivität wird durch die Praxis von Kollegialität und Leistung aufgehoben.

Im Arbeitsbereich arbeiten ca. 12 Kolleginnen und Kollegen mit dem Gruppenleiter/der Gruppenleiterin in einer Produktionsgruppe zusammen. Als Werkstatt für Menschen mit Behinderung bieten wir ein breites Angebot an verschiedenen Arbeitsplätzen in unterschiedlichen handwerklichen und industriellen Bereichen an (u. a. Metallbearbeitung, Autopflege, Gartenbau, Montage, usw.), um den Interessen, Neigungen und Fähigkeiten jeden Mitarbeiters mit Behinderung gerecht zu werden. Darüber hinaus ist jeder Bereich in Tätigkeiten mit unterschiedlichen Schwierigkeitsgraden gegliedert. Nicht alle unsere Angestellten stellen neue Produkte her; manche packen lediglich z. B. Süßigkeiten um, deren Verpackung während des Transports beschädigt worden ist und befüllen neue Tüten mit der richtigen Menge. Dies ermöglicht jeder Kollegin und jedem Kollegen, an dem Arbeitsplatz zu arbeiten, der seinem Leistungsvermögen entspricht.

GUIDANCE AND CHALLENGE FILES

FILE G26 Unit 10, Part B, Exercise 3A, p. 119 **GUIDANCE**

Before you listen to the talk, match the words (1–8) with the dictionary definitions (a–h).

1 ethnic
2 diverse
3 encounters
4 to differ
5 prejudice
6 to impose sth upon sb
7 agnostic
8 atheist

a a person who does not believe in the existence of God
b a person who believes that it is not possible to know whether God exists or not
c an unreasonable dislike or preference for a person or group, especially when it is based on their race, religion, etc.
d connected with or belonging to a nation, race or people that share a cultural tradition
e casual meetings (with people)
f to be clearly different (from one another)
g to make sb accept the same opinions, values, etc. as your own
h showing a great deal of variety or difference

FILE G27 Unit 11, Part A, Exercise 3, p. 129 **GUIDANCE**

Work with your partner and do all of the tasks below together.

1 Make sure you understand the vocabulary that is associated with working with the bereaved. Check how to pronounce the words properly.
2 Develop some questions the social worker might ask the candidate (e.g. What would you do when a child in the hospice dies? What support would you offer the family?) Make a note of the questions. Remember to keep the questions focused on the job of working with the bereaved.
3 Decide together how the ideal candidate might answer the questions. Make a note of the answers.
4 At some point in the interview, the candidate should be asked about the skills and qualities he/she has that will make him/her a good candidate for the job. Decide together what these qualities and skills might be. Make a list.
5 Use the notes you have written above to role-play the interview.

FILE G28 Unit 11, Part B, Exercise 1B, p. 130 **GUIDANCE**

Before you listen to Mr Watson, copy the outline below into your notebook or computer, then use it to structure your notes.

1 Earlier experiences of problems

2 Symptoms
   a The first sign
   b The next thing
   c After that,

3 Mr Watson would like …

182

Guidance and challenge files

| FILE G29 | Unit 11, Part C, Exercise 4B, p. 133 | GUIDANCE |

Complete the text with words from the box to make a short print advertisement for the high-tech headstones.

anecdotes • authorization • bereaved • buried • codes • headstones • memory •
scannable • smartphone • technology

Your loved ones may be ⬤1, but a new ⬤2 is ensuring they won't be forgotten. Our Austrian-based company, Aspetos, is using ⬤3 gravestone codes, so anyone with a ⬤4 and proper ⬤5 can unlock the memories of a person's past. These QR ⬤6 can display everything from ⬤7 to eulogies.

We know that ⬤8 is the most important thing for the ⬤9.

With our high-tech ⬤10, the memories last more than a lifetime.

| FILE G30 | Unit 12, Part A, Exercise 4, p. 141 | GUIDANCE |

Use the sentence beginnings below to structure and write your enquiry or your unsolicited application.

Option 1: Enquiry
- We saw your company's stand at …
- We are a group of …
- We are interested in …
- Please let us have details of …
- Many thanks in advance for your attention to our enquiry.

Option 2: Unsolicited application
- I attended one of your lectures at …
- I am writing to enquire whether you might have a vacancy for …
- At present, I am studying … at … college.
- Many thanks for considering my application.
- Enc. CV

| FILE G31 | Unit 4, Part A, Exercise 2B, p. 45 | GUIDANCE |

Match these English words and phrases with their German equivalents to help you prepare for writing your German summary.

1 Understanding unspoken signs

warnings signs • domestic violence •
physical violence • injuries •
bruises • to keep sb away •
to be restricted by sb • limited access •
low self-esteem

*Anzeichen • Blutergüsse •
eingeschränkter Zugang •
geringes Selbstwertgefühl •
häusliche Gewalt • jdn fernhalten •
körperliche Gewalt • Verletzungen •
von jdm eingeschränkt werden*

2 The cycle of violence in domestic abuse

cycle of violence • abuser • victim •
punching • kicking • to make excuses •
to put the blame on sb • to provoke abuse •
violent • addicted

*die Schuld auf jdn schieben • gewalttätig •
Faustschläge • Fußtritte •
Missbrauch auslösen • Opfer •
sich herausreden •
Spirale/Kreislauf der Gewalt •
süchtig • Täter*

183

GUIDANCE AND CHALLENGE FILES

| FILE C1 | Unit 2, Part C, Exercise 2, p. 25 | CHALLENGE! |

Partner A
You are the candidate. Follow the steps below to prepare for and then do a telephone role-play.

1. First work with Partner B (the interviewer) to choose a job that you are interviewing for. You might want to find an appropriate job advert and study it together.
2. Re-read the section "Understand the questions" in the tips text on page 24 and make up three more questions you might like to ask the interviewer asks if you have any questions.
   - I was wondering if …
   - Could you possibly tell me a bit more about …?
   - Why does the company …?
3. When you and your partner are ready, role-play the telephone interview.

| FILE C2 | Unit 4, Part C, Exercise 2B, p. 48 | CHALLENGE! |

Listen to the telephone call again and make a note of phrases and sentences that the counsellor uses to:

a make suggestions   b show empathy   c ask for more information

| FILE C3 | Unit 7, Part A, Exercise 1D, p. 80 | CHALLENGE! |

Post your own opinion by responding to one or more of the posts on page 80. Say if you agree or disagree with the writer(s) of the original post(s) and explain your thinking.

> I'd like to add something to (*name*)'s statement.
> As far as I am concerned, …
> I completely agree/disagree with (*name*)'s point of view.
> (*Name*) is right. I also think/feel/believe that …
> Sorry, I disagree with what (*name*) wrote.

| FILE C4 | Unit 7, Part C, Exercise 3B, p. 85 | CHALLENGE! |

Analyse Olli's use of language in order to reveal the atmosphere of the department.

- Listen out for words which express his personal feelings.
- Pay attention to how Olli describes the articles which are being packed. What might the employees feel while handling these goods?
- Note down words that Olli uses to describe the benefits of the work for his team.
- Describe how the team copes with challenges.

| FILE C5 | Unit 8, Part A, Exercise 1B, p. 92 | CHALLENGE! |

Draw your own food plate showing what you eat every day.
Describe your plate to a partner and ask him/her to comment on it.

Guidance and challenge files

| **FILE C6** | **Unit 8, Part C, Exercise 3C, p. 97** | **CHALLENGE!** |

Work with a partner. Report on what the various speakers said.

- The reporter
- Dan Clay, instructor
- Stafford Hamilton, participant
- Kristie Webster, participant

Use your notes to make a short radio clip on the same subject.

| **FILE C7** | **Unit 11, Part A, Exercise 1C, p. 128** | **CHALLENGE!** |

After you have completed the exercise on page 128, find a partner who has taken the challenge and do the tasks below together.

1   Use your dictionary to define these terms:
    - bereavement ● grief ● loss ● mourning

2   Use the words in four sentences or a short paragraph to show that you completely understand what each term means.

| **FILE C8** | **Unit 2, Part C, Exercise 2, p. 25** | **CHALLENGE!** |

Partner B
You are the interviewer. Follow the steps below to prepare for and then do a telephone role-play.

1   First work with Partner A (the candidate) to choose a job that he/she is interviewing for. You might want to study a job advert together before working on your own.

2   Re-read the section "Understand the questions" in the tips text on page 24 and make up three more questions you might like to ask the applicant.
    - Explain why … ● Tell me about … ● Why did you …?

3   When you and your partner are ready, role-play the telephone interview.

185

CORRESPONDENCE

Writing formal letters

[1] Leonie Kuhn
Domkloster 6 • 50667 Cologne
Germany
Tel. +49 17764813780
Fax +49 30 6976860
Email leo_ni.kuhn@gmail.de

04 October 2014 **[2]**

CONFIDENTIAL **[3]**

Care Disability **[4]**
62 Calder Street
GLASGOW
G42 7NQ
GREAT BRITAIN

Attn. Ann Haslam **[5]**

Dear Ms Haslam **[6]**

Work placement **[7]**

I would like to apply for a work placement at your organization as advertised in the March edition of the magazine *Caring for People*.

I am very interested in gaining experience with disabled people and their families as I feel sure this will give me the opportunity to develop both personally and professionally. I am particularly keen to work in an English-speaking country where I can apply my knowledge of English on a daily basis. **[8]**

As you can see from the enclosed CV, I am currently studying at a German vocational college. My studies include Health Studies, Biology, Social Science, Home Economics and English.

Through the experience I gained working as an au pair, I know that I enjoy helping people and can fit in well with families. My language abilities will also make me an asset to your team. My English is excellent, I am a native German speaker and, because of family ties, I also have conversational Polish.

I hope that you will consider my application and grant me an interview.

I look forward to hearing from you soon.

Yours sincerely **[9]**
Leonie Kuhn **[10]**

Leonie Kuhn

Enc: curriculum vitae **[11]**

1	Letterhead
2	Date
3	Special marking
4	Inside address
5	Attention line
6	Salutation
7	Subject line
8	Body of the letter
9	Complimentary close
10	Signature
11	Enclosure (Enc), Enclosures (Encs)

Leave a free line for each dot (•).

186

Formal letter layout

There is no standard layout for a formal letter in the English-speaking world, so a typical block form layout used in Europe is shown here. After the letterhead all the sentences are left aligned (*linksbündig*).

1 Letterhead
There are no fixed rules for the letterhead but it should include the sender's name, postal address, telephone and fax numbers, email address and website address (if there is one).

2 Date
An all-figure date can be misunderstood. In American English 04/10/14 (or 04-10-14) means April 10, 2014 but in British English it means 04 October, 2014. For this reason the month should always be written out and the year should be a four-figure number. The usual order in which a date is written in formal letters and forms is: day (in figures) – month (as a word) – year (in figures). The example in this letter is pronounced 'the fourth of October two thousand and fourteen' (or 'twenty fourteen').

3 Special marking
These include URGENT, CONFIDENTIAL, PRIVATE AND CONFIDENTIAL, PERSONAL, AIR MAIL, REGISTERED, RECORDED DELIVERY. This line can be seen over the address in a window envelope.

4 Inside address
This is the recipient's address. Always include the country because the same city names can be found in different countries. When writing to a UK address write the town or city in capital letters and the postcode on a separate line under it.

5 Attention (Attn.)
The attention line is under the inside address and close enough to it to be seen in a window envelope. If there is an attention line, the letter may be opened by the company's post department and given to the person named. However, if the inside address starts with someone's name it may only be opened by that person or their secretary.

6/9 Salutation / Complimentary close
In most cases the salutation and complimentary close can be written **without** punctuation and they are linked as shown in the table below. In general, it is always better to write to a named person than a company but if this is not possible, start the letter 'Dear Sir or Madam' and use 'Yours faithfully' as the complimentary close.

Salutation	Complimentary close	Formality	Notes
Dear Mrs Brown	Yours sincerely	Formal	The most commonly used form
Dear Sir or Madam	Yours faithfully	Formal	Only used if the name is unknown
Dear Kim Dear Kim and Jim Jim	Regards Best regards Best wishes Yours	Friendly	Used in business if the writers know each other

7 Subject line
This is written in **bold** letters or <u>underlined</u>.

8 Body of the letter
The first word always starts with a capital letter. The paragraphs are separated by an empty line.

CORRESPONDENCE

10 Signature
Signatures are often hard to read, so write the signatory's name and position under the signature. As there is no real English equivalent to *Sachbearbeiter/-in*, it is best to name the department where the signatory works (e.g. Sales Department for *Verkaufssachbearbeiter*).

11 Enclosure
It is sometimes enough just to write Enc or Encs but if necessary, details of the enclosure(s) can be listed like this:
Enc: Ticket or Encs: Tickets

Writing emails

More than 90% of organizations use email because it is quick, convenient and cheap. Here are some important things to remember before you hit 'send'.

Subject (Betreff):
This is the same as for a formal letter. Begin with a capital letter and keep it short.

Cc: 'carbon copy' (Kopie)

```
To:
Subject:
Cc:
Attachment(s):

Salutation
Body
Complimentary close
```

Writing the email
Most mistakes are made here: *Emails are not always informal.* Like formal letters they can be formal or informal but unlike formal letters they can be sent to thousands of recipients by mistake.

Salutation / Complimentary close
If you do not know the recipient, use one of the polite forms below. If the relationship becomes more friendly, your partner will start using informal forms and you should then do the same. Let your partner take the initiative.

	Salutation	Complimentary close
Polite	Dear Ms Brown Dear Mrs Brown Dear Miss Brown Dear Mr Brown Dear Dr Brown	Regards Best regards Best wishes Yours sincerely
Friendly	Good morning James Dear Kim Dear Kim and Jim	Regards Best regards Best wishes
Informal	Hello Kim Hi Kim Kim	All the best (Atb) Best Cheers Must rush

Body of the email
Tips for better communication:
- Start the email with a capital letter.
- Never use text message short forms (CUL8R, etc.).
- Write in paragraphs separated by a free line.

- If you write back in the spaces between the lines of the original email and/or in a different colour,
  - do not use red
  - do not underline words
  - do not write in **bold letters**
  - do not write in CAPITALS
  - do not use exclamation marks!

  because it sounds as if you are angry or think the reader is stupid.

Most emails are read on-screen, so keep yours as short as possible.

Points of style

Use short forms to be friendly (I've, we'll, he'd, etc.) and long forms to be more formal.

Finishing the email

If you know the recipient well, it is enough to sign off with your first name. If you do not, add your position and the name of your company under it.

Writing emails	
Starting an email	
How are things?	Wie läuft's? / Wie geht's?
I hope you're well.	Hoffentlich geht es dir/Ihnen gut.
I hope you had a good trip to …	Hoffentlich hattest du / hatten Sie eine gute Reise nach …
I am writing to … (ask for information on … / book a room for … / confirm that …).	Ich schreibe … (mit der Bitte um Informationen über … / um ein Zimmer für … zu reservieren / um zu bestätigen, dass …).
Answering or forwarding an email	
I was delighted to receive your mail.	Ich habe mich sehr über deine/Ihre E-Mail gefreut.
Many thanks for your mail … (about … / inviting me to …).	Vielen Dank für deine/Ihre E-Mail (über … / mit einer Einladung zu …).
I've just got … (your email / an email from … / a phone call from …).	Eben habe ich … (deine/Ihre E-Mail / eine E-Mail von … / einen Anruf von …) erhalten.
Getting to the point	
I'd/We'd/They'd like to know … (if/what/…, e.g. if you'll be arriving after midnight).	Ich/Wir/Sie möchte(n) wissen, (ob/was/…, z. B. ob Sie nach Mitternacht eintreffen werden).
I'm pleased/delighted to accept (your invitation / your offer).	(Sehr) gerne nehme ich (deine/Ihre Einladung / dein/Ihr Angebot) an.
Request	
Please let me have some information on …	Bitte schicken Sie mir Informationen zu …
Could you tell me if/what/…?	Würden Sie mir bitte mitteilen, ob/was/…?
Could someone … (e.g. pick me/us up at the airport)?	Könnte jemand … (z. B. mich/uns am Flughafen abholen)?
Would you send us …, please?	Würden Sie uns bitte … schicken?

PHRASE BANK

Introductions

Introducing people

I would like to introduce … / This is …	Ich würde gern … vorstellen. / Das ist …
He/She decided to be a carer because …	Er/Sie entschied sich für den Beruf des Betreuers / der Betreuerin, weil …
He/She hopes to work as a/an …	Er/Sie hofft, als … arbeiten zu können.
He/She would like to work with adults.	Er/Sie würde gern mit Erwachsenen arbeiten.

Introductions and greetings

Hi, I'm … / my name is … I'm the …	Hallo, ich bin … / mein Name ist … Ich bin der/die …
Nice to meet you.	Es freut mich, Sie kennen zu lernen.
Nice to meet you, too. / You too.	Mich auch. / Ebenso.
Hello. How are you?	Hallo. Wie geht es Ihnen?
Very well, thanks. And you?	Sehr gut, danke. Und Ihnen?

Small talk

Do you come from around here?	Kommen Sie hier aus der Gegend?
As a matter of fact, I …	In der Tat … ich …
What about you? Where do you live?	Was ist mit Ihnen? Wo wohnen Sie?
Nice weather today.	Schönes Wetter heute.
Yes. It's great. I hope it stays like this.	Ja, es ist großartig. Ich hoffe, es bleibt so.
It's nice weather for a walk, isn't it?	Es ist gutes Wetter, um einen Spaziergang zu machen, finden Sie nicht auch?
Did you find us all right?	Haben Sie gut zu uns gefunden?
So, you had no trouble finding us, then?	Also hatten Sie keine Schwierigkeiten, zu uns zu finden?
No, no trouble at all.	Nein, überhaupt nicht.

Talking about your workplace

My name is …	Mein Name ist … / Ich heiße …
I'm a/an (*job title*) at (*name of organization*).	Ich bin (*Berufsbezeichnung*) bei (*Name des Unternehmens*).
It's located in …	Es befindet sich / ist ansässig in …
I work for … (*e.g. the city council*)	Ich arbeite für … (*z.B. Stadtrat*)
(*Name of organization*) was set up in (*year*) by … to …	(*Name des Unternehmens*) wurde (*im Jahr*) von … gegründet, mit dem Ziel, …
We look after …	Wir kümmern uns um …
We have a staff of … (*number*).	Wir beschäftigen … (*Anzahl*) Personen.
I'm responsible for …	Ich bin für … verantwortlich.
My responsibilities include …	Meine Verantwortlichkeiten beinhalten …

Describing yourself and your job

I am responsible for …	Ich bin für … verantwortlich.
I report to …	Ich unterstehe …
… often/sometimes/never …	… oft/manchmal/nie …
… like/love/enjoy (…+ *ing* …)	… mag/liebe/genieße es, … zu …
… hate/dislike (…+ *ing* …)	… hasse/mag es gar nicht, … zu …

190

… joined the company … years ago / in (*year*) …	… habe vor … Jahren / (*Jahr*) … im Unternehmen angefangen.
… have been with the company since (*year*) …	… arbeite seit (*Jahr*) im Unternehmen.
Showing someone around	
If you look over here, you'll see …	Wenn Sie hierhin schauen, sehen Sie …
This is where the employees …	Dort … die Angestellten.
This area is used for …	Dieser Bereich wird für … verwendet.
The kitchen is opposite / next to / on the right/ left of …	Die Küche befindet sich gegenüber / neben / rechts/ links von …

Job titles

care assistant	Pfleger/in (in einem Heim)
case worker	Sozialarbeiter/in
childminder	Kinderbetreuer/in
classroom assistant	Assistent/in im Unterricht
community support worker	Sozialarbeiter/in (in einer Gemeinde)
counsellor	Berater/in
day care centre assistant	Pfleger/in in einer Tagesstätte (für Kinder, ältere Menschen oder Kranke)
geriatric assistant / care worker	Altenpfleger/in
healthcare assistant	Gesundheits(pflege)assistent/in
homecare worker	Hauspflegekraft / Hauspflegedienstleister/in
kindergarten assistant / teacher	pädagogische/r Assistent/in / Kindergärtner/in
maternity support worker	Mutterschaftshilfe
midwife	Hebamme
nursery / kindergarten nurse	Erzieher/in, Kinderpfleger/in
nutritionist	Ernährungsberater/in
occupational therapist	Beschäftigungstherapeut/in, Ergotherapeut/in
orthopaedic technician	Orthopädietechniker/in
paediatric assistant / nurse	pädiatrische/r Assistent/in
personal assistant	persönliche/r Assistent/in
physiotherapist	Physiotherapeut/in, Krankengymnast/in
school nurse	Krankenpfleger/-schwester in einer Schule
social administrator	Verwalter/in für soziale Angelegenheiten
social worker	Sozialarbeiter/in
speech and language therapy assistant	Sprachtherapeut/in
substance abuse counsellor	Berater/in in der Suchtkrankenhilfe
teaching assistant for children with special needs	Unterrichtshilfskraft für Schüler/innen mit Behinderung
telephone counsellor	Telefonberater/in
youth and community worker	Jugend- und Sozialarbeiter/in

PHRASE BANK

Telephoning

Introducing yourself

Hello, this is … (speaking).	Hallo, hier spricht …
I'm calling from …	Ich rufe im Namen von (*Name des Unternehmens*) an.
Can I speak to …, please? / Is this …?	Kann ich bitte … sprechen? / Spreche ich mit …?
I was wondering if …	Ich wollte fragen, ob …
Is … available at the moment?	Ist … gerade zu sprechen?
Speaking. / This is …	Am Apparat. / Hier spricht …
How can I help you?	Wie kann ich Ihnen helfen?

Putting the caller through

Could you put me through to …, please?	Können Sie mich bitte zu … durchstellen?
Just hold on one moment and I'll try to connect you.	Bitte warten Sie einen Moment. Ich versuche, Sie zu verbinden.
I'll put you through to (*name*).	Ich stelle Sie zu (*Name*) durch.

Asking for more information/clarification

Can I ask who's calling, please?	Wer spricht, bitte?
Could you repeat your name / that, please?	Können Sie Ihren Namen / das bitte wiederholen?
I'm sorry. How do you spell that?	Entschuldigung, könnten Sie mir das bitte buchstabieren?
I'm sorry, I didn't understand that.	Entschuldigung, ich habe das nicht verstanden.
Can I have your phone number, please?	Können Sie mir bitte Ihre Telefonnummer geben?
Are you still there?	Sind Sie noch da?

Saying that the call isn't possible

I'm afraid (*name*) isn't in his/her office / at his/her desk at the moment.	Leider ist (*Name*) gerade nicht im Büro / nicht erreichbar.
I'm sorry, but Mr/Ms …'s line is engaged at the moment. Would you like to try again later?	Es tut mir leid, aber der Anschluss von Herrn/Frau … ist gerade besetzt. Möchten Sie es später noch mal versuchen?
Can I take a message?	Kann ich etwas ausrichten?
No, thanks. I'll try again later.	Nein, danke. Ich versuche es später noch mal.

Leaving/Taking a message

Do you have a pen and paper?	Haben Sie einen Stift und Papier?
Do you want me to spell that?	Wollen Sie, dass ich das buchstabiere?
Shall I repeat that?	Soll ich das noch einmal sagen?
I'll just read that back to you.	Ich wiederhole noch mal.
Thanks, I think I've got all that / everything.	Danke, ich glaube, ich habe alles verstanden.
I'll pass on your message.	Ich leite Ihre Nachricht weiter.
(*Name*) will phone you as soon as he/she can.	(*Name*) ruft Sie an, sobald er/sie Zeit hat.

Arranging and changing appointments

I'd like to arrange an appointment, please.	Ich möchte bitte einen Termin vereinbaren.
When would be convenient for you?	Wann würde es Ihnen passen?
Would late afternoon on the second of April suit you?	Wäre es Ihnen am Spätnachmittag des 2. April recht?
How about Wednesday the twenty-first at 10.30?	Wie wäre es mit Mittwoch, dem 21. um 10.30 Uhr?

192

How about Friday afternoon instead?	Wie wäre es stattdessen mit Freitagnachmittag?
I'm afraid I've had to change my plans.	Leider haben sich meine Pläne verändert.
I'm going to have to cancel the appointment.	Ich muss den Termin absagen.
I'm sorry but I've already got an appointment then.	Es tut mir leid, aber da habe ich schon einen Termin.
That works fine by me.	Das passt mir gut.
Making complaints	
It's about … / There seems to be a problem with …	Es geht um … / Es gibt anscheinend ein Problem mit …
The problem is (that) …	Das Problem ist, (dass) …
There's no point in … (+ -*ing*)	Es macht keinen Sinn, … zu …
Thanks for solving the problem so quickly.	Danke, dass Sie das Problem so schnell gelöst haben.
Could you send me an email confirming this (so we have a record)?	Könnten Sie mir das per E-Mail bestätigen (damit wir es dokumentiert haben)?
Answering complaints	
I'm very sorry to hear that. / I do apologize for this.	Es tut mir leid, das zu hören. / Ich bitte dafür um Entschuldigung.
Oh, no. That sounds like someone has …	Oh nein. Das klingt, als hätte jemand …
These things can happen, I'm afraid.	Leider kann so etwas passieren.
Let me talk to my boss / sort this out and I'll get back to you straight away.	Lassen Sie mich das mit meinem Chef besprechen / die Sache in Ordnung bringen. Ich melde mich dann gleich noch mal bei Ihnen.
We'll double-check to make sure that this sort of mix-up doesn't happen again.	Wir werden genau nachprüfen, um sicher zu sein, dass ein solches Durcheinander nicht mehr vorkommt.
Ending the call	
Is there anything else that I can do for you?	Kann ich noch etwas für Sie tun?
Thank you for calling / for your call.	Danke für Ihren Anruf.
Have a nice day.	Ich wünsche Ihnen noch einen schönen Tag.

International spelling alphabet

A	Alpha	N	November
B	Bravo	O	Oscar
C	Charlie	P	Papa
D	Delta	Q	Quebec
E	Echo	R	Romeo
F	Foxtrot	S	Sierra
G	Golf	T	Tango
H	Hotel	U	Uniform
I	India	V	Victor
J	Juliet	W	Whiskey
K	Kilo	X	X-ray
L	Lima	Y	Yankee
M	Mike	Z	Zulu

PHRASE BANK

Job interviews

Why you want the job

I'm particularly interested in / keen to …	Ich interessiere mich besonders für / möchte unbedingt …
I always keep up to date with …	Ich halte mich immer bezüglich … auf dem neuesten Stand.
I have always wanted to work in this field.	Ich wollte schon immer in diesem Gebiet arbeiten.
I was able to get some good experience in/with …	Ich konnte hilfreiche Erfahrungen in/mit … sammeln.
I would like to develop my … skills.	Ich würde gerne meine …-fähigkeiten weiterentwickeln.
I really enjoyed that job / working in a team.	Ich mochte die Arbeit wirklich sehr / mochte es, in einem Team zu arbeiten.
I enjoy the challenges of my job.	Ich mag die Herausforderungen meiner Arbeit.
I am really interested in this job because I want to gain experience in this area / it sounds really interesting.	Ich bin sehr interessiert an dieser Stelle, weil ich in diesem Bereich Erfahrung sammeln möchte / es sehr interessant klingt.
I am honest and hard-working.	Ich bin ehrlich und fleißig.

Strengths and weaknesses

My language skills are very good: I can speak …	Meine Sprachkenntnisse sind sehr gut: Ich kann … sprechen.
I am a team player / I am good at working as part of a team.	Ich bin teamfähig / arbeite gut als Teil eines Teams.
I am very personable and empathetic.	Ich bin sehr umgänglich und einfühlsam.
My strengths include working independently / good organization skills / taking responsibility …	Meine Stärken sind das selbstständige Arbeiten / gute organisatorische Fähigkeiten / die Übernahme von Verantwortung …
I think my greatest weakness is probably setting my own standards too high / my lack of experience.	Ich denke, meine größte Schwäche ist (es) wahrscheinlich, zu hohe Anforderungen an mich selbst zu stellen / das Fehlen an Erfahrung.

Expectations of the job

I hope that the job will be challenging and that I will be able to take on some responsibility.	Ich hoffe, dass die Arbeit herausfordernd sein wird und ich etwas Verantwortung übernehmen kann.
I hope to gain my first experiences of …	Ich hoffe, erste Erfahrungen im Bereich … zu sammeln/ sammeln zu können.
I expect the job to provide me with a good insight into … (*field or work / specific place of work*).	Ich erwarte von dem Job, dass ich einen guten Einblick in … (*Arbeitsbereich / bestimmten Arbeitsplatz*) bekomme.

Future plans

In the future, I would like to be promoted to Senior Social Worker.	Ich würde später gerne zum/zur leitenden Sozialarbeiter/in befördert werden.
In ten years' time, I see myself …	Ich sehe mich in zehn Jahren …
I am very ambitious and I hope to gain as much experience and knowledge as I can.	Ich bin sehr ehrgeizig und hoffe, möglichst viel Erfahrung zu sammeln und viel neues Wissen zu erlangen.

Further questions

Would there be further opportunities available at the end of the internship?	Gibt es weitere zur Verfügung stehende Möglichkeiten am Ende des Praktikums?
I was wondering what/if …	Ich wollte fragen, was/ob …
What would my typical tasks be?	Was wären typische Aufgaben für mich?

Phrase bank

Presentations	
Introducing yourself / the topic	
Welcome to …	Willkommen in/bei …
My name is … and I'm here to tell you about …	Mein Name ist … und ich möchte Ihnen heute über … berichten.
Thank you for coming today.	Danke, dass Sie heute gekommen sind.
Today I'd like to talk about …	Ich würde heute gerne über … sprechen.
The purpose of my presentation is to …	Meine Präsentation soll dazu dienen, … zu …
Explaining the structure of the talk	
I've divided my presentation into three/four main parts: …	Ich habe meine Präsentation in drei/vier Hauptteile untergliedert: …
I've planned in time to answer any questions you might have at the end of my presentation.	Ich habe genügend Zeit eingeplant, sodass ich Ihre Fragen, die möglicherweise aufkommen, am Ende meiner Präsentation beantworten werde/kann.
If you have any questions, just shout them out / feel free to interrupt.	Falls Sie irgendwelche Fragen haben (sollten), rufen Sie einfach dazwischen / können Sie mich gerne (kurz) unterbrechen.
In the first part of my talk …	Im ersten Teil meines Vortrags …
Then I will go on to …	Dann werde ich mich … zuwenden.
Putting things in sequence	
First, …	Als Erstes / Zuerst …
Second, …	Zweitens …
Then, …	Dann …
After that, …	Danach …
Next, …	Als Nächstes …
Finally, …	Zum Schluss …
Moving from one point to the next	
Moving on, …	Kommen wir zum nächsten Thema, …
Now I would like to move on to the next point: …	Ich würde jetzt gerne zum nächsten Punkt kommen/übergehen: …
The next topic I'm going to talk about is …	Das nächste Thema, über das ich sprechen werde, ist …
Presenting a website	
We've divided the website into the following pages: …	Wir haben die Website in folgende Seiten unterteilt: …
On our home page we have …	Auf unserer Homepage haben wir …
As you can see, most of the jobs are in the … sector.	Wie Sie sehen, sind die meisten der Arbeitsstellen im …-bereich.
If you click on …, you can see a list of …	Wenn Sie … anklicken, können Sie eine Liste von … sehen.
So, that's our website. Does anyone have any questions?	Das ist also unsere Website. Haben Sie (noch) Fragen?
Dealing with questions	
Are there any questions?	Gibt es (noch) Fragen?
If you have any questions, I'd be happy to answer them now.	Falls Sie (noch) Fragen haben (sollten), bin ich jetzt gerne bereit, sie zu beantworten.

PHRASE BANK

Summarizing/Concluding	
So to sum up, my main points were …	Um alles zusammenzufassen, meine Hauptpunkte waren …
In conclusion, I would like to say …	Zum Schluss würde ich gerne sagen …
In summary, I think it is clear that …	Zusammenfassend denke ich, dass es klar/verständlich ist, dass …
Finally, I would like to point out that …	Zu guter Letzt würde ich gerne darauf hinweisen / erwähnen, dass …
Finishing the presentation	
Thank you very much for your attention. / Thank you for listening.	Vielen Dank für Ihre Aufmerksamkeit.

Discussions

Asking for and giving opinions	
I think that … . What about you?	Ich denke, dass … . Was meinen Sie?
I don't agree. How do you feel about …?	Ich stimme dem nicht zu. Was halten Sie von …?
Don't you agree that …?	Sind Sie nicht der Meinung, dass …?
Yes, you're probably right.	Ja, vermutlich haben Sie Recht.
What do you think of …?	Was halten Sie von …?
I'm not sure. How about … instead?	Ich weiß nicht so recht. Wie wäre es stattdessen mit …?
Why don't we do it this way?	Warum machen wir es nicht einfach so?
We shouldn't forget that …	Wir sollten nicht vergessen, dass …
Active listening	
What's the problem?	Was ist das Problem?
Shall we talk about it?	Sollen wir uns darüber unterhalten?
I understand.	Ich verstehe.
Take your time.	Nehmen Sie sich Zeit.
So, you feel as if …?	Haben Sie also das Gefühl, als ob …?
If I understand you correctly, …	Wenn ich Sie richtig verstehe, …
I'm sorry, but I don't understand what you mean by …	Entschuldigen Sie, aber ich verstehe nicht (ganz), was Sie mit … sagen wollen.
Is it true that …?	Stimmt es, dass …?
I hear what you're saying.	Ich verstehe, was Sie sagen.
Could you give me an example / explain that, please?	Könnten Sie bitte ein Beispiel nennen / das bitte erklären?
Giving advice	
It's a good idea to …	Es ist eine gute Idee, … zu …
If you can, you should …	Wenn Sie können, sollten Sie …
Try not to …	Versuchen Sie, … nicht zu …
Perhaps you could think about …	Vielleicht können Sie über … nachdenken.
It might not be a bad idea to …	Es ist vielleicht keine schlechte Idee, … zu …
Have you ever considered talking to …?	Haben Sie sich jemals überlegt, mit … zu sprechen?
Why don't you try speaking to …?	Warum versuchen Sie nicht, mit … zu sprechen?

Phrase bank

The language of meetings

Starting and making introductions

Good morning. Everyone seems to be here, so let's get started straight away, shall we?	Guten Morgen. Da alle anwesend zu sein scheinen, können wir gleich anfangen, oder?
I'd like to begin by welcoming … to … . Thank you for coming.	Ich würde zuerst gerne … bei … willkommen heißen. Vielen Dank, dass Sie gekommen sind.
Just to make sure that we all know who's who, my name is … and I'm the …	Damit wir alle Bescheid wissen, wer wer ist: Mein Name ist … und ich bin der/die …
Perhaps the two of you would like to introduce yourselves as well?	Vielleicht könnten Sie beide sich auch kurz persönlich vorstellen?

Introducing items on the agenda

As you can see on the agenda, the first point is …	Wie Sie auf der Tagesordnung sehen können, ist der erste Punkt …
So, if we move on quickly to the second point on the agenda: …	Lassen Sie uns jetzt rasch zum zweiten Punkt auf der Tagesordnung kommen/übergehen: …
Could we look at the third/next point on our agenda: …	Widmen wir uns nun dem dritten/nächsten Tagesordnungs- punkt: …
That brings us on to the next item on today's agenda: …	Das führt uns zum nächsten Punkt der heutigen Tagesordnung: …
OK, that clearly belongs under the next point on the agenda: …	Gut, das gehört eindeutig zum nächsten Punkt auf der Tagesordnung: …
The final item on the agenda is …	Der letzte Punkt auf der Tagesordnung ist …

Inviting someone to speak

(Name), is there anything you would like to add to that?	(Name), gibt es irgendetwas, was Sie dem gerne hinzufügen würden?
Perhaps I can bring … in now.	Vielleicht kann ich jetzt … zur Sprache bringen / einbringen.
(Name), how do you see the situation?	(Name), wie beurteilen/sehen Sie die Situation/Lage?

Closing the meeting

I think we've covered all the main points on the agenda, so I suggest that we bring the meeting to a close.	Ich denke, wir haben alle Hauptpunkte auf der Tagesordnung abgehandelt, daher schlage ich vor, dass wir das Meeting beenden.
OK, I think we've covered all we can on that point.	Okay, ich denke, wir haben alles angesprochen, was es zu diesem Punkt zu sagen gibt.
We'll write up the minutes of what we've discussed and will email them to you tomorrow, just for the record.	Wir werden all das, was heute besprochen wurde, zu Protokoll bringen und Ihnen dann morgen mailen, nur um das festzuhalten.
Thank you all for coming and we'll see you again on Friday.	Vielen Dank fürs Kommen und wir sehen uns dann wieder am Freitag.

Writing a record of a meeting

(Name) explained/suggested/recommended that …	(Name) erklärte/schlug vor/empfahl, dass …
It was decided/agreed that …	Es wurde entschieden/vereinbart, dass …
(Name) is to talk to / meet with …	(Name) wird mit … sprechen / wird sich mit … treffen.

PHRASE BANK

Working with clients

Describing a case

The client

The client's name is …	Der Name des Klienten/der Klientin ist …
He/She is … years old.	Er/Sie ist … Jahre alt.
He/She lives …	Er/Sie lebt …

The family background

The client's family is …	Die Familie des Klienten/der Klientin ist …
He/She was looked after by his/her …	Sein(e)/Ihr(e) … kümmerte(n) sich um ihn/sie.
When he/she was … years old, …	Als er/sie … Jahre alt war, …

Client's assessment of the situation

The client is (not) able to understand his/her situation.	Der Klient/Die Klientin kann seine/ihre Situation (nicht) verstehen.
He/She would (not) like to …	Er/Sie würde (nicht) gerne …

The current situation

We are looking into …	Wir untersuchen gerade …
We have spoken to … and are currently …	Wir haben (bereits) mit … gesprochen und sind gerade dabei, …

Making referrals

I would recommend that the person call …	Ich würde vorschlagen, dass die Person … anruft.
I'd suggest that the client get in touch with …	Ich schlage vor, dass sich der/die Klient/in mit … in Verbindung setzt.
I think he/she should call …	Ich denke, er/sie sollte … anrufen.
I would contact …	Ich würde … kontaktieren.
the police	die Polizei
a counsellor	einen/eine Berater/in
the youth protection service	die Jugendschutzbehörde
a doctor	einen Arzt/eine Ärztin
his/her therapist	seine/n / ihre/n Therapeuten/Therapeutin
his/her general practitioner (GP)	seine/n / ihre/n Arzt/Ärztin für Allgemeinmedizin

Giving reassurance

There's nothing to worry about.	Es gibt keinen Grund zur Beunruhigung.
Everything will be fine.	Alles wird gut.
Don't worry, it's just a/an …	Machen Sie sich keine Sorgen, das ist nur ein/e …
It's just a routine operation/test.	Es ist nur eine Routineoperation / eine Routineuntersuchung.
It's perfectly normal to feel like that.	Es ist ganz normal, dass Sie sich so fühlen.

Asking delicate questions

Could you tell me / explain …?	Können Sie mir sagen/erklären, …?
Do you happen to remember when …?	Erinnern Sie sich (zufällig) daran, wann …?
Would you mind telling me how …?	Können Sie mir erzählen, wie …?
…, if you don't mind me asking.	…, wenn ich fragen darf.

Phrase bank

Writing enquiries

Giving the source of the address

We saw your advertisement in … / your stand/catalogue at the … trade fair.	Wir haben Ihre Anzeige in/im … / Ihren Stand/Katalog auf der …-messe gesehen.
I was most impressed by the products/services you showed me on your stand at the … trade fair.	Die Produkte/Dienstleistungen, die Sie mir an Ihrem Stand auf der …-messe gezeigt haben, haben mich sehr beeindruckt.
When we visited your website, we were interested to see that you …	Als wir uns Ihre Webseite angeschaut haben, haben wir mit Interesse zur Kenntnis genommen, dass Sie …
We have your address from (*business partner/ organization*)	Wir haben Ihre Adresse von (*Geschäftspartner/in / Organisation*)

Stating the purpose of your enquiry

I am writing on behalf of (*name of organization*) where I'm a/an (*job title*).	Ich schreibe Ihnen im Auftrag/Namen von (*Name des Unternehmens*). Dort arbeite ich als (*Jobbezeichnung*).
We are putting together kits for …	Wir stellen Pakete für … zusammen.
Our aim is to …	Unser Ziel ist es, … zu …
As a well-known manufacturer of (*product*), we are sure you would like to contribute …	Als ein gutbekannter Hersteller von (*Produkt*) möchten Sie sicherlich gern … beisteuern.
We are looking specifically for (*items*).	Wir suchen insbesondere nach (*Waren*).
We are looking for a supplier of … .	Wir sind auf der Suche nach einem Lieferanten von … .
We are interested in your new range of … .	Wir haben Interesse an Ihrer neuen Auswahl an … .

Making requests

Please send us samples of … / your latest catalogue and price list.	Senden Sie uns bitte Muster/Warenproben / Ihren neuesten Katalog und Ihre Preisliste zu.
Please give us a quotation for … .	Legen Sie uns bitte ein Angebot an … vor.
Could you please let us have details of all discounts available?	Könnten Sie uns bitte Details all Ihrer verfügbaren Preis-nachlässe/Rabatte mitteilen?
Full details of your terms of payment and delivery would also be appreciated.	Vollständige Angaben Ihrer Zahlungsbedingungen und der Lieferung wären ebenfalls wünschenswert.
We would be grateful if you could send us your current export price list.	Wir wären Ihnen verbunden, wenn Sie uns Ihre aktuelle Export-Preisliste zukommen lassen könnten.
Delivery would be required within … days/weeks/months.	Die Lieferung wäre innerhalb von … Tagen/Wochen/ Monaten erforderlich.

Closing the letter

We look forward to hearing from you soon / in the next few days.	Wir freuen uns, bald / in den nächsten Tagen von Ihnen zu hören.
We look forward to receiving your offer/quotation/reply in due course.	Wir freuen uns auf den Erhalt Ihres Angebots / Ihrer Antwort zu gegebener Zeit.

PHRASE BANK

Writing offers

Referring to an enquiry

We refer to / With reference to your enquiry of … .	Wir verweisen auf / Mit Bezug auf Ihre Anfrage des/von … .
Thank you for your letter/email / telephone call of … enquiring about … .	Vielen Dank für Ihren Brief/Ihre E-Mail / Ihren Telefonanruf vom … bezüglich/über … .
We were delighted to receive your enquiry dated … about our … .	Wir waren erfreut darüber, Ihre Anfrage vom … bezüglich/über unser/e … zu erhalten.
I am pleased to let you have details of our offer in writing.	Ich freue mich, Ihnen Details über unser Angebot in schriftlicher Form zukommen zu lassen.

Referring to information/samples (for general enquiry)

We are enclosing out latest brochure/flyer and current price list.	Wir fügen unsere aktuelle Broschüre/unseren aktuellen Flyer und die aktuelle Preisliste bei.
We would like to draw your attention to our latest special offer / new range of … .	Wir würden Ihre Aufmerksamkeit gerne auf unser aktuelles Sonderangebot / neues Sortiment/Angebot an … richten.

Giving details (for specific enquiry)

We are pleased to send you / submit the following offer/quotation: …	Gerne schicken / unterbreiten wir Ihnen das folgende Angebot: …

Giving further information

Our delivery date is approximately … days/weeks after receipt of order.	Unser Liefertermin ist ungefähr … Tage / Wochen nach Auftragseingang.
We can guarantee delivery within … days/weeks of receipt of order.	Wir können eine Lieferung innerhalb von … Tagen / Wochen nach Auftragseingang garantieren.

Closing the letter

If you have any questions, please get in contact with me.	Falls Sie Fragen haben (sollten), setzen Sie sich bitte mit mir in Verbindung.
We feel sure that a trial order will convince you of the quality of our products.	Wir sind überzeugt davon, dass ein Probeauftrag Sie von der Qualität unserer Produkte überzeugen wird.
Thank you for your interest. We look forward to receiving your order in due course.	Vielen Dank für Ihr Interesse. Wir sehen dem Erhalt Ihrer Bestellung zu gegebener Zeit entgegen.
We look forward to doing business with you in the future / to hearing from you soon.	Wir freuen uns, in Zukunft mit Ihnen Geschäfte zu machen / bald von Ihnen zu hören.

Placing and acknowledging orders

Placing orders

Thank you for your offer/quotation of … for … .	Vielen Dank für Ihr Angebot von/vom … für … .
With reference to your offer of … .	Unter Bezugnahme auf Ihr Angebot von/vom … .
We are pleased to place an order / a trial order for …	Gerne geben wir eine Bestellung / einen Probeauftrag für …
Payment is to be made by (*date*).	Zahlung soll bis zum (*Datum*) geleistet werden.
Please acknowledge receipt of this order by fax/email.	Bitte bestätigen Sie den Erhalt dieser Bestellung per Fax/E-Mail.
Could you please also let us know exactly when we can expect delivery?	Könnten Sie uns bitte ebenfalls den genauen Termin mitteilen, wann wir mit der Lieferung rechnen können?
We look forward to receiving the consignment in due course / soon.	Wir freuen uns auf den (baldigen) Erhalt der Sendung/Lieferung / in angemessener Zeit.

We trust that you will give this order careful / your prompt attention.	Wir vertrauen darauf / gehen davon aus, dass Sie der Bestellung Sorgfalt entgegenbringen / Ihre unverzügliche Aufmerksamkeit widmen.
We look forward to receiving your confirmation of order and advice of dispatch soon.	Wir freuen uns auf den baldigen Erhalt Ihrer Auftragsbestätigung und Versandanzeige.
Acknowledging orders	
Thank you / Many thanks for your order of … for … .	Vielen / Herzlichen Dank für Ihre Bestellung vom … über … .
We acknowledge receipt of your order of (*date*) for …	Wir nehmen den Eingang Ihrer Bestellung vom (*Datum*) über …
We note that we can expect payment by (*method of payment*) on receipt of our invoice / within 30 days of delivery.	Wir stellen fest, dass wir die Zahlung per (*Zahlungsmethode*) bei Erhalt unserer Rechnung / innerhalb von 30 Tagen nach Lieferung erwarten können.
The consignment will be dispatched on (*date*) by … .	Die Sendung wird am (*Datum*) durch/per … verschickt.
We expect to complete your order within approximately … days and will inform you as soon as the goods are ready.	Wir gehen davon aus, Ihre Bestellung innerhalb von etwa … Tagen vervollständigen zu können, und werden Sie dann sofort darüber informieren, wenn die Waren auslieferbereit sind.
We are sure that you will be satisfied with the goods/consignment.	Wir sind zuversichtlich, dass Sie mit den Waren/der Lieferung zufrieden sein werden.
If you have any questions about your order, please do not hesitate to contact us.	Falls Sie Fragen bezüglich Ihrer Bestellung haben (sollten), zögern Sie bitte nicht, uns zu kontaktieren.
We look forward to hearing from you again.	Wir freuen uns darauf, noch einmal von Ihnen zu hören.

SKILLS FILE

Schwierige Texte lesen
> Beispiele und Übungen, S. 16

Wenn Sie einen Text zum Lösen einer Verständnisfrage oder einer Prüfungsaufgabe lesen, sollten Sie sich darauf konzentrieren, so schnell wie möglich die Informationen zu finden, die für die Beantwortung der Fragen nötig sind.

1. Lesen Sie den Titel, Untertitel und/oder die Einleitung sorgfältig.
2. Überfliegen (*skim*) Sie den Text, um sich einen Überblick zu verschaffen und die allgemeine Aussage des Textes herauszufinden. Lesen Sie nur den ersten und letzten Abschnitt ganz sowie jeweils den ersten Satz in jedem verbleibenden Abschnitt.
3. Nachdem Sie den Text überflogen haben, lesen Sie nun die Verständnisfragen sorgfältig. Suchen Sie nach Schlüsselwörtern in den Verständnisfragen.
4. Lesen Sie den Text sorgfältig und haben Sie dabei immer die Fragen im Hinterkopf. Die Informationen können jederzeit im Text auftauchen. In diesem Fall könnten Sie einige der Fragen bereits zu diesem Zeitpunkt beanworten.
5. Nachdem Sie mit dem Lesen fertig sind, durchsuchen Sie schnell (*scan*) den Text, um diesen gezielt auf Antworten zu durchsuchen, die Sie während des Lesens nicht entdeckt haben.

Mit unbekannten Wörtern umgehen
> Beispiele und Übungen, S. 28

Mit unbekannten Wörtern umgehen zu können ist eine sehr wichtige Kompetenz. Wenn Sie einen Text lesen, werden Sie sicherlich auf Wörter stoßen, die Sie nicht kennen. Das ist jedoch kein Grund, in Panik zu geraten. Man muss nicht jedes einzelne Wort kennen, um den ganzen Text zu verstehen. Verbringen Sie nicht lange damit, einen Satz wieder und wieder zu lesen, weil Sie ein bestimmtes Wort nicht verstehen. Denken Sie über die allgemeine Aussage des Satzes nach und stellen Sie eine Vermutung an, welche Bedeutung das Wort haben könnte.

1. Oft können Sie die Bedeutung eines Wortes aus den umliegenden Wörtern erschließen.
2. Sie können einen Teil des Wortes identifizieren. Betrachten Sie das Präfix (erster Teil eines zusammengesetzten Wortes) oder das Suffix (letzter Teil eines zusammengesetzten Wortes) und überlegen Sie, ob Sie es verstehen.
3. Sie können ein Wort als Bestandteil einer Wendung identifizieren.
4. Das Wort oder die Wendung könnte im Text erklärt sein. Wenn ein Ausdruck ungewöhnlich, aber wichtig für die übergeordnete Bedeutung ist, steht die Erklärung häufig im Text.
5. Sie wissen wahrscheinlich, ob das Wort ein Substantiv, Verb, Adjektiv oder Adverb ist. Dieses Wissen kann Ihnen helfen, die übergeordnete Bedeutung des Satzes zu verstehen.
6. Wenn ein Wort mit einem Großbuchstaben beginnt, bezeichnet es sehr wahrscheinlich einen Eigennamen. Manchmal wird die Person oder Institution usw. näher erklärt.

Textproduktion: Umgang mit Operatoren
> Beispiele und Übungen, S. 40

In einer Prüfung kann es vorkommen, dass Sie einen Text lesen und dazu Textproduktionsaufgaben bearbeiten sollen, die Arbeitsanweisungen, sog. „Operatoren", enthalten. Es ist wichtig, sich mit diesen Begriffen vertraut zu machen und zu wissen, was bei den einzelnen Operatoren verlangt wird. Operatoren sind in drei „Anforderungsbereiche" unterteilt: I – Inhalt, II – Analyse und III – Interpretation.

> Liste der Operatoren, S. 203

1. Überfliegen Sie den Text, damit Sie einen Eindruck vom Inhalt bekommen. Lesen Sie dann die Textproduktionsaufgaben. Behalten Sie diese im Hinterkopf und lesen Sie den Text gründlich. Durchsuchen Sie danach den Text auf Informationen, die für die erste Aufgabe relevant sind.

> Schwierige Texte lesen, S. 202

2 Die Operatoren im Anforderungsbereich I untersuchen, wie gut Sie den Inhalt des Textes verstehen und wie genau und klar Sie diesen wiedergeben können. Es ist jedoch erforderlich, dass Sie Ihre eigenen Worte verwenden.

3 Wenn die Aufgabe eine längere Antwort erfordert, empfiehlt es sich, Ihre Ideen vor dem Schreiben zu organisieren und sich eine Struktur für Ihren Text zu überlegen.

> *Mindmaps und Gliederungen erstellen, S. 207*

4 Bei Operatoren im Anfordertungsbereich II müssen Sie untersuchen, wie der Autor / die Autorin den Text aufgebaut hat, um einen bestimmten Zweck zu erreichen. Der Zweck eines Textes könnte sein, zu informieren, überzeugen, beschreiben, Anweisungen zu erteilen oder ein Thema zu erörtern. Wenn Sie einen Text analysieren, sollten Sie die verwendeten Mittel und deren Wirkung verknüpfen und die einzelnen Aspekte mit Beispielen aus dem Text stützen.

5 Operatoren aus den Anforderungsbereichen I und II verlangen sachliche Antworten. Ihre persönliche Meinung über den Text sollten Sie nicht mit hineinbringen.

6 Bei Operatoren im Anforderungsbereich III müssen Sie „zwischen den Zeilen lesen" und sowohl die explizite als auch die implizite Bedeutung oder Absicht erklären. Oft kann es auch vorkommen, dass Sie Vor- und Nachteile aufzeigen und eine persönliche Beurteilung geben müssen.

> *Einen Aufsatz oder eine Stellungnahme schreiben, S. 208*

1. Operatoren mit Bezug auf den Inhalt

Die folgenden Operatoren fordern Sie dazu auf, sich auf die Hauptideen des Autors / der Autorin zu konzentrieren.

Operator	Deutsche Entsprechung	Was Sie machen sollen	Tipps
Summarize	zusammen-fassen	Geben Sie die Hauptideen des Textes kurz und bündig in Ihren eigenen Worten wieder. Beziehen Sie nicht Beispiele, Abbildungen oder Ihre eigene Meinung mit ein.	● Beachten Sie auch den Abschnitt über das Schreiben einer Zusammenfassung. > *Eine Stellungnahme schreiben, S. 208*
Outline	darstellen	Beschreiben Sie die wesentlichen Sachverhalte. Sie können dabei Ihre Darstellung in zentrale und untergeordnete Punkte unterteilen.	● **Bevor Sie zu schreiben beginnen:** Sammeln Sie Ihre Ideen in einem Flussdiagramm (wenn die Fragestellung eine Entwicklung oder einen Prozess einbezieht) oder in einer Mindmap (wenn es sich um einen argumentativen Text handelt). > *Mindmaps erstellen, S. 207*
Point out	aufzeigen	Beziehen Sie sich auf ausgewählte wichtige Aspekte/Ideen des Textes und zeigen Sie deren Bedeutsamkeit auf.	● **Bevor Sie zu schreiben beginnen:** Heben Sie die Passagen in dem Text mit einem Textmarker hervor.

SKILLS FILE

Say what the text is about	sagen, worum es im Text geht	Geben Sie den Inhalt kurz und in Ihren eigenen Worten wieder. Das, was Sie schreiben, kann kürzer und weniger detailgenau als eine Zusammenfassung sein.	• **Bevor Sie zu schreiben beginnen:** Lesen Sie den Text durch und machen Sie sich dann kurze Notizen zu den im Text vorkommenden Hauptideen. • **Wenn Sie am Schreiben sind:** Verwenden Sie eigene Formulierungen, indem Sie den Satzbau ändern oder Synonyme gebrauchen.

Die folgenden Operatoren werden häufig gebraucht, um zu kontrollieren, ob Sie den Text richtig verstanden haben. Sie fordern Sie dazu auf, in den Text (oder einzelne Passagen) zu schauen und Bericht über bestimmte Aspekte zu erstatten.

Operator	Deutsche Entsprechung	Was Sie machen sollen	Tipps
Describe	beschreiben	Sagen Sie, wie etwas ist, indem Sie Angaben über eine Person, Situation oder einen Gegenstand machen.	• **Bevor Sie zu schreiben beginnen:** Sammeln Sie alle Aspekte, die Sie erwähnen möchten, in einer Mindmap. • **Wenn Sie am Schreiben sind:** Verwenden Sie viele Adjektive, sodass sich der Leser / die Leserin ein klares Bild machen kann. • **Hilfreiche Redewendung:** *In the following, I shall describe …* › *Mindmaps erstellen, S. 207*
Define	bestimmen, umreißen, definieren	Beschreiben Sie eine Situation, ein Problem, die Bedeutung eines Begriffes, etc. genau.	• **Wenn Sie am Schreiben sind:** Seien Sie so präzise wie möglich. Benennen Sie den Begriff, der definiert werden soll, und geben Sie an, welcher Gruppe er zuzuordnen ist. Legen Sie die besonderen Charakteristika des Begriffes dar.
Say/State/ Explain why … or State the reasons for …	sagen / angeben / erklären, warum … die Gründe angeben für …	Erklären Sie, warum jemand etwas getan hat oder warum etwas geschehen ist.	• **Bevor Sie zu schreiben beginnen:** Machen Sie eine Liste mit allen Gründen auf einem Blatt Papier. • **Hilfreiche Redewendungen:** *To state the reasons for …, one has to look at…; The text gives a number of reasons why …; because / as a result / therefore / consequently / for this reason*

204

| Find evidence in the text to show ... | Belege im Text finden für ... | Suchen Sie nach Tatsachen, Gegenständen oder Anzeichen, um zu zeigen, dass etwas wahr ist. | • **Bevor Sie zu schreiben beginnen:** Heben Sie alle relevanten Textpassagen mit einem Marker hervor. |

2. Operatoren zum Vergleich oder der Gliederung von im Text vorkommenden Themenaspekten

Die folgenden Operatoren kommen in Prüfungen häufig zum Einsatz und erfordern eine sehr exakte Antwort.

Operator	Deutsche Entsprechung	Was Sie machen sollen	Tipps
Compare	vergleichen	Beschreiben Sie die Ähnlichkeiten und Unterschiede zwischen zwei Sachen / Vorstellungen / Systemen, etc.	• **Bevor Sie zu schreiben beginnen:** Erstellen Sie eine Tabelle mit zwei Spalten, um einzelne Aspekte zu vergleichen.
Name the similarities and differences between ...	die Ähnlichkeiten und Unterschiede benennen		• **Hilfreiche Redewendungen:** *On the one hand, ... On the other hand, ...; The first point the author makes about ... is that ... . However, the text goes on to say that ...; both of ... / neither of ...*
Contrast	gegenüberstellen	Zeigen Sie die Unterschiede zwischen zwei Sachen / Vorstellungen / Systemen, etc. auf.	
Point out	beschreiben	Stellen Sie auf sachliche Art und Weise die Vor- und Nachteile von etwas, wie sie im Text präsentiert werden, dar.	
Discuss the advantages and disadvantages of ...	die Vor- und Nachteile erörtern		

3. Operatoren zur Analyse eines Textes

Die folgenden Operatoren verlangen von Ihnen, dass Sie die eindeutigen Ideen, die im Text vorzufinden sind, erläutern, aber auch, dass Sie ‚zwischen den Zeilen lesen' und implizite Bedeutungen erklären.

Operator	Deutsche Entsprechung	Was Sie machen sollen	Tipps
Analyse	analysieren	Beschreiben und erklären Sie bestimmte Aspekte im Detail.	• **Bevor Sie zu schreiben beginnen:** Achten Sie besonders auf die Gliederung Ihres Textes. Erstellen Sie eine Übersicht, in der Sie planen, was Sie in den einzelnen Paragrafen sagen möchten.
Describe and explain	beschreiben und erklären		• **Hilfreiche Redewendungen:** *This suggests ... / This seems to suggest ... / This implies ...*
Examine	untersuchen		

SKILLS FILE

Der folgende Operator fordert Sie dazu auf, sowohl explizite als auch implizite Bedeutungen zu erklären, sowie eine Bewertung vorzunehmen.

Interpret	interpretieren	Erklären Sie die genaue Bedeutung oder ‚Botschaft' einer Äußerung, eines Konzepts, einer Karikatur, etc. Beziehen Sie dabei Ihr Hintergrundwissen mit ein und nehmen Sie Stellung.	• **Hilfreiche Redewendungen:** *The author wishes to communicate ...; The author's thesis is that ...; ... can be interpreted in the following manner.*

4. Operatoren zur Stellungnahme oder Diskussion eines Aspektes

Die folgenden Operatoren fordern Sie dazu auf, selbst eine Meinung zu erörtern.

Operator	Deutsche Entsprechung	Was Sie machen sollen	Tipps
Assess	beurteilen	Geben Sie ein Urteil ab, nachdem Sie sorgfältig über etwas nachgedacht haben, und stützen Sie Ihre Meinung mit Beweisen.	• **Wenn Sie am Schreiben sind:** Erörtern Sie Ihren Fall, aber erwähnen Sie immer auch Gegenargumente, um zu zeigen, dass Sie diese ebenfalls verstehen. • **Hilfreiche Redewendungen:** Wendungen zur Meinungsäußerung, z. B. *It seems to me that ...; considering these arguments; I agree that ...* › *Eine Stellungnahme schreiben, S. 208*
Evaluate	einschätzen, bewerten		
Comment on	Stellung nehmen zu		

Der folgende Operator erfordert von Ihnen Objektivität.

Discuss	erörtern	Wägen Sie beide Seiten eines Themas ab, indem Sie Gründe nennen, die für und gegen etwas sprechen.	• **Bevor Sie zu schreiben beginnen:** Rufen Sie sich in Erinnerung, dass *discuss* bedeutet, dass Sie beide Seiten eines Themas betrachten. Es ist nützlich, Ihre Ideen erst zu strukturieren, z. B. mithilfe einer Mindmap oder einer Übersicht. • **Hilfreiche Redewendungen:** *On the one hand, ... On the other hand, ...; While it is true that ..., one can also say that ...* › *Mindmaps erstellen, S. 207* › *Eine Stellungnahme schreiben, S. 208*

Skills file

Mit Hör-/Sehverstehensaufgaben umgehen

> *Beispiele und Übungen, S. 52*

Üblicherweise werden Hörverstehensaufgaben oder Videos zweimal abgespielt. Der erste Durchgang ist dazu bestimmt, eine allgemeine Vorstellung vom Inhalt zu bekommen oder die Kernaussage zu verstehen. Beim zweiten Hören/Sehen sollten Sie sich mehr auf bestimmte Details konzentrieren.

Vor dem ersten Hören/Sehen:

1   Der Titel, das Thema und der Inhalt können Ihnen einen Hinweis über den zu erwartenden Wortschatz geben.
2   Lesen Sie die Aufgabe sorgfältig und halten Sie nach Schlüsselwörtern Ausschau. Achten Sie darauf, dass Sie verstanden haben, welche Informationen Sie benötigen. Denken Sie dazu über die Fragen nach, die Ihnen gestellt werden. Was wissen Sie bereits über diese Themen? Worüber könnten die Personen sprechen?

Während des ersten Hörens/Sehens:

1   Denken Sie daran, dass es nicht notwendig ist, jedes einzelne Wort zu verstehen. Versuchen Sie, die Wörter, die Sie nicht verstehen, zu ignorieren. Nutzen Sie Ihr Allgemeinwissen, um die Bedeutung zu erschließen.   > *Mit unbekannten Wörtern umgehen, S. 202*
2   Richten Sie Ihre Aufmerksamkeit auf Fakten und Schlüsselwörter. Machen Sie sich Notizen, um Ihr Gedächtnis zu entlasten.
3   Schreiben Sie beim Hören/Sehen mit. Tragen Sie Ihre Antworten danach in den Antwortbogen ein.

Vor dem zweiten Hören/Sehen:

Lesen Sie die Fragen noch einmal. Konnten Sie alle Fragen beantworten? Wenn ja, überprüfen Sie Ihre Antworten. Wenn nicht, ermitteln Sie, auf welche Informationen Sie beim erneuten Hören/Sehen achten müssen.

Während des zweiten Hörens/Sehens:

Beantworten Sie die Fragen detaillierter und ergänzen Sie fehlende Informationen.

Der Vorteil bei einem Video ist, dass Ihnen zusätzlich die Bilder helfen. Körpersprache, Mimik, Gestik und der Schauplatz können Ihnen Hinweise auf die Handlung geben.

Mindmaps und Gliederungen erstellen

> *Beispiele und Übungen, S. 76*

Bevor Sie Texte jeglicher Art verfassen, sollten Sie Inhalt und Struktur Ihres Textes vorbereiten. Mindmaps eignen sich, um schnell viele Ideen niederzuschreiben (Brainstorming) und diese gleichzeitig zu strukturieren. Mithilfe einer Grobgliederung teilen Sie das, was Sie schreiben möchten, in mehrere Sinnabschnitte auf. Die einzelnen Gliederungspunkte helfen, einen Text inhaltlich zu strukturieren und somit übersichtlicher zu machen.

1   Schreiben Sie das Thema in die Mitte eines Blatt Papiers.
2   Notieren Sie die wichtigsten Gedanken zu diesem Thema ringsherum und verbinden Sie diese jeweils mit dem Hauptthema durch zweigartige Linien. Die Begriffe dieser Verästelungen können die Grundlage für die einzelnen Paragraphen Ihres Textes darstellen.
3   Fügen Sie jedem Unterbegriff weitere Wörter und Gedanken hinzu. Das ist das Gerüst, das Sie benötigen, um Ihre Ideen auszuarbeiten.
4   Verwenden Sie diese Gedanken-Landkarte als Grundlage für das, was Sie schreiben wollen.

SKILLS FILE

Einen Aufsatz oder eine Stellungnahme schreiben
> *Beispiele und Übungen, S. 88*

Textproduktionsaufgaben fordern Sie heraus, nicht nur grammatikalisch korrektes, sondern auch gut strukturiertes und klares Englisch zu gebrauchen. Bei den meisten Aufgaben zur Textproduktion sollen Sie objektiv über ein Thema schreiben, ohne Ihre Meinung zu äußern. Wenn eine Aufgabe jedoch den Operator *„comment"* enthält, ist Ihre eigene Meinung, eine Beurteilung oder eine Erörterung erforderlich.   > *Textproduktion: Umgang mit Operatoren, S. 202*

Bevor Sie beginnen:
1. Lesen Sie sich die Aufgabe mehrmals durch und vergewissern Sie sich, was gefordert ist.
   - Um einen Aufsatz zu schreiben, müssen Sie Argumente finden, die diese Aussage sowohl stützen als auch bestreiten.
   - Wenn Sie eine Stellungnahme schreiben, müssen Sie Ihre eigene Meinung äußern und diese auch untermauern.
2. Brainstorming: Schreiben Sie alle Gedanken auf, die Ihnen in den Sinn kommen, wenn Sie über das Thema nachdenken, und ordnen Sie diese in einer Struktur an. Grobgliederungen und Mindmaps eignen sich dafür sehr gut.   > *Mindmaps und Gliederungen erstellen, S. 207*

Den Aufsatz oder die Stellungnahme schreiben:
3. Schreiben Sie einen Einleitungssatz, der das Thema/Problem und die darauf zurückzuführende Situation darstellt. Beschreiben Sie dann das Thema mit anderen Worten und äußern Sie Ihre Meinung. Geben Sie Ihren Lesern abschließend einen Überblick Ihrer Argumente, die Sie anführen wollen.
4. Schreiben Sie nun den Hauptteil Ihres Aufsatzes. Behandeln Sie jedes Argument in einem eigenen Abschnitt. Stützen Sie Ihre Argumente mit Fakten und Beispielen. Stellen Sie sicher, dass Ihre Argumente logisch und leicht nachvollziehbar sind. Verwenden Sie Wörter und Wendungen, die die Struktur Ihres Textes klarer machen.
5. Schreiben Sie in der Schlussfolgerung eine Zusammenfassung dessen, was Sie bereits geschrieben haben. Führen Sie hier keine neuen Argumente ein. Unterstreichen Sie Ihren Standpunkt kurz und knapp in einem Schlusssatz. Dieser sollte in einer Stellungnahme Ihre eigene Meinung widerspiegeln.

Das Geschriebene bearbeiten:
6. Überprüfen Sie Ihren Entwurf auf Rechtschreib- und Grammatikfehler hin. Achten Sie besonders auf mögliche Fehler bei der Wortstellung.
7. Vorsicht vor „falschen Freunden" – das sind englische Wörter, die deutschen Wörtern ähnlich sind, aber etwas anderes bedeuten.
8. Überlegen Sie, ob Sie Ihren Text verbessern können, indem Sie abwechslungsreicheres Vokabular verwenden.

Einen Text zusammenfassen
> *Beispiele und Übungen, S. 64*

Die Kompetenz, einen Text zusammenzufassen, ist wichtig, um einen Text vollständig zu verstehen, und um einen Text auf seine wesentlichsten Informationen zu kürzen.

1. Lesen Sie den Text gründlich. Behalten Sie während des Lesens die Kernideen im Kopf.
     > *Schwierige Texte lesen, S. 202*
2. Lesen Sie und machen Sie sich Notizen. Um sicherzugehen, welche Informationen wichtig sind, formulieren und beantworten Sie *Wh*-Fragen.
3. Nun können Sie beginnen, Ihre Zusammenfassung anhand Ihrer Notizen zu schreiben. Beachten Sie dabei folgende Grundsätze:

- Beschreiben Sie in einem oder zwei einleitenden Sätzen, um was es geht.
- Wenn Sie die Zusammenfassung schreiben, lassen Sie alles weg, was nicht von Bedeutung ist. Das sind unter anderem Beispiele, Auflistungen, Namen, Zitate und Statistiken.
- Äußern Sie nicht Ihre Meinung.
- Gebrauchen Sie Ihre eigenen Worte.
- Wenn Sie jemanden aus dem Text zitieren möchten, schreiben Sie das Zitat um, indem Sie indirekte Rede verwenden. ❯ *Reported speech, S. 217*

4 Überprüfen Sie Ihre Zusammenfassung auf Fehler, und stellen Sie sicher, dass Sie alle relevanten Aspekte des Textes mit einbezogen haben.

Präsentieren ❯ *Beispiele und Übungen, S. 100*

Die Kompetenz, eine wirkungsvolle Präsentation vor einem Publikum zu halten, ist in fast jedem Lebensstadium von Bedeutung, angefangen von der Schule bis hin zum Arbeitsleben. Nicht nur der Inhalt ist wichtig, sondern auch, wie klar und verständlich dieser vorgetragen wird.

1 Bereiten Sie Ihr Thema sorgfältig vor und stellen Sie sicher, dass die Webseiten, die Sie wählen, glaubwürdige Quellen darstellen. Überlegen Sie sich angemessene Begriffe, nach denen Sie suchen können, damit Sie nicht bloß im Netz surfen. Verlassen Sie sich nicht auf die ersten Informationen, die Sie finden. Wenn eine URL auf .org, .edu oder .gov endet, ist sie höchstwahrscheinlich eine glaubwürdige Quelle. Prüfen Sie auch den „*About us*"-Link und finden Sie heraus, wer für den Inhalt verantwortlich ist.

2 Schreiben Sie Ihre Notizen, die Sie für Ihre Präsentation verwenden, auf Englisch. Kopieren Sie nicht ganze Informationsabschnitte aus dem Internet oder Büchern. Ganz gleich, ob Sie sich bei Ihrer Präsentation mit Karteikarten behelfen oder frei sprechen, sollten Sie Ihre eigenen Worte verwenden.

3 Prüfen Sie die Korrektheit Ihrer Notizen in Bezug auf Informationsgehalt und Sprache. Am wichtigsten ist es, dass Sie alle Wörter richtig aussprechen können. Wenn Sie sich nicht sicher sind, hören Sie sich Beispiele in einem Online-Wörterbuch wie Leo oder Pons an, oder suchen Sie nach Videos, die diesen Begriff enthalten.

4 Machen Sie Ihre Präsentation für Ihre Zuhörer einprägsam mithilfe von angemessenem Anschauungsmaterial.
- Wenn Sie ein Flipchart oder Whiteboard benutzen: Überlegen Sie, wie dieses am Ende der Präsentation aussehen soll, und denken Sie daran, sauber und ordentlich zu schreiben.
- Wenn Sie Ihre Präsentation in PowerPoint erstellen: Überfrachten Sie die Folien nicht mit zu vielen Informationen. Die Aufmerksamkeit sollte auf Ihnen liegen, nicht auf den Folien.
- Auch Gegenstände können effektives Anschauungsmaterial sein. Besorgen Sie für Ihre Präsentation, wenn möglich, reale Gegenstände, wie z. B. Souvenirs, Flyer, etc.

5 Machen Sie Ihre Präsentation lebendig und interessant.
- Probieren Sie eine Live-Vorführung aus, führen Sie etwas auf, oder erzählen Sie eine Geschichte, einen Witz oder eine persönliche Anekdote.
- Überhäufen Sie Ihre Zuhörer nicht mit Zahlen und Daten. Verwenden Sie so wenige wie möglich, und entlasten Sie Ihr Publikum, indem Sie sie in schriftlicher Form zeigen.
- Interagieren Sie mit Ihrem Publikum. Halten Sie Blickkontakt und stellen Sie ab und zu Fragen.

6 Üben Sie so oft wie möglich. Üben Sie, ruhig zu stehen, ohne dabei zu zappeln oder sich unnötig zu bewegen. Bleiben Sie auf der Stelle. Üben Sie das, was Sie vortragen möchten, möglichst oft, um einen Blackout zu vermeiden. Proben Sie Ihre Präsentation zunächst vor einem Spiegel, dann vor einem imaginären Publikum und schließlich vor Freunden. Sie können gar nicht oft genug üben!

SKILLS FILE

Bilder und Cartoons beschreiben und analysieren
> *Beispiele und Übungen, S. 112*

Wenn Sie ein Bild oder einen Cartoon beschreiben, sollten Sie sich auf die Hauptaussage konzentrieren und sich nicht in Details verlieren. Vermeiden Sie „um die Ecke zu denken", sondern bleiben Sie im Rahmen des Themas.

1. Beschreiben Sie das Bild: Schauen Sie sich alle Aspekte der Abbildung an, gehen Sie jedoch nur auf die Elemente ein, die für die Aussage wichtig sind. Geben Sie an, welches Objekt Sie beschreiben, indem Sie genau bestimmen, wo es sich im Bild befindet. Verwenden Sie die Verlaufsform *present progressive*, um den Inhalt der Abbildung darzustellen. Achtung: *be, seem, look, show* und *describe* werden i. d. R. nicht in der Verlaufsform verwendet.
2. Interpretieren Sie das Bild: Wenn Sie der Meinung sind, dass die Darstellung nicht viel aussagt, erwähnen Sie dies in Ihrer Interpretation. Bezeichnen Sie die Abbildung als mehrdeutig oder unklar.
3. Stellen Sie dar, welche Auswirkung das Bild auf Sie hat: Fassen Sie die Hauptaussage zusammen und geben Sie Ihre eigene Meinung wieder.
4. Falls ein unabhängiger Text dazu einbezogen werden kann, vergleichen Sie die Abbildung mit dem Inhalt des Textes: Sagen Sie, ob das Bild die Aussage des Textes unterstützt oder ihr widerspricht.

Schaubilder und Statistiken beschreiben und analysieren
> *Beispiele und Übungen, S. 136*

In einer Prüfung kann es vorkommen, dass Sie statistische Daten beschreiben sollen, die in einer Grafik, einem Diagramm oder einer Tabelle dargestellt sind. Am besten bereiten Sie sich darauf vor, indem Sie lernen, wie Sie Ihre Beschreibung/Analyse strukturieren, und sich signifikante Wörter bzw. Phrasen zur Beschreibung und Erläuterung statistischer Daten verinnerlichen.

1. Beschreiben Sie zunächst, worum es in der Statistik geht.
2. Fassen Sie dann kurz die Entwicklung oder die Entwicklungstendenz zusammen. Wenn es mehrere Informationen gibt, vergleichen Sie diese.
3. Schreiben Sie zum Schluss eine kurze Schlussfolgerung der Informationen. Äußern Sie nicht Ihre Meinung.

An Diskussionen teilnehmen
> *Beispiele und Übungen, S. 124*

Ganz gleich, ob Sie an einer Gruppendiskussion, Debatte oder einem Rollenspiel teilnehmen, ist es wichtig, sich aktiv zu beteiligen und auf die anderen Teilnehmer/innen zu reagieren. Es ist eine gute Möglichkeit, frei zu sprechen, aber denken Sie daran, beim Thema zu bleiben.

1. Bereiten Sie sich inhaltlich vor, indem Sie sich einzelne Aspekte des Themas noch einmal ins Gedächtnis rufen und Schlüsselbegriffe auf Englisch notieren.
2. Legen Sie sich, falls genügend Zeit ist, ein paar Fragen/Antworten zum Thema zurecht.
3. Denken Sie nach, bevor Sie anfangen zu sprechen, aber versuchen Sie, spontan zu sein. Sie können sich nicht auf alles vorbereiten! Wenn Sie also mit unerwarteten Fragen konfrontiert werden, klinken Sie sich einfach in das Gespräch ein.
4. Äußern Sie Ihre Meinung und begründen Sie das, was Sie sagen.
5. Fragen Sie andere nach ihrer Meinung und ob sie Ihnen zustimmen oder nicht.
6. Stimmen Sie anderen zu und seien Sie anderer Meinung.
7. Prüfen Sie, ob Sie verstanden wurden und ob Sie die anderen verstanden haben.
8. Haben Sie keine Hemmungen, jemanden zu unterbrechen, der die Diskussion gerade beherrscht.
9. Versuchen Sie, schüchterne oder ruhige Teilnehmer/innen in das Gespräch mit einzubeziehen.

10 Verwenden Sie genügend Ausdrücke, um Interesse, Überraschung oder andere emotionale Reaktionen auszudrücken. Das macht die Diskussion lebhafter.

11 Bleiben Sie beim Thema und schweifen Sie nicht ab.

12 Gehen Sie auf Ihre/n Gesprächspartner/in ein und halten Sie Blickkontakt.

Mediation

> *Beispiele und Übungen, S. 148*

Mediation bedeutet „Vermittlung". In einer Mediationsaufgabe übermittelt man die Informationen aus fremdsprachlichen Quellen an jemanden, der die Fremdsprache nicht beherrscht. Sprachmittlung ist in der alltäglichen und beruflichen Kommunikation von großer Bedeutung. Bei einer Übersetzung muss man sich möglichst getreu nach dem Original richten; bei einer Mediation dagegen geht es lediglich darum, die wesentlichen Informationen im Originaltext zu verstehen und in die andere Sprache sinngemäß und adressantenbezogen zu übertragen. Form und Inhalt Ihrer Zusammenfassung hängen von folgenden Faktoren ab, die in der Aufgabenstellung vorgegeben werden:

- Adressat (Mitschüler/innen, Kunden einer Firma usw.)
- Medium (Info-Broschüre, E-Mail usw.)
- Ort (Schule, Arbeitsplatz, Jugendgruppe usw.)
- Zweck (Infos/Ratschläge/Argumente zu einem spezifischen Thema aufbereiten)

1 Lesen Sie den Text schnell durch, um sich einen Überblick zu verschaffen. Lesen Sie bei kleineren Verständnisproblemen einfach weiter – wahrscheinlich ergibt sich der Sinn schwieriger Stellen aus dem Kontext.

2 Lesen Sie die Aufgabenstellung genau durch – sie gibt Auskunft über den Zweck der Zusammenfassung, den Adressaten, das Ausgangs- bzw. Zielmedium sowie darüber, welche Informationen aus dem Text benötigt werden.

3 Gehen Sie den Text jetzt Absatz für Absatz durch und unterstreichen Sie die wesentlichen Sätze und Satzteile. Folgende Textstellen können bei einer Mediationsaufgabe als unwesentlich betrachtet werden: Wiederholungen (oft eingeleitet durch *in other words*, *to put it another way*), Anekdoten und Exkurse (oft eingeleitet durch *by the way*, *incidentally*) und unnötige Statistiken.

4 Fassen Sie die unterstrichenen Teile zusammen (auf Englisch bei Mediation D–E und auf Deutsch bei Mediation E–D). Übersetzen Sie nicht Wort für Wort. Beachten Sie dabei folgende Punkte:

- Vergewissern Sie sich, dass Ihr Text adressaten- und mediumgerecht ist, z. B. muss eine E-Mail an einen Freund deutlich informeller als ein Bericht für Ihren Chef sein.
- Gebrauchen Sie so weit wie möglich Ihre eigenen Worte. Verwenden Sie ein Wörterbuch, um Synonyme oder Antonyme für Wörter aus dem Originaltext zu finden und diese so umschreiben zu können.
- Nehmen Sie keine Stellung zum Text. Dies gehört in der Regel nicht zur Aufgabenstellung.
- Berücksichtigen Sie, dass eventuell bestimmte kulturelle Aspekte aus dem Originaltext in Ihrer Zusammenfassung erklärt werden müssen.
- Mit Beispielen und Zitaten müssen Sie etwas vorsichtiger umgehen. Manchmal werden Zitate nur angeführt, um eine Ausführung zu veranschaulichen, bei journalistischen Texten sind jedoch manchmal Kernaussagen des Textes in Zitaten enthalten. Auf jeden Fall sollte ein Zitat auf seine Kernaussage reduziert und in indirekte Rede umgewandelt werden. In manchen Zieltexten ist es unangebracht, den Originaltext zu zitieren. > *Reported speech, p. 217*

5 Gehen Sie alle Textteile, die Sie unterstrichen haben, nochmals durch. Vergewissern Sie sich, dass Sie sie alle in Ihrem Text berücksichtigt haben.

6 Prüfen Sie: Ist der Aufbau klar? Sind die Sätze vollständig? Ist die Rechtschreibung korrekt?

GRAMMAR SUMMARY

The simple present

1 I **go** to meetings twice a week.
2 We **live** in Bavaria.
3 Mr Brown **teaches** us English every day.
4 I **don't like** team meetings.
5 **Does** he **like** travelling?

- Man gebraucht das **simple present** für regelmäßige, sich wiederholende Ereignisse oder Handlungen (1, 3) und für Dauerzustände (2, 4, 5).
- Mit Ausnahme der 3. Person Singular (*he, she, it*) hat das **simple present** dieselbe Form wie der Infinitiv (1, 2).
  ❗ Die **3. Person Singular** endet auf *-(e)s* (3).
- Die **Verneinung** und **Fragen** werden mit der entsprechenden Form von *to do* gebildet (4, 5).

Das **simple present** wird häufig mit den folgenden **Zeitangaben** benutzt:

- *always, never, often, rarely, seldom, sometimes*
- *generally, mostly, normally, regularly, usually*
- *every day/week/month/…, every morning/afternoon/…*
- *on Mondays/Tuesdays/…, on weekdays*
- *in (the) summer/winter/…*
- *at Christmas/Easter, at weekends*

The present progressive

1 I**'m calling** to say that Ben is ill.
2 He**'s working** from home today.
3 The computer **isn't working**.
4 **Are** you **eating** lunch?

- Man benutzt das **present progressive** (auch **present continuous** genannt) für Vorgänge oder Handlungen, die im Moment des Sprechens oder Schreibens passieren und noch nicht abgeschlossen sind (1, 3, 4).
- Es wird auch für vorübergehende Situationen gebraucht (2).
- Das **present progressive** wird mit dem Präsens von *to be* und der *-ing-*Form des Vollverbs gebildet.
- Die **Verneinung** wird mit *not/n't* gebildet (3).
- Fragen werden durch Umstellung gebildet (4).

Das **present progressive** wird oft mit den folgenden **Zeitangaben** benutzt:

at the moment, at present, now, this week/month, currently

❗ Diese Verben bilden normalerweise **keine progressive form**:

be, believe, doubt, feel (meinen)*, hate, hear, imagine, know, like/dislike, love, mean, notice, prefer, realize, recognize, remember, see* (begreifen)*, seem, suppose, think* (meinen)*, understand, want, wish*

212

The simple past

1 We **wanted** to go to the USA last year.
2 She **went** on a training course in London.
3 Jasmin **did not enjoy** her holiday in Rimini last summer.
4 Where **did** you **go** last year?

- Man benutzt das **simple past**, um über Vergangenes zu berichten.
- Das **simple past** wird auch gebraucht, wenn man sagen will, **wann** etwas geschehen ist (1, 3, 4).
- Bei **regelmäßigen** Verben wird das **simple past** durch das Anhängen von -ed an den Infinitiv gebildet (1).
  ⚠ Die unregelmäßigen Verben haben eine Sonderform (2), die man sich merken – auswendig lernen! – muss.   ❯ *Irregular Verbs, p. 294*
- Man bildet die **Verneinung** und **Fragen** mit did/didn't (3, 4).

Das **simple past** wird häufig mit den folgenden **Zeitangaben** benutzt:

- *yesterday, the day before yesterday, the week/month/… before last*
- *last night/week/month/summer/December/Easter/…*
- *two/three/… hours/days/years/… ago*
- *in 2005 / in the 20th century …*
- *at that time, in those days*

The past progressive

1 The boss **was talking** to Heather **throughout the presentation**.
2 The carers **were starting** their shifts when a fire alarm (suddenly) **rang**.
3 I **wasn't doing** anything particular when he **arrived**.
4 **Were** you **having** breakfast when I **phoned**?

- Wenn man ausdrücken möchte, dass eine Handlung zu einem bestimmten Zeitpunkt oder während eines bestimmten Zeitraumes in der Vergangenheit **im Gange** war, benutzt man das **past progressive** (auch **past continuous** genannt) (1).
- Das **past progressive** wird auch benutzt, um zu verdeutlichen, dass eine Handlung im Gange war, als ein neues Ereignis (plötzlich) eintrat (2–4).
- Man bildet das **past progressive** mit was/were und der -ing-Form des Vollverbs (1).
- Die **Verneinung** wird mit was not / wasn't bzw. were not / weren't gebildet (3).
- **Fragen** bildet man durch Umstellung (4).
  ⚠ Einige Verben haben normalerweise keine progressive form (siehe die Liste unter **present progressive**).

GRAMMAR SUMMARY

The present perfect

1 I**'ve bought** a new computer.
2 I **haven't seen** the new care home yet.
3 How long **have** you **owned** a laptop?
4 We**'ve had** snow **for** two weeks.
5 She**'s been** ill since December.

- Wenn man ausdrücken will, dass etwas geschehen ist, ohne dass der genaue Zeitpunkt des Ereignisses wichtig ist, wird das **present perfect** benutzt (1, 2).
- Man gebraucht das **present perfect** auch, um zu sagen, seit wann oder wie lange ein Zustand oder eine Handlung schon andauert (3–5). Dafür wird sehr oft *for* bzw. *since* verwendet. (Im Deutschen steht dafür oft „seit" plus Gegenwart.)
- Das **present perfect** wird mit *have/has* und der 3. Form des Vollverbs gebildet (1, 4, 5).
  ❗ Die unregelmäßigen Verben haben eine Sonderform (1, 2, 4, 5), die man auswendig lernen muss. ▸ *Irregular Verbs, p. 294*
- Die **Verneinung** wird durch das Einfügen von *not/n't* nach *have/has* gebildet (2).
- **Fragen** bildet man durch Umstellung (3).

Das **present perfect** wird oft mit den folgenden Zeitangaben benutzt:

- *already, still (not), (not) yet*
- *(not) ever, just, lately, never, recently*
- *so far this week/month/…, till/until now*

The present perfect progressive

1 I**'ve been learning** English since I was ten.
2 They **haven't been speaking** to each other lately.
3 **Has** he **been planning** the meeting for long?

- Das **present perfect progressive** (auch **present perfect continuous** genannt) benutzt man für Handlungen und Vorgänge, die in der Vergangenheit begonnen haben und zum Zeitpunkt des Sprechens bzw. Schreibens noch nicht beendet sind.
- Das **present perfect progressive** wird mit *have/has been* und der *-ing*-Form des Vollverbs gebildet (1).
- Die **Verneinung** bildet man durch das Einfügen von *not/n't* unmittelbar nach *have/has* (2).
- Fragen werden durch Umstellung gebildet (3).
  ❗ Einige Verben haben normalerweise **keine progressive form** (siehe die Liste unter **present progressive**, S. 220).

The past perfect

1 Laura couldn't pay. She **had forgotten** her purse.
2 Nina **had** already **left** the coffee bar by the time I arrived.
3 When I visited John in hospital, he **had been** there for ten days.

- Mit Hilfe des **past perfect** drückt man aus, dass zwei Handlungen oder Vorgänge in der Vergangenheit aufeinander folgten (1, 2). Die Handlung, die zeitlich vorranging, steht im **past perfect**.

- Das **past perfect** wird auch verwendet, um auszudrücken, dass ein Zustand vor einem Zeitpunkt der Vergangenheit begann und zu diesem Zeitpunkt noch andauerte (3).
  ❗ Wenn zwei oder mehrere kurze Handlungen in der Vergangenheit direkt aufeinander folgen, wird für alle Handlungen das **simple past** verwendet:
  *The cat **ran** out when Joanne **opened** the door.*

The past perfect progressive

1   Rod **had been preparing** for his interview for three weeks when he got another job offer.
2   When I found Mary, I could see that she **had been crying**.

- Das **past perfect progressive** (auch **past perfect continuous** genannt) wird verwendet, wenn man ausdrücken will, dass eine Handlung oder ein Vorgang vor einem Zeitpunkt in der Vergangenheit begonnen hatte und bis (oder fast bis) zu diesem Zeitpunkt andauerte.

The future

A will-future

1   In the future people **will use** public transport more often.
2   We can only hope that everyone **will accept** this shift in attitudes.
3   You've forgotten your purse? Don't worry. I'**ll lend** you some money.
4   Ms Smith **will not be** at the meeting this afternoon.
5   I **won't come** either.
6   **Will** he **get** the job?

- Das **will-future** benutzt man, um Vorhersagen zu machen (1) oder Vermutungen über die Zukunft zu äußern (2).
- Man benutzt es auch, wenn man sich spontan zu etwas entschließt, Angebote oder Versprechen macht (3).
- Das **will-future** wird mit *will* + Infinitiv des Vollverbs gebildet. Es hat für alle Personen die gleiche Form (1–3).
- Die **Verneinung** bildet man durch das Einfügen von not unmittelbar nach *will* (4).
  Im gesprochenen Englisch sagt man häufig won't (5).
- **Fragen** werden durch Umstellung gebildet (6).

Das **will-future** kommt häufig mit den folgenden einleitenden Verben und Ausdrücken vor:

- *believe, expect, forecast, hope, imagine, suppose, think*
- *It's clear/obvious that …, There's no doubt that …*

B going to-future

1   Look at these clouds. It'**s going to rain** soon.
2   This time I'**m going to get** good marks in the class test.
3   Tom **isn't going to work** at the club any more.
4   When **are** you **going to take** your driving test?

- Das **going to-future** benutzt man für Ereignisse und Situationen, die nach Meinung des Sprechers bald eintreten werden (weil es bereits Anzeichen dafür gibt) (1).
- Es wird auch für Pläne und Absichten gebraucht (2).
- Das **going to-future** wird mit *am/is/are* + *going to* + Infinitiv gebildet (1, 2).

GRAMMAR SUMMARY

- Die **Verneinung** bildet man durch das Einfügen von *not*/*n't* unmittelbar nach *am*/*is*/*are* (3).
- **Fragen** werden durch Umstellung gebildet (4).

  ❗ Auch wenn in vielen Situationen sowohl das **will-future** als auch das **going to-future** ohne Unterschiede in der Bedeutung verwendet werden kann, ist es für Lernende ratsam, sich nach den oben angegebenen Gebrauchsmöglichkeiten zu richten.

C The present progressive / The simple present

1 We**'re leaving** the house at 10.30.
2 The bus **goes** at 11 o'clock.

- Man kann das **present progressive** auch **mit einer Zeitbestimmung der Zukunft** (*at 10.30, this afternoon, on Sunday*) für bereits feststehende Pläne und Verabredungen verwenden (1).
- Genau wie im Deutschen wird auch im Englischen das **simple present mit einer Zeitangabe** benutzt, um fest terminierte Vorgänge (Fahrpläne, Stundenpläne, Programme usw.) anzugeben (2).

Modal auxiliary verbs

1 He **can speak** several languages.
2 You **must accept** your new situation.
3 We **can't go** to work today.
4 **May** I **interrupt** you?

- Um zu sagen, was geschehen kann, muss, darf, soll usw., benutzt man ein modales Hilfsverb in Verbindung mit einem Vollverb (1–4).
- Modale Hilfsverben – nicht jedoch die Ersatzverben (siehe unten) – haben bei allen Personen immer die gleiche Form, einschließlich der 3. Person Singular (keine -s-Endung) (1, 2).

  ❗ Wenn man *must* verneint, ändert sich die Bedeutung.
  – I **mustn't** miss that film ⟶ Ich darf den Film nicht verpassen.
  "Nicht müssen" heißt *not have to*, z. B. *I don't habe to go to school today. It's Sunday.*

- Die **Verneinung** wird durch das Einfügen von *not*/*n't* unmittelbar nach dem Hilfsverb gebildet (3).
- **Fragen** bildet man durch Umstellung (4).
- Abgesehen von *could* kann man modale Hilfsverben nur im Präsens und – mit einer geeigneten Zeitangabe – mit zukünftiger Bedeutung benutzen, zum Beispiel:
  – You **can go** home now. (Präsens)
     You **can go** home an hour early tomorrow. (Futur)
  – I **must write** these letters now. (Präsens)
     I **must write** a long report next week. (Futur)

  ❗ Um andere Zeitformen bei modalen Hilfsverben zu bilden oder um u. a. die Bedeutung (auch im Präsens) deutlich zu machen, werden Ersatzwerben eingesetzt.

  must   The provider **had to block** access to the internet last December.
         I really **must write** to Jill. I'll do it now. (Zwang konnt vom Sprecher)
         I **have to go** to work now. (Zwang kommt von außen)
  can   I **couldn't drive** my boyfriend's car yesterday. The battery was flat. (Fähigkeit)
         We **couldn't leave** work early yesterday. There was too much to do. (Erlaubnis).
         I **wasn't able to drive** my boyfriend's car yesterday. (Fähigkeit)
         We **weren't allowed to leave** work early yesterday. (Erlaubnis)

Übersicht der modalen Hilfsverben nach Funktion

Funktion	Modale(s) Hilfsverb(en)	
Fähigkeit	He **can** speak several languages.	
	The first satellites **could** only transmit sound.	
Möglichkeit	With your qualifications you **could** work abroad.	
	The boss **may** come in at any moment.	
	He **might** ask you what you are doing.	
Bitte	**Can** I have a word with Ms Sims, please?	(neutral)
	Could I speak to Ms Sims, please?	(höflich)
	May I interrupt you?	(betont höflich)
	Might I ask you a personal question?	(äußerst höflich)
Erlaubnis	You **can** go in now.	(neutral)
	The boss is free. You **may** go in now.	(gefällig)
Verbot	We **mustn't** be late for work tomorrow.	
Pflicht	You **must** wear a white tunic when working in the hospital.	
Fehlen eines Zwangs	Most therapists **needn't** work on Sundays.	
	You **don't have to** eat the food if you don't like it.	
Empfehlung	You **should** get better qualifications.	(neutral)
	You **ought to** get better qualifications.	(betont)
	You **must** get better qualifications.	(streng)

Reported speech

A Aussagesätze

1   Some people **claim** that 'servant' robots **are putting** people out of work.
2   The speaker **reminded** his audience that there **were** some jobs robots **couldn't do**.

- Wenn man einem Dritten berichten möchte, was während eines Gespräches gesagt wurde, benutzt man die **indirekte Rede**.
- Bei Verwendung der indirekten Rede benutzt man ein einleitendes Verb wie *claim*, *say*, *remind*, *answer*, *think*, *mention* usw., um zu verdeutlichen, dass eine Äußerung wiedergegeben wird.
  Steht das einleitende Verb in der Vergangenheit – also *said*, *answered*, *mentioned* usw. –, dann verschieben sich die Zeiten wie folgt:

direkte Rede		indirekte Rede
simple present	→	simple past
she works hard		she worked hard
present progressive	→	past progressive
she is working hard		she was working hard
simple past	→	past perfect
she worked hard		she had worked hard
past progressive	→	past perfect progressive
she was working hard		she had been working hard
present perfect	→	past perfect
she has worked hard		she had worked hard

GRAMMAR SUMMARY

present perfect progressive she has been working hard	→	**past perfect progressive** she had been working hard
past perfect she had worked hard		(keine Verschiebung) –
past perfect progressive she had been working hard		(keine Verschiebung) –
will she will work hard	→	**would** she would work hard
am/is/are going to she is going to work hard	→	**was/were going to** she was going to work hard
would/might etc. she would work hard		(keine Verschiebung) –
would have/might have etc. she had been working hard		(keine Verschiebung) –

❗ Die modalen Hilfsverben werden folgendermaßen verschoben:

Modalverb	Bedeutung	indirekte Rede
can	Fähigkeit	could, was/were able to
can	Erlaubnis	was/were allowed to
may	Möglichkeit	might
may	Erlaubnis	was/were allowed to
must	Pflicht	had to
mustn't	Verbot	was/were not allowed to
needn't	freie Wahl	did not/didn't have to

● Außer wenn man über ein Gespräch berichtet, das am selben Tag stattgefunden hat, müssen fast alle **Zeit**- und einige **Ortsangaben** entsprechend der folgenden Tabelle geändert werden. (Angaben, die nicht aufgeführt sind, bleiben unverändert.)

direkte Rede		indirekte Rede
today	→	on that day
tomorrow	→	the next day
yesterday	→	the day before
the day after tomorrow	→	two days later
the day before yesterday	→	two days before
next day/Friday/week/Christmas/…	→	the following day/Friday/week/Christmas/…
last Friday/week/summer/…	→	the Friday/week/summer/… before
two years/months/weeks/… ago	→	two years/months/weeks/… before
now, at present	→	then
at the moment	→	at that moment
at this time	→	at that time
here	→	there
in this place	→	in that place
this	→	that
these	→	those

218

B Fragesätze

1 A member of the audience **asked what had led** to the widespread use of robots in hospitals.
2 She **wanted to know if/whether** her job **was endangered**.

- Bei indirekten **Fragen** unterscheidet man zwischen Fragen mit Fragewort (1) und Fragen ohne Fragewort (2).
- Bei Fragen **mit Fragewort** wird das Fragewort übernommen (1).
- Bei Fragen **ohne Fragewort** benutzt man *if* bzw. *whether* (= ob), um zu verdeutlichen, dass es sich um eine Frage handelt (2).
- Alle anderen Änderungen erfolgen wie bei den Aussagesätzen (siehe **Aussagesätze** S. 217).

C Bitten, Aufforderungen und Befehle

1 Lucy **asked the engineer to show her** the robot. (Direkte Rede: "Show me the robot, please.")
2 He **told her not to go** too close to it. (Direkte Rede: "Don't go too close to it.")

- **Bitten** werden meist durch *asked* (= bitten) (1), **Aufforderungen** und **Befehle** durch *told* (= sagen) (2) eingeleitet.
- Bei **positiven Sätzen** erscheint das Verb als *to* + Infinitiv (1).
- Bei **negativen Sätzen** wird *not* unmittelbar vor *to* gesetzt (2).

  ⚠ Die beiden Verben *to tell* und *to ask* stehen immer mit einem Objekt, das die angesprochene Person erwähnt (1, 2). Ist dies vom Kontext her nicht erkennbar, wird einfach ein passender Begriff eingesetzt:
  - *Ben said, 'Don't enter the studio when the red light is on.'*
    Ben **told everybody** *not to enter the studio when the red light was on.*

The passive

1 Measures **are being introduced** to reduce traffic pollution.
2 Pollution **is caused by** some thoughtless people.

- Ist der Verursacher einer Handlung unbekannt oder zweitrangig, benutzt man das Passiv. Im Vordergrund steht also das Ergebnis des Vorgangs (1).
- Möchte man den Verursacher doch angeben, benutzt man einen *by agent* (2).
  ⚠ Der Verursacher wird mit *by* – auf keinen Fall mit *from* – eingeleitet.
- Das Passiv wird mit einer Zeitform von *to be* und der 3. Form des Vollverbs gebildet:

Zeit	Zeitform von *to be*	3. Form
simple present	*am/is/are*	*caused*
present progressive	*am/is/are being*	*introduced*
simple past	*was/were*	*buried*
past progressive	*was/were being*	*built*
present perfect	*has/have been*	*installed*
will-future	*will be*	*blocked*
going to-future	*am/is/are going to be*	*sacked*

- Beim Gebrauch von modalen Hilfsverben wird nach folgendem Muster verfahren:

bei Aussagen	Hilfsverb + *to be* + 3. Form	*must be displayed*
bei Fragen	Hilfsverb + Subjekt + *to be* + 3. Form	*Can … be persuaded?*

GRAMMAR SUMMARY

Other passive forms

A

1. **I was told/advised** to be there early.
2. **I was allowed** to go on the trip.
3. **We were asked** to leave.

- Einige englische Verben können ein "persönliches Passiv" (*personal passive*) bilden. Bei den entsprechenden deutschen Verben geht dies nicht, z. B. Mir wurde gesagt…/Man sagte mir … und NICHT ~~Ich wurde gesagt~~ …

B

1. They gave her a book. **She was given a CD** too.
2. They promised him two months' holiday. **A pay rise was offered to him** too.

- Verben wie *give*, *promise*, *offer*, *show* haben im Aktiv gewöhnlich zwei Objekte nach sich: ein indirektes und ein direktes Objekt.
- Meist wird als Subjekt das persönliche Passiv verwendet (1).
- Seltener verwendet man ein Sachsubjekt (2).

C

1. People say that he is ill. **He is said to be ill.**
2. Everybody thinks he has cancer. **It is thought that he has cancer.**

- Von den Verben des Sagens und Denkens (z. B. *believe*, *say*, *think*) können im Englischen zwei Passivkonstruktionen gebildet werden.
- Das persönliche Passiv besteht aus Subjekt + Passivform + *to*-Infinitiv (1).
- Das unpersönliche Passiv besteht aus *it* + Passivform + *that*-Satz (2).

***If*-sentences**

1. If I **go** by bus, I**'ll (= I will) be** late.
2. If I **had** a car, I**'d (= I would) be** on time.
3. If I **had won** the lottery, I **would have bought** a car.
4. I **would have been** very happy if I **had won** the lottery.
5. If we **knew** how to cook, we **would have invited** our friends to dinner last week.
6. If people **drink** too much, they **have** a headache the next day.

- Ein **Konditionalsatz** besteht aus zwei Teilen; dem ***if*-Teil** und dem **Hauptteil**. Der ***if*-Teil** drückt eine **Bedingung** aus, der **Hauptteil** eine **Folge**.
- Bei Konditionalsätzen kommen folgende Zeitmuster am häufigsten vor:

  Typ I   *If* + simple present   + *will*-Futur (1)
  Typ II   *If* + simple past   + *would* + Infinitiv (2)
  Typ III   *If* + past perfect   + *would have* + 3. Form des Verbs (3)

- Der *if*-Teil kann hinter dem Hauptteil stehen. In diesem Fall steht kein Komma dazwischen (4).
- Es gibt auch Mischformen wie z. B. Typ II + Typ III (5).
- Wenn man ausdrücken will, dass auf eine bestimmte Handlung immer ein bestimmtes Ergebnis folgt, benutzt man in beiden Satzteilen das *simple present* (Typ 0) (6).

- *if*-Sätze werden gemäß der **Wahrscheinlichkeit** der zu erwartenden Folge eingesetzt:
  Typ I: Folge (fast) sicher.
  *If we **invest in** new technology, a lot of people **will lose** their jobs.*
  D. h. viele Leute werden (vermutlich) ihre Stellen verlieren, da wir (sehr wahrscheinlich) in die neue Technologie investieren werden.
  Typ II: Folge theoretisch möglich, aber kaum unwahrscheinlich.
  *If we **invested in** new technology, a lot of people **would lose** their jobs.*
  D. h. es ist nicht zu erwarten, dass viele Leute ihre Stellen verlieren werden, da wir (wahrschein-lich) nicht in die neue Technologie investieren werden.
  Typ III: Folge unmöglich, da die Bedingung nicht erfüllt wurde und bereits in der Vergangenheit liegt.
  *If we **had invested in** new technology, a lot of people **would have lost** their jobs.*
  D. h. der Sprecher weiß schon, dass keiner den Job verloren hat, da wir in die neue Technologie nicht investiert haben.

Gerund/Infinitive

1   Max **enjoys visiting** his customers.
2   Can you **afford to buy** that new physiotherapy equipment?
3   Cem and Julie **continued to meet** even though they were no longer colleagues.
4   Cem and Julie **continued meeting** even though they were no longer colleagues.
5   Alison **normally likes meeting** clients, but **today** she would **prefer to stay** in the office.

- Nach einigen Verben folgt immer die *-ing*-Form **(gerund)** (1).
  Am wichtigsten sind:

  > *admit, avoid, consider, deny, enjoy, finish, give up, imagine, mention, (not) mind* (etwas/nichts dagegen haben), *miss, practise, recommend, risk, stop, suggest*

- **Nach einigen Verben** folgt immer der Infinitiv **(infinitive)** (2).
  Die **wichtigsten** Verben dieser Gruppe sind:

  > *afford, choose, decide, expect, hope, manage, mean, plan, promise, refuse, want*

- ⚠ Nach den Verben *begin, continue, intend* und *start* kann der **Infinitiv** oder die **-*ing***-Form beliebig benutzt werden (3, 4).
- Einige Verben werden **je nach Bedeutung** entweder mit dem **Infinitiv** oder mit der **-*ing***-Form benutzt. Die **wichtigsten** Verben dieser Gruppe sind:

  > *like, love, hate, prefer*

- Nach *would like, would hate, would love, would prefer* steht **nur** der Infinitiv (5).

forget/remember

Die Struktur **forget/remember** + **-*ing***-Form bezieht sich auf die Vergangenheit. Sie drückt etwa die Idee „Ich werde nie vergessen …" aus.
⚠ „Vergangenheit" bezieht sich hier nicht auf forget/remember, sondern auf das nachfolgende Verb.
*I still **remember getting** my first job.*
*I'll never **forget going** to Japan last year.*

GRAMMAR SUMMARY

Die Struktur **forget/remember** + **Infinitiv** dagegen bezieht sich auf die Zukunft. Sie drückt etwa die Idee aus „Ich darf nicht vergessen, etwas zu tun" bzw. „Ich habe noch etwas zu tun, weil ich es bis jetzt vergessen habe".
*Dad, please **remember / don't forget to pick me up** from the station.*
*Oh dear. I **forgot / didn't remember to pick Sally up** from the station.*

regret
Die Struktur **regret + -ing-Form** drückt Bedauern über eine vergangene Situation bzw. einen vergangenen Vorfall aus. Häufig geht es dabei um verpasste Chancen.
*I really **regret leaving** school without any qualifications.*
*I know they will **regret buying** such a big, expensive car.*

Die Struktur **regret + Infinitiv** – fast immer mit einem Verb des Mitteilens wie *inform, say, tell* kombiniert – drückt eine schlechte Nachricht aus.
*I **regret to say** that I can't attend the meeting tomorrow.*
*We **regret to inform** you that the vacancy has now been filled.*

stop
Bedeutet **stop** „aufhören, etwas zu tun", steht das nachfolgende Verb in der **-ing-Form**.
Bedeutet **stop** aber „kurz anhalten, um etwas anderes zu tun", folgt ein Verb im **Infinitiv**.
*For heaven's sake **stop shouting** at me.*
*I'm a little late because I **stopped to give** somebody a lift.*

try
Bedeutet **try** „etwas ausprobieren", steht das nachfolgende Verb in der **-ing-Form**.
Bedeutet **try** aber „sich anstrengen, etwas zu tun", folgt ein Verb im **Infinitiv**.
*I **tried phoning** Ellie, but she wasn't at home.*
*We'**ll try to repair** your computer by the weekend.*

Adjectives and adverbs

1 John has a **new** printer.
2 He always buys **expensive** equipment.
3 My computer often crashes and is **usually very slow**.
4 We can make printouts **quickly** and **cheaply**.
5 That CD sounds **terrible**.
6 I **used to** go skiing but I **kept** falling over. I didn't **enjoy** it.

- Um **Personen** oder **Sachen** näher zu beschreiben, benutzt man **Adjektive** (1–4).
- Adjektive stehen **unmittelbar** vor Substantiven oder **unmittelbar nach** einer Form von *be* (bzw. *become* oder *seem*, die *be* ersetzen können) (3). Dies gilt auch für Adverbien der inbestimmten Häufigkeit wie *always, often, usually, sometimes, never*.
- Adjektive statt Adverbien werden bei folgenden Bedeutungen von *feel* (sich fühlen), *look* (aussehen), *sound* (sich anhören), *smell* (riechen, duften) und *taste* (schmecken) verwendet (5).
- Um einen **Tätigkeitsverb** näher zu beschreiben, setzt man ein Adverb **unmittelbar hinter das Verb** bzw. Verb + Objekt (5).
   ⚠ Im Englischen können ein Verb und sein Objekt – anders als im Deutschen – nicht durch ein Adverb getrennt werden. Also NICHT: ~~We can make quickly printouts~~. (siehe **Word order** S. 223)
- Adverbien werden auch benutzt, um **Adjektive, andere Adverbien** und **ganze Sätze** näher zu bestimmen:

*MP3 players have become **surprisingly cheap**.* (Adverb + Adjektiv)
*My fax machine prints out **terribly slowly**.* (Adverb + Adverb)
***Luckily** Gerd left a message on my mailbox.* (Satzadverb)

- Die meisten Adverbien werden durch Anhängen von *-ly* an das Adjektiv gebildet (4). Eine kleine Anzahl von Adverbien hat dieselbe Form wie Adjektive; die häufigsten sind *fast, hard, early late, long.* Deutsche Adverbien, z. B. „früher", „immer", „gern" werden häufig durch Verbkonstruktionen wiedergegeben (6).

Comparison of adjectives and adverbs

1 A hundred years ago life was **slower** and people may have been **happier**.
2 Which technological innovation is the **most/least important**?
3 Today elderly people can get about **more easily than** ever before.

- **Einsilbige** und **zweisilbige Adjektive**, die auf *-y* enden – zum Beispiel *easy, happy* und *lucky* –, werden mit *-(i)er/-(i)est* gesteigert (1).
- **Mehrsilbige Adjektive** und **Adverbien**, die auf *-ly* enden, werden mit *more/most* gesteigert (2, 3).

  ⚠ Die Adverbien, die dieselbe Form wie das entsprechende Adjektiv haben (*fast, hard, early* usw.), werden mit *-er/-est* gesteigert.
- Um Personen oder Sachen im Satz miteinander zu vergleichen, gibt es folgende Möglichkeiten:

Kein Unterschied	***as** good **as***	genau so gut wie
Unterschied	***not as** good **as***	nicht so gut wie
Unterschied	*better **than***	besser als

Word order – positions of adverbs of time, place and frequency

1 She does home visits **every week**.
2 The care home is situated in a small town **outside of Frankfurt**.
3 **Last year** we went to an Italian restaurant for our team Christmas party.
4 Paul and Emily went to **the USA last year**.
5 She **always finishes** work early on Fridays.
6 He **is never** in the office when I call.
7 I like to work at home **now and then**.
8 Gina acted **strangely at the health care fair last week**.

- Zeitangaben (Wann?) und Ortsangaben (Wo?, Wohin?) stehen in der Regel am Satzende (1, 2).
- Um die Zeit eines bestimmten Ereignisses hervorzuheben, kann man die Zeitangabe an die erste Stelle setzen (3).
- Stehen eine Zeitangabe und eine Ortsangabe zusammen am Satzende, dann gilt die Reihenfolge Ort vor Zeit (alphabetisch merken: O vor Z!) (4).
- Besteht eine Häufigkeitsangabe aus einem Wort, z. B. *always, often, sometimes*, steht sie unmittelbar vor dem Vollverb (5).
- Lautet das Vollverb *to be*, steht das Adverb direkt dahinter (6).
- Besteht die Häufigkeitsangabe aus mehreren Wörtern, z. B. *every day, now and then*, steht sie wie eine Zeitangabe am Satzende (7).
- Adverbien der Art und Weise stehen in der Regel am Satzende. Kommen noch Zeit- oder Ortsadverbien hinzu, lautet die Reihenfolge: Art und Weise – Ort – Zeit (AOZ) (8).

GRAMMAR SUMMARY

Relative clauses and contact clauses

1 Computer scientists are designing 'smart homes' **which/that** use data gathered from inhabitants.
2 East Asia is welcoming health tourists **who/that** are looking for a better quality of life in old age.
3 Tony filled in a job satisfaction questionnaire **(which/that)** he found on the internet.
4 Fred Foley is a is a young carer **whose** job involves helping the bereaved.
5 Care home employees, most **of whom** are quite young, work long hours.
6 Antibiotics are being incorrectly used for conditions **against which** they have no resistance.

- Relativsätze werden benutzt, um den Hauptsatz durch zusätzliche Informationen genauer zu bestimmen.
- Für **Sachen** benutzt man das Relativpronomen *which* bzw. *that* (1) und für Personen *who* bzw. *that* (2).
- Ist das Relativpronomen das **Objekt des Relativsatzes**, dann kann man es weglassen (3). Solche Relativsätze heißen **contact clauses**.
- Um **Besitz** bzw. **Zugehörigkeit** anzuzeigen, gebraucht man *whose* unmittelbar vor dem **Substantiv** bei Personen und Sachen (4).
- Steht eine **Präposition** vor dem **Relativpronomen**, wird *whom* für Personen und *which* für Sachen benutzt (5, 6). In solchen Fällen ist der Gebrauch von *that* nicht möglich.

Defining and non-defining relative clauses

1 The first Europeans **who** settled in Australia came from Britain.
2 Sydney, **which** is famous for its unusually designed opera house, is situated on the south-eastern coast of Australia.

- Im **ersten Beispielsatz** ist der Sinn des Hauptsatzes *The first Europeans came from Britain* ohne den Relativsatz *who settled in Australia* offensichtlich falsch bzw. unvollständig. Relativsätze dieser Art – die wesentlich für das Verständnis des gesamten Satzes sind – nennt man **defining relative clauses** (notwendige oder bestimmende Relativsätze).
- Im **zweiten Beispielsatz** ist die Aussage des Hauptsatzes *Sydney is situated on the south-eastern coast of Australia* ohne den Relativsatz völlig verständlich, weil der Relativsatz *which is famous for its unusually designed opera house* eine zusätzliche, also nebensächliche, Information enthält. Daher werden solche Relativsätze **non-defining relative clauses** (nicht notwendige oder nicht bestimmende Relativsätze) genannt.
  ⚠ Notwendige Relativsätze werden immer **ohne** trennende **Kommas** benutzt. Dies signalisiert, dass sie fester Bestandteil der Hauptaussage sind.

Participle constructions

1 A meal **costing** two pounds is very cheap.
2 The work **involved** with cooking a simple meal is minimal.
3 **Waiting** for the bus, the doctor thought about her patients.
4 **Weakened** by disease, many children die young.
5 **Having lost** so many people to AIDS, Africa needs our help more than ever.
6 **Despite facing** extreme poverty, many people haven't given up hope.
7 Donors should invest in projects that help local inhabitants become self-supporting, thereby **making** sure that the money isn't wasted.
8 AIDS represents a major challenge to sub-Saharan Africa, currently **killing** more than two million people every year.

Grammar summary

Die englische Sprache ist geprägt durch die häufige Verwendung von Partizipialkonstruktionen. Diese ermöglichen einen eleganteren Sprachfluss.

- Ein **present participle** kann Relativsätze verkürzen (*A meal that costs …*) (1).
- Auch ein **past participle** kann zur Verkürzung von Relativsätzen verwendet werden (*The work that is involved …*) (2).
- Participles werden auch verwendet, um adverbial Nebensätze zu verkürzen (3, 4).
- Auch das **perfect participle** wird verwendet (5).
- Manchmal sind Konjunktionen unerlässlich, um den logischen Zusammenhang herauszustellen (6, 7).
- Schließlich verknüpft man mit einer Partizipialkonstruktion zwei Hauptsätze zu einem einzigen Satz, und zwar ausnahmslos mittels **present participle** (8).

Countable and uncountable nouns

1 Visit our website for more **information** on our care services.　　NICHT ~~informations~~
2 Have you read the paper today? The political **news** is interesting.　　NICHT ~~news are~~
3 Where can I get some **advice**?　　NICHT ~~an advice~~
4 **Fewer people** learn French nowadays. **More people** learn Spanish than French. **Most people** learn English. **The fewest** students in Germany learn Russian.
5 We have **more bread** than butter and **less cola** than orange juice. We have brought **the least cola** and **the most bread** to the party.

- Einige wichtige **Substantive** sind **zählbar im Deutschen, nicht jedoch im Englischen**. Diese Substantive können also nicht ohne weiteres mit dem unbestimmten Artikel *a/an* oder mit einem Zahlwort benutzt werden.
  Hier ist eine Liste solcher Wörter, die Sie auswendig lernen sollten:

  > *advice, baggage, damage, data, equipment, evidence, furniture, information, knowledge, luck, luggage, machinery, news, progress, research, rubbish, work (housework, homework)*

- Um diese Substantive im Plural zu verwenden, muss *some*, *a bit of* bzw. *a piece of* hinzugefügt werden (3).
  ❶ Wenn *most* die Mehrheit allgemein bedeutet, benutzt man keinen Artikel *the*. (*Most dogs like bones*). *Most* (und auch *fewest*) kann mit oder ohne Artikel stehen, wenn es superlative Bedeutung (höchste Steigerungsstufe) hat. (*I have (the) most computer games of anybody in my class.*)

Some and any

1 **Some** teams prefer to hold regular weekly meetings.
2 They haven't got **any** women working in their organization.
3 Have you got **any** information about arrival times?
4 Can I have **some** more coffee, please?
5 Would you like **some** mineral water?
6 There's **something** I need to do but I can't remember what it is.
7 He can't find that letter **anywhere**. Maybe **somebody** took it.

- Wir verwenden *some* in **bejahten Aussagen** (1) und *any* in **verneinten Aussagen** (2) und **„echten" Fragen** (3).

GRAMMAR SUMMARY

- Drückt die Frage eine höfliche **Bitte** (4) bzw. ein **Angebot** (5) aus, worauf eine positive Antwort erwartet wird, verwenden wir ebenfalls *some*.
- Wir verwenden die Zusammensetzungen von *some* and *any* – also *somebody/someone, something, somewhere, anybody/anyone, anything* und *anywhere* – in genau derselben Art und Weise (6–7).

The definite article

1 **Sociologists** say that **violence** is increasing among young people.
2 Is **the violence** they see in **modern films** the cause of this?
3 **Most sentences** are not tough enough.
4 Nearly **half the prisoners** in **British prisons** are under 25.
5 We had **breakfast** late this morning so we came to work **by car** instead of **by bus**.

- Hat ein Substantiv eine allgemeine, uneingeschränkte Bedeutung – also „alle ohne Ausnahme" – dann steht es ohne Artikel (1, 2, 5).
- Ist die Bedeutung eines Substantives auf bestimmte Fälle eingeschränkt, benutzt man den Artikel (2, 5).
- Ferner wird der Artikel in den folgenden Fällen und Wendungen im Englischen – z. T. anders als im Deutschen – nicht gebraucht:
  – bei *most* in der Bedeutung „die meisten" (3),
  – bei öffentlichen Gebäuden im allgemeinen Sinn (4),
  – bei Mahlzeiten (6),
  – bei Verkehrsmitteln (6),
  – bei Straßennamen.
- Der Artikel wird verwendet nach *all* und *half* (4).

The indefinite article

1 Yesterday I met **a woman** who works for **a friend** of my father's.
2 We'll have to buy **a** new **computer**.
3 That's **an** interesting **idea**.
4 Jane's **an occupational therapist**? I thought she was **a nurse**.
5 My father has been **a non-smoker** all his life.
6 How much does petrol cost **a liter**?
7 We have planning meetings four times **a month**.

- Der unbestimmten Artikel a/an steht bei einer einzelnen, nicht näher bestimmten Person (1), einer Sache (2), oder einem Begriff (3).
- Anders als im Deutschen verwenden wir im Englischen den unbestimmten Artikel in folgenden Fällen:
  – bei Berufsangaben (4),
  – bei Angaben über Nationalität, Religion, Politik oder Gruppenzugehörigkeit (5),
  – bei Maß- (6), Verpackungs-, und Zeitangaben (7),
  – bei den folgenden Wendungen:

to be in a hurry	in Eile sein, es eilig haben
to come to an end	enden
to have a bath/shower/…	sich baden/duschen/…
to have a go	es ausprobieren
to have a turn at (+ -ing-Form)	an der Reihe sein, etwas zu tun
to make a noise	Lärm machen
to take a seat	Platz nehmen
for a change	zur Abwechslung
for a long/short time	lange/kurze Zeit
in a loud/quiet voice	mit lauter/ruhiger Stimme
What a pity!	Wie schade!
without a break	ohne Pause

❗ Bei *half*, *quite*, *rather* und *such* wird der unbestimmte Artikel nachgestellt:

- The meeting starts in half **an** hour.
- We had quite **a** successful year in 2005.
- Jack can be rather **an** idiot sometimes.
- We've never had such **a** busy period.

BASIC WORD LIST

Diese Liste enthält ca. 900 Grundwörter, die in **Social Pulse** als bekannt vorausgesetzt werden. Nicht aufgeführt, jedoch vorausgesetzt sind einige sehr elementare Wörter wie einfache Präpositionen, Pronomen, Farben, Zahlen, Tage, Jahreszeiten, Staaten usw. sowie internationale Wörter wie z. B. *hotel*, *restaurant*, *email*.

A

8 a.m. 8 Uhr morgens/vormittags
to **be able to** können
about um, über, ungefähr
above über, oben, oberhalb
abroad im/ins Ausland
absolute(ly) absolut, völlig
to **accept** akzeptieren, annehmen
accident Unfall
across (hin)über; quer durch
active aktiv
activity Tätigkeit, Beschäftigung
actual(ly) eigentlich, tatsächlich
to **add** hinzufügen
to **address** adressieren, anreden; Adresse, Anrede
advice Rat(schlag)
after nach
afternoon Nachmittag
afterwards nachher, danach
again wieder
against gegen
age Alter, Zeitalter
ago vor
to **agree** zustimmen, sich einigen, vereinbaren
ahead voraus, vorn
air Luft
airline Fluggesellschaft
airport Flughafen
all alle
to **be allowed to** etw dürfen
to **allow** erlauben, gestatten
almost fast, beinah
alone allein(e)
along entlang, weiter, vorwärts
already schon, bereits
also auch, außerdem
although obwohl
always immer
amazing erstaunlich, fantastisch
ambulance Krankenwagen
among unter, zwischen
amusing lustig
angry böse, zornig, ärgerlich
animal Tier
another noch eine/r/s, ein/e andere/r/s
to **answer; answer** (be)antworten; Antwort, Lösung
any irgendetwas, irgendwelche
anybody (irgend)jemand, jeder
not anymore nicht mehr

anyone (irgend)jemand, jeder
anyone jede/r
anything (irgend)etwas; alles
anyway trotzdem, sowieso
anywhere irgendwo
apartment Wohnung
apple Apfel
to **argue** sich streiten; argumentieren
arm Arm
around ungefähr, zirka; um (… herum)
to **arrive** ankommen, eintreffen
as well (as) ebenso (wie)
to **ask** fragen, bitten
at least zumindest, wenigstens
to **attack; attack** angreifen; Angriff
to **attend** teilnehmen, besuchen, absolvieren
aunt Tante
away weg, entfernt

B

back Rücken; zurück
bad(ly) schlecht
bag Tasche, Tüte
to **bake** backen
ball Ball
bank Bank
basic Grund-, Haupt-, grundsätzlich
basically im Prinzip, im Grunde
bathroom Badezimmer
to **be** sein
beach Strand
beautiful(ly) schön, herrlich
because weil, da
to **become** werden
bed Bett
bedroom Schlafzimmer
beer Bier
before vor, vorher, zuvor, bevor
to **begin** anfangen, beginnen
behind hinter, hinten
to **believe** glauben, meinen
below unter(halb), unten
best am besten, beste/r/s
better besser, bessere/r/s
between zwischen
beyond darüber hinaus
bicycle Fahrrad
big groß
bike (Fahr-, Motor-)Rad

bird Vogel
birthday Geburtstag
a bit ein wenig, etwas
board Tafel
boat Boot, Schiff
body Körper
to **book; book** buchen; Buch
to **be/get bored** sich langweilen
boring langweilig
born geboren
boss Chef/in
both beide
bottle Flasche
bottom Unterteil, Boden, unteres Ende
box Kiste, Kasten, Karton
boy Junge
boyfriend Freund
bread Brot
breakfast Frühstück
bright hell, strahlend, glänzend
brilliant glänzend, genial, super
to **bring** bringen, mitbringen
brother Bruder
to **build** (auf)bauen
building Gebäude
to **burn** (ver)brennen
bus Bus
business Geschäft(e), Unternehmen, Wirtschafts-
busy beschäftigt, verkehrsreich, besetzt
but aber, sondern
butter Butter
to **buy** kaufen
bye Tschüs

C

calendar Kalender
to **call; call** (an)rufen; Anruf
to **be called** heißen
caller Anrufer/in
can können; Dose
car Auto
card Karte
careful(ly) vorsichtig, sorgfältig
to **carry** tragen, befördern
to **catch** fangen; packen; erreichen
to **cause; cause** hervorrufen, verursachen; Ursache, Grund
central zentral
centre Mitte, Mittelpunkt, Zentrum

228

Basic word list

certain(ly) sicher(lich), gewiss, bestimmt
chair Stuhl
chance Gelegenheit, Chance
to **change; change** wechseln, (sich ver)ändern, umsteigen; Veränderung
to **chat; chat** (mit jdm) plaudern, sich unterhalten; Schwätzchen
cheap billig, preiswert
to **check** (über)prüfen, kontrollieren
cheese Käse
child, children Kind, Kinder
chocolate Schokolade
choice Wahl, Auswahl
to **choose** wählen, aussuchen
Christmas Weihnachten
city Stadt
class Klasse, Kurs, Unterricht
classmate Klassenkamerad/in
classroom Klassenzimmer, Klassenraum
to **clean; clean** putzen, säubern; sauber
clear(ly) klar, deutlich
clever(ly) klug, gescheit, raffiniert
to **climb** klettern, steigen
to **close** schließen, zumachen
clothes (pl) Kleidung, Kleider
coast Küste
cold Kälte; kalt
to **collect** (ein)sammeln; abholen
college Hochschule, Berufsschule, Universität
colour Farbe
colourful bunt, farbenfroh
to **come** kommen, geliefert werden
comfortable bequem, angenehm, komfortabel
common üblich, verbreitet, gemeinsam
to **communicate** sich verständigen, kommunizieren
communication Kommunikation, Verständigung
to **complete; complete(ly)** abschließen, ausfüllen, vervollständigen; völlig, vollständig, komplett
conference Tagung, Konferenz
context Zusammenhang, Kontext
to **continue** weitergehen, fortsetzen, weitermachen
contract Vertrag
conversation Gespräch, Unterhaltung
to **cook** kochen, braten
cool kühl, cool
to **copy; copy** kopieren, abschreiben; Kopie, Exemplar
to **correct; correct(ly)** berichtigen; richtig, genau
corridor Gang, Flur
to **cost; cost** kosten; Kosten

to **count** zählen
country Land, Staat
countryside Land(schaft), Natur
couple (Ehe-)Paar
a **couple** ein paar, einige
course Kurs, Studiengang
crazy verrückt
creative kreativ, schöpferisch
crowd Menge, Menschenmasse
cup (of) Tasse
customer Kunde/Kundin
to **cut** schneiden
to **cycle** radeln

D

daily täglich
to **dance; dance** tanzen; Tanz
danger Gefahr
dangerous gefährlich
dark dunkel
date Datum, Verabredung
daughter Tochter
day Tag
dear liebe/r
to **decide** (sich) entscheiden, beschließen, sich entschließen
decision Entscheidung, Beschluss
deep tief
to **describe** beschreiben
desert Wüste
desk Schreibtisch
detail Einzelheit, Detail, Angabe(n)
to **develop** (sich) entwickeln
development Entwicklung
dialogue Dialog
diary Tagebuch, Terminkalender
dictionary Wörterbuch
to **die** sterben
difference Unterschied
different(ly) verschieden, unterschiedlich
difficult schwierig, schwer
difficulty Schwierigkeit
dinner Abendessen
direct(ly) direkt
direction Richtung
directions: to give ~ den Weg beschreiben
to **discuss** diskutieren, besprechen, erörtern
to **do** tun, machen
doctor Arzt/Ärztin
dog Hund
door Tür
double doppelt, Doppel-
down her-/hinunter
dream: ~; to ~ träumen, Traum
to **dress** sich kleiden, sich anziehen
to **drink; drink** trinken; Getränk
to **drive** fahren
driver Fahrer/in
during während

E

each jede/r/s, jeweils
each other einander
early früh
to **earn** verdienen
east (nach) Osten, Ost
Easter Ostern
easy, easily einfach, leicht
to **eat** essen
edition Ausgabe
effect Auswirkung, Effekt
egg Ei
either or entweder … oder
either: not … ~ auch nicht, auch kein/e
else sonst (noch), andere/r/s
empty leer
to **end; end** (be)enden; Ende, Schluss
engine Motor
to **enjoy** genießen, gefallen
to **enjoy doing sth** etw gern tun
enough genug
even sogar, noch
evening Abend
event Ereignis, Veranstaltung
ever je(mals)
every jede/r/s
everybody jede/r
everyone jede/r
everything alles
everywhere überall(hin)
exact(ly) genau, exakt
exam Prüfung
example Beispiel
for example zum Beispiel
excellent ausgezeichnet, hervorragend
except außer
excited (freudig) aufgeregt
exciting aufregend, spannend
to **excuse; excuse** entschuldigen; Ausrede
to **exercise; exercise** üben, trainieren; Übung, Training
exercise book (Schul-)Heft
to **expect** erwarten
expensive teuer
to **explain** erklären, erläutern
expression Ausdruck
extreme(ly) äußerst, extrem
eye Auge

F

face Gesicht
fact Tatsache
factory Fabrik
fair Messe; fair, gerecht
fairly ziemlich
to **fall; fall** sinken, fallen; Rückgang
false falsch

BASIC WORD LIST

family Familie
famous berühmt
fantastic fantastisch, großartig
far weit
farm Bauernhof
farm: arm arm
farmer Bauer/Bäuerin
fascinating faszinierend
fast schnell
fat dick
father Vater
favourite Lieblings-, Liebling
to **feel** (sich) fühlen, glauben
feeling Gefühl, Ansicht
few wenige
a few einige, ein paar
field Feld
to **fight; fight** (be)kämpfen; Kampf
to **file; file** ablegen; Ordner, Akte
to **fill** (aus-, be-)füllen; übernehmen; erledigen
to **fill in** ausfüllen
final letzte/r/s, End-
finally endlich, schließlich, zuletzt
financial(ly) finanziell
to **find (out)** (heraus)finden, feststellen
fine gut, schön, in Ordnung
finger Finger
to **finish; finish** zu Ende bringen, (be-, ab)schließen; Schluss
fire Feuer, Brand
first name Vorname
fish Fisch
flat Wohnung; flach
floor Etage
flower Blume, Blüte
to **fly** fliegen
following folgende/r/s
food Essen, Lebensmittel
foot, feet Fuß, Füße
football Fußball
to **forget** vergessen
forward vorwärts, nach vorn
free frei, umsonst
freedom Freiheit
fresh frisch
friend Freund/in
friendly freundlich
in front vorne, davor
in front of vor
fruit Obst, Frucht
full(y) voll, völlig
fun Spaß
funny lustig, seltsam
furniture Möbel
further weiter/e/s
future Zukunft, zukünftige/r/s

G

game Spiel
garage Werkstatt, Garage
garden Garten
gate Tor; Flugsteig
general(ly) allgemein, generell
to **get** bekommen, werden, gelangen
to **get on** vorankommen
to **get up** aufstehen
giant Riese; riesig
girl Mädchen
girlfriend Freundin
to **give** geben, schenken
to **give up** aufgeben, aufhören mit
glad froh
glass Glas
to **go** gehen, fahren
to **go on** weitermachen, fortfahren
good gut
goodbye auf Wiedersehen
grammar Grammatik
grandchildren Enkelkinder
great groß, großartig, toll
group Gruppe
to **grow** (an)wachsen
to **grow up** aufwachsen
guest Gast

H

hair Haar, Haare
half Hälfte, halb
ham Schinken
hand Hand
hand: on the one ~, on the other ~ einerseits, andererseits
to **happen** passieren, geschehen
happy glücklich, zufrieden
hard hart, schwer, schwierig
harmless harmlos
to **have to** müssen
head Kopf
health Gesundheit(szustand)
healthy gesund
to **hear** hören
heart Herz, Zentrum
heavy schwer
to **help; help** helfen; Hilfe
helpful hilfreich, hilfsbereit
here hier
high hoch
to **hold** halten
holiday Ferien, Urlaub, Feiertag
home zu/nach Hause, Zuhause
homework Hausaufgaben
to **hope; hope** hoffen; Hoffnung
hospital Krankenhaus
hour Stunde
house Haus
how wie
however doch, jedoch, aber; egal wie
hungry hungrig

I

I'm afraid leider
ice Eis
idea Idee, Gedanke, Vorstellung
if wenn, falls
ill krank
immediate(ly) unmittelbar, umgehend, sofort
important wichtig
to **improve** (sich) verbessern
indoors drinnen
to **inform** informieren, unterrichten
inside in, innen, hinein
to **interest; interest** interessieren; Interesse
to **be interested in** interessiert sein an, sich interessieren für
interesting interessant
to **introduce** einführen, vorstellen, bekanntmachen
introduction(s) Einleitung, Einführung, Vorstellung, Bekanntmachen
to **invite** einladen
island Insel

J

jacket Jacke, Jackett
jam Marmelade, Konfitüre
job Arbeit, Stelle, Arbeitsplatz
to **join** verbinden, beitreten, sich anschließen
journey Fahrt, Reise
just einfach, gerade

K

to **keep** bleiben, halten, behalten, aufbewahren, etw weiter tun
kids Kinder
kind Sorte; freundlich
king König
kitchen Küche
to **know** wissen, kennen
knowledge Wissen, Kenntnis

L

lady Dame
lake See
to **land; land** landen; Land
language Sprache
large groß, bedeutend
to **last; last** dauern; letzte/r/s
at last endlich
late verspätet
late spät
to **lead** führen
to **learn** lernen
to **leave** (ver-, hinter-, da)lassen, weggehen, abfahren
left links

230

Basic word list

leg Bein
to **lend** leihen
less weniger
to **let** lassen
letter Brief, Buchstabe
to **lie** liegen
life Leben
lift Aufzug
light hell, leicht; Licht
to **like; like** mögen, gern haben;
  (ähnlich) wie
line Linie, Zeile, Leitung
to **list; list** auflisten; Liste
to **listen (to)** (zu-, an)hören
little klein, wenig
a little ein bisschen
to **live** leben
lonely einsam
long lang
to **look; look** ansehen, aussehen; Blick
to **look after** sich kümmern um
to **look for** suchen
lorry Lastwagen
to **lose** verlieren
a lot (of) viel, viele
lots of viel, viele
to **love; love** lieben, sehr gern
  mögen; Liebe
lovely hübsch, nett
low niedrig
luck Glück
luckily glücklicherweise
lucky glücklich
to **be lucky** Glück haben
lunch Mittagessen
lunch break Mittagspause

M

madam gnädige Frau
magazine Zeitschrift
mail Post
main Haupt-, hauptsächliche/r/s
to **make** machen
man, men Mann, Männer
many viele
map Stadtplan, Landkarte
to **market; market** vermarkten;
  Markt
married verheiratet
Maths Mathematik
may dürfen, können
maybe vielleicht
meal Mahlzeit
to **mean** bedeuten, heißen, meinen
meaning Bedeutung, Sinn
meat Fleisch
to **meet** treffen, kennen lernen
meeting Sitzung, Besprechung,
  Konferenz
member Mitglied
message Nachricht, Botschaft
midday Mittag

middle mittlere/r/s
midnight Mitternacht
might könnte
mile Meile
milk Milch
minute Minute
mirror Spiegel
to **miss** vermissen, verpassen
missing fehlend
mistake Fehler
to **mix; mix** mischen; Mischung
model Modell, Beispiel
moment Moment, Augenblick
moment: at the ~ im Augenblick
money Geld
month Monat
more mehr
morning Morgen
most der/die/das meiste, die meisten
mostly größtenteils
mother Mutter
motorbike Motorrad
mountain Berg
mouse, pl. mice Maus
to **move** (sich) bewegen, umziehen,
  verlegen, versetzen
Ms Frau (allgemeine Anrede f. Frauen)
much viel
mum Mutti, Mama
must müssen
must not nicht dürfen

N

to **name; name** (be)nennen; Name
nature Nature
near nahe, in der Nähe von
nearly beinahe, fast
necessary notwendig, nötig
to **need; need** brauchen, benötigen;
  Bedarf, Bedürfnis
neighbour Nachbar/in
neither keines (von beiden), auch nicht
never nie(mals)
new neu
news Neuigkeit(en), Nachricht(en)
newspaper Zeitung
next nächste/r/s, danach
nice schön, nett
night Nacht
no one niemand, keiner
nobody niemand
non- Nicht-
none keine/r/s
normal(ly) normal(erweise)
north (nach) Norden, Nord
to **note; note** notieren, zur Kenntnis
  nehmen; Notiz
nothing nichts
to **notice** beachten, bemerken
now nun, jetzt
nowhere nirgends
number Zahl, (Telefon-) / Nummer

O

two o'clock zwei Uhr
obvious(ly) offensichtlich, klar,
  deutlich, natürlich
occasional(ly) gelegentlich
of course natürlich, selbst-
  verständlich
to **offer; offer** (an)bieten; Angebot
office Büro, Amt
often oft, häufig
oil Öl
old alt
once einmal; sobald
only nur, einzige/r/s
onto auf (hinauf)
to **open; open** (sich) öffnen, eröffnen;
  offen
opinion Meinung
opportunity Gelegenheit
opposite Gegenteil;
  gegenüber(liegend)
or oder
to **order; order** bestellen; Bestellung,
  Auftrag, Reihenfolge
in order to um ... zu
ordinary gewöhnlich, normal
other andere/r/s, weitere/r/s
otherwise sonst, ansonsten
ought to sollte
outside Außenseite; außerhalb von,
  draußen
over über, vorüber
to **own; own** besitzen; eigene/r/s

P

2 p.m. 2 Uhr nachmittags, 14 Uhr
8 p.m. 8 Uhr abends, 20 Uhr
page Seite
paint Farbe
pair Paar
paper Papier, Zeitung
paragraph Absatz, Abschnitt
parents Eltern
part Teil
particular bestimmt, besondere/r/s,
  speziell
particularly besonders, vor allem,
  insbesondere
partner Partner/in, Gesellschafter/in
past Vergangenheit; vorbei (an),
  hinter
path Weg, Pfad
to **pay; pay** (be)zahlen; Bezahlung,
  Gehalt
pen Stift, Kugelschreiber
pencil Bleistift
people Leute, Menschen
per cent Prozent
perfect vollkommen, perfekt
perhaps vielleicht
period Zeit(raum), Frist

BASIC WORD LIST

permanent(ly) dauerhaft, bleibend
person Person
to **phone; phone** telefonieren, anrufen; Telefon
photo Foto
phrase Ausdruck, Redewendung
to **pick up** abholen
picture Bild
piece Stück, Teil
place Stelle, Platz, Ort
to **plan; plan** planen; Plan
plane Flugzeug
planet Planet
to **play** spielen
player Spieler/in
pleasant angenehm, freundlich, nett
please bitte
pleased froh, erfreut
pleasure Vergnügen
pocket Tasche
to **point; point** zeigen, richten; Punkt, Argumente, Seite
police Polizei
pool Schwimmbad, Pool
poor arm, schlecht
popular beliebt, populär
possible möglich, denkbar
possibly möglicherweise
post Post
pound Pfund
practice Praxis, Verfahrensweise
practice Übung(en)
to **practise** üben, trainieren
to **prefer** vorziehen, lieber mögen
to **prepare** (sich) vorbereiten
present Gegenwart, Geschenk
pretty hübsch; ziemlich
price Preis
private privat, persönlich
probably wahrscheinlich
programme (TV-, Radio-)Sendung, Programm, Plan
to **promise; promise** versprechen; Versprechen
proper(ly) richtig, ordnungsgemäß
to **protect** schützen, beschützen
pub Kneipe
to **pull** ziehen
pupil Schüler/in
to **put** setzen, stellen, legen
to **put on** anziehen

Q

quality Qualität, Eigenschaft
queen Königin
question Frage
quick(ly) schnell
quiet(ly) still, ruhig, leise
quite ziemlich, ganz

R

to **race; race** rennen; Rennen
to **rain; rain** regnen; Regen
rather ziemlich
to **reach; reach** erreichen; Reichweite
to **read** lesen, vorlesen
ready bereit
real(ly) echt, wirklich, sehr
to **receive** erhalten, empfangen
recent jüngst, aktuell
recently neulich, kürzlich, in letzter Zeit
regular(ly) regelmäßig
to **relax** sich entspannen
to **remember** sich an etw erinnern, daran denken
to **rent; rent** mieten; Miete
to **reply; reply** antworten; Antwort
to **report; report** berichten; Bericht
to **reserve** reservieren, buchen
rest Rest
restaurant Restaurant
result Folge, Ergebnis
to **return** zurückkehren, zurückgeben, -senden
rich reich, wohlhabend
right richtig; rechts; Recht
to **risk; risk** riskieren; Risiko
river Fluss
road Straße
role Rolle
room Zimmer, Raum
round rund; (um/in …) herum
rule Regel, Vorschrift
to **run** laufen, rennen

S

sad traurig
safe sicher
safety Sicherheit
to **sail; sail** segeln, zur See fahren; Segel
salad Salat
salt Salz
same gleiche/r/s, der-, die-, dasselbe
to **say** sagen
school Schule
sea Meer, See
season Saison
seat Sitz, Platz
second-hand gebraucht, aus zweiter Hand
secretary Sekretär/in
to **see** sehen
to **seem** scheinen
to **sell** verkaufen
to **send** senden, schicken
sentence Satz
serious(ly) ernst(haft)
several etliche, einige, mehrere
shelf Regal

ship Schiff
shirt Hemd
shoe Schuh
to **shop; shop** einkaufen; Laden, Geschäft
short kurz
should sollte
shoulder Schulter
to **show** zeigen
to **shower; shower** duschen; Dusche, Schauer
sightseeing Besichtigungen
to **sign; sign** unterschreiben, unterzeichnen; Zeichen, Schild
silly albern, doof
simple (simply) einfach, schlicht
since seit, seitdem, da, weil
to **sing** singen
sir mein Herr
sister Schwester
to **sit** sitzen
to **sit down** sich setzen
size Größe
skirt Rock
to **sleep** schlafen
slow(ly) langsam
small klein
to **smell; smell** riechen; Duft, Geruch
to **smile; smile** lächeln; Lächeln
to **smoke; smoke** rauchen; Rauch
snow Schnee
so so, also
soap Seife
some etwas, einige, irgendein
somebody jemand
something etwas
sometimes manchmal
somewhere irgendwo(hin)
son Sohn
song Lied
soon bald
(I'm) sorry (es) tut mir leid
sort Art, Sorte
to **sound; sound** klingen; Klang
soup Suppe
south (nach) Süden, Süd
to **speak** sprechen
special besondere/r/s, Sonder-
spend (Zeit) verbringen, (Geld) ausgeben
sport Sport(art)
stairs Treppe
to **stand** stehen
star Stern, Star
to **start; start** beginnen, eröffnen; Anfang
station Bahnhof
to **stay** bleiben, wohnen
still noch immer
to **stop** aufhören, anhalten
storm Sturm, Unwetter
story Geschichte
straight direkt, gerade

232

Basic word list

strange seltsam
stranger Fremde/r
street Straße
strong stark
student Schüler/in, Student/in
to **study** lernen, studieren, sich etw genau ansehen, durchlesen
stupid dumm
subject Thema; (Schul-)Fach; Betreff
success Erfolg
successful(ly) erfolgreich
such solche/r/s
sudden(ly) plötzlich
sugar Zucker
summer Sommer
sun Sonne
to **suppose** glauben, annehmen, vermuten
sure sicher, freilich
to **surprise; surprise** überraschen; Überraschung
sweet süß
sweets Süßigkeiten
to **swim** schwimmen

T

table Tisch; Tabelle
to **take** (an-, ein-, mit)nehmen, dauern
to **talk** reden, sprechen
tall groß, hoch
task Aufgabe
tea Tee
teacher Lehrer/in
to **tell** sagen, erzählen
tent Zelt
terrible furchtbar, schrecklich
than als
to **thank** danken
thanks danke
that dies; der, die, das; dass; jene/r/s
then dann
there da, dort, dorthin
therefore deshalb
these diese
thief Dieb
thing Sache, Ding
to **think (of)** denken (an), halten von
this dies, diese/r/s
those jene
though obwohl, doch
through durch, hindurch
time Zeit, Mal
tired müde
title Titel, Anrede, Bezeichnung
today heute
together zusammen
toilet Toilette
tomorrow morgen
tonight heute Abend
too zu, auch
toothpaste Zahncreme

top Spitze, Anfang; Spitzen-, oberste/r/s
total(ly) völlig, total, Gesamt
towards gegen, auf … zu, (in) Richtung
town Stadt
toy Spielzeug
traffic Verkehr
train Zug
trainee Auszubildende/r
to **translate** übersetzen
to **travel; travel** reisen, fahren; Reisen
tree Baum
trip Reise, Ausflug
trouble Problem(e), Schwierigkeiten, Mühe(n)
truck Lastwagen
true wahr
to **try** versuchen, probieren
twice zweimal
twin Zwilling, Zwillings
to **type; type** tippen; Art, Sorte, Typ

U

ugly hässlich
under unter
to **understand** verstehen, begreifen
unfortunately leider, unglücklicherweise
unfriendly unfreundlich
unhappy unzufrieden, unglücklich
unhealthy ungesund
unit Einheit, Lektion, Stück
university Universität
unless wenn nicht; es sei denn, dass
unnecessary unnötig
until bis
unusual ungewöhnlich, unüblich
to **use; use** gebrauchen, benutzen; Verwendung, Gebrauch
useful nützlich
usual(ly) normal(erweise), gewöhnlich

V

vegetable Gemüse
very sehr
via über, per
village Dorf
to **visit; visit** besuchen, besichtigen; Besuch, Besichtigung
visitor Besucher/in
vocabulary Vokabular, Wortschatz

W

to **wait** warten
waiter, waitress Kellner/in
to **wake up** aufwachen

to **walk; walk** (zu Fuß) gehen; Spaziergang, Fußweg
wall Wand
to **want** wollen, mögen
warm warm
to **warn** warnen
to **wash** waschen
to **watch** zusehen, beobachten, anschauen
water Wasser
way Weg, Methode
way: this ~ hier entlang
weak schwach
to **wear** tragen
week Woche
weekday Wochentag
weekend Wochenende
weight Gewicht
to **welcome; welcome** willkommen heißen; willkommen
well also; gut
west (nach) Westen, West
what was, welche/r/s
whatever was auch immer
wheel Rad
when wenn, als, wann
where wo, wohin
whether ob
which welche/r/s
while während, solange; Weile
who wer, die, der
whoever wer auch immer
whole ganze/r/s
why warum, weshalb
why: that's ~ deshalb, darum
will will, wollen, werden; Wille
to **win** gewinnen, siegen
to **wish; wish** wünschen; Wunsch
with mit, bei
within innerhalb, binnen, in
without ohne
woman, women Frau, Frauen
to **wonder (about); wonder** sich (etw) fragen; Wunder
wonderful wunderbar
word Wort
to **work; work** arbeiten, funktionieren; Arbeit
world Welt
to **worry; worry** sich Sorgen machen; Sorge
worse schlechter, schlechte/r/s
worst am schlechtesten, schlechteste/r/s
to **write (down)** (auf-, ab)schreiben
wrong falsch

Y

year Jahr
yesterday gestern
yet schon, bereits
young jung

233

UNIT WORD LIST

Dieses Wörterverzeichnis enthält alle Wörter in **Social Pulse** in der Reihenfolge ihres Auftretens. Nicht aufgeführt sind internationale Wörter wie *hotel*, *email* usw.

Wörter, die in den Hörverständnisübungen vorkommen, sind mit einem gelben Balken, und Wörter, die in den *Partner Files bzw Guidance and Challenge Files* vorkommen, mit einem blauen Balken gekennzeichnet.

UNIT 1

page 6

pulse [pʌls]	Puls, Rhythmus
to **care for sb** ['keə fə]	jdn pflegen, betreuen, jdn mögen
caring profession ['keərɪŋ prəfeʃn]	Sozialberuf, Pflegeberuf
profession [prə'feʃn]	Beruf
to **match** [mætʃ]	zuordnen
headline ['hedlaɪn]	Schlagzeile, Überschrift
trained [treɪnd]	ausgebildet
assistant [ə'sɪstənt]	Helfer/in, Assistent/in
substance abuse ['sʌbstəns əbjuːs]	Drogenmissbrauch
substance ['sʌbstəns]	Substanz, Stoff
abuse [ə'bjuːs]	Missbrauch
increase ['ɪŋkriːs]	Erhöhung, Zunahme
unemployed [ˌʌnɪm'plɔɪd]	arbeitslos
rise (in) [raɪz]	Erhöhung, Anstieg
to **train** [treɪn]	trainieren, ausbilden, ausgebildet werden
social administrator [ˌsəʊʃl əd'mɪnɪstreɪtə]	Sozialverwalter/in, Sozialmanager/in
social ['səʊʃl]	gesellschaftlich, sozial, Sozial-
midwife, *pl* midwives ['mɪdwaɪf]	Hebamme
home birth ['həʊm bɜːθ]	Hausgeburt
geriatric care worker [dʒeriˌætrɪk 'keə wɜːkə]	Altenpfleger/in
geriatric [ˌdʒeri'ætrɪk]	geriatrisch
in demand [ɪn dɪ'mɑːnd]	(nach)gefragt, gesucht
demand [dɪ'mɑːnd]	Bedarf, Nachfrage, Anforderung
positive ['pɒzətɪv]	positiv, sicher
care [keə]	Versorgung, Fürsorge
community [kə'mjuːnəti]	Gemeinschaft, Gemeinde, Bevölkerungsgruppe
youth [juːθ]	Jugend(-), Jugendliche/r
inner city [ˌɪnə 'sɪti]	Innenstadt
male [meɪl]	Mann, männlich
kindergarten nurse ['kɪndəgɑːtn nɜːs]	Kindergärtner/in

page 7

studies *(pl)* ['stʌdiz]	Studium
... is to come [tu, tə]	... wird/soll kommen
carer ['keərə]	Betreuer/in, Pfleger/in
thought [θɔːt]	Gedanke
to **take a look at** [teɪk ə 'lʊk ət]	(sich) ansehen

organization [ˌɔːgənaɪ'zeɪʃn]	Organisation
caring ['keərɪŋ]	Versorgung, Betreuung, Pflege
to **consider** [kən'sɪdə]	nachdenken über, *sich etw* überlegen, in Erwägung ziehen
suggestion [sə'dʒestʃən]	Vorschlag
caring professional [ˌkeərɪŋ prə'feʃənl]	in einem Sozialberuf Tätige/r
professional [prə'feʃnl]	beruflich, Berufs-, professionell, Profi-
at the end [ət ðɪ 'end]	am Ende, zum Schluss
to **do research (into)** [duː rɪ'sɜːtʃ]	recherchieren, Nachforschungen anstellen (über)
to **produce** [prə'djuːs]	produzieren, herstellen, (an)fertigen
material [mə'tɪəriəl]	Material, Stoff, Angaben
to **follow** ['fɒləʊ]	folgen
goal [gəʊl]	Ziel
to **make notes** [ˌmeɪk 'nəʊts]	(sich) Notizen machen

page 8

Who cares? [huː 'keəz]	Wer sorgt/betreut/pflegt? *auch:* Wen kümmert das? Na und?
section ['sekʃn]	Abschnitt
extract ['ekstrækt]	Auszug, Extrakt
advertisement, advert, ad [əd'vɜːtɪsmənt, 'ædvɜːt, æd]	Anzeige, Inserat, Werbespot
heading ['hedɪŋ]	Überschrift
to **motivate** ['məʊtɪveɪt]	motivieren
committed (to) [kə'mɪtɪd]	engagiert (für)
social support service [ˌsəʊʃl sə'pɔːt sɜːvɪs]	soziale Leistung
support [sə'pɔːt]	Unterstützung
service ['sɜːvɪs]	Dienstleistung
to **range (from ... to ...)** [reɪndʒ]	sich erstrecken, reichen (von ... bis ...)
teen [tiːn]	Teenager, Jugendliche/r
adult ['ædʌlt]	Erwachsene/r
immense [ɪ'mens]	enorm, immens
continually [kən'tɪnjuəli]	ständig, ununterbrochen
to **provide** [prə'vaɪd]	(zur Verfügung) stellen, bereitstellen
to **draw** [drɔː]	zeichnen
to **sort** [sɔːt]	sortieren, ordnen
category ['kætəgəri]	Kategorie
worker ['wɜːkə]	Arbeiter/in
day care centre ['deɪ keə sentə]	Tagesstätte

234

Unit word list

day care [ˈdeɪ keə] — Tagesbetreuung
nursery [ˈnɜːsəri] — Kinderhort
occupational therapist [ˌɒkjuˌpeɪʃnl ˈθerəpɪst] — Ergotherapeut/in, Beschäftigungstherapeut/in
therapist [ˈθerəpɪst] — Therapeut/in
paediatric [ˌpiːdiˈætrɪk] — pädiatrisch, Kinderheilkunde-
physiotherapist [ˌfɪziəʊˈθerəpɪst] — Physiotherapeut/in, Krankengymnast/in
counsellor [ˈkaʊnsələ] — Berater/in
to support [səˈpɔːt] — unterstützen
everyday [ˈevrideɪ] — alltäglich, Alltags-
to manage [ˈmænɪdʒ] — leiten, verwalten
to assist (with) [əˈsɪst] — assistieren, helfen (bei)
(the) elderly [ˈeldəli] — Senioren/-innen, ältere (Menschen)
pregnant [ˈpregnənt] — schwanger
sector [ˈsektə] — Sektor, Bereich
information (on) (no pl) [ˌɪnfəˈmeɪʃn] — Information(en) (über), Angaben (zu)
to interview [ˈɪntəvjuː] — befragen

page 9

residence [ˈrezɪdəns] — Residenz, Anwesen
council [ˈkaʊnsl] — Rat, Gemeinderat
day nursery [ˈdeɪ nɜːsəri] — Tageskrippe
nursery nurse [ˈnɜːsəri nɜːs] — Kinderpfleger/in
National Health Service (NHS) [ˌnæʃnəl ˈhelθ sɜːvɪs] — *staatlicher Gesundheitsdienst in Großbritannien*
adolescent [ˌædəˈlesnt] — jugendlich, Jugend-, Jugendliche/r
psychiatry [saɪˈkaɪətriː] — Psychiatrie
social education worker [ˌsəʊʃl ˌedʒuˈkeɪʃn wɜːkə] — Sozialpädagoge/-pädagogin
education [ˌedʒuˈkeɪʃn] — Erziehung
to note down [ˌnəʊt ˈdaʊn] — aufschreiben, notieren
speaker [ˈspiːkə] — Redner/in, Sprecher/in
eldest [ˈeldɪst] — älteste/r/s
India [ˈɪndiə] — Indien
original(ly) [əˈrɪdʒənəli] — ursprünglich
tradition [trəˈdɪʃn] — Tradition, Brauch
culture [ˈkʌltʃə] — Kultur
to belong (to) [bɪˈlɒŋ] — gehören (zu)
calling [ˈkɔːlɪŋ] — Berufung
client [ˈklaɪənt] — Kunde/Kundin, Klient/in, Mandant/in
day-to-day [ˌdeɪ tə ˈdeɪ] — tagtäglich
mealtime [ˈmiːltaɪm] — Essenszeit
personal [ˈpɜːsənl] — persönlich
patience [ˈpeɪʃns] — Geduld
respect [rɪˈspekt] — Respekt, Achtung
worthwhile [ˌwɜːθˈwaɪl] — lohnend
pragmatic [prægˈmætɪk] — pragmatisch
no matter [ˈnəʊ mætə] — gleichgültig, egal
to be a single parent [ˈsɪŋgl peərənt] — alleinerziehend sein
to grow up [ˌgrəʊ ˈʌp] — erwachsen werden
to realize [ˈrɪəlaɪz] — (be)merken, sich klar werden
staff [stɑːf] — Personal, Belegschaft
local authority [ˌləʊkl ɔːˈθɒrəti] — Kommunalbehörde

preschool [ˈpriːskuːl] — Vorschul-, Kindergarten-
area [ˈeəriə] — Gebiet, Bereich, Feld, Gegend
attached to [əˈtætʃt] — angebunden an
local [ˈləʊkl] — örtlich, lokal
Right. [raɪt] — Gut. OK.
apart from [əˈpɑːt frəm] — außer, abgesehen von
to supervise [ˈsuːpəvaɪz] — beaufsichtigen
rest time [ˈrest taɪm] — Ruhezeit
enthusiastic [ɪnˌθjuːziˈæstɪk] — begeistert
easy-going [ˌiːziˈgəʊɪŋ] — unkompliziert, nicht so streng
strict [strɪkt] — streng, strikt
to take seriously [teɪk ˈsɪəriəsli] — ernst nehmen
attention [əˈtenʃn] — Aufmerksamkeit
eating disorder [ˈiːtɪŋ dɪsɔːdə] — Essstörung
disorder [dɪsˈɔːdə] — (Funktions-)Störung *(med.)*
adolescent psychiatric unit [ædəˌlesnt saɪkiˈætrɪk juːnɪt] — jugendpsychiatrische Station/Abteilung
psychiatric [saɪkiˈætrɪk] — psychiatrisch
state-run [ˈsteɪt rʌn] — staatlich *(von der öffentlichen Hand betrieben)*
to structure [ˈstrʌktʃə] — strukturieren
to get dressed [get ˈdrest] — sich anziehen
to guide [gaɪd] — führen, (an)leiten
sensitive (to) [ˈsensətɪv] — einfühlsam
to deal with [ˈdiːl wɪð] — sich beschäftigen mit, sich kümmern um, umgehen mit
listener [ˈlɪsnə] — Zuhörer/in
willing [ˈwɪlɪŋ] — bereit, willens, gewillt
point of view [ˌpɔɪnt əv ˈvjuː] — Standpunkt, Ansicht
to make a decision [dɪˈsɪʒn] — eine Entscheidung treffen
to stick to [ˈstɪk tə] — bleiben bei, festhalten an
at the end of the day [ət ði ˌend əv ðə ˈdeɪ] — letztendlich
to reconstruct [ˌriːkənˈstrʌkt] — rekonstruieren
long hours *(pl)* [lɒŋ ˈaʊəz] — Überstunden
full-time [ˌfʊl ˈtaɪm] — Vollzeit
part-time [ˌpɑːt ˈtaɪm] — Teilzeit-, Halbtags-
statement [ˈsteɪtmənt] — Aussage
interaction [ˌɪntərˈækʃn] — Interaktion
to find out [ˌfaɪnd ˈaʊt] — herausfinden, feststellen

page 10

to compare [kəmˈpeə] — vergleichen, sich vergleichen lassen
to contrast [kənˈtrɑːst] — gegenüberstellen
first [fɜːst] — zuerst
to predict [prɪˈdɪkt] — voraussagen, vorhersagen, prognostizieren
to skim [skɪm] — überfliegen
to cover [ˈkʌvə] — abdecken, *(Thema)* behandeln

235

UNIT WORD LIST

to **talk sth over** [tɔːk ˈəʊvə]	über etw reden, etw besprechen	**fellowship** [ˈfeləʊʃɪp]	Gesellschaft
charity [ˈtʃærəti]	Wohltätigkeitsverein, Hilfsorganisation	to **register sb as sth** [ˈredʒɪstə]	jdn als etw registrieren
relationship support [rɪˈleɪʃnʃɪp səpɔːt]	Partnerschaftshilfe	**government** [ˈgʌvənmənt]	Regierung, öffentliche Verwaltung
relationship [rɪˈleɪʃnʃɪp]	Beziehung, Verhältnis	to **inspire** [ɪnˈspaɪə]	inspirieren, anregen, anspornen
vision [ˈvɪʒn]	Vision, Blick, Sehkraft	**education** [ˌedʒuˈkeɪʃn]	(Schul-)Bildung, Ausbildung
thriving [ˈθraɪvɪŋ]	florierend, blühend	**child-centred** [ˈsentəd]	am Kind orientiert
society [səˈsaɪəti]	Gesellschaft	**qualified** [ˈkwɒlɪfaɪd]	qualifiziert, ausgebildet
skilled [skɪld]	qualifiziert, Fach-	to **nurture** [ˈnɜːtʃə]	entwickeln, pflegen, fördern
crisis, pl **crises** [ˈkraɪsɪs, ˈkraɪsiːz]	Krise		
impact (on) [ˈɪmpækt]	(Aus-)Wirkung, Folge, Einfluss (auf)	**page 11**	
ability [əˈbɪləti]	Fähigkeit	**clientele** [ˌkliːənˈtel]	Klientel, Kundenkreis
to **maintain** [meɪnˈteɪn]	aufrecht erhalten	to **outline** [ˈaʊtlaɪn]	skizzieren, beschreiben, darstellen
stable [ˈsteɪbl]	stabil, konstant	**evidence** [ˈevɪdəns]	Nachweis(e), Beweis(e), Beweismaterial
involved in [ɪnˈvɒlvd ɪn]	beteiligt an, beschäftigt mit	**competent** [ˈkɒmpɪtənt]	kompetent
mission [ˈmɪʃn]	Auftrag, Mission	to **fund** [fʌnd]	finanzieren
individual [ˌɪndɪˈvɪdʒuəl]	Einzelne/r, Individuum	**gift** [gɪft]	Spende, Schenkung
to **set up** [ˌset ˈʌp]	aufbauen, durchführen	**situation** [ˌsɪtʃuˈeɪʃn]	Situation, Lage
aim [eɪm]	Ziel, Zweck, Absicht	**employee** [ɪmˈplɔɪiː]	Angestellte/r, Beschäftigte/r
all over ... [ˌɔːl ˈəʊvə]	überall in ...	to **respect** [rɪˈspekt]	respektieren
UK [juːˈkeɪ]	Vereinigtes Königreich	**of mine/yours/...** [əv]	von mir/dir/...
network [ˈnetwɜːk]	Netz(werk)	to **apply (for)** [əˈplaɪ]	sich bewerben (um)
face-to-face [ˌfeɪs tə ˈfeɪs]	persönlich	**contrast** [ˈkɒntrɑːst]	Gegensatz
multicultural [ˌmʌltiˈkʌltʃərəl]	multikulturell	**guidance** [ˈgaɪdəns]	Anleitung, Hilfestellung
assistance [əˈsɪstəns]	Hilfe	to **turn to** [ˈtɜːn tə]	sich wenden an, (Seite) aufschlagen
to **undertake** [ˌʌndəˈteɪk]	unternehmen, in Angriff nehmen	**step** [step]	Schritt
isolated [ˈaɪsəleɪtɪd]	isoliert	to **re-read** [riːˈriːd]	nochmals lesen
to **establish** [ɪˈstæblɪʃ]	etablieren, aufbauen	to **get in touch with** [ˌget ɪn ˈtʌtʃ wɪð]	(sich) in Verbindung setzen mit
cultural(ly) [ˈkʌltʃərəl]	kulturell, Kultur-	**target group** [ˈtɑːgɪt gruːp]	Zielgruppe
appropriate [əˈprəʊpriət]	angemessen, passend, richtig	**workplace** [ˈwɜːkpleɪs]	Arbeitsplatz
minority [maɪˈnɒrəti]	Minderheit	**talk** [tɔːk]	Vortrag, Rede
ethnic [ˈeθnɪk]	ethnisch, Volks-	**option** [ˈɒpʃn]	(Wahl-)Möglichkeit
to **respond to** [rɪˈspɒnd tə]	antworten auf, reagieren auf	**practical** [ˈpræktɪkl]	praktisch, praxisbezogen
domestic [dəˈmestɪk]	Haus-, häuslich	**training** [ˈtreɪnɪŋ]	Ausbildung, Training
non-profit [ˌnɒnˈprɒfɪt]	gemeinnützig, nicht auf Gewinn ausgerichtet	**work experience** [ˈwɜːk ɪkspɪəriəns]	Praktikum/Praktika, Berufserfahrung
to **found** [faʊnd]	gründen	to **imagine** [ɪˈmædʒɪn]	sich vorstellen
bureaucracy [bjʊəˈrɒkrəsi]	Bürokratie	to **mention** [ˈmenʃn]	erwähnen, nennen, anführen
facilities (pl) [fəˈsɪlətiz]	Einrichtungen, Gelegenheit	to **invent** [ɪnˈvent]	erfinden, sich ausdenken
to **aim at / for / to do sth** [ˈeɪm ət]	zielen auf, sich richten an	to **be located in ...** [bi ləʊˈkeɪtɪd ɪn]	in ... ansässig sein, seinen/ihren Sitz in ... haben
hand-picked [ˌhændˈpɪkt]	handverlesen, sorgsam ausgewählt	**responsible (for)** [rɪˈspɒnsəbl]	verantwortlich, zuständig (für)
elders (pl) [ˈeldəz]	ältere Generation	**responsibility** [rɪˌspɒnsəˈbɪləti]	Aufgabenbereich, Zuständigkeit
to **recruit sb** [rɪˈkruːt]	jdn anwerben, jdn neu einstellen	to **include** [ɪnˈkluːd]	einbeziehen, einschließen
Welsh [welʃ]	walisisch, Waliser/in	**page 12**	
independent [ˌɪndɪˈpendənt]	unabhängig	**self-care** [ˈselfkeə]	Selbst(für)sorge, Selbstbehandlung
system [ˈsɪstəm]	System	to **cope (with)** [kəʊp]	zurechtkommen, fertig werden (mit)
six-year-olds [ˈsɪks jɪə əʊldz]	Sechsjährige	**stress** [stres]	Stress, Belastung
aged [eɪdʒd]	im Alter von		
accredited [əˈkredɪtɪd]	anerkannt, akkreditiert		

236

Unit word list

supervision [ˌsuːpəˈvɪʒn]	Überwachung, Betreuung, Supervision
to **conduct** [kənˈdʌkt]	durchführen
survey [ˈsɜːveɪ]	Umfrage, Erhebung
stress-buster [ˈstresbʌstə]	Stressbekämpfer
item [ˈaɪtəm]	Artikel, Gegenstand, Punkt
unable [ʌnˈeɪbl]	unfähig, nicht in der Lage
to **switch on/off** [swɪtʃ]	an-/abschalten
challenge [ˈtʃælɪndʒ]	Herausforderung, Aufgabe
balanced [ˈbælənst]	ausgeglichen, ausgewogen, im Gleichgewicht
to **experience** [ɪkˈspɪəriəns]	erleben, erfahren
despair [dɪˈspeə]	Verzweiflung
to **solve** (a task / a problem) [sɒlv]	(eine Aufgabe) bewältigen, (ein Problem) lösen
to **suffer from sth** [ˈsʌfə]	an etw leiden
supervisor [ˈsuːpəvaɪzə]	Betreuer/in, Vorgesetzte/r
to **scan** [skæn]	überfliegen, absuchen, scannen
licensed [ˈlaɪsnst]	amtlich zugelassen
clinical [ˈklɪnɪkl]	klinisch
responsible [rɪˈspɒnsəbl]	verantwortungsvoll
to **separate** [ˈsepəreɪt]	(sich) trennen
inability [ˌɪnəˈbɪləti]	Unfähigkeit
to **cool down** [ˌkuːl ˈdaʊn]	sich abkühlen, sich beruhigen
to **be faced with sth** [ˈfeɪst]	konfrontiert werden mit
challenging [ˈtʃælɪndʒɪŋ]	anspruchsvoll
aware of sth [əˈweə]	sich einer Sache bewusst
frequent(ly) [ˈfriːkwənt]	häufig, oft
stressful [ˈstresfl]	stressig
case [keɪs]	Fall
to **reflect on sth** [rɪˈflekt]	etw reflektieren
to **interact** [ˌɪntərˈækt]	interagieren, miteinander umgehen
conscious [ˈkɒnʃəs]	bewusst
to **teach** [tiːtʃ]	lehren
confidential [ˌkɒnfɪˈdenʃl]	vertraulich
environment [ɪnˈvaɪrənmənt]	Umfeld, Umgebung
concern [kənˈsɜːn]	Befürchtung, Bedenken, Sorge
solution (to a problem) [səˈluːʃn]	Lösung (eines Problems, für ein Problem)
balance [ˈbæləns]	Gleichgewicht, Ausgewogenheit
awareness [əˈweənəs]	Bewusstsein

page 13

to **achieve** [əˈtʃiːv]	erreichen, erzielen, erlangen
to **summarize** [ˈsʌməraɪz]	zusammenfassen
pros and cons (pl) [ˌprəʊz ənd ˈkɒnz]	Für und Wider, Pro und Contra
to **point sth out** [ˌpɔɪnt ˈaʊt]	etw (auf)zeigen, auf etw hinweisen
to **dislike** [dɪsˈlaɪk]	nicht mögen
technique [tekˈniːk]	Methode, Technik
to **beat** [biːt]	schlagen, besiegen, übertreffen

caring [ˈkeərɪŋ]	liebevoll, warmherzig
to **trust** [trʌst]	(ver)trauen
(in) a ... way [weɪ]	auf (eine) ... Art/Weise
nursing assistant [ˌnɜːsɪŋ əˈsɪstənt]	Pflegehelfer/in
nursing [ˈnɜːsɪŋ]	Pflege, Krankenpflege
not for me [ˌnɒt fə ˈmi]	nicht meine Sache
gym [dʒɪm]	Sportstudio, Fitnessstudio, Turnhalle (Schule)
to **go for a run** [rʌn]	laufen gehen
diet [ˈdaɪət]	Ernährung, Diät
exercise [ˈeksəsaɪz]	Bewegung, (körperliches) Training
to **remind (sb of sth)** [rɪˈmaɪnd]	(jdn an etw) erinnern
nasty [ˈnɑːsti]	gemein, fies, scheußlich, widerlich
personality [ˌpɜːsəˈnæləti]	Persönlichkeit
to **get in the way** [ɪn ðə ˈweɪ]	(einem) im Wege stehen
to **meditate** [ˈmedɪteɪt]	meditieren
relaxation [ˌriːlækˈseɪʃn]	Erholung
auxiliary [ɔːgˈzɪliəri]	Hilfs-, Aushilfs-
writer [ˈraɪtə]	Schreiber/in
to **disagree (with)** [ˌdɪsəˈgriː]	nicht zustimmen
response [rɪˈspɒns]	Reaktion, Antwort
stressed [strest]	gestresst
(not) at all [ət ˈɔːl]	überhaupt (nicht)
attitude [ˈætɪtjuːd]	Einstellung, (Geistes-)Haltung
as far as ... is/are concerned [kənˈsɜːnd]	was ... betrifft/angeht
to **make sth up** [ˌmeɪk ˈʌp]	etw erfinden, sich etw ausdenken
questionnaire [ˌkwestʃəˈneə]	Fragebogen

page 14

project [ˈprɒdʒekt]	Projekt
form [fɔːm]	Form, Art
description [dɪˈskrɪpʃn]	Beschreibung
nutritionist [njuˈtrɪʃənɪst]	Ernährungswissenschaftler/in, Ernährungsberater/in
to **advise** [ədˈvaɪz]	(be)raten
mobility [məʊˈbɪləti]	Beweglichkeit, Mobilität
addiction [əˈdɪkʃn]	Sucht, Abhängigkeit
to **gain** [geɪn]	erwerben, gewinnen, sammeln
skill [skɪl]	Fertigkeit, Fähigkeit
to **expand** [ɪkˈspænd]	expandieren, (sich) erweitern
horizon [həˈraɪzn]	Horizont
clinic [ˈklɪnɪk]	Klinik, Ambulanz, Sprechstunde
brackets (pl) [ˈbrækɪts]	Klammern
to **serve** [sɜːv]	servieren
resident [ˈrezɪdənt]	Bewohner/in, Einwohner/in
patient [ˈpeɪʃnt]	Patient/in
colleague [ˈkɒliːg]	Kollege/Kollegin
odd one out [ˌɒd wʌn ˈaʊt]	Außenseiter/in, nicht dazugehörig
sociable [ˈsəʊʃəbl]	gesellig, verbindlich

237

UNIT WORD LIST

gentle	['dʒentl]	sanft
calm	[kɑːm]	ruhig
talkative	['tɔːkətɪv]	gesprächig
supportive	[sə'pɔːtɪv]	hilfreich, verständnisvoll
internship	['ɪntɜːnʃɪp]	Praktikum

page 15

notebook	['nəʊtbʊk]	Notizbuch, Notebook
to design	[dɪ'zaɪn]	entwerfen, gestalten
presentation	[ˌprezn'teɪʃn]	Vorstellung, Präsentation, Referat
career	[kə'rɪə]	Karriere, Beruf
qualification	[ˌkwɒlɪfɪ'keɪʃn]	Abschluss, Qualifikation
drawback	['drɔːbæk]	Nachteil
to gather	['gæðə]	sammeln, sich versammeln
content	['kɒntent]	Inhalt
menu	['menjuː]	Menü, Speisekarte
to present	[prɪ'zent]	vorstellen, präsentieren
to divide into	[dɪ'vaɪd ɪntə]	(sich) unterteilen in
progress	['prəʊgres]	Fortschritt
to browse	[braʊz]	stöbern, sich umsehen (in/durch)
previous	['priːviəs]	vorherig
now that	['naʊ ðət]	jetzt, wo
entry	['entri]	Eintrag, Beitrag

UNIT 2

page 18

CV (= curriculum vitae)	[ˌsiː 'viː, kəˌrɪkjələm 'viːtaɪ]	Lebenslauf
sex	[seks]	Geschlecht
female	['fiːmeɪl]	Frau, weiblich
date of birth	[ˌdeɪt əv 'bɜːθ]	Geburtsdatum
birth	[bɜːθ]	Geburt
family support worker	[ˌfæməli sə'pɔːt wɜːkə]	Sozialpädagogische/r Helfer/in
covering letter	[ˌkʌvərɪŋ 'letə]	Anschreiben, Begleitschreiben
letter of application	[ˌletər əv æplɪ'keɪʃn]	Bewerbungsschreiben
application	[ˌæplɪ'keɪʃn]	Bewerbung
(work) placement	['wɜːk pleɪsmənt]	Praktikum
to advertise	[ˌædvətaɪz ə 'dʒɒb]	(eine Stelle) ausschreiben
as advertised	[əz 'ædvətaɪzd]	wie beschrieben
employment	[ɪm'plɔɪmənt]	Anstellung, Beschäftigung, Arbeit
sequence	['siːkwəns]	(richtige) Reihenfolge, Abfolge
not ... yet	[jet]	noch nicht
Same here.	[ˌseɪm 'hɪə]	Ich auch. / Mir geht's genauso.
by asking ...	[baɪ]	indem man ... fragt / du ... fragst

page 19

interview	['ɪntəvjuː]	Vorstellungsgespräch
template	['templeɪt]	Muster, Vorlage, Schablone
instruction(s)	[ɪn'strʌkʃn]	Anweisung(en)
link	[lɪŋk]	Verbindung, Link

page 20

to get started	[get 'stɑːtɪd]	anfangen, loslegen
to brainstorm	['breɪnstɔːm]	Ideen (ungeordnet) sammeln
ideal	[aɪ'dɪəl]	ideal
experience	[ɪk'spɪəriəns]	Erfahrung, Erlebnis
employer	[ɪm'plɔɪə]	Arbeitgeber/in
duty	['djuːti]	Aufgabe, Pflicht
applicant	['æplɪkənt]	Bewerber/in
disability	[ˌdɪsə'bɪləti]	Behinderung
disabled	[dɪs'eɪbld]	behindert
physical(ly)	['fɪzɪkl]	körperlich, physisch
impairment	[ɪm'peəmənt]	Beeinträchtigung
long-term	[ˌlɒŋ 'tɜːm]	langfristig, Langzeit-
condition	[kən'dɪʃn]	Leiden, Erkrankung
reliable	[rɪ'laɪəbl]	zuverlässig, verlässlich
flexible	['fleksəbl]	flexibel
social care	[ˌsəʊʃl 'keə]	Sozialfürsorge, Sozialwesen
health care	['helθ keə]	Gesundheitsfürsorge, medizinische Versorgung
driving licence BE	['draɪvɪŋ laɪsns]	Führerschein
advantage (over)	[əd'vɑːntɪdʒ]	Vorteil, Vorzug (gegenüber)
to accompany	[ə'kʌmpəni]	begleiten
to take part (in)	[ˌteɪk 'pɑːt]	teilnehmen (an)
leisure	['leʒə]	Freizeit
enjoyable	[ɪn'dʒɔɪəbl]	angenehm, schön
rewarding	[rɪ'wɔːdɪŋ]	lohnend, erfüllend
to carry out	[ˌkæri 'aʊt]	ausführen, durchführen
token	['təʊkən]	symbolisch
payment	['peɪmənt]	Bezahlung, Zahlung
expenses (pl)	[ɪk'spensɪz]	Kosten, Auslagen
(for the) attention (of) (Attn.)	[ə'tenʃn]	zu Händen
to contact	['kɒntækt]	Kontakt aufnehmen zu, sich wenden an
by telephone	[baɪ]	telefonisch, per Telefon

page 21

to be missing (from)	[bɪ 'mɪsɪŋ]	fehlen (bei/in)
article	['ɑːtɪkl]	Artikel
to grab	[græb]	packen, greifen, sich etw schnappen
to leave out	[ˌliːv 'aʊt]	weglassen, auslassen
to attach	[ə'tætʃ]	anfügen, anhängen (an ein E-Mail)
to state	[steɪt]	erklären, angeben
summary	['sʌməri]	Zusammenfassung
reader	['riːdə]	Leser/in
to make sure	[ˌmeɪk 'ʃʊə]	sicherstellen
honest	['ɒnɪst]	ehrlich

factual ['fæktʃuəl]	Sach-, sachlich
personal details (pl) [ˌpɜːsənl 'diːteɪlz]	persönliche Angaben
unlike [ˌʌn'laɪk]	anders als, im Gegensatz zu
profile ['prəʊfaɪl]	Profil, Porträt
eye-catching ['aɪ kætʃɪŋ]	auffallend, ins Auge springend
reverse [rɪ'vɜːs]	umgekehrt, entgegengesetzt
position [pə'zɪʃn]	Posten, Stellung, (Arbeits-)Stelle
achievement [ə'tʃiːvmənt]	Errungenschaft, Leistung
brief [briːf]	kurz, knapp
equivalent [ɪ'kwɪvələnt]	Äquivalent, Gegenstück
to be equivalent to [ɪ'kwɪvələnt tə]	entsprechen
vocational college BE [vəʊˌkeɪʃənl 'kɒlɪdʒ]	Fachoberschule, Berufskolleg
throughout ... [θruː'aʊt]	das ganze ... (hindurch), überall in ...
...-orientated ['ɔːriənteɪtɪd]	...orientiert
energetic [ˌenə'dʒetɪk]	kraftvoll, energisch
optional ['ɒpʃənl]	freiwillig, fakultativ, Wahl-
to party ['pɑːti]	auf Partys gehen, feiern
reference ['refrəns]	Referenz
due to ['djuː tə]	wegen, aufgrund (von)
data ['deɪtə]	Daten
protection [prə'tekʃn]	Schutz
law [lɔː]	Gesetz
available [ə'veɪləbl]	verfügbar, erhältlich, (am Telefon) zu sprechen
request [rɪ'kwest]	Anfrage, Wunsch, Bitte
permission [pə'mɪʃn]	Erlaubnis, Genehmigung
certificate [sə'tɪfɪkət]	Zeugnis, Urkunde
such as ['sʌtʃ əz]	wie (zum Beispiel)
to contain [kən'teɪn]	enthalten
space [speɪs]	Platz, Raum, Fläche
beside [bɪ'saɪd]	neben
search (for) [sɜːtʃ]	Suche (nach)

page 22

to adapt (to sth) [ə'dæpt]	sich anpassen (an etw)
candidate ['kændɪdət]	Bewerber/in, Kandidat/in
to prepare [prɪ'peə]	erstellen
highly ['haɪli]	höchst, äußerst
to seek [siːk]	suchen (nach), anstreben
fluent(ly) ['fluːənt]	fließend (Sprache)
to be good at ['gʊd ət]	gut sein in, gut beherrschen
pressure ['preʃə]	Druck
biology [baɪ'ɒlədʒi]	Biologie
Health Studies (pl) ['helθ stʌdiz]	Gesundheitswesen, Gesundheitswissenschaften
Social Studies (pl) [ˌsəʊʃl 'stʌdiz]	Sozialkunde, Sozialwissenschaften
Home Economics [ˌhəʊm iːkə'nɒmɪks]	Hauswirtschaftslehre
secondary school ['sekəndri skuːl]	weiterführende Schule, Realschule
temporary ['temprəri]	vorübergehend, zeitlich befristet

primary school ['praɪməri skuːl]	Grundschule
native speaker [ˌneɪtɪv 'spiːkə]	Muttersprachler/in
oral(ly) ['ɔːrəl]	mündlich
Polish ['pəʊlɪʃ]	polnisch, Polnisch
conversational [ˌkɒnvə'seɪʃənl]	Konversations-, gesprochenes
first aid [ˌfɜːst 'eɪd]	Erste Hilfe
referee [ˌrefə'riː]	Referenzgeber/in

page 23

to consider [kən'sɪdə]	berücksichtigen
to refer to [rɪ'fɜː]	sich beziehen auf
to be keen on sth / to do sth [kiːn]	an etw sehr interessiert sein, etw unbedingt wollen
on a daily basis [ˌdeɪli 'beɪsɪs]	jeden Tag, täglich
on a regular basis [ˌregjələ 'beɪsɪs]	regelmäßig
enclosed [ɪn'kləʊzd]	beigefügt, beiliegend
current(ly) ['kʌrənt]	aktuell, gegenwärtig
to fit in (with) [ˌfɪt 'ɪn]	sich anpassen (an), sich einfügen (in)
to be an asset (to) ['æset]	von Vorteil sein, von Wert sein (für)
because of [bɪ'kɒz əv]	wegen
tie [taɪ]	(Ver-)Bindung, Beziehung
to grant [grɑːnt]	gewähren, einräumen
to look forward to (doing sth) [ˌlʊk 'fɔːwəd tə]	sich darauf freuen (etw zu tun)
Yours sincerely [jɔːz sɪn'sɪəli]	Mit freundlichen Grüßen
Enc (enclosed) [ɪŋk, ɪn'kləʊzd]	Anlage(n)

page 24

No sweat! [swet]	Kein Problem!
sweat [swet]	Schweiß
process ['prəʊses]	Prozess, Vorgang
mediation [miːdi'eɪʃn]	Vermittlung, Sprachmittlung
scary ['skeəri]	beängstigend, gruselig
meaningful ['miːnɪŋfl]	wichtig, bedeutend, bedeutungsvoll
as ... as [əz]	(eben)so ... wie
interviewee [ˌɪntəvjuː'iː]	Befragte/r (im Interview)
clothing ['kləʊðɪŋ]	Kleidung
to do better [ˌduː 'betə]	besser abschneiden
casual(ly) ['kæʒuəl]	lässig, zwanglos, leger
wear [weə]	Bekleidung
confident ['kɒnfɪdənt]	(selbst)sicher, zuversichtlich, überzeugt
impression [ɪm'preʃn]	Eindruck
likely ['laɪkli]	geeignet
to make sb do sth [meɪk]	jdn dazu bringen etw zu tun, jdn etw tun lassen
... years from now [frəm 'naʊ]	in ... Jahren
investment [ɪn'vestmənt]	Investition
company ['kʌmpəni]	Unternehmen, Gesellschaft, Firma

UNIT WORD LIST

notepad [ˈnəʊtpæd]	Notizblock	to qualify [ˈkwɒlɪfaɪ]	einen/seinen/ihren Abschluss machen
strength [streŋθ]	Stärke	to involve [ɪnˈvɒlv]	mit sich bringen, einbeziehen, beinhalten
weakness [ˈwiːknəs]	Schwäche		
to role-play [ˈrəʊpleɪ]	im Rollenspiel darstellen	childcare [ˈtʃaɪld keə]	Kinderbetreuung
		rescue [ˈreskjuː]	Rettung(s-)
page 25		health insurance [ˈhelθ ɪnˈʃʊərəns]	Krankenversicherung
flow chart [ˈfləʊ tʃɑːt]	Flussdiagramm	value [ˈvæljuː]	Wert
to answer the phone [ˌɑːnsə ðə ˈfəʊn]	ans Telefon gehen	Yours faithfully [ˌjɔːz ˈfeɪθfəli]	Mit freundlichen Grüßen
to greet [griːt]	(be)grüßen		
to repeat [rɪˈpiːt]	wiederholen	**page 27**	
You're breaking up. [jɔː ˌbreɪkɪŋ ˈʌp]	(Telefon) Das Netz geht weg.	to print (out) [prɪnt]	(aus)drucken
in charge (of) [ɪn ˈtʃɑːdʒ]	verantwortlich (für), zuständig (für)	to proofread [ˈpruːfriːd]	Korrektur lesen
recruitment [rɪˈkruːtmənt]	Anwerbung, Einstellung (von Personal)	to pin sth up (on the wall) [ˌpɪn ˈʌp]	etw (an die Wand) heften, (an der Wand) befestigen
(in a) panic [ˈpænɪk]	in Panik	draft [drɑːft]	Entwurf
handshake [ˈhændʃeɪk]	Händedruck	formal [ˈfɔːml]	formell, förmlich
dos and don'ts (pl) [ˌduːz ən ˈdəʊnts]	Hinweise, was man tun und lassen sollte	to take turns [ˌteɪk ˈtɜːnz]	sich abwechseln
to behave [bɪˈheɪv]	sich verhalten, sich benehmen	to handle [ˈhændl]	umgehen mit, handhaben
there's more to it than … [mɔː]	es geht um mehr als … / es steckt mehr dahinter als …	effective(ly) [ɪˈfektɪv]	effektiv, wirksam, wirkungsvoll
		to suggest [səˈdʒest]	vorschlagen
in (good) time (for) [ɪn ˈtaɪm]	rechtzeitig (für/zu), beizeiten	to swap [swɒp]	(aus)tauschen
to shake hands [ˌʃeɪk ˈhændz]	sich die Hand geben, die Hände schütteln	vice versa [ˌvaɪs ˈvɜːsə]	umgekehrt
		paperwork [ˈpeɪpəwɜːk]	Formalitäten, Unterlagen
shy [ʃaɪ]	schüchtern, scheu	to simulate [ˈsɪmjuleɪt]	simulieren
mouth [maʊθ]	Mund	of your own [əv jɔːr ˈəʊn]	(Ihr/dein) eigene/r/s
to take a seat [ˌteɪk ə ˈsiːt]	Platz nehmen, sich (hin)setzen	criterion, pl criteria [kraɪˈtɪəriən, kraɪˈtɪəriə]	Kriterium
weather [ˈweðə]	Wetter	to start sb off (on sth) [ˌstɑːt ˈɒf]	jdn auf etw bringen, jdm einen Einstieg geben (für etw)
politics [ˈpɒlətɪks]	Politik		
to take place [teɪk ˈpleɪs]	stattfinden	polite [pəˈlaɪt]	höflich
partly [ˈpɑːtli]	teilweise, zum Teil		
to settle down [ˌsetl ˈdaʊn]	zur Ruhe kommen, es sich bequem machen	**UNIT 3**	
preparation [ˌprepəˈreɪʃn]	Vorbereitung	**page 30**	
to relate (to/with) [rɪˈleɪt]	(sich) verbinden, im Zusammenhang bringen (mit)	approximately (approx) [əˈprɒksɪmətli]	ungefähr, etwa, zirka (ca.)
to focus on [ˈfəʊkəs ɒn]	sich konzentrieren auf	in residential care [ˌrezɪˈdenʃl ˈkeə]	in Heimen
background [ˈbækgraʊnd]	Hintergrund(-), Herkunft	residential [ˌrezɪˈdenʃl]	Wohn-, Wohnungs-
prospect [ˈprɒspekt]	Aussicht	nursing home [ˈnɜːsɪŋ həʊm]	Pflegeheim
firm [fɜːm]	Firma	community-based [kəˈmjuːnəti beɪst]	gemeinschaftlich, von der Gemeinschaft getragen
to occur to sb [əˈkɜː tə]	jdm einfallen	at home [ət ˈhəʊm]	zu Hause
concerning [kənˈsɜːnɪŋ]	betreffend, hinsichtlich	provider [prəˈvaɪdə]	Anbieter (Firma)
out the door [aʊt]	zur Tür hinaus, durch die Tür (hinaus)	sexual [ˈsekʃuəl]	sexuell
firm [fɜːm]	fest, verbindlich	reproductive [ˌriːprəˈdʌktɪv]	Fortpflanzungs-, Reproduktions-
		nationwide [ˌneɪʃnˈwaɪd]	landesweit
page 26		caption [ˈkæpʃn]	Bildunterschrift, Überschrift
suitable [ˈsuːtəbl]	geeignet, passend		
to hurry [ˈhʌri]	sich beeilen, eilen	unwanted [ˌʌnˈwɒntɪd]	unerwünscht
to borrow [ˈbɒrəʊ]	(sich etw) borgen, (sich) (aus)leihen	pregnancy [ˈpregnənsi]	Schwangerschaft
to volunteer [ˌvɒlənˈtɪə]	sich freiwillig melden, ehrenamtlich arbeiten	to combine [kəmˈbaɪn]	verbinden, kombinieren
nearby [ˈnɪəbaɪ]	nahe gelegen, in der Nähe	divorce [dɪˈvɔːs]	Scheidung
community centre [kəˈmjuːnəti sentə]	Gemeindezentrum	to break apart [breɪk əˈpɑːt]	auseinanderbrechen
to enclose [ɪnˈkləʊz]	beifügen, beilegen		

240

equal chances [ˌiːkwəl ˈtʃɑːnsɪz]	Chancengleichheit	it used to be [ˈjuːs tə]	es war früher (üblicher- weise)
equal [ˈiːkwəl]	gleich(berechtigt), ebenbürtig	over time [ˌəʊvə ˈtaɪm]	im Laufe der Zeit
same-sex [ˈseɪmseks]	gleichgeschlechtlich	wherever [weərˈevə]	wo (auch) immer
shall [ʃæl]	sollen	homeland [ˈhəʊmlænd]	Heimatland
granny [ˈgræni]	Oma	patriarchal [ˌpeɪtriˈɑːkl]	patriarchalisch
dysfunctional [dɪsˈfʌŋkʃənl]	gestört	household [ˈhaʊshəʊld]	Haushalt, Haushalts-
traditional [trəˈdɪʃənl]	traditionell	to marry [ˈmæri]	heiraten
to adopt [əˈdɒpt]	adoptieren	marriage [ˈmærɪdʒ]	Hochzeit, Ehe
		to arrange [əˈreɪndʒ]	arrangieren, vereinbaren

page 31

according to [əˈkɔːdɪŋ tə]	(je) nach, zufolge, laut	to integrate [ˈɪntɪgreɪt]	integrieren
poll [pəʊl]	Umfrage	native [ˈneɪtɪv]	einheimisch
maternity leave [məˈtɜːnəti liːv]	Mutterschaftsurlaub	death [deθ]	Tod, Todesfall, Tote/r
to replace (with/by) [rɪˈpleɪs]	ersetzen (durch), austauschen (gegen)	to be likely to do sth [ˈlaɪkli]	etw wahrscheinlich tun werden
cover [ˈkʌvə]	Vertretung	separation [sepəˈreɪʃn]	Trennung
to illustrate [ˈɪləstreɪt]	zeigen, veranschaulichen	majority [məˈdʒɒrəti]	größter Teil, Mehrheit
familiar (to sb/with sth) [fəˈmɪliə]	(jdm/mit etw) vertraut	access [ˈækses]	Zugang
pattern [ˈpætn]	Muster, Schema	to split sth down the middle [splɪt]	etw in der Mitte aufteilen/spalten
adoption [əˈdɒpʃn]	Adoption	daughter-in-law [ˈdɔːtər ɪn lɔː]	Schwiegertochter
scene [siːn]	Szene	to sort out [ˌsɔːt ˈaʊt]	klären, lösen
scripted reality show [ˌskrɪptɪd riˈæləti ʃəʊ]	Scripted Reality, Doku- Soap (Fernsehformat: Pseudo-Dokumentation mit Laiendarstellern)	(problems) to do with ... [tə ˈduː wɪð]	(Probleme, die) mit ... zusammenhängen
		to get sth right [ˌget ˈraɪt]	etw richtig machen
i.e. [ˌaɪ ˈiː]	d. h.	especially [ɪˈspeʃəli]	besonders, insbesondere
		bond [bɒnd]	Bindung, Verbindung
		beneficial (to) [ˌbenɪˈfɪʃl]	nützlich, vorteilhaft (für)

page 32

page 33

senior [ˈsiːniə]	leitend	keyword [ˈkiːwɜːd]	Schlüsselwort
to look into [ˌlʊk ˈɪntə]	prüfen, untersuchen	to come into being [ˌkʌm ɪntə ˈbiːɪŋ]	entstehen
to face sth [feɪs]	vor etw stehen, mit etw konfrontiert werden	potential [pəˈtenʃl]	potenziell, möglich, künftig
to define [dɪˈfaɪn]	definieren, (genauer) erklären	discussion [dɪˈskʌʃn]	Diskussion, Besprechung
folder [ˈfəʊldə]	Mappe, Ordner	to exchange [ɪksˈtʃeɪndʒ]	austauschen, eintauschen, umtauschen
set-up [ˈsetʌp]	Aufbau, System		
label [ˈleɪbl]	Kennzeichnung, Etikett	circle [ˈsɜːkl]	Kreis, Clique
extended [ɪksˈtendɪd]	erweitert	beginning [bɪˈgɪnɪŋ]	Anfang
intercultural [ˌɪntəˈkʌltʃərəl]	interkulturell	millennium, pl millennia [mɪˈleniəm, mɪˈleniə]	Jahrtausend
migrant [ˈmaɪgrənt]	Migrant/in, Zuwanderer/ Zuwanderin	to connect [kəˈnekt]	verbinden, anschließen
nuclear [ˈnjuːkliə]	Kern-	state [steɪt]	Zustand
stepfamily [ˈstepfæməli]	Stieffamilie	habit [ˈhæbɪt]	(An-)Gewohnheit
grandparent [ˈgrænpeərənts]	Großvater/-mutter, pl Großeltern	sound [saʊnd]	Ton
to share [ʃeə]	teilen	off [ɒf]	ausgeschaltet
century [ˈsentʃəri]	Jahrhundert	biracial AE [ˌbaɪˈreɪʃl]	gemischtrassig
western [ˈwestən]	westlich, West-	to go through [ˌgəʊ ˈθruː]	durchmachen, erleben
European [ˌjʊərəˈpiːən]	Europäer/in, europäisch	biological [ˌbaɪəˈlɒdʒɪkl]	biologisch
husband [ˈhʌzbənd]	Ehemann	to benefit from [ˈbenɪfɪt]	profitieren von
breadwinner [ˈbredwɪnə]	Brotverdiener/in	mixed-race BE [ˌmɪkstˈreɪs]	gemischtrassig
wife, pl wives [waɪf, waɪvz]	(Ehe-)Frau, Gattin	to feel about sth [ˈfiːl əbaʊt]	denken über etw, etw empfinden
housewife, pl housewives [ˈhaʊswaɪf]	Hausfrau	modern [ˈmɒdn]	modern
the one [ðə ˈwʌn]	der-/die-/dasjenige	to influence [ˈɪnfluəns]	beeinflussen
medium, pl media [ˈmiːdiəm, ˈmiːdiə]	Medium, Medien	discrimination (against sb) [dɪˌskrɪmɪˈneɪʃn]	Diskriminierung (eines Menschen)
to exist [ɪgˈzɪst]	existieren	racism [ˈreɪsɪzəm]	Rassismus
		tolerance [ˈtɒlərəns]	Toleranz, Verständnis
		nowadays [ˈnaʊədeɪz]	heutzutage

241

UNIT WORD LIST

relative	['relətɪv]		Verwandte/r
respectable	[rɪ'spektəbl]		angesehen, ehrbar, anständig
despite this	[dɪ'spaɪt ðɪs]		trotzdem
discriminatory	[dɪ'skrɪmɪnətəri]		benachteiligend, diskriminierend
rate	[reɪt]		Rate, Quote
side	[saɪd]		Seite

page 34

halfway	[ˌhɑːf'weɪ]		auf halbem Wege, halb(wegs)
proof	[pruːf]		Beweis
to turn sth into sth	['tɜːn ˌɪntə]		etw zu etw machen
to function	['fʌŋkʃn]		funktionieren
at some time	[ət sʌm 'taɪm]		irgendwann
e.g.	[ˌiː 'dʒiː]		z. B.
illness	['ɪlnəs]		Krankheit
to get back (to)	[get 'bæk]		zurückkommen (zu), zurückkehren (zu)
to pass	[pɑːs]		vorübergehen, vorbeigehen
to deal with sth	['diːl wɪð]		etw erledigen, etw bearbeiten
behaviour	[bɪ'heɪvjə]		Verhalten, Benehmen
to hand down	[ˌhænd 'daʊn]		weitergeben, vererben
to neglect	[nɪ'glekt]		vernachlässigen
to control	[kən'trəʊl]		kontrollieren, beherrschen
independence	[ˌɪndɪ'pendəns]		Unabhängigkeit
victim	['vɪktɪm]		Opfer
Venn diagram	['ven daɪəgræm]		Venndiagramm, Mengendiagramm
adultery	[ə'dʌltəri]		Ehebruch
alcoholism	['ælkəhɒlɪzəm]		Alkoholismus
bullying	['bʊliɪŋ]		Tyrannisieren, Mobbing
to lie (to sb)	[laɪ]		(jdn an-)lügen
manipulative	[mə'nɪpjələtɪv]		manipulativ
mental abuse	['mentəl əbjuːs]		psychische Gewalt, seelische Misshandlung
battering	['bætərɪŋ]		Prügel
to play truant	[pleɪ 'truːənt]		schwänzen, unentschuldigt fehlen
promiscuity	[ˌprɒmɪs'kjuːəti]		Promiskuität (häufiger Partnerwechsel)
to steal	[stiːl]		stehlen
soap (opera)	['səʊp ɒpərə]		Seifenoper, TV-Serie
series, pl series	['sɪəriːz]		Reihe, Serie
to appear	[ə'pɪə]		auftauchen, (er)scheinen
sibling	['sɪblɪŋ]		Bruder/Schwester, Geschwisterkind pl Geschwister
character	['kærəktə]		Charakter, Figur (Buch, Film, Comic)
television (TV)	['telɪvɪʒn]		Fernsehen
to commit	[kə'mɪt]		(Verbrechen etc.) begehen

page 35

to be afraid (of)	[ə'freɪd]		Angst haben (vor)
women's refuge	[ˌwɪmɪnz 'refjuːdʒ]		Frauenhaus
to break out (of)	[ˌbreɪk 'aʊt]		ausbrechen (aus)
lack (of)	[læk]		Mangel (an), Fehlen (von)
empathy	['empəθi]		Einfühlungsvermögen
marginalize	['mɑːdʒɪnəlaɪz]		an den Rand drängen, marginalisieren
denial	[dɪ'naɪəl]		Verdrängung
to stand by	[ˌstænd 'baɪ]		tatenlos zusehen
explanation	[ˌekspləˈneɪʃn]		Erläuterung, Erklärung
to carry over	['kæri əʊvə]		übernehmen, übertragen
to push	[pʊʃ]		schieben, stoßen, drücken
to ignore	[ɪg'nɔː]		ignorieren
refusal	[rɪ'fjuːzl]		Ablehnung, Verweigerung
painful	['peɪnfl]		schmerzhaft
unpleasant	[ʌn'plezənt]		unangenehm, unfreundlich
to be scared that	[skeəd]		fürchten, dass
scared	[skeəd]		verstört, ängstlich
conflict	['kɒnflɪkt]		Streit(igkeiten), Konflikt
to occur	[ə'kɜː]		stattfinden, geschehen
to go on	[ˌgəʊ 'ɒn]		passieren, geschehen, los sein
I see.	[aɪ 'siː]		Aha., Ich verstehe.
to abuse	[ə'bjuːz]		missbrauchen
to be left to	['left tə]		jdm überlassen bleiben
to get on with sth	[ˌget 'ɒn wɪð]		mit etw klarkommen
I'm afraid so.	[ə'freɪd]		Leider ja.
to divorce	[dɪ'vɔːs]		sich scheiden lassen
fault	[fɔːlt]		Defekt, Fehler, Mangel
to complement	['kɒmplɪmənt]		ergänzen
aggressive	[ə'gresɪv]		aggressiv
passive	['pæsɪv]		passiv, untätig
helpline	['helplaɪn]		telefonische Beratung, Telefonnotdienst
district nurse	['dɪstrɪkt nɜːs]		Gemeindeschwester, Pflegekraft in der ambulanten Pflege
to recognize	['rekəgnaɪz]		anerkennen, (wieder)erkennen
feature	['fiːtʃə]		Merkmal, Eigenschaft, Kennzeichen
over and over (again)	[ˌəʊvə ənd 'əʊvə]		immer wieder
understanding	[ˌʌndə'stændɪŋ]		Verständnis
sensitivity	[ˌsensə'tɪvəti]		Sensibilität, Einfühlungsvermögen
to pick on sb	['pɪk ɒn]		auf jdm herumhacken
to treat	[triːt]		behandeln
to come across sth	['kʌm əkrɒs]		auf etw stoßen, etw (zufällig) finden
continuous(ly)	[kən'tɪnjuəs]		kontinuierlich
to deserve	[dɪ'zɜːv]		verdienen
incest	['ɪnsest]		Inzest
to court	[tə 'kɔːt]		vor Gericht
to insist	[ɪn'sɪst]		darauf bestehen, beteuern

242

Unit word list

no idea [nəʊ aɪˈdɪə] — keine Ahnung
teenaged [ˈtiːneɪdʒd] — im Teenager-Alter
intercourse [ˈɪntəkɔːs] — Geschlechtsverkehr
like this [laɪk ˈðɪs] — so, auf diese Art/Weise
to go off [ɡəʊ ˈɒf] — weggehen
horrible [ˈhɒrəbl] — schrecklich, furchtbar, fürchterlich

to bring sb up [ˌbrɪŋ ˈʌp] — jdn aufziehen, großziehen
to look up [ˌlʊk ˈʌp] — etw nachschlagen, etw heraussuchen

bruise [bruːz] — Bluterguss, Prellung
black eye [blæk ˈaɪ] — blaues Auge
to claim [kleɪm] — angeben, behaupten
clumsy [ˈklʌmzi] — ungeschickt, schwerfällig
to cover up for sb [ˈkʌvər ʌp] — jdn decken
to call on sb [ˈkɔːl ɒn] — jdn aufsuchen
rude [ruːd] — unhöflich, unverschämt
childhood [ˈtʃaɪldhʊd] — Kindheit
manager [ˈmænɪdʒə] — Leiter/in, Manager/in
to kill [kɪl] — töten, umbringen
robbery [ˈrɒbəri] — Raub, Überfall
dependent (on) [dɪˈpendənt] — abhängig (von)
sleeping pill [ˈsliːpɪŋ pɪl] — Schlaftablette
term [tɜːm] — Trimester
to recommend [ˌrekəˈmend] — empfehlen
institution [ˌɪnstɪˈtjuːʃn] — Institution
pastoral care [ˈpɑːstərəl keə] — Seelsorge
welfare [ˈwelfeə] — Wohl(fahrt), Fürsorge
welfare department [ˈwelfeə dɪpɑːtmənt] — Sozialamt
department [dɪˈpɑːtmənt] — Abteilung, Amt

page 36

to near [nɪə] — sich nähern
to give/put sb up for adoption [ʌp fər əˈdɒpʃn] — jdn zur Adoption freigeben
to assess [əˈses] — einschätzen, beurteilen, bewerten
prospective [prəˈspektɪv] — potentiell, prospektiv
adoptive couple/ parents [əˈdɒptɪv] — Adoptiveltern
to identify [aɪˈdentɪfaɪ] — erkennen, feststellen, identifizieren
reason [ˈriːzn] — Motiv, Grund, Beweggrund
to proceed [prəˈsiːd] — voranschreiten, weitergehen
stepfather [ˈstepfɑːðə] — Stiefvater
neighbourhood [ˈneɪbəhʊd] — (Wohn-)Gegend, Nachbarschaft
to avoid [əˈvɔɪd] — (ver)meiden
figure [ˈfɪɡə] — Figur
verbal abuse [ˌvɜːbl əˈbjuːs] — Beschimpfung(en)
hostility [hɒˈstɪləti] — Feindseligkeit
grandmother [ˈɡrænmʌðə] — Großmutter
to move in (with sb) [ˈmuːv ɪn] — (bei jdm) einziehen
god [ɡɒd] — Gott
realistic [ˌriːəˈlɪstɪk] — realistisch, naturgetreu

circumstances (pl) [ˈsɜːkəmstənsɪz] — Umstände
legal [ˈliːɡl] — legal
termination [ˌtɜːmɪˈneɪʃn] — Schwangerschaftsabbruch, Beendigung
Roman Catholic [ˌrəʊmən ˈkæθlɪk] — römisch-katholisch
antenatal [ˌæntiˈneɪtl] — vorgeburtlich, pränatal
to give birth [ɡɪv ˈbɜːθ] — gebären
to liaise (with) [liˈeɪz] — zusammenarbeiten (mit), Bindeglied sein
agency [ˈeɪdʒənsi] — Agentur, Organisation
key [kiː] — Schlüssel(-), wichtige/r/s
medical [ˈmedɪkl] — Medizin-, medizinisch, ärztlich
to tend to [ˈtend] — dazu neigen
term [tɜːm] — Begriff
to induce [ɪnˈdjuːs] — einleiten
abortion [əˈbɔːʃn] — Abtreibung
traumatic [trɔːˈmætɪk] — traumatisch
precise(ly) [prɪˈsaɪs] — genau, präzise
spontaneous [spɒnˈteɪniəs] — spontan
miscarriage [ˈmɪskærɪdʒ] — Fehlgeburt
foetus [ˈfiːtəs] — Fetus

page 37

assessment [əˈsesmənt] — Prüfung, Beurteilung
to take into account [əˈkaʊnt] — berücksichtigen
to affect [əˈfekt] — sich auswirken auf, betreffen
adopter [əˈdɒptə] — Adoptierende/r
smoker [ˈsməʊkə] — Raucher/in
recommendation [ˌrekəmenˈdeɪʃn] — Empfehlung
to expose (sb to sth) [ɪkˈspəʊz] — (jdn einer Sache) aussetzen
view [vjuː] — Sicht
to refer sb to sb/sth [rɪˈfɜː] — jdn zu jdm überweisen, jdn an etw verweisen
to quit sth [kwɪt] — etw aufgeben
adviser [ədˈvaɪzə] — Berater/in
to be in one's mid-30s [mɪd] — Mitte dreißig sein
to suggest [səˈdʒest] — hinweisen auf, hindeuten auf
counselling [ˈkaʊnsəlɪŋ] — professionelle Beratung
approach [əˈprəʊtʃ] — Ansatz, Herangehensweise
consequence [ˈkɒnsɪkwəns] — Folge, Konsequenz
to place sb with sb [pleɪs] — jdn bei jdm unterbringen
to pass sth on [ˌpɑːs ˈɒn] — etw weitergeben, weiterleiten
genetic(ally) [dʒəˈnetɪk] — genetisch
convicted (for) [kənˈvɪktɪd] — verurteilt (wegen)
vandalism [ˈvændəlɪzəm] — Vandalismus
conviction [kənˈvɪkʃn] — Verurteilung
offence [əˈfens] — Straftat, Vergehen
check-up [ˈtʃekʌp] — Untersuchung
set [set] — Gruppe, Satz, Reihe
to counsel (on) [ˈkaʊnsl] — beraten (über)

UNIT WORD LIST

religious [rɪˈlɪdʒəs]	religiös	
upbringing [ˈʌpbrɪŋɪŋ]	Erziehung	
mental [ˈmentl]	geistig, psychisch, seelisch	
issue [ˈɪʃuː]	Frage, Aspekt, Problem, Streitpunkt	
similar (to) [ˈsɪmələ]	ähnlich, vergleichbar	
to come about [ˌkʌm əˈbaʊt]	passieren	
to surface [ˈsɜːfɪs]	auftauchen, aufkommen	
to perform [pəˈfɔːm]	ausführen, durchführen	
last but not least [ˌlɑːst bʌt nɒt ˈliːst]	nicht zuletzt	
gap [gæp]	Lücke	

page 38

decade [ˈdekeɪd]	Jahrzehnt
instead [ɪnˈsted]	stattdessen
to rise [raɪz]	(an)steigen
gay [geɪ]	schwul, homosexuell
childbirth [ˈtʃaɪldbɜːθ]	Geburt
drunk [drʌŋk]	betrunken
in secret [ɪn ˈsiːkrɪt]	im Geheimen
appointment [əˈpɔɪntmənt]	Termin, Verabredung
community service [kəˈmjuːnəti sɜːvɪs]	gemeinnützige Arbeit
drug [drʌg]	Droge, Rauschgift, Medikament
to terminate [ˈtɜːmɪneɪt]	beenden
home [həʊm]	Heim
follow-up [ˈfɒləʊʌp]	Folge-
to be with sb [wɪð]	mit jdm zusammen sein
not … any longer [nɒt eni ˈlɒŋgə]	nicht mehr

page 39

semi- [ˈsemi]	halb
nanny [ˈnæni]	Kindermädchen
to shout at [ˈʃaʊt ət]	anschreien
episode [ˈepɪsəʊd]	Folge (einer Serie), Episode
to rewrite [ˌriːˈraɪt]	umschreiben, neu schreiben
to act sth out [ˌækt ˈaʊt]	etw vorspielen, etw aufführen
fictional [ˈfɪkʃənl]	fiktiv, erfunden

UNIT 4

page 42

illustration [ˌɪləˈstreɪʃn]	Abbildung, Illustration
to threaten [ˈθretn]	(be)drohen
image [ˈɪmɪdʒ]	Bild, (visuelle) Vorstellung, Image
to fit (with/to) [fɪt]	passen (zu)
closely [ˈkləʊsli]	genau

page 43

depressed [dɪˈprest]	deprimiert, niedergeschlagen
way out [ˌweɪ ˈaʊt]	Ausweg, Ausgang
suicide [ˈsuːɪsaɪd]	Selbstmord
upstairs [ˌʌpˈsteəz]	(nach) oben, im oberen Stockwerk
before [bɪˈfɔː]	schon (einmal)
loud [laʊd]	laut
to act [ækt]	handeln, sich verhalten
proud [praʊd]	stolz
to hit [hɪt]	schlagen, aufprallen (auf)
to cry [kraɪ]	weinen, schreien
it's not your business [ˈbɪznəs]	es geht Sie/dich nichts an
I guess [ges]	ich nehme an, ich denke
to break sth [breɪk]	(sich) etw brechen
to throw [θrəʊ]	werfen
unspoken [ʌnˈspəʊkən]	unausgesprochen
violence [ˈvaɪələns]	Gewalt
victimization [ˌvɪktɪmaɪˈzeɪʃn]	Schikanierung
session [ˈseʃn]	Sitzung

page 44

signal [ˈsɪgnəl]	Signal, Warnzeichen
seminar [ˈsemɪnɑː]	Seminar, Fachtagung
crime [kraɪm]	Verbrechen, Kriminalität
focus [ˈfəʊkəs]	Brennpunkt, Blickpunkt
trainer [ˈtreɪnə]	Ausbilder/in
to distribute [dɪˈstrɪbjuːt]	verteilen
handout [ˈhændaʊt]	Arbeitsblatt
anxious [ˈæŋkʃəs]	unruhig, beunruhigt, ängstlich
suicidal [ˌsuːɪˈsaɪdl]	suizidal, selbstmordgefährdet
accessory [əkˈsesəri]	Accessoire
to hide [haɪd]	(sich) verbergen, (sich) verstecken
scar [skɑː]	Narbe
sunglasses (pl) [ˈsʌnglɑːsɪz]	Sonnenbrille
in public [ɪn ˈpʌblɪk]	öffentlich, in der Öffentlichkeit
credit card [ˈkredɪt kɑːd]	Kreditkarte
social occasion [ˌsəʊʃl əˈkeɪʒn]	gesellschaftliches Ereignis
occasion [əˈkeɪʒn]	Anlass, Gelegenheit
major [ˈmeɪdʒə]	groß, bedeutend
withdrawn [wɪðˈdrɔːn]	zurückgezogen
educated [ˈedʒukeɪtɪd]	(gut) ausgebildet
uneducated [ʌnˈedʒukeɪtɪd]	ungebildet
to overlook [ˌəʊvəˈlʊk]	übersehen
to deny [dɪˈnaɪ]	leugnen, bestreiten
certainty [ˈsɜːtnti]	Gewissheit
symptom [ˈsɪmptəm]	Symptom, Anzeichen
emotional abuse [ɪˌməʊʃnl əˈbjuːs]	psychischer Missbrauch, seelische Gewalt
emotional(ly) [ɪˈməʊʃnl]	emotional
to check in (with) [ˌtʃek ˈɪn]	sich melden (bei)
to go along with sb/sth [ˌgəʊ əˈlɒŋ wɪð]	jdm zustimmen, mit etw einverstanden sein
injury [ˈɪndʒəri]	Verletzung
isolation [ˌaɪsəˈleɪʃn]	Isolierung
to restrict [rɪˈstrɪkt]	beschränken, einschränken
abuser [əˈbjuːzə]	jd, der jdn/etw missbraucht, Peiniger/in

244

limited ['lɪmɪtɪd]	begrenzt
rare(ly) ['reə]	selten
psychological [ˌsaɪkə'lɒdʒɪkl]	psychologisch
self-esteem [ˌself ɪ'stiːm]	Selbstachtung, Selbstwertgefühl
to exhibit [ɪg'zɪbɪt]	zeigen, ausstellen
to spot [spɒt]	entdecken
to react (to) [ri'ækt]	reagieren (auf)

page 45

stage [steɪdʒ]	Stadium, Phase
cycle ['saɪkl]	Zyklus, Kreislauf
incomplete [ˌɪnkəm'pliːt]	unvollständig
slide [slaɪd]	Folie, Dia
to fantasize ['fæntəsaɪz]	fantasieren
to set [set]	setzen, stellen, legen
trap [træp]	Falle
to punch [pʌntʃ]	(mit Fäusten) schlagen, boxen
to kick [kɪk]	treten, kicken
to come out [ˌkʌm 'aʊt]	herauskommen
to provoke [prə'vəʊk]	provozieren, auslösen, hervorrufen
to talk sb through sth [ˌtɔːk 'θruː]	etw mit jdm durchsprechen
abusive [ə'bjuːsɪv]	missbräuchlich, Missbrauchs-
to misunderstand [ˌmɪsʌndə'stænd]	missverstehen, falsch verstehen
spouse [spaʊs, spaʊz]	Gatte/Gattin
so far [səʊ 'fɑː]	bis jetzt, bis hierher
to put the blame on sb [bleɪm]	jdm die Schuld geben
blame [bleɪm]	Schuld
jealous ['dʒeləs]	eifersüchtig
to cheat on sb ['tʃiːt ɒn]	jdn betrügen
to shift sth to sb [ʃɪft]	etw auf jdn abwälzen
to hit out [ˌhɪt 'aʊt]	drauflosschlagen
to admit [əd'mɪt]	zugeben, (ein)gestehen
surge of energy [ˌsɜːdʒ əv 'enədʒi]	Energiewelle, Energiestoß
to wear off [weə 'ɒf]	nachlassen
fix infml [fɪks]	Schuss
cigarette [ˌsɪgə'ret]	Zigarette
rush hour ['rʌʃ aʊə]	Hauptverkehrszeit
to be held up [bi ˌheld 'ʌp]	aufgehalten werden
to take (time) [teɪk]	(Zeit) brauchen
a long time [ə ˌlɒng 'taɪm]	lange
to crave sth [kreɪv]	sich nach etw sehnen
deliberately [dɪ'lɪbərətli]	absichtlich, (ganz) bewusst, vorsätzlich
mind [maɪnd]	Geist, Verstand, Gedanken, Denkweise
to remove [rɪ'muːv]	entfernen, beseitigen
usefulness ['juːsfəlnəs]	Nützlichkeit, Eignung
to blame sb [bleɪm]	jdm die Schuld geben
purpose ['pɜːpəs]	Zweck, Ziel

page 46

topic ['tɒpɪk]	Punkt, Thema
cyberbullying [ˌsaɪbə'bʊliɪŋ]	Mobbing im Netz

sexual harassment [ˌsekʃʊəl 'hærəsmənt]	sexuelle Belästigung
harassment ['hærəsmənt]	Schikane, Mobbing
to associate (with) [ə'səʊʃiət]	verbinden, assoziieren (mit)
gang [gæŋ]	Gang, Bande
weapon ['wepən]	Waffe
one-off [ˌwʌn 'ɒf]	einmalig
incident ['ɪnsɪdənt]	Vorfall, Begebenheit, Sachverhalt
to victimize ['vɪktɪmaɪz]	schikanieren
verbal ['vɜːbl]	verbal
to call sb names [kɔːl 'neɪmz]	jdn beschimpfen
to escalate ['eskəleɪt]	eskalieren
findings (pl) ['faɪndɪŋz]	Ergebnisse
to indicate ['ɪndɪkeɪt]	(an)zeigen, darauf hindeuten, hinweisen auf
to engage in sth [ɪn'geɪdʒ ɪn]	sich an etw beteiligen
to harass ['hærəs]	schikanieren, belästigen
peer [pɪə]	Gleichaltrige/r, Ebenbürtige/r
Scandinavian [ˌskændɪ'neɪviən]	skandinavisch
Sweden ['swiːdn]	Schweden
to investigate [ɪn'vestɪgeɪt]	untersuchen
user ['juːzə]	(Be-)Nutzer/in
hurtful ['hɜːtfl]	verletzend
to post [pəʊst]	bekannt geben, posten (im Internet veröffentlichen)
naked ['neɪkɪd]	nackt
worrying ['wʌriɪŋ]	besorgniserregend
who are known to ... [nəʊn]	von denen man weiß, dass ...
to attempt [ə'tempt]	versuchen
to be ashamed (of) [bi ə'ʃeɪmd]	sich schämen (für)
stigmatized ['stɪgmətaɪzd]	stigmatisiert
to fear [fɪə]	(be)fürchten
to be frightened ['fraɪtnd]	Angst haben (vor)
to punish ['pʌnɪʃ]	bestrafen
relatively ['relətɪvli]	relativ, verhältnismäßig
to survey [sə'veɪ]	untersuchen, erfassen
aggressor [ə'gresə]	Aggressor/in, Angreifer/in
to take advantage of [ˌteɪk əd'vɑːntɪdʒ əv]	(sich) zunutze machen, ausnutzen
power ['paʊə]	Macht, Kraft, Stärke
reaction [ri'ækʃn]	Reaktion
occurrence [ə'kʌrəns]	Ereignis, Vorkommen
build-up ['bɪldʌp]	Anhäufung
anger ['æŋgə]	Zorn, Wut
frustration [frʌ'streɪʃn]	Frustration
humiliation [hjuːˌmɪli'eɪʃn]	Demütigung
shooting ['ʃuːtɪŋ]	Schießerei
fear [fɪə]	Angst
insecurity [ˌɪnsɪ'kjʊərəti]	Unsicherheit
assault [ə'sɔːlt]	Überfall, Angriff
to witness ['wɪtnəs]	Zeuge sein, (mit)erleben
worse [wɜːs]	schlimmer

UNIT WORD LIST

availability [ə,veɪlə'bɪləti] — Verfügbarkeit
knife, pl knives [naɪf, naɪvz] — Messer
gun [gʌn] — Schusswaffe
to agree on sth [ə'griː ɒn] — sich auf / über etw einigen
psychologist [saɪ'kɒlədʒɪst] — Psychologe/Psychologin
to conclude [kən'kluːd] — (ab)schließen
to be on the increase ['ɪŋkriːs] — ansteigen
sweater ['swetə] — Pullover
peer pressure [,pɪə 'preʃə] — Gruppendruck, -zwang, Einfluss der Clique
music ['mjuːsɪk] — Musik
concert ['kɒnsət] — Konzert
tough [tʌf] — hart, grob, brutal
guy [gaɪ] — Typ, Kerl
influence ['ɪnfluəns] — Einfluss
viewer ['vjuːə] — Zuschauer/in
to laugh (at) ['lɑːf] — lachen (über), (aus)lachen
hurt [hɜːt] — verletzt
celebrity [sə'lebrəti] — Prominente/r
to force [fɔːs] — drängen, zwängen, zwingen
humiliating [hjuː'mɪlieɪtɪŋ] — erniedrigend
to ridicule sb ['rɪdɪkjuːl] — jdn lächerlich machen
entertainment [,entə'teɪnmənt] — Unterhaltung
site [saɪt] — (kurz für) Website
platform ['plætfɔːm] — Plattform
unsuitable [ʌn'suːtəbl] — ungeeignet, unpassend
thoughtless ['θɔːtləs] — gedankenlos, unbedacht
to go viral [gəʊ 'vaɪrəl] — viral (verbreitet) werden
to turn (into) ['tɜːn ɪntə] — werden (zu)
problematic [,prɒblə'mætɪk] — problematisch
to access ['ækses] — zugreifen auf
to glorify ['glɔːrɪfaɪ] — verherrlichen
to upload [,ʌp'ləʊd] — hochladen
home-made [,həʊm'meɪd] — selbstgemacht
exposure [ɪk'spəʊʒə] — Ausgesetztsein
violent ['vaɪələnt] — gewalttätig
to snigger ['snɪgə] — kichern
to hand sth around [,hænd ə'raʊnd] — etw herumreichen
stuff [stʌf] — Zeug, Sachen
parenting ['peərəntɪŋ] — Kindererziehung
when it comes to … [,wen ɪt 'kʌmz tə] — wenn es um … geht
to arrest [ə'rest] — verhaften
to care about ['keə əbaʊt] — sich interessieren für
blunt(ly) [blʌnt] — geradeheraus
to fail [feɪl] — versagen, durchfallen
messed-up [,mest'ʌp] — verkorkst
by far [baɪ 'fɑː] — bei weitem
mystery ['mɪstri] — Rätsel, Geheimnis
attribute [ə'trɪbjuːt] — Attribut, Eigenschaft
object ['ɒbdʒɪkt] — Objekt, Gegenstand, Ziel(scheibe)
masculine ['mæskjəlɪn] — maskulin, männlich

effeminate [ɪ'femɪnət] — feminin, effeminiert, unmännlich
teacher's pet [,tiːtʃəz 'pet] — Lieblingsschüler/in, Streber/in

page 47
choir ['kwaɪə] — Chor
mark BE [mɑːk] — Zensur, (Schul-)Note
to drop [drɒp] — fallen (lassen), verlieren
extra-curricular [,ekstrə kə'rɪkjələ] — außerschulisch
migraine ['miːgreɪn] — Migräne, pl Migräneanfälle
to bully ['bʊli] — tyrannisieren, mobben
to scratch [skrætʃ] — (zer)kratzen, sich kratzen
till [tɪl] — bis
to bleed [bliːd] — bluten
scratch [skrætʃ] — Kratzer
comment (about/on) ['kɒment] — Bemerkung (zu/über), Kommentar (zu)
dispute [dɪ'spjuːt] — Streit, Disput, Kampf
to date sb [deɪt] — mit jdm gehen, eine Beziehung haben
to weigh [weɪ] — wiegen
leader ['liːdə] — Anführer/in, Leiter/in
to prove [pruːv] — nachweisen, beweisen
to stab sb [stæb] — auf jdn einstechen, jdn niederstechen
out of … ['aʊt əv] — aus … (heraus/hinaus)
to come up with sth [,kʌm 'ʌp wɪð] — sich etw ausdenken, etw vorschlagen
to stamp sth out [,stæmp 'aʊt] — etw ausmerzen
action ['ækʃn] — Handlung, Aktion, Maßnahme(n)
to prevent [prɪ'vent] — (ver)hindern, vorbeugen

page 48
referral [rɪ'fɜːrəl] — Empfehlung, Überweisung
anonymity [,ænə'nɪməti] — Anonymität
to call in [,kɔːl 'ɪn] — anfordern, hinzuziehen
emergency [ɪ'mɜːdʒənsi] — Notfall
to rape [reɪp] — vergewaltigen
alcoholic [,ælkə'hɒlɪk] — Alkoholiker, alkoholisch
to swallow ['swɒləʊ] — (ver)schlucken
to get off [,get 'ɒf] — aussteigen aus, loskommen von
general practitioner [,dʒiː 'piː] — niedergelassene/r Allgemeinarzt/-ärztin, Hausarzt/-ärztin
to encourage [ɪn'kʌrɪdʒ] — ermutigen, ermuntern, motivieren
recording [rɪ'kɔːdɪŋ] — Aufnahme, Aufzeichnung
curtain ['kɜːtn] — Vorhang, Gardine
close (to) [kləʊs] — eng, nah, dicht (an/bei)
closeness ['kləʊsnəs] — Nähe
grief [griːf] — Kummer, Leid
self-help [,self'help] — Selbsthilfe
to get better [,get 'betə] — sich erholen, gesund werden
to pay attention (to) [peɪ ə'tenʃn] — aufpassen, achten (auf)

Unit word list

page 49

feedback ['fiːdbæk] — Rückmeldung
vital(ly) ['vaɪtl] — (lebens)wichtig
encounter [ɪn'kaʊntə] — Begegnung
disappointed [ˌdɪsə'pɔɪntɪd] — enttäuscht
matter ['mætə] — Angelegenheit, Sache
to concentrate (on) ['kɒnsntreɪt] — sich konzentrieren (auf)
uninteresting [ʌn'ɪntrəstɪŋ] — uninteressant
non-verbal [nɒn'vɜːbl] — nonverbal
to reassure [ˌriːə'ʃʊə] — beruhigen
indeed [ɪn'diːd] — in der Tat, wirklich
at ease [ət 'iːz] — bequem, zwanglos, unverkrampft
to enable [ɪ'neɪbl] — ermöglichen, befähigen
to master sth ['mɑːstə] — etw meistern, bewältigen
silence ['saɪləns] — Schweigen, Stille
patient ['peɪʃnt] — geduldig
to explore [ɪk'splɔː] — erforschen, erkunden
to work up [ˌwɜːk 'ʌp] — verarbeiten, ausarbeiten
to jump in [ˌdʒʌmp 'ɪn] — hineinspringen, eingreifen
to judge [dʒʌdʒ] — (be)urteilen, ermessen
unthreatening [ʌn'θretnɪŋ] — nicht bedrohlich
to nod [nɒd] — nicken
to remain [rɪ'meɪn] — (ver)bleiben
neutral ['njuːtrəl] — neutral
non-judgemental [ˌnɒndʒʌdʒ'mentl] — nicht wertend, vorurteilsfrei
to take sides [ˌteɪk 'saɪdz] — Partei ergreifen
role-play ['rəʊlpleɪ] — Rollenspiel
flatmate ['flætmeɪt] — Mitbewohner/in
to get to know [ˌget tə 'nəʊ] — kennenlernen
fall [fɔːl] — Sturz
to be in trouble [ɪn 'trʌbl] — Ärger haben, in Schwierigkeiten stecken
overweight [ˌəʊvə'weɪt] — übergewichtig
to tear [teə] — (zer)reißen
head teacher ['hed tiːtʃə] — Direktor/in, Schulleiter/in
to complain to sb (about) [kəm'pleɪn] — sich bei jdm beschweren, sich bei jdm beklagen (über)
to make things worse [meɪk θɪŋz 'wɜːs] — alles verschlimmern
to record [rɪ'kɔːd] — aufnehmen, aufzeichnen

page 50

to apologize [ə'pɒlədʒaɪz] — sich entschuldigen
apology [ə'pɒlədʒi] — Entschuldigung
affair [ə'feə] — Affäre, Verhältnis
to jumble ['dʒʌmbl] — durcheinander bringen
to unjumble [ʌn'dʒʌmbl] — (das Wirrwarr) ordnen
apart [ə'pɑːt] — auseinander, getrennt
to move out [ˌmuːv 'aʊt] — ausziehen

page 51

daytime TV ['deɪtaɪm] — Nachmittags-, Vorabendprogramm (Fernsehen)
authority [ɔː'θɒrəti] — Autorität, Befugnis, Kompetenz(en)
tolerant ['tɒlərənt] — tolerant

to employ [ɪm'plɔɪ] — beschäftigen
security personnel [sɪˌkjʊərəti pɜːsə'nel] — Sicherheitspersonal
to say sth out loud [ˌseɪ aʊt 'laʊd] — etw laut (aus-, vor)sprechen
speech [spiːtʃ] — Rede, Vortrag
natural ['nætʃrəl] — natürlich, echt
script [skrɪpt] — Drehbuch
to perform sth [pə'fɔːm] — etw aufführen
to interpret [ɪn'tɜːprɪt] — interpretieren
related to [rɪ'leɪtɪd] — verbunden mit
to resolve [rɪ'zɒlv] — lösen, auflösen
concept ['kɒnsept] — Idee, Konzept
attentive [ə'tentɪv] — aufmerksam
observation [ˌɒbzə'veɪʃn] — Beobachtung
interpersonal [ˌɪntə'pɜːsənl] — zwischenmenschlich

UNIT 5

page 54

homeless ['həʊmləs] — wohnungslos, obdachlos
to binge drink ['bɪndʒ drɪŋk] — komasaufen
shelter ['ʃeltə] — (Obdachlosen-)Asyl, Schutzraum, Unterschlupf
to reach out to sb [ˌriːtʃ 'aʊt tə] — die Hand nach jdm ausstrecken
at-risk [ət'rɪsk] — Risiko-, gefährdet
shocking ['ʃɒkɪŋ] — schockierend
asylum seeker [ə'saɪləm siːkə] — Asylsuchende/r
asylum [ə'saɪləm] — Asyl

page 55

route [ruːt] — Route, Strecke, Weg
homelessness ['həʊmləsnəs] — Obdachlosigkeit
facility [fə'sɪləti] — Einrichtung
refugee [ˌrefju'dʒiː] — Flüchtling
throughout [θruː'aʊt] — überall (in), in ganz
to manufacture [ˌmænju'fæktʃə] — herstellen, produzieren
alcohol ['ælkəhɒl] — Alkohol
kit [kɪt] — Ausrüstung, Kit
decriminalization [diːˌkrɪmɪnəlaɪ'zeɪʃn] — Entkriminalisierung
to give a presentation [ˌgɪv ə prezn'teɪʃn] — ein Referat halten
troubled ['trʌbld] — mit Problemen belastet, geplagt

page 56

greeting ['griːtɪŋ] — Gruß(formel), Begrüßung
small talk ['smɔːl tɔːk] — Smalltalk
by the way [baɪ ðə 'weɪ] — übrigens, nebenbei (bemerkt)
nice to meet you [ˌnaɪs tə 'miːt ju] — schön, dich/Sie kennenzulernen, sehr erfreut
as a matter of fact [æz ə ˌmætər əv 'fækt] — tatsächlich
around the corner [əˌraʊnd ðə 'kɔːnə] — um die Ecke

UNIT WORD LIST

it takes me five minutes [ɪt ˈteɪks mi]	ich brauche fünf Minuten	to experiment [ɪkˈsperɪmənt]	experimentieren
to drive sb over [ˌdraɪv ˈəʊvə]	jdn vorbeifahren, herbringen	to go along with the crowd infml [ˌgəʊ əˌlɒŋ wɪð ðə ˈkraʊd]	mit der Herde mitgehen, mit dem Strom schwimmen
to drive in [ˌdraɪv ˈɪn]	hineinfahren, hereinfahren	vodka [ˈvɒdkə]	Wodka
motorway [ˈməʊtəweɪ]	Autobahn	instead of [ɪnˈsted əv]	anstatt, anstelle von
satnav [ˈsætnæv]	Navi(gationsgerät)	to organize [ˈɔːgənaɪz]	organisieren
latecomer [ˈleɪtkʌmə]	Nachzügler/in	to go right off the rails infml [ˌraɪt ɒf ðə ˈreɪlz]	auf die schiefe Bahn gelangen, aus dem Gleis geraten
to take it in turns [ˌteɪk ɪt ɪn ˈtɜːnz]	sich abwechseln	hangover [ˈhæŋəʊvə]	Kater, Hangover
to take notes (on) [teɪk ˈnəʊts]	(sich) Notizen machen (zu)	park [pɑːk]	Park
one … or another [wʌn ɔːr əˈnʌðə]	der/die/das eine oder andere …	to hang out [ˌhæŋ ˈaʊt]	rumhängen
to drop out of sth [ˌdrɒp ˈaʊt]	aus etw aussteigen, etw abbrechen	to sleep rough [ˌsliːp ˈrʌf]	im Freien übernachten, auf der Straße leben
combination [ˌkɒmbɪˈneɪʃn]	Kombination, Verbindung	to end up [ˌend ˈʌp]	(schließlich) gelangen, landen, enden
individual(ly) [ˌɪndɪˈvɪdʒuəl]	einzeln, individuell	to put sb in touch with [ˌpʊt ɪn ˈtʌtʃ]	für jdn den Kontakt herstellen mit
broad [brɔːd]	breit	sheltered [ˈʃeltəd]	geschützt, behütet
specific(ally) [spəˈsɪfɪk]	bestimmt, speziell, spezifisch	accommodation [əˌkɒməˈdeɪʃn]	Unterkunft, Unterbringung
priority [praɪˈɒrəti]	Priorität	one-to-one [ˌwʌn tə ˈwʌn] therapy [ˈθerəpi]	Einzel-Therapie
entitled [ɪnˈtaɪtld]	berechtigt	GCSE (= General Certificate of Secondary Education) [ˌdʒiː siː es ˈiː]	Prüfung für Schüler ab 15, mittlerer Schulabschluss
in the first place [ɪn ðə ˈfɜːst pleɪs]	überhaupt (erst mal), am Anfang (schon), an erster Stelle	not all that (brilliant) infml [nɒt ˈɔːl ðæt]	nicht ganz so (toll)
for [fə]	wegen	to pass [pɑːs]	(Prüfung) bestehen, schaffen
voluntary [ˈvɒləntri]	freiwillig, spontan	hairdresser [ˈheədresə]	Friseur/in
to re-establish [ˌriːɪˈstæblɪʃ]	wiederherstellen	salon [ˈsælən]	Salon
to reunite [ˌriːjuːˈnaɪt]	wiedervereinigen	to be fun [bi ˈfʌn]	Spaß machen
to take sth up [ˌteɪk ˈʌp]	etw aufnehmen, mit etw (neu) anfangen	back in touch [bæk ɪn ˈtʌtʃ]	wieder in Kontakt
participant [pɑːˈtɪsɪpənt]	Teilnehmer/in	to destroy [dɪˈstrɔɪ]	zerstören, vernichten
figure [ˈfɪgə]	Zahl, Ziffer	property [ˈprɒpəti]	Eigentum
to overcome [ˌəʊvəˈkʌm]	überwinden	uncomfortable [ʌnˈkʌmftəbl]	ungemütlich, unwohl
improvement [ɪmˈpruːvmənt]	Verbesserung	condition [kənˈdɪʃn]	Bedingung, Zustand
in terms of … [ɪn ˈtɜːmz əv]	was … angeht	unacceptable [ˌʌnəkˈseptəbl]	unannehmbar, inakzeptabel
to harm [hɑːm]	schaden, verletzen	similarity [ˌsɪməˈlærəti]	Ähnlichkeit
to poison [ˈpɔɪzn]	vergiften	prostitute [ˈprɒstɪtjuːt]	Prostituierte/r
self-harm [ˈselfhɑːm]	Selbstverletzung	to pick up sb [ˌpɪk ˈʌp]	jdn aufgreifen
to get to grips with sth infml [ˌget tə ˈgrɪps]	etw in den Griff bekommen	probation [prəˈbeɪʃn]	Bewährung
criminal [ˈkrɪmɪnl]	Verbrecher/in, Kriminelle/r, kriminell, strafbar	probation officer [prəˈbeɪʃn ɒfɪsə]	Bewährungshelfer/in
to offend [əˈfend]	straffällig werden	shared flat [ˌʃeəd ˈflæt]	Wohngemeinschaft
perspective [pəˈspektɪv]	Perspektive	illegal(ly) [ɪˈliːgl]	illegal, verboten, gesetzwidrig
typical (of) [ˈtɪpɪkl]	typisch (für)	building site [ˈbɪldɪŋ saɪt]	Baustelle
percentage [pəˈsentɪdʒ]	Anteil, Prozentsatz	wage [weɪdʒ]	Lohn, Gehalt
page 57		young offender institution [jʌŋ əˈfendə ɪnstɪtjuːʃn]	Jugendgefängnis
to chuck sb out infml [ˌtʃʌk ˈaʊt]	jdn rausschmeißen	to report to sb [rɪˈpɔːt tə]	sich bei jdm melden
constantly [ˈkɒnstənt]	ständig	vocational school [vəʊˌkeɪʃənl ˈskuːl]	Berufsschule, berufsbildende Schule
warning (against) [ˈwɔːnɪŋ]	Warnung (vor), Verwarnung	mechatronics [ˌmekəˈtrɒnɪks]	Mechatronik
to vandalize [ˈvændəlaɪz]	mutwillig beschädigen, zerstören	hygiene [ˈhaɪdʒiːn]	Hygiene
youth court [ˈjuːθ kɔːt]	Jugendgericht		
mate infml [meɪt]	Freund, Kumpel		

248

Unit word list

page 58

sponsor ['spɒnsə] — Geldgeber/in, Sponsor/in
to announce [ə'naʊns] — ankündigen, bekanntgeben

for good [fə 'gʊd] — für immer
strategy ['strætədʒi] — Strategie
to persuade [pə'sweɪd] — überreden, überzeugen
trust [trʌst] — Vertrauen
dignity ['dɪgnəti] — Würde
Urdu ['ʊədu:] — Urdu (Landessprache in Pakistan und weiten Teilen Indiens)

to live rough [lɪv 'rʌf] — auf der Straße leben
disagreement [ˌdɪsə'gri:mənt] — Meinungsverschiedenheit

unwilling to do sth [ˌʌn'wɪlɪŋ] — nicht bereit, etw zu tun

in case [ɪn 'keɪs] — für den Fall, dass
moreover [mɔːr'əʊvə] — außerdem, zudem
suspicious [sə'spɪʃəs] — misstrauisch
persuasion [pə'sweɪʒn] — Überzeugung, Überzeugungskunst

to view sth/sb [vju:] — sich etw/jdn anschauen, etw/jdn betrachten

to retain [rɪ'teɪn] — behalten
to travel ['trævl] — reisen
to examine [ɪg'zæmɪn] — untersuchen, prüfen
in privacy [ɪn 'prɪvəsi] — diskret
medication [ˌmedɪ'keɪʃn] — Arzneimittel
to put together [ˌpʊt tə'geðə] — zusammenstellen
rehabilitation [ˌri:əˌbɪlɪ'teɪʃn] — Rehabilitation
rehab ['ri:hæb] — Reha, Drogenentzug
to tackle a problem ['tækl] — ein Problem angehen
to make up one's mind [ˌmeɪk ʌp wʌnz 'maɪnd] — sich entscheiden

page 59

schedule ['ʃedju:l] — Terminplan, Zeitplan
on duty [ɒn 'dju:ti] — im Dienst
to write up [raɪt 'ʌp] — verfassen
AA [eɪ 'eɪ] — anonyme Alkoholiker
to review [rɪ'vju:] — bewerten, prüfen
media centre ['mi:diə sentə] — Medienzentrum
catalogue ['kætəlɒg] — Katalog
contribution (to) [ˌkɒntrɪ'bju:ʃn] — Beitrag (zu)
to contribute [kən'trɪbju:t] — beitragen
to display [dɪ'spleɪ] — anzeigen, ausstellen, präsentieren
on behalf of [ɒn bɪ'hɑːf əv] — in Namen
well known [ˌwel 'nəʊn] — bekannt
manufacturer [ˌmænju'fæktʃərə] — Hersteller/in, Produzent/in

page 60

to assign [ə'saɪn] — zuweisen, zuteilen
case worker ['keɪs wɜ:kə] — Sachbearbeiter/in
to specialize (in) ['speʃəlaɪz] — sich spezialisieren (auf), sich spezialisiert haben (auf)

---

to fill sb in on sth [fɪl 'ɪn] — jdn über etw informieren
graph [græf] — Diagramm, Graph
to depict [dɪ'pɪkt] — darstellen, aufzeigen
by age [ˌbaɪ 'eɪdʒ] — nach Alter (aufgeschlüsselt)

to represent [ˌreprɪ'zent] — vertreten, repräsentieren
scale [skeɪl] — Skala
amongst [ə'mʌŋst] — zwischen, unter
level ['levl] — Ebene, Niveau, Höhe
consumption [kən'sʌmpʃn] — Verbrauch, Konsum
to reach a high/low [ri:tʃ] — einen Höhepunkt/ Tiefpunkt erreichen
to decrease (by) [dɪ'kri:s] — fallen, abnehmen, verringern (um)
to increase (by) [ɪn'kri:s] — steigern, erhöhen (um)
slight(ly) ['slaɪtli] — geringfügig, leicht
to plunge [plʌndʒ] — fallen, stürzen
to soar [sɔ:] — steigen, emporschnellen
legalization [ˌli:gəlaɪ'zeɪʃən] — Legalisierung

to overtake [ˌəʊvə'teɪk] — überholen
to legalize ['li:gəlaɪz] — legalisieren
marijuana [ˌmærə'wɑːnə] — Marihuana
to doubt [daʊt] — bezweifeln
Dutch [dʌtʃ] — Holländer/in, holländisch
lenient ['li:niənt] — milde, nachsichtig
forbidden [fə'bɪdn] — verboten
foreigner ['fɒrənə] — Ausländer/in
tourism ['tʊərɪzəm] — Tourismus
cannabis ['kænəbɪs] — Cannabis
amount [ə'maʊnt] — Menge, Betrag
policy ['pɒləsi] — Politik, Vorgehensweise, Regelung

to adopt [ə'dɒpt] — anwenden, sich entscheiden für

analysis, pl analyses [ə'næləsɪs, ə'næləsi:z] — Analyse
huge [hju:dʒ] — gewaltig, riesig

page 61

to decriminalize [di:'krɪmɪnəlaɪz] — entkriminalisieren
argument ['ɑːgjumənt] — Argument, Streit
incorrect [ˌɪnkə'rekt] — falsch, unrichtig
jail [dʒeɪl] — Gefängnis
treatment ['tri:tmənt] — Behandlung
Portuguese [ˌpɔːtʃu'gi:z] — portugiesisch, Portugiese/Portugiesin

to comment on ['kɒment ɒn] — kommentieren
infection [ɪn'fekʃn] — Infektion
to decline [dɪ'klaɪn] — abnehmen, zurückgehen
(drug) trafficking ['træfɪkɪŋ] — (Drogen-)Handel
resounding success [rɪˌzaʊndɪŋ sək'ses] — durchschlagender Erfolg
turnaround ['tɜːnəraʊnd] — Aufschwung, Kehrtwendung

dramatic [drə'mætɪk] — dramatisch
liberal ['lɪbrəl] — liberal
possession [pə'zeʃn] — Besitz, Besitztum
panel ['pænl] — Gremium, Jury
to refuse [rɪ'fju:z] — ablehnen

249

UNIT WORD LIST

jail sentence ['dʒeɪl sentəns]	Gefängnisstrafe	
punishable ['pʌnɪʃəbl]	strafbar	
steadily ['stedɪli]	stetig, kontinuierlich	
to leap up [ˌliːp 'ʌp]	hochschnellen	
to save [seɪv]	(ein)sparen	
prison ['prɪzn]	Gefängnis	
to be unlikely to do sth [ʌn'laɪkli]	etw wohl kaum tun werden	
spokesperson, (pl) spokespersons/spokespeople ['spəʊkspɜːsn, 'spəʊkspiːpl]	Sprecher/in	
to reduce (by) [rɪ'djuːs]	reduzieren, verringern (um)	
to crack down [ˌkræk 'daʊn]	hart durchgreifen	
addict ['ædɪkt]	Abhängige/r	
abridged [ə'brɪdʒd]	(ab)gekürzt	
debate [dɪ'beɪt]	Debatte	

page 62

addicted (to) [ə'dɪktɪd]	süchtig (nach), abhängig (von)	
to beg sb for sth ['beg fə]	jdn um etw anbetteln	
shoplifting ['ʃɒplɪftɪŋ]	Ladendiebstahl	
shopkeeper ['ʃɒpkiːpə]	Ladenbesitzer/in	
to hand over [ˌhænd 'əʊvə]	übergeben, überantworten	
motor mechanic ['məʊtə məkænɪk]	Kraftfahrzeugmechaniker/in	
distribution [ˌdɪstrɪ'bjuːʃn]	Verteilung, (Aus-)Lieferung	
region ['riːdʒən]	Region	

page 63

prompt [prɒmpt]	Stichwort, Vorgabe	
to sit in (on) [ˌsɪt 'ɪn]	anwesend sein (bei)	
to bother sb ['bɒðə]	jdn stören, jdn belästigen	
to allocate ['æləkeɪt]	verteilen, zuordnen	
visuals (pl) ['vɪʒuəlz]	Anschauungsmaterial	
audience ['ɔːdiəns]	(die) Zuhörer, Zuschauer, (das) Publikum	
to mediate ['miːdieɪt]	vermitteln, (sprachlich) inhaltlich wiedergeben	
to put sth forward [ˌpʊt 'fɔːwəd]	(Argumente) vorbringen, zur Diskussion stellen	
competence ['kɒmpɪtəns]	Kompetenz	

UNIT 6

page 66

to promote sb [prə'məʊt]	jdn befördern	
skin [skɪn]	Haut, Schale	
to freak sb out [ˌfriːk 'aʊt]	jdn aufregen, ausflippen lassen	
racial ['reɪʃl]	Rassen-, rassisch	
speech bubble ['spiːtʃbʌbl]	Sprechblase	
to analyse ['ænəlaɪz]	analysieren, untersuchen	
cartoonist [kɑː'tuːnɪst]	Zeichner (von Cartoons/Karikaturen)	

page 67

to pile up [ˌpaɪl 'ʌp]	sich häufen, sich auftürmen, (sich) (auf)stapeln	
legal ['liːgl]	Rechts-, juristisch	
intimidation [ɪnˌtɪmɪ'deɪʃn]	Einschüchterung	
depression [dɪ'preʃn]	Depression(en)	
inner ['ɪnə]	innere/r/s	
resignation [ˌrezɪg'neɪʃn]	Resignation	
mediator ['miːdieɪtə]	Vermittler/in	
record ['rekɔːd]	Aufzeichnung, Nachweis	
restructuring [ˌriː'strʌktʃərɪŋ]	Umstrukturierung	
to create [kri'eɪt]	erstellen, (er)schaffen	
guideline ['gaɪdlaɪn]	Richtlinie	
resource [rɪ'sɔːs]	(Hilfs-)Mittel, Ressource	
core [kɔː]	Basis(-), Kern(-), Schwerpunkt(-)	
to draw on ['drɔː ɒn]	zurückgreifen auf, schöpfen aus	

page 68

engineer [ˌendʒɪ'nɪə]	Ingenieur/in, Techniker/in	
Russia ['rʌʃə]	Russland	
Human Resources (HR) [ˌhjuːmən rɪ'sɔːsɪz]	Personalabteilung	
to be to do sth ['bi tə]	etw tun sollen	
to hold [həʊld]	(Veranstaltungen) abhalten, (Gespräche) führen	
to familiarize sb/yourself with [fə'mɪliəraɪz]	sich/jdn vertraut machen mit	
translation [træns'leɪʃn]	Übersetzung	
document ['dɒkjumənt]	Dokument	
joke [dʒəʊk]	Witz, Scherz	
orientation [ˌɔːriən'teɪʃn]	Orientierung	
offensive [ə'fensɪv]	beleidigend, anstößig	
remark [rɪ'mɑːk]	Bemerkung	
suggestive [sə'dʒestɪv]	zweideutig, anzüglich	
gesture ['dʒestʃə]	Geste	
to stare (at) ['steər ət]	(an)starren	
manner ['mænə]	Art (und Weise)	
lewd [luːd]	unanständig, anzüglich	
to touch [tʌtʃ]	berühren, anfassen	
inappropriate [ˌɪnə'prəʊpriət]	ungeeignet, unpassend, unangemessen	
Is that OK with you? [əʊ'keɪ wɪð]	Ist dir/Ihnen das recht?	
that good ['ðæt gʊd]	so gut	
to go over sth [ˌgəʊ 'əʊvə]	etw durchgehen, durchsehen	
to pretend [prɪ'tend]	so tun, als ob	
to bring along [ˌbrɪŋ ə'lɒŋ]	mitbringen	
attractive [ə'træktɪv]	attraktiv, reizvoll	
to make sb's life hell/difficult [meɪk ˌlaɪf 'hel, meɪk ˌlaɪf 'dɪfɪkəlt]	jdm das Leben zur Hölle/schwer machen	
to discriminate against [dɪ'skrɪmɪneɪt əgenst]	diskriminieren	
to be open about sth ['əʊpən əbaʊt]	offen umgehen mit	
homosexual [ˌhəʊmə'sekʃuəl]	homosexuell, Homosexuelle/r	
even though [ˌiːvn 'ðəʊ]	auch wenn, selbst wenn	
to hang up [ˌhæŋ 'ʌp]	aufhängen	
dirty ['dɜːti]	schmutzig	

250

Unit word list

things like that [ˌθɪŋz laɪk ˈðæt] — solche Dinge
disgusting [dɪsˈɡʌstɪŋ] — ekelhaft, widerlich, abscheulich
photograph [ˈfəʊtəɡrɑːf] — Foto(grafie)
gapped [ɡæpt] — mit Lücken versehen

page 69

to perceive [pəˈsiːv] — wahrnehmen, erkennen
conclusion [kənˈkluːʒn] — Fazit, Schluss
to delete [dɪˈliːt] — löschen
witness [ˈwɪtnəs] — Zeuge/Zeugin
complaint [kəmˈpleɪnt] — Beschwerde, Klage, Reklamation
to guarantee [ˌɡærənˈtiː] — garantieren
to make a complaint [ˌmeɪk ə kəmˈpleɪnt] — sich beschweren
to get on with sth [ˌɡet ˈɒn wɪð] — etw erledigen, mit etw weitermachen, vorankommen
at the same time [ət ðə seɪm ˈtaɪm] — zur selben Zeit, um die gleiche Zeit
to highlight [ˈhaɪlaɪt] — hervorheben, markieren
to take on [ˌteɪk ˈɒn] — annehmen, übernehmen

page 70

to evaluate [ɪˈvæljueɪt] — einschätzen, bewerten, auswerten
to relate to [rɪˈleɪt tə] — sich beziehen auf, im Zusammenhang stehen mit
evaluation [ɪˌvæljuˈeɪʃn] — Auswertung, Bewertung
responsibility [rɪˌspɒnsəˈbɪləti] — Verantwortung
unclear [ˌʌnˈklɪə] — unklar
to satisfy [ˈsætɪsfaɪ] — zufriedenstellen, befriedigen
a great deal (of) [ə ˌɡreɪt ˈdiːl] — viel, eine Menge
co-worker [ˈkəʊ wɜːkə] — Arbeitskollege/-kollegin
say (in) [seɪ] — Mitspracherecht (in/bei)
headache [ˈhedeɪk] — Kopfschmerzen
muscle [ˈmʌsl] — Muskel
tension [ˈtenʃn] — Verspannung(en), Spannung
neck [nek] — Hals, Halsausschnitt
stomach [ˈstʌmək] — Magen, Bauch
pain [peɪn] — Schmerz(en)
indigestion [ˌɪndɪˈdʒestʃən] — Magenprobleme, Magenschmerzen
digestive [daɪˈdʒestɪv] — Verdauungs-
tranquilizer [ˈtræŋkwəlaɪzə] — Beruhigungsmittel
caffeinated [ˈkæfɪneɪtɪd] — koffeinhaltig
beverage [ˈbevərɪdʒ] — Getränk
to add up [ˌæd ˈʌp] — zusammenrechnen
to have sb do sth [ˌhæv ˈduː] — jdn etw tun lassen
to take a break [ˌteɪk əˈbreɪk] — (eine) Pause machen
to disturb [dɪsˈtɜːb] — stören
concentration [ˌkɒnsnˈtreɪʃn] — Konzentration
tense [tens] — angespannt, verkrampft
(at) lunchtime [ˈlʌntʃtaɪm] — (zur) Mittagszeit

---

canteen [kænˈtiːn] — Kantine
nice and (quiet) [ˈnaɪs ən] — schön (leise)
for heaven's sake [fə ˌhevnz ˈseɪk] — um Himmels willen
to be up to sb [bi ˈʌp tə] — jds Sache sein
overall [ˌəʊvərˈɔːl] — allgemein, (ins)gesamt, Gesamt-
score [skɔː] — Ergebnis, Punktestand
average [ˈævərɪdʒ] — durchschnittlich, Durchschnitt
to lower [ˈləʊə] — senken
as soon as [əz ˈsuːn əz] — sobald
excerpt [ˈeksɜːpt] — Auszug, Ausschnitt
IT (Information Technology) [ˌaɪ ˈtiː, ˌɪnfəˌmeɪʃn tekˈnɒlədʒi] — Informationstechnologie
to force sb to do sth [fɔːs] — jdn zwingen etw zu tun
waste (of time) [weɪst] — (Zeit-)Verschwendung
so-called [ˌsəʊ ˈkɔːld] — sogenannt
intelligence [ɪnˈtelɪdʒəns] — Intelligenz
performance [pəˈfɔːməns] — Leistung
to keep to [ˈkiːp tə] — sich halten an, einhalten, bleiben bei
and so on [ənd ˈsəʊ ɒn] — und so weiter
to have time off [ɒf] — nicht da sein, nicht auf/bei der Arbeit sein

page 71

to put yourself in sb's shoes [ɪn ˌsʌmbədiz ˈʃuːz] — sich in jds Lage versetzen
graduate [ˈɡrædʒuət] — Absolvent/in
to quit [kwɪt] — kündigen
appreciation [əˌpriːʃiˈeɪʃn] — Anerkennung
recognition [ˌrekəɡˈnɪʃn] — (An-)Erkennung, (Wieder-)Erkennen
to make a note of sth [ˌmeɪk ə ˈnəʊt əv] — sich etw notieren
upset [ʌpˈset] — aufgeregt, mitgenommen, bestürzt
programming [ˈprəʊɡræmɪŋ] — Programmierung, Programmier-
approval [əˈpruːvl] — Zustimmung
to be off sick [ɒf ˈsɪk] — krankgeschrieben sein
lately [ˈleɪtli] — in letzter Zeit
to get your act together [ˌɡet jɔːr ˈækt təɡeðə] — sich zusammenreißen
in fact [ɪn ˈfækt] — tatsächlich, eigentlich
to set up (a meeting/a session) [ˌset ˈʌp] — (ein Treffen/eine Sitzung) planen, arrangieren, vereinbaren
to take it easy [ˌteɪk ɪt ˈiːsi] — es ruhig angehen, sich schonen
technology [tekˈnɒlədʒi] — Technik, Technologie
to graduate [ˈɡrædʒueɪt] — den Abschluss machen
What's wrong with …? [ˈrɒŋ] — Was stimmt nicht mit …? / Was ist das Problem mit …?
promotion [prəˈməʊʃn] — Beförderung, Aufstieg
professional [prəˈfeʃənl] — Fachmann/-frau, in einem gehobenen Beruf Tätige/r
to be involved with [ɪnˈvɒlvd wɪð] — in einer Beziehung stehen mit, zu tun haben mit
accurate(ly) [ˈækjərət] — genau, präzise

251

UNIT WORD LIST

to **meet with** sb ['miːt wɪð]	sich mit jdm treffen	to **stay on** [ˌsteɪ 'ɒn]	noch (da) bleiben
transcript ['trænskrɪpt]	Niederschrift, Protokoll	to **axe** [æks]	entlassen, streichen
unfair (to sb) [ˌʌn'feə]	unfair, ungerecht (jdm gegenüber)	to **retrain** [ˌriː'treɪn]	umschulen, sich umschulen lassen
director [dəˈrektə]	Geschäftsführer/in, Chef/in	**teleworker** ['teliwɜːkə]	Telearbeiter/in
head [hed]	Leiter/in, Chef/in	**atmosphere** ['ætməsfɪə]	Atmosphäre, Stimmung
smooth(ly) [smuːð]	glatt, reibungslos, problemlos	**insensitive(ly)** [ɪnˈsensətɪv]	gefühllos, unsensibel
to **transfer (sb/sth)** [trænsˈfɜː]	(jdn) versetzen, (etw) verlegen	to **finish up** [ˌfɪnɪʃ 'ʌp]	fertig machen, beenden
demotivation [ˌdiːməʊtɪˈveɪʃn]	Demotivation	**in the end** [ɪn ði 'end]	schließlich, letztendlich
on time [ɒn 'taɪm]	pünktlich	**…, though.** [ðəʊ]	… aber …, … trotzdem …, (in Fragen) … (aber) wenigstens …
page 72		**freelance** ['friːlɑːns]	selbstständig, freiberuflich
closure ['kləʊʒə]	Abschluss, Schließung, Stilllegung	to **go freelance** ['friːlɑːns]	sich selbstständig machen, freiberuflich arbeiten
multinational [ˌmʌltiˈnæʃnəl]	multinational, multinationaler Konzern	to **do well** [ˌduː 'wel]	gut laufen, erfolgreich sein
to **restructure** [ˌriːˈstrʌktʃə]	umstrukturieren	to **outsource** [ˈaʊtsɔːs]	(Arbeit) auslagern, outsourcen
downsizing [ˈdaʊnsaɪzɪŋ]	Personalabbau	**telework(ing)** ['teliwɜːk]	Telearbeit
to **lay sb off** [ˌleɪ 'ɒf]	jdn entlassen, jdm betriebsbedingt kündigen	to **intend to do sth** [ɪnˈtend]	beabsichtigen / vorhaben, etw zu tun
cut [kʌt]	(Ver-)Kürzung, Schnitt	**page 73**	
to **do badly** [ˌduː 'bædli]	schlecht laufen, keinen Erfolg haben	**quote** [kwəʊt]	Zitat
severance package/pay ['sevərəns pækɪdʒ, 'sevərəns peɪ]	Abfindung	**control** [kənˈtrəʊl]	Kontrolle, Regulierung, Steuerung
to **calculate** ['kælkjuleɪt]	ausrechnen, berechnen, kalkulieren	**entire(ly)** [ɪnˈtaɪə]	gesamte/r/s, ganz, vollständig
to **keep doing sth** [kiːp]	etw dauernd/immer wieder tun	**superior** [suːˈpɪəriə]	Vorgesetzte/r
to **invest in** [ɪnˈvest]	investieren in	to **be mistaken (about)** [mɪˈsteɪkən]	sich irren, sich täuschen (in)
bulletin board [ˈbʊlətɪn bɔːd]	Anschlagtafel, Schwarzes Brett	**CEO (Chief Executive Officer)** [ˌsiː iː 'əʊ, ˌtʃiːf ɪgˈzekjətɪv ɒfɪsə]	Geschäftsführer/in, Vorstandsvorsitzende/r
lay-off ['leɪɒf]	Entlassung	**freelancer** ['friːlɑːnsə]	Freiberufler/in
circular ['sɜːkjələ]	rund, Rund-	**tool** [tuːl]	Werkzeug, Instrument
to **benefit sb** ['benɪfɪt]	jdm nützen, zugutekommen	**alternative** [ɔːlˈtɜːnətɪv]	Alternative, alternativ
in two weeks' time [ɪn ˌtuː wiːks 'taɪm]	in zwei Wochen	**compensation** [ˌkɒmpənˈseɪʃn]	Schaden(s)ersatz, Entschädigung, Kompensation
to **do/work overtime** ['əʊvətaɪm]	Überstunden machen	**survivor** [səˈvaɪvə]	Überlebende/r
delivery [dɪˈlɪvəri]	Lieferung	**flexitime** ['fleksitaɪm]	Gleitzeit, flexible Arbeitszeit(en)
to **work on sth** [ˈwɜːk ɒn]	arbeiten an	to **find closure (with sth)** [ˌfaɪnd ˈkləʊʒə]	abschließen (mit etw), (etw) hinter sich lassen
to **be back to square one** [ˌbæk tə skweə ˈwʌn]	wieder von vorne anfangen müssen	**loss** [lɒs]	Verlust
line [laɪn]	(Warte-)Schlange	**earnings** (pl) [ˈɜːnɪŋz]	Verdienst, Einkommen, Einnahmen
to **stand/wait in line (for)** [ɪn 'laɪn]	Schlange stehen, sich anstellen (für/nach)	**affected by** [əˈfektɪd baɪ]	betroffen, beeinflusst, beeindruckt von
to **hire sb** ['haɪə]	jdn engagieren, einstellen, beauftragen	**page 74**	
smart [smɑːt]	intelligent, geschickt	**after-work (activities)** [ˌɑːftə 'wɜːk]	(Aktivitäten) nach Feierabend
rival ['raɪvl]	Konkurrenz, Rivale/Rivalin	**economic** [ˌiːkəˈnɒmɪk]	wirtschaftlich, Wirtschafts-
to **downsize** ['daʊnsaɪz]	(sich) verkleinern, Personal abbauen	**overworked** [ˌəʊvəˈwɜːkt]	überarbeitet
to **fire sb** ['faɪə]	jdn (fristlos) entlassen, jdn feuern	**rumour** [ˈruːmə]	Gerücht
to **keep sb on** [ˌkiːp 'ɒn]	jdn weiterbeschäftigen	to **propose** [prəˈpəʊz]	vorschlagen, unterbreiten, darlegen
school-aged (children) ['skuːl eɪdʒd]	(Kinder) im Schulalter	to **come as a/no surprise** [səˈpraɪz]	es ist eine/keine Überraschung

252

to **call a meeting** [ˌkɔːl ə ˈmiːtɪŋ]	eine Sitzung/ein Meeting einberufen
to **keep a close eye on sth** [kiːp ə kləʊs ˈaɪ ɒn]	jdn/etw genau beobachten, auf jdn/etw scharf aufpassen

page 75

to **publish** [ˈpʌblɪʃ]	veröffentlichen
dissatisfied [dɪsˈsætɪsfaɪd]	unzufrieden
to **formulate** [ˈfɔːmjuleɪt]	formulieren
to **express** [ɪkˈspres]	ausdrücken, zum Ausdruck bringen
separate [ˈseprət]	getrennt
openness [ˈəʊpənnəs]	Offenheit, Aufgeschlossenheit
to **peer-review** [ˌpɪə rɪˈvjuː]	die Arbeit von Mitschülern/Mitschülerinnen bewerten, prüfen
to what extent …? [ɪkˈstent]	in welchem Maß(e) …?
insight (into) [ˈɪnsaɪt]	Einblick (in), Verständnis (von)
to **arise** [əˈraɪz]	sich ergeben, entstehen, auftreten

UNIT 7

page 78

United Nations (UN) [juːˌnaɪtɪd ˈneɪʃnz]	Vereinte Nationen (UN)
convention [kənˈvenʃn]	Abkommen, Konvention
principle [ˈprɪnsəpl]	Prinzip, Grundsatz
inherent [ɪnˈhɪərənt]	angeboren, innewohnend, eigen
autonomy [ɔːˈtɒnəmi]	Autonomie, Unabhängigkeit
participation [pɑːˌtɪsɪˈpeɪʃn]	Teilnahme, Beteiligung
inclusion [ɪnˈkluːʒn]	Aufnahme, Einbeziehung, Inklusion
acceptance [əkˈseptəns]	Akzeptanz, Annahme
human [ˈhjuːmən]	menschlich, Mensch
diversity [daɪˈvɜːsəti]	Vielfalt
humanity [hjuːˈmænəti]	Menschheit, Menschlichkeit
equality [iˈkwɒləti]	Gleichberechtigung, Gleichheit
accessibility [əkˌsesəˈbɪləti]	Zugänglichkeit, Barrierefreiheit
to **evolve** [ɪˈvɒlv]	sich weiter entwickeln
capacity [kəˈpæsəti]	Fähigkeit, Leistungsvermögen
to **preserve** [prɪˈzɜːv]	bewahren, erhalten
identity [aɪˈdentəti]	Identität
challenged [ˈtʃælɪndʒd]	behindert
possibility [ˌpɒsəˈbɪləti]	Möglichkeit
requirement [rɪˈkwaɪəmənt]	Anforderung, Bedarf, Wunsch
citizen [ˈsɪtɪzn]	Bürger/in

page 79

Italy [ˈɪtəli]	Italien
differently-abled [ˌdɪfrəntli ˈeɪbld]	behindert (anders begabt), Menschen mit besonderen Bedürfnissen

mainstream [ˈmeɪnstriːm]	konventionell, regulär
advance [ədˈvɑːns]	Fortschritt
schooling [ˈskuːlɪŋ]	Schulbildung
billion [ˈbɪliən]	Milliarde
to **correspond to** [ˌkɒrəˈspɒnd tə]	entsprechen, übereinstimmen mit
population [ˌpɒpjuˈleɪʃn]	Bevölkerung
global(ly) [ˈgləʊbl]	global, weltweit
significant(ly) [sɪgˈnɪfɪkənt]	deutlich, spürbar, erheblich
despite [dɪˈspaɪt]	trotz
proposal [prəˈpəʊzl]	Vorschlag, Antrag
scheme [skiːm]	Plan, Programm
to **put sth into action** [ˌpʊt ɪntu ˈækʃn]	etw in die Tat umsetzen
to **be prepared to do sth** [bi prɪˈpeəd tə]	bereit sein, etw zu tun

page 80

trisomy [ˈtrɪsəmi]	Trisomie
Down's/Down syndrome [ˈdaʊnz sɪndrəʊm]	Down-Syndrom
academic [ˌækəˈdemɪk]	Schul-, akademisch, Akademiker/in
expectation [ˌekspekˈteɪʃn]	Erwartung
able [ˈeɪbl]	fähig, kompetent
developmental [dɪˌveləpˈmentəl]	Entwicklungs-
cerebral palsy [ˌserəbrəl ˈpɔːlzi]	spastische Lähmung
sleepover [ˈsliːpəʊvə]	Pyjamaparty, Party mit Übernachtung
abled [ˈeɪbld]	normal (nicht behindert)
day after day [ˌdeɪ ɑːftə ˈdeɪ]	Tag für Tag
lesson [ˈlesn]	Unterricht(sstunde), Lektion
specialist [ˈspeʃəlɪst]	Fach-, Spezial-, Spezialist
to **suit sb/sth** [suːt]	jdm passen, jdm stehen, zu etw passen, etw entsprechen
to **cater for sb** [ˈkeɪtə fə]	jdm gerecht werden
deaf [def]	gehörlos, taub

page 81

to **defend** [dɪˈfend]	verteidigen
scholarship [ˈskɒləʃɪp]	Stipendium, Freiplatz
unknown [ˌʌnˈnəʊn]	unbekannt
national [ˈnæʃnəl]	national, staatlich
hero [ˈhɪərəʊ]	Held/in
benefactor [ˈbenɪfæktə]	Wohltäter/in
ever since [ˌevə ˈsɪns]	seit, seitdem, seither
to **break** [breɪk]	zuerst veröffentlicht werden (Nachricht)
tip [tɪp]	Trinkgeld
donation [dəʊˈneɪʃn]	Spende, Schenkung
to **stand up for sb/sth** [ˌstænd ˈʌp fə]	sich für jdn/etw einsetzen, für jdn/etw eintreten
to **present** [prɪˈzent]	überreichen, schenken
motive [ˈməʊtɪv]	Motiv, Beweggrund
to **recreate** [ˌriːkriˈeɪt]	nachbilden
to **raise** [reɪz]	erhöhen, (an)heben, steigern

UNIT WORD LIST

tourist attraction [ˌtʊərɪst əˈtrækʃn]	Touristenattraktion	blindness [ˈblaɪndnəs]	Blindheit
graduation [ˌgrædʒuˈeɪʃn]	Schulabschluss	to limit [ˈlɪmɪt]	beschränken, einschränken, begrenzen
voice-over [ˈvɔɪsəʊvə]	Begleitkommentar	function [ˈfʌŋkʃn]	Funktion
		to damage [ˈdæmɪdʒ]	(be)schädigen, schaden
page 82		vision impairment [ˈvɪʒn ɪmˈpeəmənt]	Beeinträchtigung der Sehkraft
enterprise [ˈentəpraɪz]	Unternehmen	speech impediment [ˈspiːtʃ ɪmpedɪmənt]	Sprachfehler, Sprachstörung
impaired [ɪmˈpeəd]	beeinträchtigt		
absence [ˈæbsəns]	Abwesenheit	impediment [ɪmˈpedɪmənt]	Behinderung, Hindernis
based on [ˈbeɪst ɒn]	auf der Basis von, basierend auf, aufgrund	invisible [ɪnˈvɪzəbl]	unsichtbar
		diabetes [ˌdaɪəˈbiːtiːz]	Diabetes (Zuckerkrankheit)
gender [ˈdʒendə]	Geschlecht		
origin [ˈɒrɪdʒɪn]	Ursprung, Herkunft	inflammatory bowel disease [ɪnˌflæmətri ˈbaʊəl dɪziːz]	entzündliche Darmerkrankung (M. Crohn, Colitis ulcerosa)
religion [rɪˈlɪdʒən]	Religion(szugehörigkeit)		
widely used [ˌwaɪdli ˈjuːzd]	weitverbreitet	epilepsy [ˈepɪlepsi]	Epilepsie
		as opposed to [əz əˈpəʊzd tə]	im Gegensatz zu, gegenüber
visual impairment [ˌvɪʒuəl ɪmˈpeəmənt]	Sehbehinderung		
handicapped [ˈhændɪkæpt]	behindert, versehrt	visible [ˈvɪzəbl]	sichtbar
worldwide [ˈwɜːldwaɪd]	weltweit	to require [rɪˈkwaɪə]	benötigen, erfordern, verlangen
rapid(ly) [ˈræpɪd]	schnell, rasch		
to age [eɪdʒ]	altern, alt werden (lassen)	**page 83**	
chronic [ˈkrɒnɪk]	chronisch	long-lasting [ˌlɒŋ ˈlɑːstɪŋ]	langlebig, lang anhaltend, dauerhaft
statistics (pl) [stəˈtɪstɪks]	Statistik(en), statistische Angabe(n)	to cure [kjʊə]	heilen
		to disable [dɪsˈeɪbl]	behindern, ausschalten
disproportionate(ly) [ˌdɪsprəˈpɔːʃənət]	unverhältnismäßig	to enter [ˈentə]	hineinkommen, betreten
		prejudice [ˈpredʒudɪs]	Vorurteil
vulnerable [ˈvʌlnərəbl]	verletzlich, verwundbar	form [fɔːm]	Formular
to campaign (for/against) [kæmˈpeɪn]	kämpfen, sich einsetzen (für/gegen)	symbol (of) [ˈsɪmbl]	Symbol (für), Siegel (z. B. Güte-, Bio-)
stereotypical [ˌsteriəˈtɪpɪkl]	stereotyp, klischeehaft	as long as [əz ˈlɒŋ əz]	solange
		to meet requirements [ˌmiːt rɪˈkwaɪəmənts]	Anforderungen erfüllen
wheelchair [ˈwiːltʃeə]	Rollstuhl		
range [reɪndʒ]	Umfang, Auswahl, Kollektion	to favour [ˈfeɪvə]	bevorzugen
		chain [tʃeɪn]	Kette
mild [maɪld]	mild	cognitive [ˈkɒgnətɪv]	kognitiv
severe(ly) [sɪˈvɪə]	schwer(wiegend), stark, schlimm	producer [prəˈdjuːsə]	Produzent/in
		opening [ˈəʊpnɪŋ]	offene Stelle
gradation [grəˈdeɪʃn]	Abstufung, Einteilung	data entry [ˈdeɪtə entri]	Dateneingabe
to object (to sth) [əbˈdʒekt]	Einwände haben (gegen etw), etw ablehnen	characteristic [ˌkærəktəˈrɪstɪk]	Eigenschaft, (charakteristisches) Merkmal
deafness [ˈdefnəs]	Taubheit	perfectionism [pəˈfekʃənɪzəm]	Perfektionismus
autism [ˈɔːtɪzəm]	Autismus		
intellectual [ˌɪntəˈlektʃuəl]	intellektuell, geistig	repetition [ˌrepəˈtɪʃn]	Wiederholung
to characterize [ˈkærəktəraɪz]	charakterisieren	competitive [kəmˈpetətɪv]	Wettbewerbs-, Konkurrenz-
		equal-opportunity law [ˌiːkwəl ˌɒpəˈtjuːnəti lɔː]	Chancengleichheitsgesetz
routine [ruːˈtiːn]	Tagesablauf, Routine		
to originate [əˈrɪdʒɪneɪt]	entstehen, seinen Ursprung haben	hesitant [ˈhezɪtənt]	zögerlich, zögernd
		to be aimed at sth [ˈeɪmd ət]	zu etw dienen, etw tun sollen
to result (from) [rɪˈzʌlt]	entstehen (aus)		
stimulation [ˌstɪmjuˈleɪʃn]	Stimulierung, Anreiz	to come up [ˌkʌm ˈʌp]	aufgeworfen werden, aufkommen
responsiveness [rɪˈspɒnsɪvnəs]	Ansprechbarkeit, Entgegenkommen	prejudiced [ˈpredʒədɪst]	befangen, voreingenommen
motor neuron disease (MND) [ˌməʊtə ˈnjʊərɒn dɪziːz]	Amyotrophe Lateralsklerose (ALS)	stereotype [ˈsteriətaɪp]	Klischee(vorstellung)
		unreliable [ˌʌnrɪˈlaɪəbl]	unzuverlässig
disease [dɪˈziːz]	Krankheit, Erkrankung	to stick in one's mind [ˌstɪk ɪn ˈmaɪnd]	im Gedächtnis haften (bleiben)
multiple sclerosis [ˌmʌltɪpl skləˈrəʊsɪs]	Multiple Sklerose (MS)		
paraplegia [ˌpærəˈpliːdʒə]	Querschnittslähmung	moderate [ˈmɒdərət]	moderat, mäßig
quadriplegia [ˌkwɒdrɪˈpliːdʒə]	Tetraplegie (Lähmung aller vier Gliedmaßen)	catering [ˈkeɪtərɪŋ]	Gastronomie(-)
to amputate [ˈæmpjuteɪt]	amputieren		
limb [lɪm]	Extremität, Glied(maße)		

254

Unit word list

page 84

workshop ['wɜːkʃɒp]	Werkstatt, Workshop	
invitation [ˌɪnvɪ'teɪʃn]	Einladung	
open day ['əʊpən deɪ]	Tag der offenen Tür	
to run [rʌn]	betreiben	
empowerment [ɪm'paʊəmənt]	Bevollmächtigung, Ermächtigung (Übertragung von Verantwortung auf Untergebene)	
printout ['prɪntaʊt]	Ausdruck	
variety [və'raɪəti]	Vielfalt	
tour [tʊə]	Rundgang, Führung	
reception [rɪ'sepʃn]	Empfang, Rezeption	
floor plan ['flɔː plæn]	Grundriss, Lageplan	
ladies and gentlemen [ˌleɪdiz ənd 'dʒentlmən]	meine Damen und Herren	
welcoming ['welkəmɪŋ]	einladend	
painting ['peɪntɪŋ]	Bild, Gemälde	
plant [plɑːnt]	Pflanze	
cube [kjuːb]	Würfel	
to the right/left [tə ðə 'raɪt, tə ðə 'left]	nach rechts/links, zur Rechten/Linken	
fire exit ['faɪə eksɪt]	Notausgang	
exit ['eksɪt]	Ausgang, Ausfahrt	
entrance ['entrəns]	Eingang	
to evacuate [ɪ'vækjueɪt]	evakuieren	
drill [drɪl]	Drill, Exerzieren, Übung	
seating area ['siːtɪŋ eəriə]	Wartebereich	
to turn left/right [ˌtɜːn 'left, ˌtɜːn 'raɪt]	links/rechts abbiegen	
storage ['stɔːrɪdʒ]	Aufbewahrung, Lagerung	
far [fɑː]	weit entfernt	
corner ['kɔːnə]	Ecke	
soft [sɒft]	weich	
to package ['pækɪdʒ]	(ver)packen	
see-through [siː'θruː]	durchsichtig, transparent	
packaging ['pækɪdʒɪŋ]	Verpackung	
sock [sɒk]	Socke	
storeroom ['stɔːruːm]	Lagerraum	

page 85

goods (pl) [ɡʊdz]	Güter, Ware(n)
to pack [pæk]	(ver)packen
to take sth off [ˌteɪk 'ɒf]	etw ausziehen
coat [kəʊt]	Mantel, Jacke, Kittel
hairnet ['heənet]	Haarnetz
net [net]	Netz
confectionery [kən'fekʃənəri]	Süßwaren
Easter bunny ['iːstə bʌni]	Osterhase
shift [ʃɪft]	Schicht(-)
sense of purpose [ˌsens əv 'pɜːpəs]	Zielstrebigkeit
self-confidence [ˌself 'kɒnfɪdəns]	Selbstsicherheit, Selbstvertrauen
initiative [ɪ'nɪʃətɪv]	Initiative, Eigeninitiative
togetherness [tə'ɡeðənəs]	Zusammengehörigkeit
to reveal sth [rɪ'viːl]	etw zeigen, verraten
to listen out for sth [ˌlɪsn 'aʊt fə]	(beim Zuhören) auf etw achten
benefit ['benɪfɪt]	Nutzen, Vorteil
decision-making [dɪ'sɪʒnmeɪkɪŋ]	Entscheidungsfindung

page 86

integration [ˌɪntɪ'ɡreɪʃn]	Integration
fulfilling [fʊl'fɪlɪŋ]	erfüllend
presence ['prezns]	Anwesenheit, Präsenz
to shine [ʃaɪn]	glänzen, leuchten
to promote [prə'məʊt]	fördern, unterstützen, bewerben
praise [preɪz]	Lob, Anerkennung
sb is diagnosed with … ['daɪəɡnəʊzd]	bei jdm wird … festgestellt, diagnostiziert
to diagnose ['daɪəɡnəʊz]	eine Diagnose stellen, diagnostizieren
working age ['wɜːkɪŋ 'eɪdʒ]	erwerbsfähiges Alter
long-running survey [ˌlɒŋrʌnɪŋ 'sɜːveɪ]	Langzeitstudie
climate ['klaɪmət]	Klima

page 87

after-school (programme) [ˌɑːftə 'skuːl]	(Programm) nach Unterrichtsschluss
to discard [dɪs'kɑːd]	verwerfen

UNIT 8

page 90

to bombard [bɒm'bɑːd]	bombardieren
skinny ['skɪni]	mager, dürr
obsession [əb'seʃn]	Besessenheit, Wahn, Zwang
beauty ['bjuːti]	Schönheit
attractiveness [ə'træktɪvnəs]	Attraktivität, Reiz
grade AE [ɡreɪd]	Klasse, Schuljahr
to lose weight [luːz 'weɪt]	abnehmen (Körpergewicht reduzieren)
clinically (overweight) ['klɪnɪkli]	krankhaft (übergewichtig)
hang-up (about) ['hæŋ ʌp]	Komplex (wegen)
height [haɪt]	Höhe, Größe (bei Menschen)
wrinkle ['rɪŋkl]	Falte
excess ['ekses]	überschüssig
body hair ['bɒdi heə]	Körperbehaarung
boobs (pl, infml) [buːb]	Busen, (weibliche) Brust
abs (= abdominals) (pl) [æbz, æb'dɒmɪnlz]	Bauchmuskeln
belly ['beli]	Bauch
love handles (pl) ['lʌv hændlz]	Hüftgold (Fettpölsterchen an der Taille)
to come to mind [ˌkʌm tə 'maɪnd]	einem einfallen
infographic [ˌɪnfə'ɡræfɪk]	Infografik

page 91

anorexia [ˌænə'reksiə]	Anorexie, Magersucht
obesity [əʊ'biːsəti]	Fettleibigkeit
malnutrition [ˌmælnjuː'trɪʃn]	Unterernährung, falsche Ernährung
sb can't be bothered to do sth [ˌkɑːnt bi 'bɒðəd tə]	jd hat keine Lust, etw zu tun
lazy ['leɪzi]	faul, träge, nachlässig

255

UNIT WORD LIST

to **pressurize sb (into sth, into doing sth)** ['preʃəraɪz] — jdn (zu etw) drängen, jdn drängen (etw zu tun)
campaign [kæm'peɪn] — Kampagne

page 92

nutrition [nju'trɪʃn] — Ernährung
plate [pleɪt] — Teller, Platte
bean [biːn] — Bohne
dairy ['deəri] — Molkerei, Milch-, Molkerei-
source [sɔːs] — Quelle
protein ['prəʊtiːn] — Protein, Eiweiß
high in … ['haɪ ɪn] — reich an …, mit hohem …-Gehalt

rice [raɪs] — Reis
potato, pl **potatoes** [pə'teɪtəʊ] — Kartoffel
starchy ['stɑːtʃi] — stärkehaltig
only ever ['əʊnli evə] — (immer) nur
ready meal [ˌredi 'miːl] — Fertiggericht
stepmum ['stepmʌm] — Stiefmutter
convenience food [kən'viːniəns fuːd] — Fertignahrung
convenience [kən'viːniəns] — Bequemlichkeit, Annehmlichkeit
factory-farmed ['fæktri fɑːmd] — aus Massentierhaltung
chicken ['tʃɪkɪn] — Huhn, Hühnerfleisch
beef [biːf] — Rind(fleisch)
chemical ['kemɪkl] — Chemikalie, chemisch
granddad, grandad ['grændæd] — Opa
home-cooked ['həʊm kʊkt] — selbst gekocht, hausgemacht
free-range (eggs) [ˌfriː 'reɪndʒ] — Eier von frei laufenden Hühnern
processed food ['prəʊsest] — verarbeitete Lebensmittel
to **process** ['prəʊses] — (weiter)verarbeiten
farming ['fɑːmɪŋ] — Landwirtschaft, Anbau
ingredient [ɪn'griːdiənt] — Zutat, Inhaltsstoff
microwave (oven) [ˌmaɪkrəweɪv 'ʌvn] — Mikrowellenherd
to **last** [lɑːst] — halten, frisch bleiben (Nahrungsmittel)
frozen ['frəʊzn] — (tief)gefroren, Tiefkühl-
to **freeze** [friːz] — (ge)frieren
canned [kænd] — Dosen-
hot [hɒt] — heiß, warm (Mahlzeit)
livestock ['laɪvstɒk] — Vieh
to **feed** [fiːd] — füttern, ernähren

page 93

from scratch [skrætʃ] — ganz von vorne, von Grund auf
recipe ['resəpi] — (Koch-)Rezept
equipment [ɪ'kwɪpmənt] — Ausstattung, Ausrüstung, Geräte
base [beɪs] — Basis, Boden (Kuchen, Pizza)
altogether [ˌɔːltə'geðə] — insgesamt
topping ['tɒpɪŋ] — Überzug, Belag (z. B. Pizza)
to **grate** [greɪt] — reiben, raspeln
teaspoonful ['tiːspuːnfʊl] — Teelöffel

yeast [jiːst] — Hefe
handful ['hændfʊl] — Handvoll
to **chop** [tʃɒp] — (klein) schneiden
basil ['bæzl] — Basilikum
olive ['ɒlɪv] — Olive
clove (of garlic) [kləʊv] — (Knoblauch-)Zehe
garlic ['gɑːlɪk] — Knoblauch
to **crush** [krʌʃ] — (zer)quetschen, (aus)pressen

tin [tɪn] — Dose, Büchse
tomato, pl **tomatoes** [tə'mɑːtəʊ] — Tomate
cherry ['tʃeri] — Kirsche
to **halve** [hɑːv] — halbieren, sich halbieren
paste [peɪst] — Paste, (Tomaten-)Mark, Brei
leaf, pl **leaves** [liːf, liːvz] — Blatt
flour ['flaʊə] — Mehl
dough [dəʊ] — Teig
to **rise** [raɪz] — gehen (Hefeteig)
to **knead** [niːd] — kneten
crisp [krɪsp] — knusprig, knackig
additional [ə'dɪʃənl] — zusätzlich
to **smooth (sth over sth)** [smuːð] — glätten, (etw über etw) streichen, gleichmäßig verteilen

spoon [spuːn] — Löffel
to **scatter** ['skætə] — verteilen, verstreuen
to **sprinkle** ['sprɪŋkl] — (be)streuen, (be)träufeln
mixture ['mɪkstʃə] — Mischung, Gemisch
baking paper ['beɪkɪŋ peɪpə] — Backpapier
on top of sth [ɒn 'tɒp əv] — auf etw (oben) drauf
to **preheat** [ˌpriː'hiːt] — vorheizen
baking sheet, baking tray ['beɪkɪŋ ʃiːt, 'beɪkɪŋ treɪ] — Backblech
to **blend** [blend] — mischen, verrühren
to **rub sth in** [ˌrʌb 'ɪn] — etw (hin)einkneten (Zutaten in Teig)
to **pour** [pɔː] — (aus-, ein)gießen
oven ['ʌvn] — Ofen, Herd
to **flour** ['flaʊə] — mit Mehl bestäuben
rolling pin ['rəʊlɪŋ pɪn] — Teigrolle, Nudelholz
to **roll sth out** [ˌrəʊl 'aʊt] — etw ausrollen
round [raʊnd] — Kreis, Runde
across [ə'krɒs] — im Durchmesser
thin [θɪn] — dünn
to **lift** [lɪft] — heben, hochheben
to **drain** [dreɪn] — abgießen, abtropfen (lassen)
temperature ['temprətʃə] — Temperatur
at room temperature [ət] — bei Raumtemperatur
to **shape** [ʃeɪp] — formen
to **turn** [tɜːn] — (um)drehen, kippen, stürzen (Teig)

light(ly) [laɪt] — leicht, hell
bowl [bəʊl] — Schale, Schüssel
cloth [klɒθ] — Stoff, Tuch
nugget ['nʌgɪt] — paniertes Klößchen
mechanical [mɪ'kænɪkl] — mechanisch, Maschinen-
cut (of meat) [kʌt] — Stück (Fleisch)
carcass ['kɑːkəs] — Kadaver
high-pressure [ˌhaɪ 'preʃə] — Hochdruck-
sieve [sɪv] — Sieb

256

Unit word list

to **speculate** [ˈspekjuleɪt]	spekulieren	
product [ˈprɒdʌkt]	Produkt, Erzeugnis	
unnatural [ʌnˈnætʃrəl]	unnatürlich	
derivative [dɪˈrɪvətɪv]	Derivat, Abkömmling	
TBHQ [ˌti: bi: eɪtʃ ˈkju:]	tert-Butylhydrochinon (TBHQ)	
PDMS [ˌpi: di: em ˈes]	Polydimethylsiloxan (PDMS)	
to **waste** [weɪst]	vergeuden, verschwenden	
to **gleam** [gli:m]	glänzen, strahlen	
stainless steel [ˌsteɪnləs ˈsti:l]	Edelstahl, rostfreier Stahl	
foodstuff [ˈfu:dstʌf]	Nahrungsmittel	
to **chop sth up** [ˌtʃɒp ˈʌp]	etw klein schneiden	
blender [ˈblendə]	Mixer (Küchengerät)	
to **be made up of** [bi ˌmeɪd ˈʌp əv]	bestehen aus	
flavouring [ˈfleɪvərɪŋ]	Aroma(stoff)	
corn [kɔ:n]	Getreide, (AE) Mais	
You had me worried (there). (infml) [ˈwʌrid]	Sie haben mir einen Schrecken eingejagt.	
industry [ˈɪndəstri]	Industrie, Branche	
industrial [ɪnˈdʌstriəl]	industriell, Industrie-	
petroleum [pəˈtrəʊliəm]	Erdöl	
silicone [ˈsɪlɪkəʊn]	Silikon	
mouthful (infml) [ˈmaʊθfʊl]	langes Wort, Zungenbrecher	
crude oil [ˌkru:d ˈɔɪl]	Rohöl	
to **frighten** [ˈfraɪtn]	erschrecken, Angst einjagen	
frightening [ˈfraɪtnɪŋ]	beängstigend	
preferably [ˈprefrəbli]	vorzugsweise, am liebsten	
organic [ɔ:ˈgænɪk]	Bio-, organisch	
blood [blʌd]	Blut	
bone [bəʊn]	Knochen	
bone marrow [ˈbəʊn mærəʊ]	Knochenmark	
AMR meat (= advanced meat recovery) [ˌeɪ em ˈɑ:]	Separatorenfleisch (vom Knochen gewonnenes Fleisch)	
to **scrape** [skreɪp]	(ab)kratzen, schaben	
yuck [jʌk]	Ekel-, igitt!	
trace [treɪs]	Spur	
growth [grəʊθ]	Wachstum	
hormone [ˈhɔ:məʊn]	Hormon	
vaccine [ˈvæksi:n]	Impfstoff	
to **medicate** [ˈmedɪkeɪt]	mit Medikamenten behandeln	
pharmaceuticals (pl) [ˌfɑ:məˈsu:tɪklz]	Arzneimittel	
to **contaminate** [kənˈtæmɪneɪt]	verseuchen, verunreinigen	
pesticide [ˈpestɪsaɪd]	Schädlingsbekämpfungsmittel	
delicious [dɪˈlɪʃəs]	köstlich, lecker	
food for thought [fu:d fə ˈθɔ:t]	ein Denkanstoß	
educator [ˈedʒukeɪtə]	Pädagoge/Pädagogin	

page 94

to **be dying to do sth** [ˈdaɪɪŋ]	etw unbedingt tun wollen, darauf brennen etw zu tun

slim [slɪm]	schlank	
French [frentʃ]	französisch, Französisch, Franzose/Französin	
battle (for/against) [ˈbætl]	Kampf, Schlacht (um/gegen)	
starvation [stɑ:ˈveɪʃn]	Hunger(tod)	
at the age of (28) [eɪdʒ]	im Alter von (28) Jahren	
to **photograph** [ˈfəʊtəgrɑ:f]	fotografieren	
controversial [ˌkɒntrəˈvɜ:ʃl]	kontrovers, umstritten	
to **promote sth** [prəˈməʊt]	fördern, unterstützen, Werbung machen für etw	
metre [ˈmi:tə]	Meter	
campaigner [kæmˈpeɪnə]	Aktivist/in	
skeletal [ˈskelətl]	Skelett-, skelettartig	
criticism [ˈkrɪtɪsɪzəm]	Kritik	
disgusted (by) [dɪsˈgʌstɪd]	angewidert (von), empört (über)	
to **shock** [ʃɒk]	schockieren	
unvarnished [ʌnˈvɑ:nɪʃt]	unlackiert, ungeschminkt (Wahrheit, Bild)	
psoriasis [səˈraɪəsɪs]	Schuppenflechte (med., Hauterkrankung)	
to **be pigeon-chested** [ˌpɪdʒɪn ˈtʃestɪd]	eine Kielbrust/Hühnerbrust haben (med.)	
Italian [ɪˈtæljən]	italienisch, Italiener/in, Italienisch	
photographer [fəˈtɒgrəfə]	Fotograf/in	
to **shoot** [ʃu:t]	(Film) drehen, Aufnahmen machen	
hard-hitting [ˌhɑ:d ˈhɪtɪŋ]	schonungslos	
to **diet** [ˈdaɪət]	eine Schlankheitskur machen, weniger essen	
Milan [mɪˈlæn]	Mailand	
eve (of) [i:v]	Vortag, Vorabend (von)	
fashion [ˈfæʃn]	Mode	
shock wave [ˈʃɒk weɪv]	Druckwelle, Erschütterung	
to **ban** [bæn]	verbieten, verbannen, sperren	
watchdog [ˈwɒtʃdɒg]	Überwachungsbeauftragte/r, Überwachungsgremium	
to **fuel** [ˈfju:əl]	anheizen, anfachen	
bulimia [buˈlɪmiə]	Bulimie (med., Ess-Brech-Sucht)	
kilogram [ˈkɪləgræm]	Kilo(gramm)	
sufferer [ˈsʌfərə]	Opfer, Kranke/r, Leidende/r	
tailbone [ˈteɪlbəʊn]	Steißbein	
wound [wu:nd]	Wunde	
tooth, pl **teeth** [tu:θ, ti:θ]	Zahn	
dry [draɪ]	trocken	
breast [brest]	Brust	
to **fall** [fɔ:l]	sinken, sich (ab)senken	
to **model** [ˈmɒdl]	als Fotomodell arbeiten	
high school USA [ˈhaɪ sku:l]	Gymnasium, Oberstufenschule	
frail [freɪl]	zart, zerbrechlich, gebrechlich	
physique [fɪˈzi:k]	Körperbau, Statur	
never once [ˈnevə wʌns]	nicht ein (einziges) Mal	

UNIT WORD LIST

modelling agency ['mɒdəlɪŋ eɪdʒənsi]	Fotoagentur	supplement ['sʌplɪmənt]	Ergänzung
to put on weight [ˌpʊt ɒn 'weɪt]	zunehmen (Körpergewicht erhöhen)	vitamin supplement ['vɪtəmɪn sʌplɪmənt]	Vitaminpräparat
association [əˌsəʊsi'eɪʃn]	Verband, Vereinigung	transformation [ˌtrænsfə'meɪʃn]	Umwandlung, (grundlegende) Veränderung
acute [ə'kjuːt]	akut	**page 97**	
respiratory [rə'spɪrətri]	Atmungs-, Atem-, die Atemwege betreffend (med.)	to put sth across (to sb) [ˌpʊt ə'krɒs]	(jdm) etw vermitteln
role model ['rəʊl mɒdl]	Vorbild	boot camp ['buːt kæmp]	Ausbildungslager
to place [pleɪs]	stellen, legen, setzen (etw wohin) tun	to boom [buːm]	blühen (Wirtschaft, Geschäft)
alongside [əˌlɒŋ'saɪd]	neben, entlang	Australian [ɒ'streɪliən]	australisch, Australier/in
page 95		outdoors [ˌaʊt'dɔːz]	im Freien, (nach) draußen, die freie Natur
a matter of opinion [ə ˌmætər əv ə'pɪniən]	Ansichtssache	to guess [ges]	(er)raten
to trigger ['trɪɡə]	auslösen	interval ['ɪntəvl]	(Zeit-)Abschnitt, Abstand, Intervall
mass [mæs]	Masse(n-)	push-up ['pʊʃ ʌp]	Liegestütz
to consist of [kən'sɪst əv]	bestehen aus	refreshment [rɪ'freʃmənt]	Erfrischung
mathematical [ˌmæθə'mætɪkl]	mathematisch	sprint [sprɪnt]	(Kurzstrecken-)Lauf, Spurt
formula ['fɔːmjələ]	Formel	squat [skwɒt]	Kniebeuge
objective [əb'dʒektɪv]	objektiv	(training) session ['seʃn]	(Trainings-)Stunde, Einheit
equation [ɪ'kweɪʒn]	Gleichung	Australia [ɒ'streɪliə]	Australien
research (into/on) [rɪ'sɜːtʃ]	Forschung, Untersuchungen (über/zu), Recherche(n)	latest ['leɪtɪst]	neueste/r/s
		over the last ... years ['əʊvə]	im Lauf der letzten ... Jahre
to suspect [sə'spekt]	vermuten	to be stuck (in) [stʌk]	festsitzen (in), stecken bleiben, nicht weiterkommen
in total [ˌɪn 'təʊtl]	insgesamt		
socio-economic [ˌsəʊsiəʊ ˌiːkə'nɒmɪk]	sozioökonomisch (sozial und wirtschaftlich)	style [staɪl]	Stil
to search [sɜːtʃ]	durchsuchen, suchen	(boot-camp) style [staɪl]	im Stil (eines Ausbildungslagers)
foundation [faʊn'deɪʃn]	Stiftung	powerful ['paʊəfl]	kräftig, stark, mächtig
well-known [ˌwel'nəʊn]	sehr bekannt, berühmt	initial(ly) [ɪ'nɪʃl]	erste(r, s), Anfangs-, anfänglich
page 96		satisfaction [ˌsætɪs'fækʃn]	Zufriedenheit, Befriedigung
on offer [ɒn 'ɒfə]	im Angebot	earth [ɜːθ]	(die) Erde
for sale [fə 'seɪl]	zu verkaufen	front line [ˌfrʌnt 'laɪn]	vorderste Front, vorderste Linie
to throw sth up [ˌθrəʊ 'ʌp]	aufwerfen, zu Tage bringen	to bulge [bʌldʒ]	hervortreten, sich (vor)wölben, prall gefüllt sein
aimed at sb ['eɪmd ət]	an jdn gerichtet, für jdn		
to get in(to) shape [ˌɡet ɪn 'ʃeɪp]	fit werden, sich in Form bringen	various ['veəriəs]	(mehrere) verschiedene
workout ['wɜːkaʊt]	(Fitness-)Training, Work-out	instructor [ɪn'strʌktə]	Lehrer/in, Ausbilder/in
		to give it a try [ˌɡɪv ɪt ə 'traɪ]	es mal versuchen, ausprobieren
sleek [sliːk]	geschmeidig, schlank	letter to the editor [ˌletə tə ði 'edɪtə]	Leserbrief
lean [liːn]	schlank, hager, mager (Fleisch)		
to boost [buːst]	stärken, unterstützen, Auftrieb geben	enquiry [ɪn'kwaɪəri]	Anfrage, Erkundigung
		to draft [drɑːft]	entwerfen, abfassen
supposed(ly) [sə'pəʊzdli]	angeblich	representation [ˌreprɪzen'teɪʃn]	Darstellung
to hate [heɪt]	hassen, überhaupt nicht mögen		
sluggish ['slʌɡɪʃ]	träge, schwerfällig	organizer ['ɔːɡənaɪzə]	Organisator/in
to tone [təʊn]	straffen	**page 98**	
spotlight ['spɒtlaɪt]	Rampenlicht, Scheinwerfer(licht)	I'll have ... [aɪl 'hæv]	ich nehme ... (beim Essen, im Restaurant)
efficient [ɪ'fɪʃnt]	effizient, rationell	syrup ['sɪrəp]	Sirup
to work out [ˌwɜːk 'aʊt]	trainieren	artificial [ˌɑːtɪ'fɪʃl]	künstlich
lifestyle ['laɪfstaɪl]	Lebensweise, Lebensführung, Lebensstil	flavour ['fleɪvə]	Geschmack(srichtung), Geschmacksstoff
to keep a log [ˌkiːp ə 'lɒɡ]	Buch führen	assorted [ə'sɔːtɪd]	gemischt, verschieden
calorie ['kæləri]	Kalorie		

awful ['ɔːfl]	furchtbar, schrecklich	
to **take exercise** [ˌteɪk 'eksəsaɪz]	sich Bewegung verschaffen	
vegetarian [ˌvedʒə'teəriən]	vegetarisch, Vegetarier/in	

page 99

to **target** ['tɑːgɪt]	zielen auf, ins Visier nehmen
billboard ['bɪlbɔːd]	Reklametafel, Plakatwand
spot [spɒt]	(Werbe-)Spot
commercial [kə'mɜːʃl]	Werbespot
European Union (EU) [ˌjʊərəpiːən 'juːniən, ˌiː 'juː]	Europäische Union (EU)
depending on [dɪ'pendɪŋ ɒn]	abhängig von, je nach
catchy ['kætʃi]	eingängig (Lied, Slogan)
tune [tjuːn]	Song, Lied
detailed ['diːteɪld]	ausführlich, detailliert
sketch [sketʃ]	Skizze, Entwurf
engaging [ɪn'geɪdʒɪŋ]	fesselnd, spannend
to arouse [ə'raʊz]	wecken, erregen
to demonstrate ['demənstreɪt]	vorführen, zeigen, demonstrieren
desire [dɪ'zaɪə]	Wunsch, Verlangen
to **desire sth** [dɪ'zaɪə]	sich etw wünschen, etw begehren
helper [helpə]	Helfer/in

UNIT 9

page 102

for a lifetime [fər ə 'laɪftaɪm]	lebenslang
proverb ['prɒvɜːb]	Sprichwort
author ['ɔːθə]	Verfasser/in, Autor/in
enemy ['enəmi]	Feind/in, Gegner/in
volunteer organization [ˌvɒləntɪə ˌɔːgənaɪ'zeɪʃn]	Freiwilligenorganisation
volunteer [ˌvɒlən'tɪə]	freiwillig, ehrenamtlich, Freiwillige/r, Volontär/in
disadvantage [ˌdɪsəd'vɑːntɪdʒ]	Nachteil

page 103

disadvantaged [ˌdɪsəd'vɑːntɪdʒd]	benachteiligt
Moldova [mɒl'dəʊvə]	Moldawien
unto ['ʌntə]	auf, zu, nach (archaisch)
to **clean up** [ˌkliːn 'ʌp]	säubern, aufräumen
inflatable [ɪn'fleɪtəbl]	aufblasbar
distress [dɪ'stres]	Not, Notlage
typhoon [taɪ'fuːn]	Taifun (tropischer Wirbelsturm)
mosquito [mə'skiːtəʊ]	Stechmücke
experiential learning [ɪkspɪəri,enʃl 'lɜːnɪŋ]	Erlebnispädagogik
outdoor ['aʊtdɔː]	Outdoor-, im Freien
adventure [əd'ventʃə]	Abenteuer
excursion [ɪk'skɜːʃn]	Ausflug, Exkursion
purposeful(ly) ['pɜːpəsfl]	zielgerichtet, zielstrebig
to **engage with sb** [ɪn'geɪdʒ wɪð]	mit jdm interagieren

page 104

inexpensive [ˌɪnɪk'spensɪv]	preisgünstig, preiswert
tourist industry ['tʊərɪst ɪndəstri]	Tourismus-Industrie
quotation [kwəʊ'teɪʃn]	Zitat
to **cater to sb** ['keɪtə tə]	auf jdn ausgerichtet sein
adventurous [əd'ventʃərəs]	abenteuerlustig
stay [steɪ]	Aufenthalt
gap year ['gæp jɪə]	das Jahr zwischen Schulabgang und Studienbeginn
traveller ['trævələ]	Reisende/r
underdeveloped [ˌʌndədɪ'veləpt]	unterentwickelt
developing country [dɪˌveləpɪŋ 'kʌntri]	Entwicklungsland
non-governmental organization (NGO) [ˌnɒn gʌvənˌmentl ɔː gənaɪ'zeɪʃn]	Nichtregierungsorganisation
to **dig** [dɪg]	graben
well [wel]	Quelle, Brunnen
environmental [ɪnˌvaɪrən'mentl]	Umwelt-
reforestation [ˌriːfɒrɪ'steɪʃn]	(Wieder-)Aufforstung
orphan ['ɔːfn]	Waise
poverty ['pɒvəti]	Armut
privileged ['prɪvəlɪdʒd]	privilegiert
history ['hɪstri]	Geschichte (vergangene Zeiten)
distinct [dɪ'stɪŋkt]	deutlich, unterschiedlich
division [dɪ'vɪʒn]	Trennung
benevolent [bə'nevələnt]	gütig, wohlwollend
giver ['gɪvə]	Geber/in
to **cast** [kɑːst]	besetzen (eine Rolle)
cast as ... ['kɑːst əz]	in die Rolle des/der ... gesetzt
grateful (to sb) ['greɪtfl]	(jdm) dankbar
receiver [rɪ'siːvə]	Empfänger/in
charity ['tʃærəti]	Nächstenliebe, Wohltätigkeit
preconception [ˌpriː kən'sepʃn]	Vorurteil
reinforced [ˌriːɪn'fɔːst]	verstärkt
divide [dɪ'vaɪd]	Kluft
relief [rɪ'liːf]	Erleichterung, Linderung
to **exploit** [ɪk'splɔɪt]	benutzen, ausnutzen, ausbeuten
root cause ['ruːt kɔːz]	Grundursache
root [ruːt]	Wurzel
sustainability [səˌsteɪnə'bɪləti]	Nachhaltigkeit
energy ['enədʒi]	Energie
mutual ['mjuːtʃuəl]	gegenseitig
funding ['fʌndɪŋ]	Finanzausstattung, (finanzielle) Mittel, Finanzierung
indirect [ˌɪndə'rekt]	indirekt
accreditation [əˌkredɪ'teɪʃn]	Akkreditierung
to **sign up** [ˌsaɪn 'ʌp]	sich anmelden
database ['deɪtəbeɪs]	Datenbank

UNIT WORD LIST

page 105

to **donate** [dəʊˈneɪt]		spenden, schenken
admiration [ˌædməˈreɪʃn]		Bewunderung
potential [pəˈtenʃl]		Potenzial, Möglichkeit(en)
tour company [ˈtʊə kʌmpəni]		Touristikunternehmen
to **make a difference** [meɪk ə ˈdɪfrəns]		etw verändern
Poland [ˈpəʊlənd]		Polen
award [əˈwɔːd]		Auszeichnung, Preis
to **participate (in)** [pɑːˈtɪsɪpeɪt]		teilnehmen (an), sich beteiligen (an)
to **make sth up** [ˌmeɪk ˈʌp]		etw ausmachen, bilden

page 106

to **get down to work** [get ˌdaʊn tə ˈwɜːk]		sich an die Arbeit machen
Romania [ruːˈmeɪniə]		Rumänien
theme [θiːm]		Thema
geographical [ˌdʒiːəˈɡræfɪkl]		geographisch
flyer [ˈflaɪə]		Flugzettel, Flyer
to **mail** [meɪl]		(zu)schicken, (zu)senden, mailen
weekly [ˈwiːkli]		wöchentlich
grant [ɡrɑːnt]		Zuschuss, Stipendium
grant proposal [ˈɡrɑːnt prəpəʊzl]		Zuschussantrag
administrative [ədˈmɪnɪstrətɪv]		Verwaltungs-
biking [ˈbaɪkɪŋ]		Radfahren
hiking [ˈhaɪkɪŋ]		Wandern
white-water rafting [ˌwaɪtwɔːtə ˈrɑːftɪŋ]		Wildwasserrafting
cross-country skiing [ˌkrɒs ˈkʌntri skiːɪŋ]		Skilanglauf
to **facilitate sth** [fəˈsɪlɪteɪt]		etw vermitteln, vereinfachen
debriefing [ˌdiːˈbriːfɪŋ]		Nachbesprechung
to **attain** [əˈteɪn]		erreichen, erlangen

page 107

to **take a message** [ˌteɪk ə ˈmesɪdʒ]		eine Nachricht entgegennehmen
Irish [ˈaɪrɪʃ]		irisch, Iren (pl)
administration [ədˌmɪnɪˈstreɪʃn]		Verwaltung
surname [ˈsɜːneɪm]		Nachname, Familienname
country code [ˈkʌntri kəʊd]		Ländervorwahl
to **read sth back** [ˌriːd ˈbæk]		etw wiedergeben
My pleasure. [maɪ ˈpleʒə]		Es war mir ein Vergnügen. (höfliche Antwort, wenn sich jemand bedankt hat)
to **confirm** [kənˈfɜːm]		bestätigen
to **hold on** [ˌhəʊld ˈɒn]		warten, dranbleiben
in person [ɪn ˈpɜːsn]		persönlich
cooperation [kəʊˌɒpəˈreɪʃn]		Zusammenarbeit
sometime [ˈsʌmtaɪm]		irgendwann
hardly [ˈhɑːdli]		kaum
flight [flaɪt]		Flug

to **call (a flight)** [kɔːl]		(einen Flug) aufrufen
to **cancel** [ˈkænsl]		stornieren
all day [ɔːl ˈdeɪ]		den ganzen Tag
cancellation [ˌkænsəˈleɪʃn]		Stornierung, Absage
to **spell** [spel]		buchstabieren, schreiben
regarding [rɪˈɡɑːdɪŋ]		bezüglich, betreffend
convenient [kənˈviːniənt]		passend, praktisch, angenehm
arrangement [əˈreɪndʒmənt]		Termin, Abmachung, Vereinbarung
instructional [ɪnˈstrʌkʃənl]		Lehr-, Schulungs-
leadership [ˈliːdəʃɪp]		Führung
technical [ˈteknɪkl]		technisch
judgement [ˈdʒʌdʒmənt]		Urteil
informative [ɪnˈfɔːmətɪv]		informativ
ecological(ly) [ˌiːkəˈlɒdʒɪkl]		ökologisch, Umwelt-
inclusive [ɪnˈkluːsɪv]		einschließlich, inbegriffen
ethnicity [eθˈnɪsəti]		Ethnizität, Volkszugehörigkeit
to **acquire** [əˈkwaɪə]		erwerben

page 108

to **be on duty** [ɒn ˈdjuːti]		Dienst haben
to **go wrong** [ˌɡəʊ ˈrɒŋ]		schiefgehen
abseiling [ˈæbseɪlɪŋ]		Abseilen
orienteering [ˌɔːriənˈtɪərɪŋ]		Orientierungslauf
rock climbing [ˈrɒk klaɪmɪŋ]		Klettern
diving [ˈdaɪvɪŋ]		Tauchen
underground [ˈʌndəɡraʊnd]		unterirdisch
navigating [ˈnævɪɡeɪtɪŋ]		Navigieren
swamp [swɒmp]		Sumpf
treetop [ˈtriːtɒp]		Baumkrone
to **wander** [ˈwɒndə]		(umher-)wandern
tobogganing [təˈbɒɡənɪŋ]		Schlittenfahren
disused [ˌdɪsˈjuːzd]		stillgelegt
coal [kəʊl]		Kohle
mine [maɪn]		Bergwerk, Mine
antibiotic [ˌæntibaɪˈɒtɪk]		antibiotisch, Antibiotikum
ointment [ˈɔɪntmənt]		Salbe
antihistamine [ˌæntiˈhɪstəmiːn]		Antihistaminikum
assortment [əˈsɔːtmənt]		Sortiment, Auswahl
bandage [ˈbændɪdʒ]		Bandage, Verband
blanket [ˈblæŋkɪt]		Decke
hypothermia [ˌhaɪpəˈθɜːmiə]		Unterkühlung
iodine [ˈaɪədiːn]		Jod(tinktur)
adhesive [ədˈhiːsɪv]		(selbst-)klebend
tape [teɪp]		Band, Klebeband
gauze [ɡɔːz]		Gaze, Mull
safety pin [ˈseɪfti pɪn]		Sicherheitsnadel
scissors (pl) [ˈsɪzəz]		Schere
tweezers (pl) [ˈtwiːzəz]		Pinzette
for all eventualities [ɪˌventʃuˈælətiz]		für alle Eventualitäten
needle [ˈniːdl]		Nadel, Kanüle
cream [kriːm]		Creme
glove [ɡlʌv]		Handschuh
splint [splɪnt]		Schiene (med)

260

Unit word list

to **relieve** [rɪ'liːv]	erleichtern, (Druck) verringern, lindern
bite [baɪt]	Biss, (Insekten-)Stich
sting [stɪŋ]	Biene-, Wespen-)Stich, Brennen
rash [ræʃ]	(Haut-)Ausschlag
allergic reaction (to) [ə‚lɜːdʒɪk ri'ækʃn]	allergische Reaktion (auf)
to **stabilize** ['steɪbəlaɪz]	stabilisieren
break [breɪk]	Bruch
sprain [spreɪn]	Verstauchung, Distorsion
fever ['fiːvə]	Fieber
inflammation [‚ɪnflə'meɪʃn]	Entzündung
anticoagulant [‚æntikəʊ'ægjələnt]	Gerinnungshemmer
to **clot** [klɒt]	klumpen, gerinnen
painkiller ['peɪnkɪlə]	Schmerzmittel
fitted ['fɪtɪd]	eingepasst
tube [tjuːb]	Rohr, Röhrchen
nut [nʌt]	Nuss
insect ['ɪnsekt]	Insekt
heat [hiːt]	Wärme, Hitze
to **attend to sb** [ə'tend tə]	sich um jdn kümmern
injured ['ɪndʒəd]	verletzt
dirt [dɜːt]	Schmutz, Dreck
infected [ɪn'fektɪd]	infiziert
to **roll sth up** [‚rəʊl 'ʌp]	etw aufrollen
strip [strɪp]	Streifen
polythene (BE) ['pɒlɪθiːn]	Polyäthylen
foam [fəʊm]	Schaum
coating [kəʊtɪŋ]	Beschichtung
to **unroll** [ʌn'rəʊl]	ausrollen
to **fold** [fəʊld]	falten, zusammenlegen
rigid ['rɪdʒɪd]	starr, hart, unnachgiebig
to **immobilize** [ɪ'məʊbəlaɪz]	ruhigstellen
to **assemble** [ə'sembl]	zusammenstellen
seaside ['siːsaɪd]	(Meeres-)Küste, Strand
trek [trek]	Reise, Treck
senior ['siːnɪə]	Rentner/in
night-time ['naɪttaɪm]	nächtlich, Nacht-

page 109

to **injure** ['ɪndʒə]	(sich) verletzen
to **administer first aid** [əd'mɪnɪstə]	erste Hilfe leisten
admission [əd'mɪʃn]	Aufnahme
to **take measures** ['meʒəz]	Maßnahmen ergreifen
helmet ['helmɪt]	(Schutz-)Helm
consciousness ['kɒnʃəsnəs]	Bewusstsein
forest ['fɒrɪst]	Wald
to **snow** [snəʊ]	schneien
to **interrupt** [‚ɪntə'rʌpt]	unterbrechen, ins Wort fallen
pace [peɪs]	Tempo, Schritt, Geschwindigkeit
to **ski** [skiː]	skilaufen
logical order [‚lɒdʒɪkl 'ɔːdə]	logische Reihenfolge
mobile phone [‚məʊbaɪl 'fəʊn]	Mobiltelefon, Handy
next of kin [‚nekst əv 'kɪn]	nächste/r Angehörige/r
allergy ['ælədʒi]	Allergie

principal diagnosis [‚prɪnsəpl ‚daɪəg'nəʊsɪs]	Hauptdiagnose
diagnosis, pl **diagnoses** [‚daɪəg'nəʊsɪs, ‚daɪəg'nəʊsiːz]	Diagnose
to **account for** [ə'kaʊnt fə]	ausmachen, erklären, ergeben
to **think of sth** ['θɪŋk əv]	sich etw überlegen, ausdenken
contraceptive pill [‚kɒntrə'septɪv pɪl]	Verhütungsmittel, Antibabypille
to **ride** [raɪd]	reiten, fahren (mit)
right now [‚raɪt 'naʊ]	zur Zeit, im Augenblick
horse [hɔːs]	Pferd
pollen ['pɒlən]	Pollen, Blütenstaub
penicillin [‚penɪ'sɪlɪn]	Penizillin
to **submit** [səb'mɪt]	einreichen
outcome [aʊtkʌm]	Ergebnis, Ausgang, Resultat

page 110

wildlife ['waɪldlaɪf]	Tiere (in freier Wildbahn), Tierwelt
to **get off the ground** [get ɒf ðə 'graʊnd]	in Gang kommen
to **lack** [læk]	fehlen, (er)mangeln
to **enrol (with)** [ɪn'rəʊl]	sich verpflichten (bei), sich anmelden (bei)
to **hike** [haɪk]	wandern

page 111

to **soothe sth** [suːð]	etw lindern, mildern
bug [bʌg]	Wanze, Insekt
logistics (pl) [lə'dʒɪstɪks]	Logistik
length [leŋθ]	Länge, Dauer
confidence ['kɒnfɪdəns]	(Selbst-)Vertrauen
to **take along** [‚teɪk ə'lɒŋ]	mitnehmen
rope [rəʊp]	Seil, Tau
gear [gɪə]	Ausrüstung
competition [‚kɒmpə'tɪʃn]	Konkurrenz, Wettkampf
critical(ly) ['krɪtɪkl]	kritisch
persuasive(ly) [pə'sweɪsɪv]	überzeugend
to **clarify sth** ['klærəfaɪ]	etw klären, klarstellen

UNIT 10

page 114

foreign ['fɒrən]	Auslands-, ausländisch, fremd
migration [maɪ'greɪʃn]	Migration, Zu-/Aus-/Abwanderung
long-standing [‚lɒŋ 'stændɪŋ]	langjährig, schon lange bestehend
federal ['fedərəl]	Bundes-, auf Bundesebene geltend
statistical [stə'tɪstɪkl]	statistisch
to **immigrate** ['ɪmɪgreɪt]	einwandern
immigrant ['ɪmɪgrənt]	Einwanderer/-in
migrant background [‚maɪgrənt 'bækgraʊnd]	Migrationshintergrund
chart [tʃɑːt]	Schaubild, Diagramm, Grafik
to **leave sth behind** [‚liːv bɪ'haɪnd]	etw hinter sich lassen

261

UNIT WORD LIST

page 115

demographic [ˌdeməˈgræfɪk]	demografisch
to select [sɪˈlekt]	auswählen
free movement [ˌfriː ˈmuːvmənt]	Freizügigkeit
movement [ˈmuːvmənt]	Bewegung
descent [dɪˈsent]	Herkunft, Abstammung
to migrate [maɪˈgreɪt]	(aus-/ein-)wandern
political [pəˈlɪtɪkl]	politisch
anew [əˈnjuː]	von neuem, erneut
Chilean [ˈtʃɪliən]	Chilene/-in, chilenisch
facet [ˈfæsɪt]	Facette, Aspekt

page 116

agenda [əˈdʒendə]	Agenda, Tagesordnung
Greece [griːs]	Griechenland
boom [buːm]	Boom, Hochkonjunktur
euro [ˈjʊərəʊ]	Euro
overwhelming [ˌəʊvəˈwelmɪŋ]	überwältigend
sharp [ʃɑːp]	scharf, deutlich, steil
enlargement [ɪnˈlɑːdʒmənt]	Erweiterung, Ausweitung, Ausdehnung
working class [ˌwɜːkɪŋ ˈklɑːs]	Arbeiterklasse, Arbeiter-
burden [ˈbɜːdn]	Last, Belastung
nor [nɔː]	auch nicht, ebensowenig, noch
budget [ˈbʌdʒɪt]	Budget, Haushalt, Etat
estate agent [ɪˈsteɪt eɪdʒənt]	Makler/in
learner [ˈlɜːnə]	Lerner/in
forever [fəˈrevə]	für immer, ewig
diploma [dɪˈpləʊmə]	Diplom, Abschlusszeugnis
Greek [griːk]	Grieche/Griechin, griechisch

page 117

immigration [ˌɪmɪˈgreɪʃn]	Einwanderung
self-conscious [selfˈkɒnʃəs]	unsicher
flea market [ˈfliː mɑːkɪt]	Flohmarkt
Naples [ˈneɪpəlz]	Neapel
to start with [tə ˈstɑːt wɪð]	zunächst, anfangs
to tease [tiːz]	(auf)reizen, ärgern
to hit out (at sb) [ˌhɪt ˈaʊt]	(auf jdn) einschlagen
to annoy [əˈnɔɪ]	ärgern
Russian [ˈrʌʃn]	Russe/Russin, russisch, Russisch
to survive [səˈvaɪv]	überleben
manual [ˈmænjuəl]	Handbuch
to take revenge (on) [rɪˈvendʒ]	Rache nehmen (an)
chess [tʃes]	Schach

page 118

musical [ˈmjuːzɪkl]	Musik-
folk dance [ˈfəʊk dɑːns]	Volkstanz
belief [bɪˈliːf]	Glaube, Überzeugung
taboo subject [təˈbuː sʌbdʒɪkt]	Tabuthema
mourner [ˈmɔːnə]	Trauernde/r
funeral [ˈfjuːnərəl]	Beerdigung, Begräbnis
to celebrate [ˈselɪbreɪt]	feiern
worship [ˈwɜːʃɪp]	Anbetung, Verehrung
dementia [dɪˈmenʃə]	Demenz
mother tongue [ˈmʌðə tʌŋ]	Muttersprache
fortunate [ˈfɔːtʃənət]	glücklich, günstig
multilingual [ˌmʌltiˈlɪŋgwəl]	mehrsprachig
to read out [ˌriːd ˈaʊt]	(laut) vorlesen

page 119

miracle [ˈmɪrəkl]	Wunder
bilateral [ˌbaɪˈlætərəl]	bilateral, zweiseitig
agreement [əˈgriːmənt]	Vereinbarung, Abkommen
construction [kənˈstrʌkʃn]	(Auf-)Bau
large-scale [ˈlɑːdʒskeɪl]	groß, groß angelegt
flow [fləʊ]	Fluss, Strom
wave [weɪv]	Welle
federal republic [ˌfedərəl rɪˈpʌblɪk]	Bundesrepublik
developmental aid [dɪˌveləpˌmentl ˈeɪd]	Entwicklungshilfe
fixed [fɪkst]	fest, fix
democratic [ˌdeməˈkrætɪk]	demokratisch
GDR [ˌdʒiː diː ˈɑː]	DDR
shortage [ˈʃɔːtɪdʒ]	Mangel, Knappheit
labour [ˈleɪbə]	Arbeit, Arbeitskräfte
Eastern bloc [ˈiːstən blɒk]	Ostblock
Cuba [ˈkjuːbə]	Kuba
solidarity [ˌsɒlɪˈdærəti]	Solidarität
fellow [ˈfeləʊ]	Mit-, andere, befreundete
communist [ˈkɒmjənɪst]	kommunistisch, Kommunist/in
reunification [ˌriːjuːnɪfɪˈkeɪʃn]	Wiedervereinigung
former [ˈfɔːmə]	ehemalige/r/s
deportation [ˌdiːpɔːˈteɪʃn]	Deportation, Abschiebung
premature [ˈpremətʃə]	vorzeitig
discontinuation [ˌdɪskənˌtɪnjuˈeɪʃn]	Wegfall, Einstellung
work permit [ˈwɜːk pɜːmɪt]	Arbeitserlaubnis
guest worker [ˈgest wɜːkə]	Gastarbeiter/in
xenophobia [ˌzenəˈfəʊbiə]	Fremdenfeindlichkeit, Ausländerhass
lecturer [ˈlektʃərə]	Dozent/in, Hochschullehrer/in
diverse [daɪˈvɜːs]	unterschiedlich, vielfältig
to differ [ˈdɪfə]	sich unterscheiden
to impose sth on sb [ɪmˈpəʊz]	jdm etw auferlegen
agnostic [ægˈnɒstɪk]	Agnostiker/in, agnostisch
atheist [ˈeɪθiɪst]	Atheist/in
existence [ɪgˈzɪstəns]	Existenz
unreasonable [ʌnˈriːznəbl]	unvernünftig, unangemessen
preference [ˈprefrəns]	Präferenz, Vorliebe
nation [ˈneɪʃn]	Staat, Nation
Ireland [ˈaɪələnd]	Irland
today's [təˈdeɪz]	heutig, von heute
element [ˈelɪmənt]	Element, Bestandteil

262

Unit word list

one by one [ˌwʌn baɪ ˈwʌn]	Stück für Stück, eins nach dem anderen
tendency ['tendənsi]	Neigung
to assume [ə'sjuːm]	annehmen, glauben, davon ausgehen
to draw on sth [ˌdrɔː 'ɒn]	von etw zehren, aus etw schöpfen
to make sense [ˌmeɪk 'sens]	sinnvoll sein
automatic(ally) [ˌɔːtə'mætɪk]	automatisch
to conform to [kən'fɔːm tə]	entsprechen
custom [kʌstəm]	Gewohnheit, Brauch, Sitte
to be considered (as) [kən'sɪdəd]	gelten (als)
to discover [dɪ'skʌvə]	entdecken

page 120

nationality [ˌnæʃə'næləti]	Nationalität
unqualified [ˌʌn'kwɒlɪfaɪd]	un-, nicht qualifiziert, ungelernt
human rights [ˌhjuːmən 'raɪts]	Menschenrechte
violation [ˌvaɪə'leɪʃn]	Verstoß, Verletzung (von Gesetzen, Rechten)
traumatized ['trɔːmətaɪzd]	traumatisiert
war [wɔː]	Krieg
ethnic cleansing [ˌeθnɪk 'klenzɪŋ]	ethnische Säuberung(en)
torture ['tɔːtʃə]	Folter
harmful ['hɑːmfl]	schädlich
mentor [mentə]	Mentor
to attract [ə'trækt]	anziehen, anlocken
to convey [kən'veɪ]	vermitteln, übermitteln

page 121

voicemail ['vɔɪsmeɪl]	Anrufbeantworter
computing [kəm'pjuːtɪŋ]	Informatik
exchange (programme) [ɪks'tʃeɪndʒ]	Austausch(programm)

page 122

sensible ['sensəbl]	vernünftig, sinnvoll
absorbed [əb'sɔːbd]	vertieft

page 123

gallery ['gæləri]	Galerie

UNIT 11

page 126

communicable [kə'mjuːnɪkəbl]	übertragbar
cancer ['kænsə]	Krebs
infectious disease [ɪnˌfekʃəs dɪ'ziːz]	Infektionskrankheit
health complications ['helθ kɒmplɪkeɪʃnz]	gesundheitliche Probleme
complication [ˌkɒmplɪ'keɪʃn]	Komplikation
cardiovascular [ˌkɑːdiəʊ'væskjələ]	kardiovaskulär, Herz-Kreislauf-

disaster [dɪ'zɑːstə]	Katastrophe, Unglück, Desaster
ischaemic [ɪ'skiːmɪk]	ischämisch (Durchblutungsmangel-)
smallpox ['smɔːlpɒks]	Pocken
afterglow ['ɑːftəgləʊ]	Nachleuchten, angenehme Erinnerung, Abendröte
memory ['meməri]	Gedächtnis, Erinnerung
echo, pl echoes ['ekəʊ]	Echo
to whisper ['wɪspə]	flüstern
sunny ['sʌni]	sonnig
tear [tɪə]	Träne
to grieve [griːv]	trauern
word cloud ['wɜːd klaʊd]	Schlagwortwolke
purple ['pɜːpl]	lila, violett
diarrhoea [ˌdaɪə'rɪə]	Durchfall
famine ['fæmɪn]	Hungersnot, Hunger
stroke [strəʊk]	Schlaganfall

page 127

blues [bluːz]	Blues
clock [klɒk]	Uhr
to cut sth off [ˌkʌt 'ɒf]	etw abstellen, ausschalten
to bark [bɑːk]	bellen
juicy ['dʒuːsi]	saftig
to silence ['saɪləns]	zum Schweigen bringen, abdämpfen
piano [pi'ænəʊ]	Klavier
muffled ['mʌfld]	gedämpft, umhüllt
drum [drʌm]	Trommel
coffin ['kɒfɪn]	Sarg
aeroplane BE ['eərəpleɪn]	Flugzeug
to circle ['sɜːkl]	kreisen
to moan [məʊn]	stöhnen, jammern, klagen
overhead [ˌəʊvə'hed]	droben, am Himmel
to scribble ['skrɪbl]	kritzeln, hinkritzeln
sky [skaɪ]	Himmel
dead [ded]	tot, Tote/r, die Toten
crepe [kreɪp]	Krepp
bow [bəʊ]	Schleife
public ['pʌblɪk]	öffentlich, allgemein
dove [dʌv]	Taube
policeman, pl policemen [pə'liːsmən]	Polizist
cotton ['kɒtn]	Baumwolle
rest [rest]	Ruhe
noon [nuːn]	Mittag
to be wrong [ˌbi 'rɒŋ]	sich irren
to put sth out [ˌpʊt 'aʊt]	etw löschen
to pack sth up [ˌpæk 'ʌp]	etw einpacken, etw zusammenpacken
moon [muːn]	Mond
to dismantle [dɪs'mæntl]	abbauen, abreißen
to pour away [ˌpɔːr ə'weɪ]	wegschütten
ocean ['əʊʃn]	Ozean, Weltmeer
to sweep up [ˌswiːp 'ʌp]	auffegen, auskehren
wood [wʊd]	Wald, Holz
for [fɔː]	denn
sorrow ['sɒrəʊ]	Kummer, Leid
sadness ['sædnəs]	Traurigkeit
condolence [kən'dəʊləns]	Beileid
bereavement [bɪ'riːvmənt]	Verlust, Trauerfall

263

UNIT WORD LIST

sympathy ['sɪmpəθi]	Sympathie, Mitgefühl	**page 130**	
remembrance [rɪ'membrəns]	Erinnerung, Andenken	arrival [ə'raɪvl]	Ankunft, Ankömmling
mortality [mɔː'tæləti]	Sterblichkeit	grandson ['grænsʌn]	Enkel
mourning ['mɔːnɪŋ]	Trauern, Trauerarbeit	transient ['trænzɪənt]	vorübergehend
eulogy ['juːlədʒi]	Grabrede, Laudatio	to quote [kwəʊt]	zitieren, nennen, angeben
poem ['pəʊɪm]	Gedicht	blockage ['blɒkɪdʒ]	Verstopfung, Blockierung
relevance ['reləvəns]	Relevanz	dizzy ['dɪzi]	schwindelig, benommen
bereaved [bɪ'riːvd]	Hinterbliebene/r, hinterblieben, trauernd	numb [nʌm]	taub (Gefühl), gefühllos
		numbness [nʌmnəs]	Taubheit, Benommenheit
celebration [ˌselɪ'breɪʃn]	Feier	to manage ['mænɪdʒ]	es schaffen
to make for sth ['meɪk fə]	sorgen für etw, zu etw führen	ailment ['eɪlmənt]	Krankheit, Leiden
		cataract ['kætərækt]	Katarakt, grauer Star
page 128		macular degeneration [ˌmækjʊlə dɪˌdʒenə'reɪʃn]	Makuladegeneration
hospice ['hɒspɪs]	Hospiz, Sterbeklinik	atherosclerosis [ˌæθərəʊskləˈrəʊsɪs]	Atherosklerose, Arteriosklerose
terminally ill ['tɜːmɪnəli ɪl]	unheilbar krank	arthritis [ɑː'θraɪtɪs]	Arthritis
unsure [ˌʌn'ʃʊə]	unsicher	osteoporosis [ˌɒstiəʊpə'rəʊsɪs]	Osteoporose
FAQs (frequently asked questions) [ˌef eɪ 'kjuːz]	häufig gestellte Fragen	hypertension [ˌhaɪpə'tenʃn]	Bluthochdruck
assurance [ə'ʃʊərəns]	Sicherheit, Zuversicht	roughly ['rʌfli]	ungefähr, etwa
laughter ['lɑːftə]	Lachen	per [pə]	pro, per
friendship ['frendʃɪp]	Freundschaft	to industrialize [ɪn'dʌstriəlaɪz]	industrialisieren
humble ['hʌmbl]	demütig, bescheiden		
kindness ['kaɪndnəs]	Güte, Freundlichkeit	incidence ['ɪnsɪdəns]	Inzidenz, Auftreten, Häufigkeit
to coordinate [kəʊ'ɔːdɪneɪt]	koordinieren		
therapeutic [ˌθerə'pjuːtɪk]	therapeutisch	**page 131**	
biography [baɪ'ɒgrəfi]	Biografie	chief administrator [ˌtʃiːf əd'mɪnɪstreɪtə]	Verwaltungschef/in
to honour ['ɒnə]	ehren, annehmen	grandfather ['grænfɑːðə]	Großvater
greatly ['greɪtli]	sehr, stark	medicine, med ['medsn, med]	Medizin, Medikament
page 129		confusion [kən'fjuːʒn]	Verwirrung
palliative ['pæliətɪv]	palliativ, lindernd	delicate ['delɪkət]	delikat, heikel
to come to terms (with sth) [ˌkʌm tə 'tɜːmz]	sich (mit etw) arrangieren, (mit etw) zurechtkommen	sympathetic [ˌsɪmpə'θetɪk]	verständnisvoll, wohlwollend
		to split up [ˌsplɪt 'ʌp]	sich trennen
to spread [spred]	verteilen, verbreiten, sich ausbreiten	to rest [rest]	sich ausruhen
to confuse [kən'fjuːz]	verwirren, verwechseln	to prescribe [prɪ'skraɪb]	verschreiben, verordnen
guilt [gɪlt]	Schuld	dictation [dɪk'teɪʃn]	Diktat
parental [pə'rentl]	Eltern-, elterlich	to dictate [dɪk'teɪt]	diktieren
intense [ɪn'tens]	intensiv	punctuation [ˌpʌŋktʃu'eɪʃn]	Interpunktion, Zeichensetzung
ground [graʊnd]	Boden, Grund	involvement [ɪn'vɒlvmənt]	Engagement, Beteiligung, Einbindung
to rip out [ˌrɪp 'aʊt]	herausreißen		
abandoned [ə'bændənd]	verlassen	to get sb wrong [ˌget 'rɒŋ]	jdn missverstehen
to assure [ə'ʃʊə]	versichern, zusichern	army ['ɑːmi]	Armee
at times [ət 'taɪmz]	zeitweise	to discharge [dɪs'tʃɑːdʒ]	entlassen
at the same time [ət ðə seɪm 'taɪm]	gleichzeitig, zugleich	to be in a mess infml [ɪn ə 'mes]	in der Tinte sitzen, in der Patsche sein
emotion [ɪ'məʊʃn]	Emotion, Gefühl	eventually [ɪ'ventʃuəli]	letztendlich, schließlich
comforting ['kʌmfətɪŋ]	tröstlich		
comfort ['kʌmfət]	Komfort, Trost, Hilfe	**page 132**	
intimate ['ɪntɪmət]	intim, eng, persönlich	to his bedside ['bedsaɪd]	an sein Bett
interdisciplinary [ˌɪntə'dɪsəplɪnəri]	interdisziplinär, fachübergreifend	burial ['beriəl]	Beerdigung, Erdbestattung
to pronounce [prə'naʊns]	aussprechen	cremation [krə'meɪʃn]	Einäscherung, Feuerbestattung
reflection [rɪ'flekʃn]	Reflexion, Nachdenken, Überlegung	to bury ['beri]	begraben, vergraben
		to cremate [krə'meɪt]	einäschern

264

Unit word list

ethical ['eθɪkl]   ethisch, (moralisch) verantwortlich

to burn out [ˌbɜːn 'aʊt]   ausbrennen, verbrennen

to fade away [ˌfeɪd ə'weɪ]   verschwinden, verhallen

lyric ['lɪrɪk]   Lyrik, Text

greenhouse gas (GHG) [ˌgriːnhaʊs 'gæs]   Treibhausgas(e)

emission [ɪ'mɪʃn]   Emission, Abgas(e), Ausstoß

somewhat ['sʌmwɒt]   etwas

thorny ['θɔːni]   dornig, heikel

versus, vs. ['vɜːsəs]   gegen

environmentalist [ɪnˌvaɪrən'mentəlɪst]   Umweltschützer/in

to compost ['kɒmpɒst]   kompostieren

cremator [krə'meɪtə]   Krematoriumsofen

kilowatt-hour ['kɪləwɒt]   Kilowattstunde

electricity [ɪˌlek'trɪsəti]   Strom, Elektrizität

on average [ɒn 'ævərɪdʒ]   im Durchschnitt

aside from [ə'saɪd frəm]   außer, abgesehen von

considerable [kən'sɪdərəbl]   erheblich, beträchtlich

mercury ['mɜːkjəri]   Quecksilber

pollution [pə'luːʃn]   (Umwelt-)Verschmutzung

dental filling [ˌdentl 'fɪlɪŋ]   Zahnfüllung

crematorium, pl crematoria [ˌkremə'tɔːriəm, ˌkremə'tɔːriə]   Krematorium

ironically [aɪ'rɒnɪkli]   ironischerweise, paradoxerweise

thereby [ˌðeə'baɪ]   dabei, dadurch

wooden ['wʊdn]   hölzern, Holz-

solid ['sɒlɪd]   fest, solide

oak [əʊk]   Eiche, Eichenholz

pine [paɪn]   Kiefer, Pinie, Kiefernholz

veneered [və'nɪəd]   furniert

chipboard ['tʃɪpbɔːd]   Spanplatte

to bond [bɒnd]   verbinden, einschweißen

formaldehyde [fɔː'mældɪhaɪd]   Formaldehyd

resin ['rezɪn]   Harz

to embalm [ɪm'bɑːm]   einbalsamieren

watercourse ['wɔːtəkɔːs]   Gewässer

eco ['iːkəʊ]   öko

to frown on sth ['fraʊn ɒn]   etw missbilligen

fishfood ['fɪʃfuːd]   Fischfutter

navy ['neɪvi]   Marine, Schifffahrt

granted ['grɑːntɪd]   gestattet

location [ləʊ'keɪʃn]   (Stand-)Ort

woodland ['wʊdlənd]   Waldgebiet

increasingly [ɪn'kriːsɪŋli]   zunehmend, in zunehmendem Maße

biodegradable [ˌbaɪəʊdɪ'greɪdəbl]   biologisch abbaubar

cemetery ['semətri]   Friedhof

unmarked [ʌn'mɑːkt]   nicht gekennzeichnet, anonym

marked [mɑːkt]   gekennzeichnet, markiert

planting ['plɑːntɪŋ]   Bepflanzung

wild [waɪld]   wild

cardboard ['kɑːdbɔːd mɑːkt]   Pappe, Karton

wicker ['wɪkə]   Korbgeflecht

naturally-minded [ˌnætʃrəli 'maɪndɪd]   naturbewusst, natürlich gesinnt

sustainable [sə'steɪnəbl]   nachhaltig, umweltgerecht

to afford [ə'fɔːd]   (es) sich leisten (können)

to supersede [ˌsuːpə'siːd]   verdrängen, ersetzen, ablösen

to diminish [dɪ'mɪnɪʃ]   (sich) verringern, abnehmen

post-war [ˌpəʊst 'wɔː]   Nachkriegs-

to freeze-dry [friːzdraɪ]   gefriertrocknen

brittle [brɪtl]   spröde, brüchig

compostable [kɒm'pɒstəbl]   kompostierbar

remains (pl) [rɪ'meɪnz]   Überbleibsel, Rückstände

liquid ['lɪkwɪd]   Flüssigkeit, flüssig

nitrogen ['naɪtrədʒən]   Stickstoff

solar-powered ['səʊlə paʊəd]   solarbetrieben

tonne [tʌn]   Tonne (metrische Gewichtseinheit = 1.000 kg)

viable ['vaɪəbl]   realisierbar, durchführbar

modest ['mɒdɪst]   bescheiden

least [liːst]   wenigste/r/s, am wenigsten

page 133

disposal [dɪ'spəʊzl]   Entsorgung

to dispose of sth [dɪ'spəʊz əv]   etw beseitigen, entsorgen

formality [fɔː'mæləti]   Förmlichkeit, Formalität

headstone ['hedstəʊn]   Grabstein

anecdote ['ænɪkdəʊt]   Anekdote

authorization [ˌɔːθəraɪ'zeɪʃn]   Genehmigung

scannable ['skænəbl]   abtastbar, mit einem Scanner ablesbar

Austrian-based ['ɔːstriən beɪst]   in Österreich ansässig

to ensure [ɪn'ʃʊə]   sicherstellen

gravestone ['greɪvstəʊn]   Grabstein

to unlock [ʌn'lɒk]   freischalten, entsperren

intrigued [ɪn'triːgd]   fasziniert

regulations (pl) [ˌregju'leɪʃnz]   Vorschriften, Bestimmungen

to remark on sth [rɪ'mɑːk]   eine Bemerkung zu etw machen, etw zu etw anmerken

state [steɪt]   Land, Staat, staatlich

page 134

advancement [əd'vɑːnsmənt]   Weiterentwicklung

to reformulate [ˌriː'fɔːmjuleɪt]   umformulieren

unconscious [ʌn'kɒnʃəs]   bewusstlos, unbewusst

page 135

thematic(ally) [θɪ'mætɪk]   thematisch

town hall [ˌtaʊn 'hɔːl]   Rathaus

to surround [sə'raʊnd]   umgeben

265

UNIT WORD LIST

UNIT 12

page 138
aid [eɪd]	Hilfe, Hilfsmittel
homecare ['həʊmkeə]	häusliche Pflege
residential care home [ˌrezɪˌdenʃl 'keə həʊm]	Pflegeheim
part-residential care [ˌpɑːt rezɪˌdenʃl 'keə]	teilstationäre Pflege
to be in need of sth [ɪn 'niːd əv]	etw brauchen, benötigen, nötig haben

page 139
robot ['rəʊbɒt]	Roboter
to increase in (popularity) [ɪn'kriːs ɪn]	zunehmen an (Beliebtheit)
popularity [ˌpɒpju'lærəi]	Beliebtheit, Popularität
destination [ˌdestɪ'neɪʃn]	Ziel(ort)
Czech Republic [tʃek rɪ'pʌblɪk]	Tschechische Republik
United Arab Emirates [juːˌnaɪtɪd ˌærəb 'emɪrəts]	Vereinigte Arabische Emirate
bionic [baɪ'ɒnɪk]	bionisch (nach dem Vorbild biologischer Funktionen)
wearer ['weərə]	Träger/in
to be well placed (for sth / to do sth) [pleɪst]	in einer guten Lage sein, gute Möglichkeiten haben (für etw / etw zu tun)
to be in the habit of doing sth ['hæbɪt]	daran gewöhnt sein etw zu tun, gewöhnlich etw tun
lecture ['lektʃə]	Vorlesung, Vortrag
threat (to) [θret]	Bedrohung, Gefahr (für)

page 140
trade fair ['treɪd feə]	Handelsmesse
exhibitor [ɪg'zɪbɪtə]	Aussteller/in
stand [stænd]	Stand
handicap ['hændɪkæp]	Behinderung, Nachteil
capability [ˌkeɪpə'bɪləti]	Fähigkeit, Potenzial
innovation [ˌɪnə'veɪʃn]	Innovation, Neuerung
prosthetics [prɒs'θetɪks]	Prothetik, Prothesen
trial ['traɪəl]	Probe, Test, Versuch
appliance [ə'plaɪəns]	Gerät, Anwendung
self-reliant [ˌself rɪ'laɪən]	selbstständig
reliant on [rɪ'laɪənt ɒn]	angewiesen auf, abhängig von
wellness ['welnəs]	Gesundsein, Wohlbefinden
adjustment [ə'dʒʌstmənt]	Anpassung, Veränderung
comprehensive [ˌkɒmprɪ'hensɪv]	umfassend
to direct [də'rekt]	leiten, regeln, Regie führen
standard ['stændəd]	Standard, Norm(al)-
to collate [kə'leɪt]	zusammentragen, zusammenstellen
to monitor ['mɒnɪtə]	überwachen, verfolgen
equitable ['ekwɪtəbl]	gerecht
essential [ɪ'senʃl]	(absolut) notwendig, wesentlich
collective(ly) [kə'lektɪv]	gemeinsam, kollektiv

defence (against) [dɪ'fens]	Verteidigung, Schutz (gegen)
transnational [ˌtrænz'næʃnəl]	transnational, grenzübergreifend

page 141
pandemic [pæn'demɪk]	Seuche, Pandemie, seuchenartig, pandemisch
outbreak ['aʊtbreɪk]	Ausbruch (Krankheit, Regenschauer)
epidemic [ˌepɪ'demɪk]	Epidemie, epidemisch (seuchenartig)
antiviral [ˌænti'vaɪrəl]	antiviral, Virostatikum (Wirkstoff gegen Viren)
ever-(expanding) ['evə]	ständig (wachsend)
resources (pl) [rɪ'sɔːsɪz]	Ressourcen, Rohstoffe
localized ['ləʊkəlaɪzd]	lokal, (örtlich) begrenzt
full-blown [ˌfʊl 'bləʊn]	regelrecht, komplett, voll ausgebildet
to exceed [ɪk'siːd]	übersteigen, überschreiten
Spanish ['spænɪʃ]	Spanisch, spanisch
influenza, flu [ˌɪnflu'enzə, fluː]	Grippe
up to date [ˌʌp tə 'deɪt]	aktuell, auf dem/den neuesten Stand
China ['tʃaɪnə]	China
avian ['eɪviən]	Vogel-
swine [swaɪn]	Schwein, Schweine-
not anywhere / nowhere near [nɪə]	bei weitem nicht, nicht annähernd
vaccination [ˌvæksɪ'neɪʃn]	(Schutz-)Impfung
to eradicate [ɪ'rædɪkeɪt]	ausrotten
virus, pl viruses ['vaɪrəs]	Virus
bacteria [bæk'tɪəriə]	Bakterien
resistant (to) [rɪ'zɪstənt]	resistent, widerstandsfähig (gegen)
identification [aɪˌdentɪfɪ'keɪʃn]	Identifizierung, Bestimmung
to research (into/on) [rɪ'sɜːtʃ]	(er)forschen, recherchieren
researcher [rɪ'sɜːtʃə]	Forscher/in, Wissenschaftler/in
workforce ['wɜːkfɔːs]	Beschäftigte, Erwerbstätige, Belegschaft
working hours (pl) [ˌwɜːkɪŋ 'aʊəz]	Arbeitszeit(en)
polio ['pəʊliəʊ]	Polio, Kinderlähmung
cure (for) [kjʊə]	Heilung, (Heil-)Mittel (gegen)
to reverse [rɪ'vɜːs]	umkehren, rückgängig machen
prediction [prɪ'dɪkʃn]	Vorhersage, Voraussage, Prophezeiung
intention [ɪn'tenʃn]	Absicht
unsolicited application [ˌʌnsəˌlɪsɪtɪd ˌæplɪ'keɪʃn]	Initiativbewerbung, Blindbewerbung
in advance [ɪn əd'vɑːns]	im Voraus
to enquire (about) [ɪn'kwaɪə]	fragen, sich erkundigen (nach/wegen)
vacancy ['veɪkənsi]	freie/offene Stelle
at present [ət 'preznt]	momentan, derzeit, zurzeit

Unit word list

page 142

to **pick up** [ˌpɪk ˈʌp]	etw mitbringen, kaufen, sich etw holen
caregiver [ˈkeəɡɪvə]	pflegende/r Angehörige/r, Betreuer/in
to **be on the rise** [ˌɒn ðə ˈraɪz]	zunehmen, wachsen
to **be expected to …** [ɪkˈspektɪd]	… sollen/müssen, es wird erwartet, dass …
to **double** [ˈdʌbl]	(sich) verdoppeln
to **triple** [ˈtrɪpl]	(sich) verdreifachen
scientist [ˈsaɪəntɪst]	(Natur-)Wissenschaftler/in
to **enhance** [ɪnˈhɑːns]	verbessern, stärken
limitation [ˌlɪmɪˈteɪʃn]	Grenze, Einschränkung
expert (in) [ˈekspɜːt]	Experte/Expertin (für)
equipped with [ɪˈkwɪpt wɪð]	ausgestattet mit
to **equip** [ɪˈkwɪp]	ausrüsten, ausstatten
sensor [ˈsensə]	Sensor
motion [ˈməʊʃn]	Bewegung
inch [ɪntʃ]	Zoll, Inch (= 2,54 cm)
1 inch by 2 inches [baɪ]	1 Zoll mal 2 Zoll
to **install** [ɪnˈstɔːl]	einbauen, einrichten, aufbauen
to **track** [træk]	(zurück-, nach)verfolgen, beobachten
cooker [ˈkʊkə]	Herd
to **predetermine** [ˌpriːdɪˈtɜːmɪn]	vorher festlegen, im Voraus bestimmen
both … and … [bəʊθ]	sowohl … als auch …
for instance [fər ˈɪnstəns]	zum Beispiel
remote(ly) [rɪˈməʊt]	fern, Fern-, abgelegen
to **estimate** [ˈestɪmeɪt]	schätzen
to **retrofit** [ˈretrəʊfɪt]	nachträglich einbauen/umbauen/umrüsten
chapter [ˈtʃæptə]	Ortsgruppe
to **computerize** [kəmˈpjuːtəraɪz]	mit Computern ausstatten
technological [teknəˈlɒdʒɪkl]	technologisch

page 143

to **take a tour of sth** [ˌteɪk ə ˈtʊə]	etw besichtigen, einen Rundgang machen durch etw
impact [ˈɪmpækt]	Aufprall, Stoß, Einschlag
importance [ɪmˈpɔːtns]	Bedeutung, Wichtigkeit

page 144

to **head** [hed]	*(in Richtung von etw)* gehen, fahren
interactive [ˌɪntərˈæktɪv]	interaktiv
screen [skriːn]	Bildschirm, Leinwand
at the front (of) [frʌnt]	vorne (an/in), an der Vorderseite (von)
implication [ˌɪmplɪˈkeɪʃn]	Auswirkung, Konsequenz

page 145

to **rank (by)** [ræŋk]	einstufen, anordnen (nach)
likely [ˈlaɪkli]	wahrscheinlich
maker [ˈmeɪkə]	Hersteller/in
holistic [həʊˈlɪstɪk]	holistisch, ganzheitlich
globe [ɡləʊb]	Globus
taste [teɪst]	Geschmack, Kostprobe
in store [ɪn ˈstɔː]	vorgesehen, geplant
futurologist [ˌfjuːtʃəˈrɒlədʒɪst]	Futurologe/Futurologin
compassion [kəmˈpæʃn]	Mitgefühl
to **be the best bet** [bet]	am besten sein, der beste Tipp sein
remedy (for/to) [ˈremədi]	(Heil-)Mittel, Abhilfe (gegen),
consultant [kənˈsʌltənt]	Berater/in, Gutachter/in
to **personalize** [ˈpɜːsənəlaɪz]	persönlich/individuell gestalten
caring animal [ˈkeərɪŋ ænɪml]	*Tiere, die Menschen mit Behinderungen helfen/ assistieren*
blind [blaɪnd]	blind
to **be around** [bi əˈraʊnd]	da sein, existieren
companion [kəmˈpæniən]	Begleiter/in, Gefährte/Gefährtin
owner [ˈəʊnə]	Besitzer/in, Inhaber/in
monkey [ˈmʌŋki]	Affe
offspring [ˈɒfsprɪŋ]	Nachwuchs, Sprössling
apothecary [əˈpɒθəkəri]	Apotheker/in
tailor-made (for) [ˌteɪlə ˈmeɪd]	maßgeschneidert, zugeschnitten (auf)
entitled [ɪnˈtaɪtld]	mit dem Titel
questionable [ˈkwestʃənəbl]	fraglich, fragwürdig

page 147

announcement [əˈnaʊnsmənt]	Ankündigung, Durchsage
to **map** [mæp]	aufzeigen, erfassen
component [kəmˈpəʊnənt]	Bestandteil, Komponente
visual [ˈvɪʒuəl]	visuell, optisch
where … should go [ɡəʊ]	wo … hin(gehören) soll/sollen
to **sketch** [sketʃ]	skizzieren
to **adjust** [əˈdʒʌst]	anpassen
graphics *(pl)* [ˈɡræfɪks]	Grafiken
complex [ˈkɒmpleks]	kompliziert, komplex
to **condense** [kənˈdens]	kondensieren, zusammenfassen
to **get sth across** [ˌɡet əˈkrɒs]	etw klarmachen, etw vermitteln, etw rüberbringen

A–Z WORD LIST

Dieses Wörterverzeichnis enthält alle Wörter in **Social Pulse** in alphabetischer Reihenfolge. Nicht aufgeführt sind internationale Wörter wie *hotel*, *email* usw.

Wörter, die in den Hörverständnisübungen vorkommen, sind mit einem *t*, und Wörter, die in den *Partner Files* bzw. *Guidance and Challenge Files* vorkommen, mit einem *f* hinter der Seitenzahl gekennzeichnet.

A

AA 59 anonyme Alkoholiker
abandoned 129t verlassen
ability 10 Fähigkeit
able 80 fähig, kompetent
abled 80 normal *(nicht behindert)*
abortion 36 Abtreibung
abridged 61 (ab)gekürzt
abs (= abdominals) *(pl)* 90 Bauchmuskeln
abseiling 108 Abseilen
absence 82 Abwesenheit
absorbed 122 vertieft
abuse 6 Missbrauch
to **abuse** 35t missbrauchen
abuser 44 jd, der jdn/etw missbraucht, Peiniger/in
abusive 45t missbräuchlich, Missbrauchs-
academic 80 Schul-, akademisch, Akademiker/in
acceptance 78 Akzeptanz, Annahme
access 32 Zugang
to **access** 46t zugreifen auf
accessibility 78 Zugänglichkeit, Barrierefreiheit
accessory 44 Accessoire
accommodation 57t Unterkunft, Unterbringung
to **accompany** 20 begleiten
according to 31 (je) nach, zufolge, laut
to **account for** 109f ausmachen, erklären, ergeben
accreditation 104 Akkreditierung
accredited 10 anerkannt, akkreditiert
accurate(ly) 71 genau, präzise
to **achieve** 13 erreichen, erzielen, erlangen
achievement 21 Errungenschaft, Leistung
to **acquire** 107 erwerben
across 93f im Durchmesser
across: to get sth ~ 147 etw klarmachen, etw vermitteln
to **act** 43 handeln, sich verhalten
to **act sth out** 39 etw vorspielen, etw aufführen
action 47 Handlung, Aktion, Maßnahme(n)

action: to put sth into ~ 79 etw in die Tat umsetzen
acute 94 akut
to **adapt (to sth)** 22 sich anpassen (an etw)
to **add up** 70 zusammenrechnen
addict 61 Abhängige/r
addicted (to) 62 süchtig (nach), abhängig (von)
addiction 14 Sucht, Abhängigkeit
additional 93f zusätzlich
adhesive 108 (selbst-)klebend
to **adjust** 147 anpassen
adjustment 140 Anpassung, Veränderung
to **administer first aid** 109 erste Hilfe leisten
administration 107t Verwaltung
administrative 106 Verwaltungs-
admiration 105 Bewunderung
admission 109 Aufnahme
to **admit** 45t zugeben, (ein)gestehen
adolescent 9 jugendlich, Jugend-, Jugendliche/r
adolescent psychiatric unit 9t jugendpsychiatrische Station/ Abteilung
to **adopt** 30; 60t adoptieren; anwenden, sich entscheiden für
adopter 37 Adoptierende/r
adoption 31 Adoption
adoption: to give/put sb up for ~ 36 jdn zur Adoption freigeben
adoptive couple/parents 36 Adoptiveltern
adult 8 Erwachsene/r
adultery 34 Ehebruch
advance 79 Fortschritt
advance: in ~ 141f im Voraus
advancement 134 Weiterentwicklung
advantage (over) 20 Vorteil, Vorzug (gegenüber)
adventure 103 Abenteuer
adventurous 104 abenteuerlustig
to **advertise** 18 *(eine Stelle)* ausschreiben
as advertised 18 wie beschrieben
advertisement, advert, ad 8 Anzeige, Inserat, Werbespot
to **advise** 14 (be)raten
adviser 37f Berater/in

affair 50 Affäre, Verhältnis
to **affect** 37 sich auswirken auf, betreffen
affected by 73 betroffen, beeinflusst, beeindruckt von
to **afford** 132 (es) sich leisten (können)
afraid so: I'm ~ 35t Leider ja.
to **be afraid (of)** 35 Angst haben (vor)
afterglow 126 Nachleuchten, angenehme Erinnerung, Abendröte
after-school (programme) 87 (Programm) nach Unterrichtsschluss
after-work (activities) 74 (Aktivitäten) nach Feierabend
age: by ~ 60 nach Alter (aufgeschlüsselt)
age: at the ~ of (28) 94 im Alter von (28) Jahren
to **age** 82 altern, alt werden (lassen)
aged 10 im Alter von
agency 36 Agentur, Organisation
agenda 116 Agenda, Tagesordnung
aggressive 35t aggressiv
aggressor 46f Aggressor/in, Angreifer/in
agnostic 119 Agnostiker/in, agnostisch
to **agree on sth** 46 sich auf / über etw einigen
agreement 119f Vereinbarung, Abkommen
aid 138 Hilfe, Hilfsmittel
ailment 130 Krankheit, Leiden
aim 10 Ziel, Zweck, Absicht
to **aim at / for / to do sth** 10 zielen auf, sich richten an
aimed: to be ~ at sth 83t zu etw dienen, etw tun sollen
aimed at sb 96 an jdn gerichtet, für jdn
alcohol 55 Alkohol
alcoholic 48 Alkoholiker, alkoholisch
alcoholism 34 Alkoholismus
all: (not) at ~ 13f überhaupt (nicht)
all over ... 10 überall in ...
all: not ~ that (brilliant) *infml* 57t nicht ganz so (toll)
all day 107t den ganzen Tag
allergic reaction (to) 108 allergische Reaktion (auf)

268

A–Z word list

allergy *109f* Allergie
to **allocate** *63* verteilen, zuordnen
alongside *94* neben, entlang
alternative *73* Alternative, alternativ
altogether *93f* insgesamt
aluminium *108t* Aluminium
among(st) *60* zwischen, unter
amount *60t* Menge, Betrag
to **amputate** *82* amputieren
AMR meat (= advanced meat recovery) *93t* Separatorenfleisch *(vom Knochen gewonnenes Fleisch)*
to **analyse** *66* analysieren, untersuchen
analysis, *pl* **analyses** *60* Analyse
and so on *70t* und so weiter
anecdote *133f* Anekdote
anew *115* von neuem, erneut
anger *46f* Zorn, Wut
to **announce** *58* ankündigen, bekanntgeben
announcement *147* Ankündigung, Durchsage
to **annoy** *117t* ärgern
anonymity *48* Anonymität
anorexia *91* Anorexie, Magersucht
to **answer the phone** *25* ans Telefon gehen
antenatal *36* vorgeburtlich, pränatal
antibiotic *108* antibiotisch, Antibiotikum
anticoagulant *108t* Gerinnungs-hemmer
antihistamine *108* Antihistaminikum
antiviral *141* antiviral, Virostatikum *(Wirkstoff gegen Viren)*
anxious *44* unruhig, beunruhigt, ängstlich
apart *50* auseinander, getrennt
apart from *9t* außer, abgesehen von
to **apologize** *50* sich entschuldigen
apology *50* Entschuldigung
apothecary *145* Apotheker/in
to **appear** *34* auftauchen, (er)scheinen
appliance *140* Gerät, Anwendung
applicant *20* Bewerber/in
application *18* Bewerbung
application: unsolicited ~ *141* Initiativbewerbung, Blindbewerbung
to **apply (for)** *11* sich bewerben (um)
appointment *38* Termin, Verabredung
appreciation *71t* Anerkennung
approach *37f* Ansatz, Heran-gehensweise
appropriate *10* angemessen, passend, richtig
approval *71t* Zustimmung
approximately (approx) *30* ungefähr, etwa, zirka (ca.)

area *9t* Gebiet, Bereich, Feld, Gegend
argument *61* Argument, Streit
to **arise** *75* sich ergeben, entstehen, auftreten
army *131t* Armee
around: to be ~ *145* da sein, existieren
around: to hand sth ~ *46t* etw herumreichen
to **arouse** *99* wecken, erregen
to **arrange** *32* arrangieren, vereinbaren
arrangement *107f* Termin, Abmachung, Vereinbarung
to **arrest** *46t* verhaften
arrival *130* Ankunft, Ankömmling
arthritis *130* Arthritis
article *21* Artikel
artificial *98* künstlich
as *36* als, wie, während, weil
as … as *24* (eben)so … wie
as soon as *70f* sobald
as long as *83t* solange
ashamed: to be ~ (of) *46f* sich schämen (für)
aside from *132* außer, abgesehen von
assault *46f* Überfall, Angriff
to **assemble** *108* zusammenstellen
to **assess** *36* einschätzen, beurteilen, bewerten
assessment *37* Prüfung, Beurteilung
asset: to be an ~ (to) *23* von Vorteil sein, von Wert sein (für)
to **assign** *60* zuweisen, zuteilen
to **assist (with)** *8* assistieren, helfen (bei)
assistance *10* Hilfe
assistant *6* Helfer/in, Assistent/in
to **associate (with)** *46* verbinden, assoziieren (mit)
association *94* Verband, Vereinigung
assorted *98* gemischt, verschieden
assortment *108* Sortiment, Auswahl
to **assume** *119t* annehmen, glauben, davon ausgehen
assurance *128* Sicherheit, Zuversicht
to **assure** *129t* versichern, zusichern
asylum *54* Asyl
asylum seeker *54* Asylsuchende/r
at ease *49* bequem, zwanglos, unverkrampft
at present *141f* momentan, zurzeit
at home *30* zu Hause
at room temperature *93f* bei Raumtemperatur
at some time *34* irgendwann
at the end of the day *9t* letztendlich
atheist *119* Atheist/in

atherosclerosis *130* Atherosklerose, Arteriosklerose
atmosphere *72* Atmosphäre, Stimmung
at-risk *54* Risiko-, gefährdet
to **attach** *21* anfügen, anhängen *(an ein E-Mail)*
attached to *9t* angebunden an
to **attain** *106* erreichen, erlangen
to **attempt** *46f* versuchen
to **attend to sb** *108t* sich um jdn kümmern
attention *9t* Aufmerksamkeit
attention: to pay ~ (to) *48* aufpassen, achten (auf)
attention: (for the) ~ (of) (Attn.) *20* zu Händen
attentive *51* aufmerksam
attitude *13f* Einstellung, (Geistes-) Haltung
to **attract** *120* anziehen, anlocken
attractive *68t* attraktiv, reizvoll
attractiveness *90* Attraktivität, Reiz
attribute *46t* Attribut, Eigenschaft
audience *63* *(die)* Zuhörer, Zuschauer, *(das)* Publikum
author *102* Verfasser/in, Autor/in
authority *51* Autorität, Befugnis, Kompetenz(en)
authority: local ~ *9t* Kommunal-behörde, kommunal-
authorization *133f* Genehmigung
autism *82* Autismus
automatic(ally) *119t* automatisch
autonomy *78* Autonomie, Unabhängigkeit
auxiliary *13* Hilfs-, Aushilfs-
availability *46f* Verfügbarkeit
available *21* verfügbar, erhältlich, *(am Telefon)* zu sprechen
average *70f* durchschnittlich, Durchschnitt
avian *141t* Vogel-
to **avoid** *36* (ver)meiden
award *105* Auszeichnung, Preis
aware of sth *12* sich einer Sache bewusst
awareness *12* Bewusstsein
awful *98* furchtbar, schrecklich
to **axe** *72* schließen, streichen, entlassen

B

back in touch *57t* wieder in Kontakt
background *25f* Hintergrund(-), Herkunft
background: migrant ~ *114* Migrationshintergrund
bacteria *141t* Bakterien
baking paper *93f* Backpapier
baking sheet, baking tray *93f* Backblech

269

A–Z WORD LIST

balance 12 Gleichgewicht, Ausgewogenheit
balanced 12t ausgeglichen, ausgewogen, im Gleichgewicht
to **ban** 94 verbieten, verbannen, sperren
bandage 108 Bandage, Verband
to **bark** 127 bellen
base 93f Basis, Boden (Kuchen, Pizza)
based: Austrian-~ 133f in Österreich ansässig
based on 82 auf der Basis von, basierend auf, aufgrund
basil 93f Basilikum
basis: on a daily ~ 23 jeden Tag, täglich
basis: on a regular ~ 23 regelmäßig
battering 34 Prügel
battle (for/against) 94 Kampf, Schlacht (um/gegen)
to **be to do sth** 68 etw tun sollen
bean 92 Bohne
to **beat** 13 schlagen, besiegen, übertreffen
beauty 90 Schönheit
because of 23 wegen
bedside: to his ~ 132 an sein Bett
beef 92 Rind(fleisch)
before 43 schon (einmal)
to **beg sb for sth** 62 jdn um etw anbetteln
beginning 33 Anfang
on behalf of 59 in Namen
to **behave** 25f sich verhalten, sich benehmen
behaviour 34 Verhalten, Benehmen
belief 118 Glaube, Überzeugung
belly 90 Bauch
to **belong (to)** 9t gehören (zu)
benefactor 81 Wohltäter/in
beneficial (to) 32 nützlich, vorteilhaft (für)
benefit 85f Nutzen, Vorteil
to **benefit from** 33f profitieren von
to **benefit sb** 72 jdm nützen, zugutekommen
benevolent 104 gütig, wohlwollend
bereaved 127 Hinterbliebene/r, hinterblieben, trauernd
bereavement 127 Verlust, Trauerfall
beside 21f neben
bet: to be the best ~ 145 am besten sein, der beste Tipp sein
beverage 70 Getränk
biking 106 Radfahren
bilateral 119f bilateral, zweiseitig
billboard 99 Reklametafel, Plakatwand
billion 79 Milliarde
to **binge drink** 54 komasaufen
biodegradable 132 biologisch abbaubar

biography 128 Biografie
biological 33f biologisch
biology 22 Biologie
bionic 139 bionisch (nach dem Vorbild biologischer Funktionen)
biracial AE 33f gemischtrassig
birth 18 Geburt
bite 108 Biss, (Insekten-)Stich
black eye 35f blaues Auge
blame 45t Schuld
blame: to put the ~ on sb 45t jdm die Schuld geben
to **blame sb** 45 jdm die Schuld geben
blanket 108 Decke
to **bleed** 47 bluten
to **blend** 93f mischen, verrühren
blender 93t Mixer (Küchengerät)
blindness 82 Blindheit
blockage 130t Verstopfung, Blockierung
blood 93t Blut
blues 127 Blues
blunt(ly) 46t geradeheraus
body hair 90 Körperbehaarung
to **bombard** 90 bombardieren
bond 32 Bindung, Verbindung
to **bond** 132 verbinden, einschweißen
bone 93t Knochen
bone marrow 93t Knochenmark
boobs (pl, infml) 90 Busen, (weibliche) Brust
boom 116 Boom, Hochkonjunktur
to **boom** 97 blühen (Wirtschaft, Geschäft)
to **boost** 96 stärken, unterstützen, Auftrieb geben
boot camp 97 Ausbildungslager
to **borrow** 26 (sich etw) borgen, (sich) (aus)leihen
both ... and ... 142 sowohl ... als auch ...
to **bother sb** 63 jdn stören, jdn belästigen
bothered: sb can't be ~ to do sth 91 jd hat keine Lust, etw zu tun
bow 127 Schleife
bowl 93f Schale, Schüssel
brackets (pl) 14 Klammern
to **brainstorm** 20 Ideen (ungeordnet) sammeln
breadwinner 32 Brotverdiener/in
break 108 Bruch
to **break** 81 zuerst veröffentlicht werden (Nachricht)
to **break apart** 30 auseinanderbrechen
to **break out (of)** 35 ausbrechen (aus)
to **break sth** 43 (sich) etw brechen
breaking: You're ~ up. 25 (Telefon) Das Netz geht weg.

breast 94 Brust
brief 21 kurz, knapp
to **bring along** 68t mitbringen
to **bring sb up** 35 jdn aufziehen, großziehen
brittle 132 spröde, brüchig
broad 56t breit
to **browse** 15 stöbern, sich umsehen (in/durch)
bruise 35f Bluterguss, Prellung
budget 116 Budget, Haushalt, Etat
bug 111 Wanze, Insekt
building site 57f Baustelle
build-up 46f Anhäufung
to **bulge** 97f hervortreten, sich (vor)wölben, prall gefüllt sein
bulimia 94 Bulimie (med., Ess-Brech-Sucht)
bulletin board 72 Anschlagtafel, Schwarzes Brett
to **bully** 47 tyrannisieren, mobben
bullying 34 Tyrannisieren, Mobbing
burden 116 Last
bureaucracy 10 Bürokratie
burial 132 Beerdigung, Erdbestattung
to **burn out** 132 ausbrennen, verbrennen
to **bury** 132 begraben, vergraben
business: it's not your ~ 43 es geht Sie/dich nichts an
by 79 bis
by: 1 inch ~ 2 inches 142 1 Zoll mal 2 Zoll
by telephone 20 telefonisch, per Telefon
by the way 56t übrigens, nebenbei (bemerkt)

C

caffeinated 70 koffeinhaltig
to **calculate** 72 ausrechnen, berechnen, kalkulieren
to **call a meeting** 74 eine Sitzung/ein Meeting einberufen
to **call sb names** 46f jdn beschimpfen
to **call (a flight)** 107t (einen Flug) aufrufen
to **call in** 48 anfordern, hinzuziehen
to **call on sb** 35f jdn aufsuchen
calling 9t Berufung
calm 14 ruhig
calorie 96 Kalorie
campaign 91 Kampagne
to **campaign (for/against)** 82 kämpfen, sich einsetzen (für/gegen)
campaigner 94 Aktivist/in
to **cancel** 107t stornieren
cancellation 107t Stornierung, Absage
cancer 126 Krebs

A–Z word list

candidate *22* Bewerber/in, Kandidat/in
canned *92* Dosen-
canteen *70f* Kantine
capability *140* Fähigkeit, Potenzial
capacity *78* Fähigkeit, Leistungsvermögen
caption *30* Bildunterschrift, Überschrift
carcass *93f* Kadaver
cardboard *132* Pappe, Karton
cardiovascular *126* kardiovaskulär, Herz-Kreislauf-
care *6* Versorgung, Fürsorge
to **care about** *46t* sich interessieren für
to **care for sb** *6* jdn pflegen, betreuen, jdn mögen
career *15* Karriere, Beruf
caregiver *142* pflegende/r Angehörige/r, Betreuer/in
carer *7* Betreuer/in, Pfleger/in
caring *7* Versorgung, Betreuung, Pflege
caring *13* liebevoll, warmherzig
caring animal *145* Tiere, die Menschen mit Behinderungen helfen/ assistieren
caring profession *6* Sozialberuf, Pflegeberuf
caring professional *7* in einem Sozialberuf Tätige/r
to **carry out** *20* ausführen, durchführen
to **carry over** *35f* übernehmen, übertragen
cartoonist *66* Zeichner *(von Cartoons/Karikaturen)*
case *12* Fall
case worker *60* Sachbearbeiter/in
case: in ~ *58* für den Fall, dass
to **cast** *104* besetzen *(eine Rolle)*
cast as … *104* in die Rolle des/der … gesetzt
casual(ly) *24* lässig, zwanglos, leger
catalogue *59* Katalog
cataract *130* Katarakt, grauer Star
catchy *99* eingängig *(Lied, Slogan)*
category *8* Kategorie
to **cater for sb** *80* jdm gerecht werden
to **cater to sb** *104* auf jdn ausgerichtet sein
catering *83t* Gastronomie(-)
to **celebrate** *118* feiern
celebration *127* Feier
celebrity *46t* Prominente/r
cemetery *132* Friedhof
century *32* Jahrhundert
CEO (Chief Executive Officer) *73* Geschäftsführer/in, Vorstandsvorsitzende/r

cerebral palsy *80* spastische Lähmung
certainty *44* Gewissheit
certificate *21* Zeugnis, Urkunde
chain *83t* Kette
challenge *12* Herausforderung, Aufgabe
challenged *78* behindert
challenging *12* anspruchsvoll
chapter *142* Ortsgruppe
character *34* Charakter, Figur *(Buch, Film, Comic)*
characteristic *83t* Eigenschaft, (charakteristisches) Merkmal
to **characterize** *82* charakterisieren
charge: in ~ (of) ~ *25* verantwortlich (für), zuständig (für)
charity *10; 104* Wohltätigkeitsverein, Hilfsorganisation; Nächstenliebe, Wohltätigkeit
chart *114* Schaubild, Diagramm, Grafik
to **cheat on sb** *45t* jdn betrügen
to **check in (with)** *44* sich melden (bei)
check-up *37f* Untersuchung
chemical *92* Chemikalie, chemisch
cherry *93f* Kirsche
chess *117* Schach
chicken *92* Huhn, Hühnerfleisch
chief administrator *131* Verwaltungschef/in
childbirth *38* Geburt
childcare *26* Kinderbetreuung
childhood *35f* Kindheit
chipboard *132* Spanplatte
choir *47* Chor
to **chop** *93f* (klein) schneiden
to **chop sth up** *93t* etw klein schneiden
chronic *82* chronisch
to **chuck sb out** *infml 57t* jdn rausschmeißen
cigarette *45t* Zigarette
circle *33* Kreis, Clique
to **circle** *127* kreisen
circular *72* rund, Rund-
circumstances *(pl) 36* Umstände
citizen *78* Bürger/in
to **claim** *35f* angeben, behaupten
to **clarify sth** *111* etw klären, klarstellen
to **clean up** *103* säubern, aufräumen
client *9t* Kunde/Kundin, Klient/in, Mandant/in
clientele *11* Klientel, Kundenkreis
climate *86* Klima
clinic *14* Klinik, Ambulanz, Sprechstunde
clinical *12* klinisch
clinically (overweight) *90* krankhaft (übergewichtig)

clock *127* Uhr
close (to) *48t* eng, nah, dicht (an/bei)
closely *42* genau
closeness *48t* Nähe
closure *72* Abschluss, Schließung, Stilllegung
to **clot** *108t* klumpen, gerinnen
cloth *93f* Stoff, Tuch
clothing *24* Kleidung
clove (of garlic) *93f* (Knoblauch-) Zehe
clumsy *35f* ungeschickt, schwerfällig
coal *108* Kohle
coat *85t* Mantel, Jacke, Kittel
coating *108t* Beschichtung
coffin *127* Sarg
cognitive *83t* kognitiv
to **collate** *140* zusammentragen, zusammenstellen
colleague *14* Kollege/Kollegin
collective(ly) *140* gemeinsam, kollektiv
combination *56t* Kombination, Verbindung
to **combine** *30* verbinden, kombinieren
to **come as a/no surprise** *74* es ist eine/keine Überraschung
to **come to mind** *90* einem einfallen
to **come about** *37f* passieren
to **come across sth** *35t* auf etw stoßen, etw (zufällig) finden
to **come into being** *33* entstehen
to **come out** *45* herauskommen
to **come to terms (with sth)** *129t* sich (mit etw) arrangieren, (mit etw) zurechtkommen
to **come up** *83t* aufgeworfen werden, aufkommen
to **come up with sth** *47* sich etw einfallen lassen, sich etw ausdenken, etw vorschlagen
comes: when it ~ to … *46t* wenn es um … geht
comfort *129t* Komfort, Trost, Hilfe
comforting *129t* tröstlich
comment about/on *47* Bemerkung (zu/über), Kommentar (zu)
to **comment on** *92f* kommentieren
commercial *99* Werbespot
to **commit** *34* *(Verbrechen etc.)* begehen
committed (to) *8* engagiert (für)
communicable *126* übertragbar
communist *119f* kommunistisch, Kommunist/in
community *6* Gemeinschaft, Gemeinde, Bevölkerungsgruppe
community centre *26* Gemeindezentrum

271

A–Z WORD LIST

community service 38 gemeinnützige Arbeit
community-based 30 gemeinschaftlich, von der Gemeinschaft getragen
companion 145 Begleiter/in, Gefährte/Gefährtin
company 24 Unternehmen, Gesellschaft, Firma
to **compare** 10 vergleichen, sich vergleichen lassen
compassion 145 Mitgefühl
compensation 73 Schaden(s)ersatz, Entschädigung, Kompensation
competence 63 Kompetenz
competent 11 kompetent
competition 111 Konkurrenz, Wettkampf
competitive 83t Wettbewerbs-, Konkurrenz-
to **complain to sb (about)** 49f sich bei jdm beschweren, sich bei jdm beklagen (über)
complaint 69t Beschwerde, Klage, Reklamation
to **complement** 35t ergänzen
complex 147 kompliziert, komplex
complication 126 Komplikation
complications: health ~ 126 gesundheitliche Probleme
component 147 Bestandteil, Komponente
to **compost** 132 kompostieren
compostable 132 kompostierbar
comprehensive 140 umfassend
to **computerize** 142 auf Computer umstellen, mit Computern ausstatten
computing 121t Informatik
to **concentrate (on)** 49 sich konzentrieren (auf)
concentration 70f Konzentration
concept 51 Idee, Konzept
concern 12 Bedenken, Sorge
concerned: as far as ... is/are ~ 13f was ... betrifft/angeht
concerning 25f betreffend, hinsichtlich
concert 46t Konzert
to **conclude** 46t (ab)schließen
conclusion 69 Fazit, Schluss
to **condense** 147 kondensieren, zusammenfassen
condition 20; 57f Leiden, Erkrankung; Bedingung, Zustand
condolence 127 Beileid
to **conduct** 12 durchführen
confectionery 85t Süßwaren
confidence 111 (Selbst-)Vertrauen
confident 24 (selbst)sicher, zuversichtlich, überzeugt
confidential 12 vertraulich
to **confirm** 107 bestätigen

conflict 35t Streit(igkeiten), Konflikt
to **conform to** 119t entsprechen
to **confuse** 129t verwirren, verwechseln
confusion 131 Verwirrung
to **connect** 33 verbinden, anschließen
conscious 12 bewusst
consciousness 109 Bewusstsein
consequence 37f Folge, Konsequenz
to **consider** 7; 23 nachdenken über, sich etw überlegen, in Erwägung ziehen; berücksichtigen
considerable 132 erheblich, beträchtlich
to **be considered (as)** 119t gelten (als)
to **consist of** 95 bestehen aus
constantly 57t ständig
construction 119f (Auf-)Bau
consultant 145 Berater/in, Gutachter/in
consumption 60 Verbrauch, Konsum
to **contact** 20 Kontakt aufnehmen zu, sich wenden an
to **contain** 21f enthalten
to **contaminate** 93t verseuchen, verunreinigen
content 15 Inhalt
continually 8 ständig, ununterbrochen
continuous(ly) 35t kontinuierlich
contraceptive pill 109f Verhütungsmittel, Antibabypille
contrast 11 Gegensatz
to **contrast** 10 gegenüberstellen
to **contribute** 59 beitragen
contribution (to) 59 Beitrag (zu)
control 73 Kontrolle, Regulierung, Steuerung
to **control** 34 kontrollieren, beherrschen
controversial 94 kontrovers, umstritten
convenience 92 Bequemlichkeit, Annehmlichkeit
convenience food 92 Fertignahrung
convenient 107f passend, praktisch, angenehm
convention 78 Abkommen, Konvention
conversational 22 Konversations-, gesprochenes
to **convey** 120 vermitteln, übermitteln
convicted (for) 37f verurteilt (wegen)
conviction 37f Verurteilung
cooker 142 Herd
to **cool down** 12 sich abkühlen, sich beruhigen
cooperation 107t Zusammenarbeit
to **coordinate** 128 koordinieren

to **cope (with)** 12 zurechtkommen, fertig werden (mit)
core 67 Basis(-), Kern(-), Schwerpunkt(-)
corn 93t Getreide, (AE) Mais
corner 84t Ecke
corner: around the ~ 56t um die Ecke
to **correspond to** 79 entsprechen, übereinstimmen mit
cotton 127 Baumwolle
council 9 Rat, Gemeinderat
to **counsel (on)** 37 beraten (über)
counselling 37f professionelle Beratung
counsellor 8 Berater/in
country code 107t Ländervorwahl
court: to 35t vor Gericht
court: youth ~ 57t Jugendgericht
cover 31 Vertretung
to **cover** 10 abdecken, (Thema) behandeln
to **cover up for sb** 35f jdn decken
covering letter 18 Anschreiben, Begleitschreiben
co-worker 70 Arbeitskollege/-kollegin
to **crack down** 61 hart durchgreifen
to **crave sth** 45t sich nach etw sehnen
cream 108 Creme
to **create** 67 erstellen, (er)schaffen
credit card 44 Kreditkarte
to **cremate** 132 einäschern
cremation 132 Einäscherung, Feuerbestattung
cremator 132 Krematoriumsofen
crematorium, pl **crematoria** 132 Krematorium
crepe 127 Krepp
crime 44 Verbrechen, Kriminalität
criminal 56t Verbrecher/in, Kriminelle/r, kriminell, strafbar
crisis, pl **crises** 10 Krise
crisp 93t knusprig, knackig
criterion, pl **criteria** 27 Kriterium
critical(ly) 111 kritisch
criticism 94 Kritik
cross-country skiing 106 Skilanglauf
crowd: to go along with the ~ infml 57t mit der Herde mitgehen, mit dem Strom schwimmen
crude oil 93t Rohöl
to **crush** 93f (zer)quetschen, (aus)pressen
to **cry** 43 weinen, schreien
cube 84t Würfel
cultural(ly) 10 kulturell, Kultur-
culture 9t Kultur
to **cure** 83 heilen
cure (for) 141 Heilung, (Heil-)Mittel (gegen)

A–Z word list

current(ly) *23* aktuell, gegenwärtig
curtain *48t* Vorhang, Gardine
custom *119t* Gewohnheit, Brauch, Sitte
cut *72* (Ver-)Kürzung, Schnitt
cut (of meat) *93f* Stück (Fleisch)
to **cut sth off** *127* etw abstellen, ausschalten
CV (= curriculum vitae) *18* Lebenslauf
cyberbullying *46* Mobbing im Netz
cycle *45* Zyklus, Kreislauf

D

dairy *92* Molkerei, Milch-, Molkerei-
to **damage** *82* (be)schädigen, schaden
data *21* Daten
data entry *83t* Dateneingabe
database *104* Datenbank
to **date sb** *47* mit jdm gehen, eine Beziehung haben
date of birth *18* Geburtsdatum
daughter-in-law *32* Schwiegertochter
day care *8* Tagesbetreuung
day care centre *8* Tagesstätte
day nursery *9* Tageskrippe
day after day *80* Tag für Tag
daytime TV *51* Nachmittags-, Vorabendprogramm *(Fernsehen)*
day-to-day *9t* tagtäglich
dead *127* tot, Tote/r, die Toten
deaf *80* gehörlos, taub
deafness *82* Taubheit
deal: a great ~ (of) *70* viel, eine Menge
to **deal with** *9t* sich beschäftigen mit, sich kümmern um, umgehen mit
to **deal with sth** *34* etw erledigen, etw bearbeiten
death *32* Tod, Todesfall, Tote/r
debate *61* Debatte
debriefing *106* Nachbesprechung
decade *38* Jahrzehnt
decision-making *85f* Entscheidungsfindung
to **decline** *61* abnehmen, zurückgehen
to **decrease (by)** *60* fallen, abnehmen, verringern (um)
decriminalization *55* Entkriminalisierung
to **decriminalize** *61* entkriminalisieren
defence (against) *140* Verteidigung, Schutz (gegen)
to **defend** *81* verteidigen
to **define** *32* definieren, (genauer) erklären

degeneration: macular ~ *130* Makuladegeneration
to **delete** *69t* löschen
deliberately *45t* absichtlich, (ganz) bewusst, vorsätzlich
delicate *131* delikat, heikel
delicious *93t* köstlich, lecker
delivery *72* Lieferung
demand *6* Bedarf, Nachfrage, Anforderung
demand: in ~ *6* (nach)gefragt
dementia *118* Demenz
democratic *119f* demokratisch
demographic *115* demografisch
to **demonstrate** *99* vorführen, zeigen, demonstrieren
demotivation *71f* Demotivation
denial *35* Verdrängung
dental filling *132* Zahnfüllung
to **deny** *44* leugnen, bestreiten
department *35* Abteilung, Amt
dependent (on) *35f* abhängig (von)
depending on *99* abhängig von, je nach
to **depict** *60* darstellen, aufzeigen
deportation *119f* Deportation, Abschiebung
depressed *43* deprimiert, niedergeschlagen
depression *67* Depression(en)
derivative *93* Derivat, Abkömmling
descent *115* Herkunft, Abstammung
description *14* Beschreibung
to **deserve** *35t* verdienen
to **design** *15* entwerfen, gestalten
desire *99* Wunsch, Verlangen
to **desire sth** *99* sich etw wünschen, etw begehren
despair *12* Verzweiflung
despite *79* trotz
despite this *33f* trotzdem
destination *139* Ziel(ort)
to **destroy** *57f* zerstören, vernichten
detailed *99* ausführlich, detailliert
details: personal ~ *(pl) 21* persönliche Angaben
developing country *104* Entwicklungsland
developmental *80* Entwicklungs-
developmental aid *119f* Entwicklungshilfe
to **diagnose** *86* eine Diagnose stellen, diagnostizieren
diagnosed: sb is ~ with … *86* bei jdm wird … festgestellt, diagnostiziert
diagnosis, *pl* **diagnoses** *109f* Diagnose
diagram: Venn ~ *34* Venndiagramm, Mengendiagramm
diarrhoea *126* Durchfall
to **dictate** *131* diktieren
dictation *131* Diktat

diet *13* Ernährung, Diät
to **diet** *94* eine Schlankheitskur machen, weniger essen
to **differ** *119* sich unterscheiden
differently-abled *79* behindert *(anders begabt)*, Menschen mit besonderen Bedürfnissen
difficult *68t* schwer
to **dig** *104* graben
digestive *70* Verdauungs-
dignity *58* Würde
to **diminish** *132* (sich) verringern, abnehmen
diploma *116* Diplom, Abschlusszeugnis
to **direct** *140* leiten, regeln, Regie führen
director *71f* Geschäftsführer/in, Chef/in
dirt *108t* Schmutz, Dreck
dirty *68t* schmutzig
disability *20* Behinderung
to **disable** *83* behindern, ausschalten
disabled *20* behindert
disadvantage *102* Nachteil
disadvantaged *103* benachteiligt
to **disagree (with)** *13* nicht zustimmen
disagreement *58* Meinungsverschiedenheit
disappointed *49* enttäuscht
disaster *126* Unglück, Desaster
to **discard** *87* verwerfen
to **discharge** *131t* entlassen
discontinuation *119f* Wegfall, Einstellung
to **discover** *119t* entdecken
to **discriminate against** *68t* diskriminieren
discrimination (against sb) *33f* Diskriminierung (eines Menschen)
discriminatory *33f* benachteiligend, diskriminierend
discussion *33* Diskussion, Besprechung
disease *82* Krankheit, Erkrankung
disgusted (by) *94* angewidert (von), empört (über)
disgusting *68t* ekelhaft, widerlich, abscheulich
to **dislike** *13* nicht mögen
to **dismantle** *127* abbauen, abreißen
disorder *9t* (Funktions-)Störung *(med.)*
to **display** *59* anzeigen, ausstellen, präsentieren
disposal *133* Entsorgung
to **dispose of sth** *133* etw beseitigen, entsorgen
disproportionate(ly) *82* unverhältnismäßig
dispute *47* Streit, Disput, Kampf
dissatisfied *75* unzufrieden

A–Z WORD LIST

distinct 104 deutlich, unterschiedlich
distress 103 Not, Notlage
to **distribute** 44 verteilen
distribution 62 Verteilung, (Aus-)Lieferung
district nurse 35t Gemeindeschwester, Pflegekraft in der ambulanten Pflege
to **disturb** 70f stören
disused 108 stillgelegt
diverse 119 unterschiedlich, vielfältig
diversity 78 Vielfalt
divide 104 Kluft
to **divide into** 15 (sich) unterteilen in
diving 108 Tauchen
division 104 Trennung
divorce 30 Scheidung
to **divorce** 35t sich scheiden lassen
dizzy 130t schwindelig, benommen
dos and don'ts (pl) 25 Hinweise, was man tun und lassen sollte
to **do better** 24 besser abschneiden
do: (problems) to ~ with … 32 (Probleme, die) mit … zusammenhängen
to **do badly** 72 schlecht laufen, keinen Erfolg haben
to **do research (into)** 7 recherchieren, Nachforschungen anstellen (über)
document 68 Dokument
domestic 10 Haus-, häuslich
to **donate** 105 spenden, schenken
donation 81 Spende, Schenkung
to **double** 142 (sich) verdoppeln
to **doubt** 60t bezweifeln
dough 93f Teig
dove 127 Taube
Down's/Down syndrome 80 Down-Syndrom
to **downsize** 72 (sich) verkleinern, Personal abbauen
downsizing 72 Personalabbau
draft 27 Entwurf
to **draft** 97 entwerfen, abfassen
to **drain** 93f abgießen, abtropfen (lassen)
dramatic 61 dramatisch
to **draw** 8 zeichnen
to **draw on** 67 zurückgreifen auf, schöpfen aus
to **draw on sth** 119t von etw zehren, aus etw schöpfen
drawback 15 Nachteil
drill 84t Drill, Exerzieren, Übung
to **drive in** 56t hineinfahren, hereinfahren
to **drive sb over** 56t jdn vorbeifahren, herbringen
driving licence BE 20 Führerschein
to **drop** 47 fallen (lassen), verlieren
to **drop out of sth** 56t aus etw aussteigen, etw abbrechen
drug 38 Droge, Rauschgift, Medikament
drum 127 Trommel
drunk 38 betrunken
dry 94 trocken
due to 21 wegen, aufgrund (von)
duty 20 Aufgabe, Pflicht
duty: on ~ 59 im Dienst
duty: to be on ~ 108 Dienst haben
dying: to be ~ to do sth 94 etw unbedingt tun wollen, darauf brennen etw zu tun
dysfunctional 30 gestört

E

e.g. 34 z. B.
earnings (pl) 73 Verdienst, Einkommen, Einnahmen
earth 97f (die) Erde
ease: at ~ 49 bequem, zwanglos, unverkrampft
Easter bunny 85t Osterhase
Eastern bloc 119f Ostblock
easy-going 9t unkompliziert, nicht so streng
eating disorder 9t Essstörung
eco 132 öko
ecological(ly) 107f ökologisch, Umwelt-
economic 74 wirtschaftlich, Wirtschafts-
educated 44 (gut) ausgebildet
education 9; 10 Erziehung; (Schul-)Bildung, Ausbildung
educator 93 Pädagoge/Pädagogin
effective(ly) 27 effektiv, wirksam, wirkungsvoll
effeminate 46t feminin, unmännlich
efficient 96 effizient, rationell
elderly: (the) ~ 8 Senioren/-innen, ältere (Menschen)
elders (pl) 10 ältere Generation
eldest 9t älteste/r/s
electricity 132 Strom, Elektrizität
element 119t Element, Bestandteil
to **embalm** 132 einbalsamieren
emergency 48 Notfall
emission 132 Emission, Abgas(e), Ausstoß
emotion 129t Emotion, Gefühl
emotional abuse 44 psychischer Missbrauch, seelische Gewalt
emotional(ly) 44 emotional
empathy 35 Einfühlungsvermögen
to **employ** 51 beschäftigen
employee 11 Angestellte/r, Beschäftigte/r
employer 20 Arbeitgeber/in
employment 18 Anstellung, Beschäftigung, Arbeit

empowerment 84 Bevollmächtigung, Ermächtigung (Übertragung von Verantwortung auf Untergebene)
to **enable** 49 ermöglichen, befähigen
Enc (enclosed) 23 Anlage(n)
to **enclose** 26 beifügen, beilegen
enclosed 23 beigefügt, beiliegend
encounter 49 Begegnung
to **encourage** 48 ermutigen, ermuntern, motivieren
end: at the ~ 7 am Ende, zum Schluss
end: in the ~ 72 schließlich, letztendlich
to **end up** 57t (schließlich) gelangen, landen, enden
enemy 102 Feind/in, Gegner/in
energetic 21 kraftvoll, energisch
energy 104 Energie
to **engage in sth** 46f sich an etw beteiligen
to **engage with sb** 103 mit jdm interagieren
engaging 99 fesselnd, spannend
engineer 68 Ingenieur/in, Techniker/in
to **enhance** 142 verbessern, stärken
enjoyable 20 angenehm, schön
enlargement 116 Erweiterung, Ausweitung, Ausdehnung
to **enquire (about)** 141f fragen, sich erkundigen (nach/wegen)
enquiry 97 Anfrage, Erkundigung
to **enrol (with)** 110 sich verpflichten (bei), sich anmelden (bei)
to **ensure** 133f sicherstellen
to **enter** 83 hineinkommen, betreten, einreisen
enterprise 82 Unternehmen
entertainment 46t Unterhaltung
enthusiastic 9t begeistert
entire(ly) 73 gesamte/r/s, ganz, vollständig
entitled 56t; 145 berechtigt; mit dem Titel
entrance 84t Eingang
entry 15 Eintrag, Beitrag
environment 12 Umfeld, Umgebung
environmental 104 Umwelt-
environmentalist 132 Umweltschützer/in
epidemic 141 Epidemie, epidemisch (seuchenartig)
epilepsy 82 Epilepsie
episode 39 Folge (einer Serie), Episode
equal 30 gleich(berechtigt), ebenbürtig
equal chances 30 Chancengleichheit
equality 78 Gleichberechtigung, Gleichheit
equal-opportunity law 83t Chancengleichheitsgesetz

274

A–Z word list

equation *95* Gleichung

to **equip** *142* ausrüsten, ausstatten

equipment *93* Ausstattung, Ausrüstung, Geräte

equipped with *142* ausgestattet mit

equitable *140* gerecht

equivalent *21* Äquivalent, Gegenstück

to **be equivalent to** *21* entsprechen

to **eradicate** *141t* ausrotten

to **escalate** *46f* eskalieren

especially *32* besonders, insbesondere

essential *140* (absolut) notwendig, wesentlich

to **establish** *10* etablieren, aufbauen

estate agent *116* Makler/in

to **estimate** *142* schätzen

ethical *132* ethisch, (moralisch) verantwortlich

ethnic *10* ethnisch, Volks-

ethnic cleansing *120* ethnische Säuberung(en)

ethnicity *107f* Ethnizität, Volkszugehörigkeit

eulogy *127* Grabrede, Laudatio

European *32* Europäer/in, europäisch

to **evacuate** *84t* evakuieren

to **evaluate** *70* einschätzen, bewerten, auswerten

evaluation *70* Auswertung, Bewertung

eve (of) *94* Vortag, Vorabend (von)

even though *68t* auch wenn, selbst wenn

eventualities: for all ~ *108* für alle Eventualitäten

eventually *131t* letztendlich, schließlich

ever since *81* seit, seitdem, seither

ever-(expanding) *141t* ständig (wachsend)

everyday *8* alltäglich, Alltags-

evidence *11* Nachweis(e), Beweis(e), Beweismaterial

to **evolve** *78* sich weiter entwickeln

to **examine** *58* untersuchen, prüfen

to **exceed** *141t* übersteigen, überschreiten

excerpt *70* Auszug, Ausschnitt

excess *90* überschüssig

to **exchange** *33* austauschen, eintauschen, umtauschen

exchange (programme) *121t* Austausch(programm)

excursion *103* Ausflug, Exkursion

exercise *13* Bewegung, (körperliches) Training

to **exhibit** *44* zeigen, ausstellen

exhibitor *140* Aussteller/in

to **exist** *32* existieren

existence *119f* Existenz

exit *84t* Ausgang, Ausfahrt

to **expand** *14* expandieren, (sich) erweitern, (sich) vergrößern

expectation *80* Erwartung

expected: to be ~ to … *142* … sollen/müssen, es wird erwartet, dass …

expenses *(pl)* *20* Kosten, Auslagen

experience *20* Erfahrung, Erlebnis

to **experience** *12* erleben, erfahren

experience: work ~ *11* Praktikum/Praktika, Berufserfahrung

experiential learning *103* Erlebnispädagogik

to **experiment** *57t* experimentieren

expert (in) *142* Experte/Expertin (für)

explanation *35f* Erläuterung, Erklärung

to **exploit** *104* benutzen, ausnutzen, ausbeuten

to **explore** *49* erforschen, erkunden

to **expose (sb to sth)** *37f* (jdn einer Sache) aussetzen

exposure *46t* Ausgesetztsein

to **express** *75* ausdrücken, zum Ausdruck bringen

extended *32* erweitert

extent: to what ~ …? *75* in welchem Maß(e) …?

extract *8* Auszug, Extrakt

extra-curricular *47* außerschulisch

eye-catching *21* auffallend, ins Auge springend

F

to **face sth** *32* vor etw stehen, mit etw konfrontiert werden

faced: to be ~ with sth *12* konfrontiert werden mit

facet *115* Facette, Aspekt

face-to-face *10* persönlich

to **facilitate sth** *106* etw vermitteln, vereinfachen

facilities *(pl)* *10* Einrichtungen, Gelegenheit

facility *55* Einrichtung

fact: in ~ *71t* tatsächlich, eigentlich

fact: as a matter of ~ *56t* tatsächlich

factory-farmed *92* aus Massentierhaltung

factual *21* Sach-, sachlich

to **fade away** *132* verschwinden, verhallen

to **fail** *46t* versagen, durchfallen

fall *49f* Sturz

to **fall** *94* sinken, sich (ab)senken

familiar (to sb/with sth) *31* (jdm/mit etw) vertraut

to **familiarize sb/yourself with** *68* sich/jdn vertraut machen mit

family support worker *18* Sozialpädagogische/r Helfer/in

famine *126* Hungersnot, Hunger

to **fantasize** *45* fantasieren

FAQs (frequently asked questions) *128* häufig gestellte Fragen

far *84t* weit entfernt

far: by ~ *46t* bei weitem

far: so ~ *45t* bis jetzt, bis hierher

farming *92* Landwirtschaft, Anbau

fashion *94* Mode

fault *35t* Defekt, Fehler, Mangel

to **favour** *83t* bevorzugen

fear *46f* Angst

to **fear** *46f* (be)fürchten

feature *35t* Merkmal, Eigenschaft, Kennzeichen

federal *114* Bundes-, auf Bundesebene geltend

federal republic *119f* Bundesrepublik

to **feed** *92* füttern, ernähren

feedback *49* Rückmeldung

to **feel about sth** *33f* denken über etw, etw empfinden

fellow *119f* Mit-, andere, befreundete

fellowship *10* Gesellschaft

female *18* Frau, weiblich

fever *108* Fieber

fictional *39* fiktiv, erfunden

figure *36; 56t* Figur; Zahl, Ziffer

to **fill sb in on sth** *60* jdn über etw informieren

to **find closure (with sth)** *73* abschließen (mit etw), (etw) hinter sich lassen

to **find out** *9* herausfinden, feststellen

findings *(pl)* *46f* Ergebnisse

to **finish up** *72* fertig machen, beenden

fire exit *84t* Notausgang

to **fire sb** *72* jdn (fristlos) entlassen, jdn feuern

firm *25p; 25f* Firma; fest, verbindlich

first *10* zuerst

first aid *22* Erste Hilfe

fishfood *132* Fischfutter

fit *32* fit

to **fit (with/to)** *42* passen (zu)

to **fit in (with)** *23* sich anpassen (an), sich einfügen (in)

fitted *108t* eingepasst

fix *infml* *45t* Schuss

fixed *119f* fest, fix

flatmate *49f* Mitbewohner/in

flavour *98* Geschmack(srichtung), Geschmacksstoff

flavouring *93t* Aroma(stoff)

flea market *117t* Flohmarkt

flexible *20* flexibel

275

A–Z WORD LIST

flexitime 73 Gleitzeit, flexible Arbeitszeit(en)
flight 107t Flug
floor plan 84 Grundriss, Lageplan
flour 93f Mehl
to **flour** 93f mit Mehl bestäuben
flow 119f Fluss, Strom
flow chart 25 Flussdiagramm
fluent(ly) 22 fließend (Sprache)
flyer 106 Flugzettel, Flyer
foam 108t Schaum
focus 44 Brennpunkt, Blickpunkt
to **focus on** 25f sich konzentrieren auf
foetus 36 Fetus
to **fold** 108t falten, zusammenlegen
folder 32 Mappe, Ordner
folk dance 118 Volkstanz
to **follow** 7 folgen
follow-up 38 Folge-
food for thought 93t ein Denkanstoß
foodstuff 93t Nahrungsmittel
for good 58 für immer
for heaven's sake 70f um Himmels willen
forbidden 60t verboten
to **force** 46t drängen, zwängen, zwingen
to **force sb to do sth** 70t jdn zwingen etw zu tun
foreign 114 Auslands-, ausländisch, fremd
foreigner 60t Ausländer/in
forest 109 Wald
forever 116 für immer, ewig
form 14; 83t Form, Art; Formular
formal 27 formell, förmlich
formaldehyde 132 Formaldehyd
formality 133 Förmlichkeit, Formalität
former 119f ehemalige/r/s
formula 95 Formel
to **formulate** 75 formulieren
fortunate 118 glücklich, günstig
forward: put sth ~ 63 etw vorbringen
to **found** 10 gründen
foundation 95f Stiftung
frail 94 zart, zerbrechlich, gebrechlich
to **freak sb out** 66 jdn aufregen, ausflippen lassen
free movement 115 Freizügigkeit
freelance 72 selbstständig, freiberuflich
freelancer 73 Freiberufler/in
free-range (eggs) 92 Eier von frei laufenden Hühnern
to **freeze** 92 (ge)frieren
to **freeze-dry** 132 gefriertrocknen
frequent(ly) 12 häufig, oft
friendship 128 Freundschaft

to **frighten** 93t erschrecken, Angst einjagen
frightened: to be ~ 46f Angst haben (vor)
frightening 93t beängstigend
from now: ... years ~ 24 in ... Jahren
front line 97f vorderste Front, vorderste Linie
front: at the ~ (of) 144 vorne (an/in), an der Vorderseite (von)
to **frown on sth** 132 etw missbilligen
frozen 92 (tief)gefroren, Tiefkühl-
frustration 46f Frustration
to **fuel** 94 anheizen, anfachen
fulfilling 86 erfüllend
full-blown 141t regelrecht, komplett, voll ausgebildet
full-time 9 Vollzeit
to **be fun** 57t Spaß machen
function 82 Funktion
to **function** 34 funktionieren
to **fund** 11 finanzieren
funding 104 Finanzausstattung, (finanzielle) Mittel, Finanzierung
funeral 118 Beerdigung, Begräbnis
futurologist 145 Futurologe/Futurologin

G

to **gain** 14 erwerben, gewinnen, sammeln
gallery 123 Galerie
gang 46 Gang, Bande
gap 37f Lücke
gap year 104 das Jahr zwischen Schulabgang und Studienbeginn
gapped 68f mit Lücken versehen
garlic 93f Knoblauch
to **gather** 15 sammeln, sich versammeln
gauze 108 Gaze, Mull
gay 38 schwul, homosexuell
GDR 119f DDR
gear 111 Ausrüstung
gender 82 Geschlecht
general practitioner 48 niedergelassene/r Allgemeinarzt/-ärztin, Hausarzt/-ärztin
genetic(ally) 37f genetisch
gentle 14 sanft
geographical 106 geographisch
geriatric 6 geriatrisch
geriatric care worker 6 Altenpfleger/in
gesture 68 Geste
to **get back (to)** 34 zurückkommen (zu), zurückkehren (zu)
to **get in touch with** 11f (sich) in Verbindung setzen mit

to **get in(to) shape** 96 fit werden, sich in Form bringen
to **get sb wrong** 131t jdn missverstehen
to **get started** 20 anfangen, loslegen
to **get sth right** 32 etw richtig machen
to **get better** 48t sich erholen, gesund werden
to **get down to work** 106 sich an die Arbeit machen
to **get dressed** 9t sich anziehen
to **get in the way** 13 (einem) im Wege stehen
to **get off** 48 aussteigen aus, loskommen von
to **get off the ground** 110 in Gang kommen
to **get on with sth** 35t; 69f mit etw klarkommen; etw erledigen, mit etw weitermachen, vorankommen
to **get to know** 49f kennenlernen
to **get your act together** 71t sich zusammenreißen
gift 11 Geschenk, Spende, Schenkung
to **give it a try** 97 es mal versuchen, ausprobieren
to **give birth** 36 gebären
to **give sb up for adoption** 36 jdn zur Adoption freigeben
giver 104 Geber/in
to **gleam** 93t glänzen, strahlen
global(ly) 79 global, weltweit
globe 145 Globus
to **glorify** 46t verherrlichen
glove 108 Handschuh
go: where ... should ~ 147 wo ... hin(gehören) soll/sollen
to **go along with sb/sth** 44 jdm zustimmen, mit etw einverstanden sein
to **go for a run** 13 laufen gehen
to **go freelance** 72 sich selbstständig machen, freiberuflich arbeiten
to **go off** 35t weggehen
to **go on** 35t passieren, geschehen, los sein
to **go over sth** 68t etw durchgehen, durchsehen
to **go through** 33f durchmachen, erleben
to **go viral** 46t viral (verbreitet) werden
goal 7 Ziel
god 36 Gott
good: for ~ 58 für immer
good: that ~ 68t so gut
good: to be ~ at 22 gut sein in, gut beherrschen
goods (pl) 85 Güter, Ware(n)

A–Z word list

government *10* Regierung, öffentliche Verwaltung

to **grab** *21* packen, greifen, *sich etw* schnappen

gradation *82* Abstufung, Einteilung

grade *AE 90* Klasse, Schuljahr

graduate *71t* Absolvent/in

to **graduate** *71* den Abschluss machen

graduation *81* Schulabschluss

grandad *92* Opa

grandfather *131* Großvater

grandmother *36* Großmutter

grandparent *32* Großvater/-mutter, *pl* Großeltern

grandson *130* Enkel

granny *30* Oma

grant *106* Zuschuss, Unterstützung, Stipendium

grant proposal *106* Zuschussantrag

to **grant** *23* gewähren, einräumen

granted *132* gestattet

graph *60* Diagramm, Graph

graphics *(pl) 147* Grafiken

to **grate** *93f* reiben, raspeln

grateful (to sb) *104* (jdm) dankbar

gravestone *133f* Grabstein

greatly *128* sehr, stark

greenhouse gas (GHG) *132* Treibhausgas(e)

to **greet** *25* (be)grüßen

greeting *56* Gruß(formel), Begrüßung

grief *48t* Kummer, Leid

to **grieve** *126* trauern

grips: to get to ~ with sth *infml 56t* etw in den Griff bekommen

ground *129t* Boden, Grund

to **grow up** *9t* erwachsen werden

growth *93t* Wachstum

to **guarantee** *69t* garantieren

to **guess** *97* (er)raten

guest worker *119f* Gastarbeiter/in

guidance *11* Anleitung, Hilfestellung

to **guide** *9t* führen, (an)leiten

guideline *67* Richtlinie

guilt *129t* Schuld

gun *46f* Schusswaffe

guy *46t* Typ, Kerl

gym *13* Sportstudio, Fitnessstudio, Turnhalle *(Schule)*

H

habit *33* (An-)Gewohnheit

habit: to be in the ~ of doing sth *139* daran gewöhnt sein etw zu tun, gewöhnlich etw tun

hairdresser *57t* Friseur/in

hairnet *85t* Haarnetz

halfway *34* auf halbem Wege, halb(wegs)

to **halve** *93f* halbieren, sich halbieren

to **hand sth around** *46t* etw herumreichen

to **hand down** *34* weitergeben, vererben

to **hand over** *62* übergeben, überantworten

handful *93f* Handvoll

handicap *140* Behinderung, Nachteil

handicapped *82* behindert, versehrt

to **handle** *27* umgehen mit, handhaben

handout *44* Arbeitsblatt, Thesenpapier

hand-picked *10* handverlesen, sorgsam ausgewählt

handshake *25* Händedruck

to **hang out** *57t* rumhängen

to **hang up** *68t* aufhängen

hangover *57t* Kater, Hangover

hang-up (about) *90* Komplex (wegen)

to **harass** *46f* schikanieren, belästigen

harassment *46* Schikane, Mobbing

hard-hitting *94* schonungslos

hardly *107t* kaum

to **harm** *56t* schaden, verletzen

harmful *120* schädlich

to **hate** *96* hassen, überhaupt nicht mögen

have: I'll ~ … *98* ich nehme … *(beim Essen, im Restaurant)*

head *71f* Leiter/in, Chef/in

head teacher *49f* Direktor/in, Schulleiter/in

to **head** *144* *(in Richtung von etw)* gehen, fahren

headache *70* Kopfschmerzen

heading *8* Überschrift

headline *6* Schlagzeile, Überschrift

headstone *133* Grabstein

health care *20* Gesundheitsfürsorge, medizinische Versorgung

health complications *126* gesundheitliche Probleme

health insurance *26* Krankenversicherung

Health Studies *(pl) 22* Gesundheitswesen, Gesundheitswissenschaften

heat *108t* Wärme, Hitze

height *90* Höhe, Größe *(bei Menschen)*

held: to be ~ up *45t* aufgehalten werden

hell *68t* Hölle

helmet *109* (Schutz-)Helm

helper *99* Helfer/in

helpline *35t* telefonische Beratung, Telefonnotdienst

hero *81* Held/in

hesitant *83t* zögerlich, zögernd

to **hide** *44* (sich) verbergen, (sich) verstecken

high in … *92* reich an …, mit hohem …-Gehalt

high school *USA 94* Gymnasium, Oberstufenschule

to **highlight** *69* hervorheben, markieren

highly *22* höchst, äußerst

to **hike** *110* wandern

hiking *106* Wandern

to **hire sb** *72* jdn engagieren, einstellen, beauftragen

history *104* Geschichte *(vergangene Zeiten)*

to **hit** *43* schlagen, aufprallen (auf)

to **hit out** *45t* drauflosschlagen

to **hit out (at sb)** *117t* (auf jdn) einschlagen

to **hold** *68* *(Veranstaltungen)* abhalten, *(Gespräche)* führen

to **hold on** *107f* warten, dranbleiben

holistic *145* holistisch, ganzheitlich

home *38* Heim

home birth *6* Hausgeburt

Home Economics *22* Hauswirtschaftslehre

homecare *138* häusliche Pflege

home-cooked *92* selbst gekocht, hausgemacht

homeland *32* Heimatland

homeless *54* wohnungslos, obdachlos

homelessness *55* Obdachlosigkeit

home-made *46t* selbstgemacht

homosexual *68t* homosexuell, Homosexuelle/r

honest *21* ehrlich

to **honour** *128* ehren, annehmen

horizon *14* Horizont

hormone *93t* Hormon

horrible *35t* schrecklich, furchtbar, fürchterlich

horse *109f* Pferd

hospice *128* Hospiz, Sterbeklinik

hostility *36* Feindseligkeit

hot *92* heiß, warm *(Mahlzeit)*

household *32* Haushalt, Haushalts-

housewife, *pl* **housewives** *32* Hausfrau

huge *60* gewaltig, riesig

human *78* menschlich, Mensch

Human Resources (HR) *68* Personalabteilung

human rights *120* Menschenrechte

humanity *78* Menschheit, Menschlichkeit

humble *128* demütig, bescheiden

humiliating *46t* erniedrigend

humiliation *46f* Demütigung

to **hurry** *26* sich beeilen, eilen

hurt *46t* verletzt

277

A–Z WORD LIST

hurtful *46f* verletzend
husband *32* Ehemann
hygiene *57f* Hygiene
hypertension *130* Bluthochdruck
hypothermia *108* Unterkühlung

I

i.e. *31* d.h.
idea: no ~ *35t* keine Ahnung
identification *141t* Identifizierung, Bestimmung
to identify *36* erkennen, feststellen, identifizieren
identity *78* Identität
to ignore *35f* ignorieren
illegal(ly) *57f* illegal, verboten, gesetzwidrig
illness *34* Krankheit
to illustrate *31* zeigen, veranschaulichen
illustration *42* Abbildung, Illustration
image *42* Bild, *(visuelle)* Vorstellung, Image
to imagine *11* sich vorstellen
immense *8* enorm, immens
immigrant *114* Einwanderer/-in
to immigrate *114* einwandern
immigration *117* Einwanderung
to immobilize *108t* ruhigstellen
impact *143* Aufprall, Stoß, Einschlag
impact (on) *10* (Aus-)Wirkung, Folge, Einfluss (auf)
impaired *82* beeinträchtigt
impairment *20* Beeinträchtigung
impediment *82* Behinderung, Hindernis
implication *144* Auswirkung, Konsequenz
importance *143* Bedeutung, Wichtigkeit
to impose sth on sb *119* jdm etw auferlegen
impression *24* Eindruck
improvement *56t* Verbesserung
in (good) time (for) *25f* rechtzeitig (für/zu), beizeiten
in two weeks' time *72* in zwei Wochen
inability *12* Unfähigkeit
inappropriate *68* ungeeignet, unpassend, unangemessen
incest *35t* Inzest
inch *142* Zoll, Inch (= 2,54 cm)
incidence *130* Inzidenz, Auftreten, Häufigkeit
incident *46f* Vorfall, Begebenheit, Sachverhalt
to include *11* einbeziehen, einschließen
inclusion *78* Aufnahme, Einbeziehung, Inklusion

inclusive *107f* einschließlich, inbegriffen
incomplete *45* unvollständig
incorrect *61* falsch, unrichtig
increase *6* Erhöhung, Zunahme
increase: to be on the ~ *46t* ansteigen
to increase (by) *60* steigern, erhöhen (um)
to increase in (popularity) *139* zunehmen an (Beliebtheit)
increasingly *132* zunehmend, in zunehmendem Maße
indeed *49* in der Tat, wirklich
independence *34* Unabhängigkeit
independent *10* unabhängig
to indicate *46f* (an)zeigen, darauf hindeuten, hinweisen auf
indigestion *70* Magenprobleme, Magenschmerzen
indirect *104* indirekt
individual *10* Einzelne/r, Individuum
individual(ly) *56t* einzeln, individuell
to induce *36* einleiten
industrial *93t* industriell, Industrie-
to industrialize *130* industrialisieren
industry *93t* Industrie, Branche
inexpensive *104* preisgünstig, preiswert
infected *108t* infiziert
infection *61* Infektion
infectious disease *126* Infektionskrankheit
inflammation *108t* Entzündung
inflammatory bowel disease *82* entzündliche Darmerkrankung (M. Crohn, Colitis ulcerosa)
inflatable *103* aufblasbar
influence *46t* Einfluss
to influence *33* beeinflussen
influenza, flu *141t* Grippe
infographic *90* Infografik
information (on) *(no pl) 8* Information(en) (über), Angaben (zu)
informative *107f* informativ
ingredient *92* Zutat, Inhaltsstoff
inherent *78* angeboren, innewohnend, eigen
initial(ly) *97f* erste(r, s), Anfangs-, anfänglich
initiative *85t* Initiative, Eigeninitiative
to injure *109* (sich) verletzen
injured *108t* verletzt
injury *44* Verletzung
inner *67* innere/r/s
inner city *6* Innenstadt
insect *108t* Insekt
insecurity *46f* Unsicherheit
insensitive(ly) *72* gefühllos, unsensibel
insight (into) *75* Einblick (in), Verständnis (von)

to insist *35t* darauf bestehen, beteuern
to inspire *10* inspirieren, anregen, anspornen
to install *142* einbauen, einrichten, aufbauen
instance: for ~ *142* zum Beispiel
instead *38* stattdessen
instead of *57f* anstatt, anstelle von
institution *35* Institution
instruction(s) *19* Anweisung(en)
instructional *107f* Lehr-, Schulungs-
instructor *97f* Lehrer/in, Ausbilder/in
to integrate *32* integrieren
intellectual *82* intellektuell, geistig
intelligence *70t* Intelligenz
to intend to do sth *72* beabsichtigen / vorhaben, etw zu tun
intense *129t* intensiv
intention *141* Absicht
to interact *12* interagieren, miteinander umgehen
interaction *9* Interaktion
interactive *144* interaktiv
intercourse *35t* Geschlechtsverkehr
intercultural *32* interkulturell
interdisciplinary *129* interdisziplinär, fachübergreifend
internship *14* Praktikum
interpersonal *51* zwischenmenschlich
to interpret *51* interpretieren
to interrupt *109* unterbrechen, ins Wort fallen
interval *97* (Zeit-)Abschnitt, Abstand, Intervall
interview *19* Vorstellungsgespräch
to interview *8* befragen
interviewee *24* Befragte/r (im Interview)
intimate *129t* intim, eng, persönlich
intimidation *67* Einschüchterung
intrigued *133* fasziniert
to invent *11* erfinden, sich ausdenken
to invest in *72* investieren in
to investigate *46f* untersuchen
investment *24* Investition
invisible *82* unsichtbar
invitation *84* Einladung
to involve *26* mit sich bringen, einbeziehen, beinhalten
involved in *10* beteiligt an, beschäftigt mit
involved with: to be ~ *71* in einer Beziehung stehen mit, zu tun haben mit
involvement *130* Engagement, Beteiligung, Einbindung
iodine *108* Jod(tinktur)
Ireland *119t* Irland

A–Z word list

ironically *132* ironischerweise, paradoxerweise

ischaemic *126* ischämisch (Durchblutungsmangel-)

isolated *10* isoliert

isolation *44* Isolierung

issue *37f* Frage, Aspekt, Problem, Streitpunkt

IT (Information Technology) *70* Informationstechnologie

item *12* Artikel, Gegenstand, Punkt

J

jail *61* Gefängnis

jail sentence *61* Gefängnisstrafe

jealous *45t* eifersüchtig

joke *68* Witz, Scherz

to **judge** *49* (be)urteilen, ermessen

judgement *107f* Urteil

juicy *127* saftig

to **jumble** *50* durcheinander bringen

to **jump in** *49* hineinspringen, eingreifen, sich einmischen

K

keen on sth / to do sth: to be ~ *23* an etw sehr interessiert sein, etw unbedingt wollen

to **keep a close eye on sth** *74* jdn/etw genau beobachten, auf jdn/etw scharf aufpassen

to **keep a log** *96* Buch führen

to **keep doing sth** *72* etw dauernd/immer wieder tun

to **keep sb on** *72* jdn weiterbeschäftigen

to **keep to** *70t* sich halten an, einhalten, bleiben bei

key *36* Schlüssel(-), wichtige/r/s

keyword *33* Schlüsselwort

to **kick** *45* treten, kicken

to **kill** *35f* töten, umbringen

kilogram *94* Kilo(gramm)

kilowatt-hour *132* Kilowattstunde

kin: next of ~ *109f* nächste/r Angehörige/r

kindergarten nurse *6* Kindergärtner/in

kindness *128* Güte, Freundlichkeit

kit *55* Ausrüstung, Bausatz, Kit

to **knead** *93f* kneten

knife, *pl* **knives** *46f* Messer

L

label *32* Kennzeichnung, Etikett

labour *119f* Arbeit, Arbeitskräfte

to **lack** *110* fehlen, (er)mangeln

lack (of) *35* Mangel (an), Fehlen (von)

ladies and gentlemen *84t* meine Damen und Herren

large-scale *119f* groß, groß angelegt

to **last** *92* halten, frisch bleiben (Nahrungsmittel)

last but not least *37f* nicht zuletzt

latecomer *56t* Nachzügler/in

lately *71t* in letzter Zeit

latest *97f* neueste/r/s

to **laugh (at)** *46t* lachen (über), (aus)lachen

laughter *128* Lachen

law *21* Gesetz

to **lay sb off** *72* jdn entlassen, jdm betriebsbedingt kündigen

lay-off *72* Entlassung

lazy *91* faul, träge, nachlässig

leader *47* Anführer/in, Leiter/in

leadership *107f* Führung

leaf, *pl* **leaves** *93f* Blatt

lean *96* schlank, hager, mager (Fleisch)

to **leap up** *61* hochschnellen

learner *116* Lerner/in

least *132* wenigste/r/s, am wenigsten

to **leave out** *21* weglassen, auslassen

to **leave sth behind** *114* etw hinter sich lassen

lecture *139* Vorlesung, Vortrag

lecturer *119* Dozent/in, Hochschullehrer/in

to **be left to** *35t* jdm überlassen bleiben

legal *36; 67* legal; Rechts-, juristisch

legalization *60* Legalisierung

to **legalize** *60t* legalisieren

leisure *20* Freizeit

length *111* Länge, Dauer

lenient *60t* milde, nachsichtig

lesson *80* Unterricht(sstunde), Lektion

letter of application *18* Bewerbungsschreiben

letter to the editor *97* Leserbrief

level *60* Ebene, Niveau, Höhe

lewd *68* unanständig, anzüglich

to **liaise (with)** *36* zusammenarbeiten (mit), Bindeglied sein

liberal *61* liberal

licensed *12* amtlich zugelassen

to **lie (to sb)** *34* (jdn an-)lügen

lifestyle *96* Lebensweise, Lebensführung, Lebensstil

lifetime: for a ~ *102* lebenslang

to **lift** *93f* heben, hochheben

light(ly) *93f* leicht, hell

like this *35t* so, auf diese Art/Weise

like: things ~ that *68t* solche Dinge

likely *24; 145* geeignet; wahrscheinlich

likely: to be ~ to do sth *32* etw wahrscheinlich tun werden

limb *82* Extremität, Glied(maße)

to **limit** *82* beschränken, einschränken, begrenzen

limitation *142* Grenze, Einschränkung

limited *44* begrenzt

line *72* (Warte-)Schlange

link *19* Verbindung, Link

liquid *132* Flüssigkeit, flüssig

to **listen out for sth** *85f* (beim Zuhören) auf etw achten

listener *9t* Zuhörer/in

to **live rough** *58* auf der Straße leben

livestock *92* Vieh

local *9t* örtlich, lokal

local authority *9t* Kommunalbehörde, kommunal-

localized *141t* lokal, (örtlich) begrenzt

to **be located in ...** *11* in ... ansässig sein, seinen/ihren Sitz in ... haben

location *132* (Stand-)Ort

logical order *109f* logische Reihenfolge

logistics *(pl)* *111* Logistik

long hours *(pl)* *9* Überstunden

long-lasting *83* langlebig, lang anhaltend, dauerhaft

long: a ~ time *45t* lange

long: as ~ as *83t* solange

longer: not ... any ~ *38* nicht mehr

long-running survey *86* Langzeitstudie

long-standing *114* langjährig, schon lange bestehend

long-term *20* langfristig, Langzeit-

to **look forward to (doing sth)** *23* sich darauf freuen (etw zu tun)

to **look into** *32* prüfen, untersuchen

to **look up** *35* etw nachschlagen, etw heraussuchen

to **lose weight** *90* abnehmen (Körpergewicht reduzieren)

loss *73* Verlust

loud *43* laut

love handles *(pl)* *90* Hüftgold (Fettpölsterchen an der Taille)

to **lower** *70f* senken

lunchtime: (at) ~ *70f* (zur) Mittagszeit

lyric *132* Lyrik, Text

M

macular degeneration *130* Makuladegeneration

to **be made up of** *93t* bestehen aus

to **mail** *106* (zu)schicken, (zu)senden, mailen

279

A–Z WORD LIST

mainstream 79 konventionell, regulär
to **maintain** 10 aufrecht erhalten
major 44 groß, bedeutend
majority 32 größter Teil, Mehrheit
to **make a difference** 105f etw verändern
to **make for sth** 127 sorgen für etw, zu etw führen
to **make notes** 7 (sich) Notizen machen
to **make sb's life hell/difficult** 68t jdm das Leben zur Hölle/schwer machen
to **make sense** 119t sinnvoll sein
to **make sure** 21 sicherstellen
to **make things worse** 49f alles verschlimmern
to **make up one's mind** 58 sich entscheiden
to **make a complaint** 69t sich beschweren
to **make a decision** 9t eine Entscheidung treffen
to **make sb do sth** 24 jdn dazu bringen etw zu tun, jdn etw tun lassen
to **make sth up** 13; 105 etw erfinden, sich etw ausdenken; etw ausmachen, bilden
maker 145 Hersteller/in
male 6 Mann, männlich
malnutrition 91 Unterernährung, falsche Ernährung
to **manage** 8; 130t leiten, verwalten; es schaffen
manager 35f Leiter/in, Manager/in
manipulative 34 manipulativ
manner 68 Art (und Weise)
manual 117 Handbuch
to **manufacture** 55 herstellen, produzieren
manufacturer 59 Hersteller/in, Produzent/in
to **map** 147 aufzeigen, erfassen
marginalize 35 an den Rand drängen, marginalisieren
marijuana 60t Marihuana
mark BE 47 Zensur, (Schul-)Note
marked 132 gekennzeichnet, markiert
marriage 32 Hochzeit, Ehe
to **marry** 32 heiraten
masculine 46t maskulin, männlich
mass 95 Masse(n-)
to **master sth** 49 etw meistern, bewältigen
to **match** 6 zuordnen
mate infml 57t Freund, Kumpel
material 7 Material, Stoff, Angaben
maternity leave 31 Mutterschaftsurlaub
mathematical 95 mathematisch

matter 49 Angelegenheit, Sache
matter: as a ~ of fact 56t tatsächlich
mealtime 9t Essenszeit
meaningful 24 wichtig, bedeutend, bedeutungsvoll
mechanical 93f mechanisch, Maschinen-
mechatronics 57f Mechatronik
media centre 59 Medienzentrum
to **mediate** 63 vermitteln, (sprachlich) inhaltlich wiedergeben
mediation 24 Vermittlung, Sprachmittlung
mediator 67 Vermittler/in
medical 36 Medizin-, medizinisch, ärztlich
to **medicate** 93t mit Medikamenten behandeln
medication 58 Arzneimittel
medicine, med 131 Medizin, Medikament
to **meditate** 13 meditieren
medium, pl **media** 32 Medium, Medien
to **meet requirements** 83t Anforderungen erfüllen
to **meet with sb** 71 sich mit jdm treffen
memory 126 Gedächtnis, Erinnerung
mental 37f geistig, psychisch, seelisch
mental abuse 34 psychische Gewalt, seelische Misshandlung
to **mention** 11 erwähnen, nennen, anführen
menu 15 Menü, Speisekarte
mercury 132 Quecksilber
mess: to be in a ~ infml 131t in der Tinte sitzen, in der Patsche sein
messed-up 46t verkorkst
microwave (oven) 92 Mikrowellenherd
mid-30s: to be in one's ~ 37f Mitte dreißig sein
midwife, pl **midwives** 6 Hebamme
migraine 47 Migräne, pl Migräneanfälle
migrant 32 Migrant/in, Zuwanderer/Zuwanderin
migrant background 114 Migrationshintergrund
to **migrate** 115 (aus-/ein-)wandern
migration 114 Migration, Zu-/Aus-/Abwanderung
millennium, pl **millennia** 33 Jahrtausend
mind 45t Geist, Verstand, Gedanken, Denkweise
mine 108 Bergwerk, Mine
minority 10 Minderheit
miracle 119f Wunder

miscarriage 36 Fehlgeburt
to **be missing (from)** 21 fehlen (bei/in)
mission 10 Auftrag, Mission
to **be mistaken (about)** 73 sich irren, sich täuschen (in)
to **misunderstand** 45t missverstehen, falsch verstehen
mixed-race BE 33f gemischtrassig
mixture 93f Mischung, Gemisch
to **moan** 127 stöhnen, jammern, klagen
mobile phone 109f Mobiltelefon, Handy
mobility 14 Beweglichkeit, Mobilität
to **model** 94 als Fotomodell arbeiten
modelling agency 94 Fotoagentur
moderate 83t moderat, mäßig
modern 33 modern
modest 132 bescheiden
to **monitor** 140 überwachen, verfolgen
monkey 145 Affe
moon 127 Mond
more: there's ~ to it than ... 25f es geht um mehr als ... / es steckt mehr dahinter als ...
moreover 58 außerdem, zudem
mortality 127 Sterblichkeit
mosquito 103 Stechmücke
mother tongue 118 Muttersprache
motion 142 Bewegung
to **motivate** 8 motivieren
motive 81 Motiv, Beweggrund
motor 82 motorisch
motor mechanic 62 Kraftfahrzeugmechaniker/in
motor neuron disease (MND) 82 Amyotrophe Lateralsklerose (ALS)
motorway 56t Autobahn
mourner 118 Trauernde/r
mourning 127 Trauern, Trauerarbeit
mouth 25f Mund
mouthful (infml) 93t langes Wort, Zungenbrecher
to **move in (with sb)** 36 (bei jdm) einziehen
to **move out** 50 ausziehen
movement 115 Bewegung
muffled 127 gedämpft, umhüllt
multicultural 10 multikulturell
multilingual 118 mehrsprachig
multinational 72 multinational, multinationaler Konzern
multiple sclerosis 82 Multiple Sklerose (MS)
muscle 70 Muskel
music 46t Musik
musical 118 Musik-
mutual 104 gegenseitig
mystery 46t Rätsel, Geheimnis

A–Z word list

N

naked *46f* nackt
nanny *39* Kindermädchen
nasty *13* gemein, fies, scheußlich
nation *119f* Staat, Nation
national *81* national, staatlich
nationality *120* Nationalität
nationwide *30* landesweit
native *32* einheimisch
native speaker *22* Muttersprachler/in
natural *51* natürlich, echt
naturally-minded *132* naturbewusst, natürlich gesinnt
navigating *108* Navigieren
navy *132* Marine, Schifffahrt
to **near** *36* sich nähern
near: not anywhere / nowhere ~ *141t* bei weitem nicht, nicht annähernd
nearby *26* nahe gelegen, in der Nähe
neck *70* Hals, Halsausschnitt
need: to be in ~ of sth *138* etw brauchen, benötigen, nötig haben
needle *108* Nadel, Kanüle
to **neglect** *34* vernachlässigen
neighbourhood *36* (Wohn-)Gegend, Nachbarschaft
net *85t* Netz
network *10* Netz(werk)
neuron *82* Neuron, Nervenzelle
neutral *49* neutral
never once *94* nicht ein (einziges) Mal
nice and (quiet) *70f* schön (leise)
night-time *108* nächtlich, Nacht-
nitrogen *132* Stickstoff
no idea *35t* keine Ahnung
no matter *9t* gleichgültig, egal
No sweat! *24* Kein Problem!
not ... any longer *38* nicht mehr
to **nod** *49* nicken
non-governmental organization (NGO) *104* Nichtregierungsorganisation
non-judgemental *49* nicht wertend, vorurteilsfrei
non-profit *10* gemeinnützig, nicht auf Gewinn ausgerichtet
non-verbal *49* nonverbal
noon *127* Mittag
nor *116* auch nicht, ebensowenig, noch
not for me *13* nicht meine Sache
to **note down** *9* aufschreiben, notieren
notebook *15* Notizbuch, Notebook
notepad *24* Notizblock
now that *15* jetzt, wo
nowadays *33f* heutzutage
nuclear *32* Kern-

nugget *93* paniertes Klößchen, Stück, (Gold-)Klumpen
numb *130t* taub (*Gefühl*), gefühllos
numbness *130t* Taubheit, Benommenheit
nurse *6* Arzthelfer/in, (Kranken-)Pfleger/in
nursery *8* Kinderhort
nursery nurse *9* Kinderpfleger/in
nursing *13* Pflege, Krankenpflege
nursing assistant *13* Pflegehelfer/in
nursing home *30* Pflegeheim
to **nurture** *10* entwickeln, pflegen, fördern
nut *108t* Nuss
nutrition *92* Ernährung
nutritionist *14* Ernährungswissenschaftler/in, Ernährungsberater/in

O

oak *132* Eiche, Eichenholz
obesity *91* Fettleibigkeit
object *46t* Objekt, Gegenstand, Ziel(scheibe)
to **object (to sth)** *82* Einwände haben (gegen etw), etw ablehnen
objective *95* objektiv
observation *51* Beobachtung
obsession *90* Besessenheit, Wahn, Zwang
occasion *44* Anlass, Gelegenheit
occasion: social ~ *44* gesellschaftliches Ereignis
occupational therapist *8* Ergotherapeut/in, Beschäftigungstherapeut/in
to **occur** *35t* stattfinden, passieren, geschehen
to **occur to sb** *25f* jdm einfallen
occurrence *46f* Ereignis, Vorkommen
ocean *127* Ozean, Weltmeer
odd one out *14* Außenseiter/in, nicht dazugehörig
of mine/yours/... *11* von mir/dir/...
off *33* ausgeschaltet
off: to have time ~ *70t* nicht da sein, nicht auf/bei der Arbeit sein
offence *37f* Straftat, Vergehen
to **offend** *56t* straffällig werden
offensive *68* beleidigend, anstößig
officer: probation ~ *57f* Bewährungshelfer/in
offspring *145* Nachwuchs, Sprössling
ointment *108* Salbe
on average *132* im Durchschnitt
on offer *96* im Angebot
on time *71f* pünktlich
one: the ~ *32* der-/die-/dasjenige
one ... or another *56t* der/die/das eine oder andere ...

one by one *119t* Stück für Stück, eins nach dem anderen
one-off *46f* einmalig
one-to-one *57t* Einzel-
only ever *92* (immer) nur
open about sth: to be ~ *68t* offen umgehen mit
open day *84* Tag der offenen Tür
opening *83t* offene Stelle
openness *75* Offenheit, Aufgeschlossenheit
opinion: a matter of ~ *95* Ansichtssache
opposed to: as ~ *82* im Gegensatz zu, gegenüber
option *11* (Wahl-)Möglichkeit
optional *21* freiwillig, fakultativ, Wahl-
oral(ly) *22* mündlich
order: logical ~ *109f* logische Reihenfolge
organic *93t* Bio-, organisch
organization *7* Organisation
to **organize** *57t* organisieren
organizer *97* Organisator/in
...-orientated *21* ...orientiert
orientation *68* Orientierung
orienteering *108* Orientierungslauf
origin *82* Ursprung, Herkunft
original(ly) *9t* ursprünglich
to **originate** *82* entstehen, seinen Ursprung haben
orphan *104* Waise
osteoporosis *130* Osteoporose
out: way ~ *43* Ausweg, Ausgang
out of ... *47* aus ... (heraus/hinaus)
out the door *25f* zur Tür hinaus, durch die Tür (hinaus)
outbreak *141* Ausbruch (*Krankheit, Regenschauer*)
outcome *109* Ergebnis, Ausgang, Resultat
outdoor *103* Outdoor-, im Freien
outdoors *97* im Freien, (nach) draußen, die freie Natur
to **outline** *11* skizzieren, beschreiben, darstellen
to **outsource** *72* (Arbeit) auslagern, outsourcen
oven *93f* Ofen, Herd
over the last ... years *97f* im Lauf der letzten ... Jahre
over time *32* im Laufe der Zeit
over and over (again) *35t* immer wieder
overall *70f* allgemein, (ins)gesamt, Gesamt-
to **overcome** *56t* überwinden
overhead *127* droben, am Himmel
to **overlook** *44* übersehen
to **overtake** *60t* überholen
overtime: to do/work ~ *72* Überstunden machen

281

A–Z WORD LIST

overweight 49f übergewichtig
overwhelming 116 überwältigend
overworked 74 überarbeitet
own: of your ~ 27 (Ihr/dein) eigene/r/s
owner 145 Besitzer/in, Inhaber/in

P

pace 109 Tempo, Schritt, Geschwindigkeit
to **pack** 85t (ver)packen
to **pack sth up** 127 etw einpacken, etw zusammenpacken
to **package** 84t (ver)packen
package/pay: severance ~ 72 Abfindung
packaging 84t Verpackung
paediatric 8 pädiatrisch, Kinderheilkunde-
pain 70 Schmerz(en)
painful 35f schmerzhaft
painkiller 108t Schmerzmittel
painting 84t Bild, Gemälde
palliative 129t palliativ, lindernd
pandemic 141 Seuche, Pandemie, seuchenartig, pandemisch
panel 61 Gremium, Jury
panic: (in a) ~ 25 in Panik
paperwork 27 Formalitäten, Unterlagen
paraplegia 82 Querschnittslähmung
parent: to be a single ~ 9t alleinerziehend sein
parental 129t Eltern-, elterlich
parenting 46t Kindererziehung
participant 56t Teilnehmer/in
to **participate (in)** 105 teilnehmen (an), sich beteiligen (an)
participation 78 Teilnahme, Beteiligung
partly 25f teilweise, zum Teil
part-residential care 138 teilstationäre Pflege
part-time 9 Teilzeit-, Halbtags-
to **party** 21 auf Partys gehen, feiern
to **pass** 34; 57f vorübergehen, vorbeigehen; (Prüfung) bestehen
to **pass sth on** 37f etw weitergeben, weiterleiten
passive 35t passiv, untätig
paste 93f Paste, (Tomaten-)Mark
pastoral care 35 Seelsorge
patience 9t Geduld
patient 14; 49 Patient/in; geduldig
patriarchal 32 patriarchalisch
pattern 31 Muster, Schema
to **pay attention (to)** 48 aufpassen, achten (auf)
payment 20 Bezahlung, Zahlung
PDMS 93 Polydimethylsiloxan
peer 46f Gleichaltrige/r, Ebenbürtige/r

peer pressure 46t Gruppendruck, -zwang, Einfluss der Clique
to **peer-review** 75 die Arbeit von Mitschülern/Mitschülerinnen bewerten, prüfen
penicillin 109f Penizillin
per 130 pro, per
to **perceive** 69 wahrnehmen, erkennen
percentage 56 Anteil, Prozentsatz
perfectionism 83t Perfektionismus
to **perform** 37f ausführen, durchführen
to **perform sth** 51 etw aufführen
performance 70t Leistung
permission 21 Erlaubnis, Genehmigung
person: in ~ 107t persönlich
personal 9t persönlich
personality 13 Persönlichkeit
to **personalize** 145 persönlich/individuell gestalten
personnel 51 Personal, Personal-
perspective 56t Perspektive
to **persuade** 58 überreden, überzeugen
persuasion 58 Überzeugung, Überzeugungskunst
persuasive(ly) 111 überzeugend
pesticide 93t Schädlingsbekämpfungsmittel
petroleum 93t Erdöl
pharmaceuticals (pl) 93t Arzneimittel
phone: to answer the ~ 25 ans Telefon gehen
photograph 68t Foto(grafie)
to **photograph** 94 fotografieren
photographer 94 Fotograf/in
physical(ly) 20 körperlich, physisch
physiotherapist 8 Physiotherapeut/in, Krankengymnast/in
physique 94 Körperbau, Statur
piano 127 Klavier
to **pick on sb** 35t auf jdm herumhacken
to **pick up** 142 etw mitbringen, kaufen, sich etw holen
to **pick up sb** 57f jdn aufgreifen
pigeon-chested: to be ~ 94 eine Kielbrust/Hühnerbrust haben (med.)
to **pile up** 67 sich häufen, sich auftürmen, (sich) (auf)stapeln
to **pin sth up (on the wall)** 27 etw (an die Wand) heften, (an der Wand) befestigen
pine 132 Kiefer, Pinie, Kiefernholz
to **place** 94 stellen, legen, setzen (etw wohin) tun
place: in the first ~ 56t überhaupt (erst mal), am Anfang (schon), an erster Stelle

to **place sb with sb** 37f jdn bei jdm unterbringen
placed: to be well ~ (for sth / to do sth) 139 in einer guten Lage sein, gute Möglichkeiten haben (für etw / etw zu tun)
placement: (work) ~ 18 Praktikum
plant 84t Pflanze
planting 132 Bepflanzung
plate 92 Teller, Platte
platform 46t Plattform
to **play truant** 34 schwänzen, unentschuldigt fehlen
to **plunge** 60 fallen, stürzen
poem 127 Gedicht
point of view 9t Standpunkt, Ansicht
to **point sth out** 13 etw (auf)zeigen, auf etw hinweisen
to **poison** 56t vergiften
policeman, pl **policemen** 127 Polizist
policy 60t Politik, Vorgehensweise, Regelung
polio 141 Polio, Kinderlähmung
polite 27 höflich
political 115 politisch
politics 25f Politik
poll 31 Umfrage
pollen 109f Pollen, Blütenstaub
pollution 132 (Umwelt-)Verschmutzung
polythene (BE) 108t Polyäthylen
popularity 139 Beliebtheit, Popularität
population 79 Bevölkerung
position 21 Posten, Stellung, (Arbeits-)Stelle, Position
positive 6 positiv, sicher
possession 61 Besitz, Besitztum
possibility 78 Möglichkeit
to **post** 46f bekannt geben, posten (im Internet veröffentlichen)
post-war 132 Nachkriegs-
potato, pl **potatoes** 92 Kartoffel
potential 33; 105 potenziell, möglich, künftig; Potenzial, Möglichkeit(en)
to **pour** 93f (aus-, ein)gießen
to **pour away** 127 wegschütten
poverty 104 Armut
power 46f Macht, Kraft, Stärke
powerful 97f kräftig, stark, mächtig
practical 11 praktisch, praxisbezogen
pragmatic 9t pragmatisch
praise 86 Lob, Anerkennung
precise(ly) 36 genau, präzise
preconception 104 Vorurteil
to **predetermine** 142 vorher festlegen, im Voraus bestimmen
to **predict** 10 voraussagen, vorhersagen, prognostizieren

282

A–Z word list

prediction *141* Vorhersage, Voraussage, Prophezeiung
preferably *93t* vorzugsweise, am liebsten
preference *119f* Präferenz, Vorliebe
pregnancy *30* Schwangerschaft
pregnant *8* schwanger
to **preheat** *93f* vorheizen
prejudice *83* Vorurteil
prejudiced *83t* befangen, voreingenommen
premature *119f* vorzeitig
preparation *25f* Vorbereitung
to **prepare** *22* erstellen
to **be prepared to do sth** *79* bereit sein, etw zu tun
preschool *9t* Vorschul-, Kindergarten-
to **prescribe** *131f* verschreiben, verordnen
presence *86* Anwesenheit, Präsenz
to **present** *15; 81* vorstellen, präsentieren; überreichen, schenken
presentation *15* Vorstellung, Präsentation, Referat
presentation: to give a ~ *55* ein Referat halten
to **preserve** *78* bewahren, erhalten
pressure *22* Druck
to **pressurize sb (into sth, into doing sth)** *91* jdn (zu etw) drängen, jdn drängen (etw zu tun)
to **pretend** *68t* so tun, als ob
to **prevent** *47* (ver)hindern, vorbeugen
previous *15* vorherig
primary school *22* Grundschule
principal diagnosis *109f* Hauptdiagnose
principle *78* Prinzip, Grundsatz
to **print (out)** *27* (aus)drucken
printout *84* Ausdruck
priority *56t* Priorität
prison *61* Gefängnis
privacy: in ~ *58* diskret
privileged *104* privilegiert
probation *57f* Bewährung
probation officer *57f* Bewährungshelfer/in
problematic *46t* problematisch
to **proceed** *36* voranschreiten, weitergehen
process *24* Prozess, Vorgang
to **process** *92* (weiter)verarbeiten
processed food *92* verarbeitete Lebensmittel
to **produce** *7* produzieren, herstellen, (an)fertigen
producer *83t* Produzent/in
product *93* Produkt, Erzeugnis
profession *6* Beruf

professional *71* beruflich, Berufs-, professionell, Profi-; Fachmann/-frau, in einem gehobenen Beruf Tätige/r
profile *21* Profil, Porträt
programming *71t* Programmierung, Programmier-
progress *15* Fortschritt
project *14* Projekt
promiscuity *34* Promiskuität *(häufiger Partnerwechsel)*
to **promote** *86* fördern, unterstützen, bewerben
to **promote sb** *66* jdn befördern
to **promote sth** *94* fördern, unterstützen, Werbung machen für etw
promotion *71* Beförderung, Aufstieg
prompt *63* Stichwort, Vorgabe
to **pronounce** *129f* aussprechen
proof *34* Beweis
to **proofread** *27* Korrektur lesen
property *57f* Eigentum
proposal *79* Vorschlag, Antrag
to **propose** *74* vorschlagen, unterbreiten, darlegen
pros and cons *(pl) 13* Für und Wider, Pro und Contra
prospect *25f* Aussicht
prospective *36* potentiell, prospektiv
prosthetics *140* Prothetik, Prothesen
prostitute *57f* Prostituierte/r
protection *21* Schutz
protein *92* Protein, Eiweiß
proud *43* stolz
to **prove** *47* nachweisen, beweisen
proverb *102* Sprichwort
to **provide** *8* (zur Verfügung) stellen, bereitstellen
provider *30* Anbieter *(Firma)*
to **provoke** *45* provozieren, auslösen, hervorrufen
psoriasis *94* Schuppenflechte *(med., Hauterkrankung)*
psychiatric *9t* psychiatrisch
psychiatry *9* Psychiatrie
psychological *44* psychologisch
psychologist *46* Psychologe/Psychologin
public *44; 127* Öffentlichkeit; öffentlich, allgemein
public: in ~ *44* öffentlich, in der Öffentlichkeit
to **publish** *75* veröffentlichen
pulse *6* Puls, Rhythmus
to **punch** *45* (mit Fäusten) schlagen, boxen
punctuation *131* Interpunktion, Zeichensetzung
to **punish** *46f* bestrafen
punishable *61* strafbar
purple *126* lila, violett

purpose *45* Zweck, Ziel
purposeful(ly) *103* zielgerichtet, zielstrebig
to **push** *35f* schieben, stoßen, drücken
push-up *97* Liegestütz
to **put sb in touch with** *57t* für jdn den Kontakt herstellen mit
to **put sth across (to sb)** *97* (jdm) etw vermitteln
to **put sth into action** *79* etw in die Tat umsetzen
to **put on weight** *94* zunehmen *(Körpergewicht erhöhen)*
to **put sth forward** *63* (Argumente) vorbringen, zur Diskussion stellen
to **put sth out** *127* etw löschen
to **put together** *58* zusammenstellen
to **put sb up for adoption** *36* jdn zur Adoption freigeben

Q

quadriplegia *82* Tetraplegie *(Lähmung aller vier Gliedmaßen)*
qualification *15* Abschluss, Qualifikation
qualified *10* qualifiziert, ausgebildet
to **qualify** *26* einen/seinen/ihren Abschluss machen
questionable *145* fraglich, fragwürdig
questionnaire *13* Fragebogen
to **quit** *71t* kündigen
to **quit sth** *37f* etw aufgeben
quotation *104* Zitat
quote *73* Zitat
to **quote** *130t* zitieren, nennen, angeben

R

racial *66* Rassen-, rassisch
racism *33f* Rassismus
rails: to go right off the ~ *infml 57t* auf die schiefe Bahn gelangen, aus dem Gleis geraten
to **raise** *81* erhöhen, (an)heben, steigern
range *82* Umfang, Auswahl, Kollektion
to **range (from … to …)** *8* sich erstrecken, reichen (von … bis …)
to **rank (by)** *145* einstufen, anordnen (nach)
to **rape** *48* vergewaltigen
rapid(ly) *82* schnell, rasch
rare(ly) *44* selten
rash *108* (Haut-)Ausschlag
rate *33f* Rate, Quote
to **reach a high/low** *60* einen Höhepunkt/Tiefpunkt erreichen

283

A–Z WORD LIST

to **reach out to sb** 54 die Hand nach jdm ausstrecken
to **react (to)** 44 reagieren (auf)
reaction 46f Reaktion
to **read out** 118 (laut) vorlesen
to **read sth back** 107t etw wiedergeben
reader 21 Leser/in
ready meal 92 Fertiggericht
realistic 36 realistisch, naturgetreu
to **realize** 9t (be)merken, sich klar werden
reason 36 Motiv, Grund, Beweggrund
to **reassure** 49 beruhigen
receiver 104 Empfänger/in
reception 84 Empfang, Rezeption
recipe 93 (Koch-)Rezept
recognition 71t (An-)Erkennung, (Wieder-)Erkennen
to **recognize** 35t anerkennen, (wieder)erkennen
to **recommend** 35 empfehlen
recommendation 37f Empfehlung
to **reconstruct** 9 rekonstruieren
record 67 Aufzeichnung, Nachweis
to **record** 49f aufnehmen, aufzeichnen
recording 48 Aufnahme, Aufzeichnung
to **recreate** 81 nachbilden
to **recruit sb** 10 jdn anwerben, jdn neu einstellen
recruitment 25 Anwerbung, Einstellung (von Personal)
to **reduce (by)** 61 reduzieren, verringern (um)
to **re-establish** 56t wiederherstellen
to **refer sb to sb/sth** 37f jdn zu jdm überweisen, jdn an etw verweisen
to **refer to** 23 sich beziehen auf
referee 22 Referenzgeber/in
reference 21 Referenz
referral 48 Empfehlung, Überweisung
to **reflect on sth** 12 etw reflektieren
reflection 129 Betrachtung, Reflexion, Nachdenken, Überlegung
reforestation 104 (Wieder-)Aufforstung
to **reformulate** 134 umformulieren
refreshment 97 Erfrischung
refugee 55 Flüchtling
refusal 35f Ablehnung, Verweigerung
to **refuse** 61 ablehnen
regarding 107f bezüglich, betreffend
region 62 Region
to **register sb as sth** 10 jdn als etw registrieren
regulations (pl) 133 Vorschriften, Bestimmungen

rehab 58 Reha, Drogenentzug
rehabilitation 58 Rehabilitation
reinforced 104 verstärkt
to **relate (to/with)** 25f (sich) verbinden, im Zusammenhang bringen (mit)
to **relate to** 70 sich beziehen auf, im Zusammenhang stehen mit
related to 51 verbunden mit
relationship 10 Beziehung, Verhältnis
relationship support 10 Partnerschaftshilfe
relative 33f Verwandte/r
relatively 46f relativ, verhältnismäßig
relaxation 13 Erholung
relevance 127 Relevanz
reliable 20 zuverlässig, verlässlich
reliant on 140 angewiesen auf, abhängig von
relief 104 Erleichterung, Entlastung, Linderung
to **relieve** 108 erleichtern, (Druck) verringern, lindern
religion 82 Religion(szugehörigkeit)
religious 37f religiös
to **remain** 49 (ver)bleiben
remains (pl) 132 Überreste, Überbleibsel, Rückstände
remark 68 Bemerkung
to **remark on sth** 133 eine Bemerkung zu etw machen, etw zu etw anmerken
remedy (for/to) 145 (Heil-)Mittel, Abhilfe (gegen),
remembrance 127 Erinnerung, Andenken
to **remind (sb of sth)** 13 (jdn an etw) erinnern
remote(ly) 142 fern, Fern-, abgelegen
to **remove** 45t entfernen, beseitigen
to **repeat** 25 wiederholen
repetition 83t Wiederholung
to **replace (with/by)** 31 ersetzen (durch), austauschen (gegen)
to **report to sb** 57f sich bei jdm melden
to **represent** 60 vertreten, repräsentieren
representation 97 Darstellung
reproductive 30 Fortpflanzungs-, Reproduktions-
request 21 Anfrage, Wunsch, Bitte
to **require** 82 benötigen, erfordern, verlangen
requirement 78 Anforderung, Bedarf, Wunsch
requirements: to meet ~ 83t Anforderungen erfüllen
to **re-read** 11f nochmals lesen
rescue 26 Rettung(s-)

research (into/on) 95 Forschung, Untersuchungen (über/zu), Recherche(n)
to **research (into/on)** 141t (er)forschen, recherchieren
researcher 141t Forscher/in, Wissenschaftler/in
residence 9 Residenz, Anwesen
resident 14 Bewohner/in, Einwohner/in
residential 30 Wohn-, Wohnungs-
residential care home 138 Pflegeheim
residential care: in ~ 30 in Heimen
resignation 67 Resignation
resin 132 Harz
resistant (to) 141t resistent, widerstandsfähig (gegen)
to **resolve** 51 lösen, auflösen
resounding success 61 durchschlagender Erfolg
resource 67 (Hilfs-)Mittel, Ressource
resources (pl) 141t Ressourcen, Rohstoffe
respect 9t Respekt, Achtung
to **respect** 11 respektieren
respectable 33f angesehen, ehrbar, anständig
respiratory 94 Atmungs-, Atem-, die Atemwege betreffend (med.)
to **respond to** 10 antworten auf, reagieren auf
response 13f Reaktion, Antwort
responsibility 11; 70 Aufgabenbereich, Zuständigkeit; Verantwortung
responsible 12 verantwortungsvoll
responsible (for) 11 verantwortlich, zuständig (für)
responsiveness 82 Ansprechbarkeit, Entgegenkommen
rest 127 Ruhe
rest time 9t Ruhezeit
to **rest** 131f sich ausruhen
to **restrict** 44 beschränken, einschränken
to **restructure** 72 umstrukturieren
restructuring 67 Umstrukturierung
to **result (from)** 82 entstehen (aus)
to **retain** 58 behalten
to **retrain** 72 umschulen, sich umschulen lassen
to **retrofit** 142 nachträglich einbauen/umbauen/umrüsten
reunification 119f Wiedervereinigung
to **reunite** 56t wiedervereinigen
to **reveal sth** 85f etw zeigen, verraten
revenge: to take ~ (on) 117 Rache nehmen (an)
reverse 21 umgekehrt, entgegengesetzt

284

A–Z word list

to **reverse** *141* umkehren, rück-
gängig machen
to **review** *59* bewerten, prüfen
rewarding *20* lohnend, erfüllend
to **rewrite** *39* umschreiben, neu
schreiben
rice *92* Reis
to **ride** *109f* reiten, fahren (mit)
to **ridicule sb** *46t* jdn lächerlich
machen
right now *109f* zur Zeit,
im Augenblick
Right. *9t* Gut. OK.
rigid *108t* starr, hart, unnachgiebig
to **rip out** *129t* herausreißen
to **rise** *38; 93f* (an)steigen; gehen
(Hefeteig)
rise: to be on the ~ *142* zunehmen,
wachsen
rise (in) *6* Erhöhung, Anstieg
rival *72* konkurrierend, Konkurrenz,
Rivale/Rivalin
robbery *35f* Raub, Überfall
robot *139* Roboter
rock climbing *108* Klettern
role model *94* Vorbild
to **roll sth out** *93f* etw ausrollen
to **roll sth up** *108t* etw aufrollen
rolling pin *93f* Teigrolle, Nudelholz
Roman Catholic *36* römisch-
katholisch
root *104* Wurzel
root cause *104* Grundursache
rope *111* Seil, Tau
roughly *130* ungefähr, etwa
round *93f* Kreis, Runde
route *55* Route, Strecke, Weg
routine *82* Tagesablauf, Routine
to **rub sth in** *93f* etw (hin)einkneten
(Zutaten in Teig)
rude *35f* unhöflich, unverschämt
rumour *74* Gerücht
to **run** *84* betreiben
rush hour *45t* Hauptverkehrszeit

S

sadness *127* Traurigkeit
safety pin *108* Sicherheitsnadel
sale: for ~ *96* zu verkaufen
salon *57t* Salon
Same here. *18* Ich auch. / Mir geht's
genauso.
same-sex *30* gleichgeschlechtlich
satisfaction *97f* Zufriedenheit,
Befriedigung
to **satisfy** *70* zufriedenstellen,
befriedigen
satnav *56t* Navi(gationsgerät)
to **save** *61* (ein)sparen
say (in) *70* Mitspracherecht (in/bei)
to **say sth out loud** *51* etw laut
(aus-, vor)sprechen

scale *60* Skala
to **scan** *12* überfliegen, absuchen,
scannen
scannable *133f* abtastbar, mit einem
Scanner ablesbar
scar *44* Narbe
scared *35f* verstört, ängstlich
to **be scared that** *35f* fürchten, dass
scary *24* beängstigend, gruselig
to **scatter** *93f* verteilen, verstreuen
scene *31* Szene
schedule *59* Terminplan, Zeitplan
scheme *79* Plan, Programm
scholarship *81* Stipendium, Freiplatz
school-aged (children) *72* (Kinder)
im Schulalter
schooling *79* Schulbildung
scientist *142* (Natur-)Wissen-
schaftler/in
scissors *(pl)* *108* Schere
score *70f* Ergebnis, Punktestand
to **scrape** *93t* (ab)kratzen, schaben
scratch *47* Kratzer
to **scratch** *47* (zer)kratzen, sich
kratzen
scratch: from ~ *93* ganz von vorne,
von Grund auf
screen *144* Bildschirm, Leinwand
to **scribble** *127* kritzeln, hinkritzeln
script *51* Drehbuch
scripted reality show *31* Scripted
Reality, Doku-Soap *(Fernsehformat:
Pseudo-Dokumentation mit Laien-
darstellern)*
to **search** *95* durchsuchen, suchen
search (for) *21* Suche (nach)
seaside *108* (Meeres-)Küste, Strand
seating area *84t* Wartebereich
secondary school *22* weiter-
führende Schule, Realschule
secret: in ~ *38* im Geheimen
section *8* Abschnitt
sector *8* Sektor, Bereich
security *51* Sicherheit
security personnel *51* Sicherheitspersonal
to **seek** *22* suchen (nach),
anstreben
see-through *84t* durchsichtig,
transparent
to **select** *115* auswählen
self-care *12* Selbst(für)sorge,
Selbstbehandlung
self-confidence *85t* Selbstsicher-
heit, Selbstvertrauen
self-conscious *117t* unsicher
self-esteem *44* Selbstachtung,
Selbstwertgefühl
self-harm *56t* Selbstverletzung
self-help *48t* Selbsthilfe
self-reliant *140* selbstständig
semi- *39* halb
seminar *44* Seminar, Fachtagung

senior *32; 108* leitend; Rentner/in
sense of purpose *85t* Zielstrebigkeit
sensible *122* vernünftig, sinnvoll
sensitive (to) *9t* einfühlsam
sensitivity *35t* Sensibilität, Einfühlungsvermögen
sentence: jail ~ *61* Gefängnisstrafe
separate *75* getrennt
to **separate** *12* (sich) trennen
separation *32* Trennung
sequence *18* *(richtige)* Reihenfolge,
Abfolge
series, *pl* **series** *34* Reihe, Serie
to **serve** *14* servieren
service *8* Dienstleistung
session *43* Sitzung
session: (training) ~ *97* (Trainings-)
Stunde, Einheit
set *37* Gruppe, Satz, Reihe
to **set** *45* setzen, stellen, legen
to **set up** *10* aufbauen, durchführen
to **set up (a meeting/a session)** *71t*
(ein Treffen/eine Sitzung) planen,
arrangieren, vereinbaren
to **settle down** *25f* zur Ruhe kommen, es sich bequem machen
set-up *32* Aufbau, System
severance package/pay *72*
Abfindung
severe(ly) *82* schwer(wiegend),
stark, schlimm
sex *18* Geschlecht
sexual *30* sexuell
sexual harassment *46* sexuelle
Belästigung
to **shake hands** *25f* sich die Hand
geben, die Hände schütteln
shall *30* sollen
to **shape** *93f* formen
to **share** *32* teilen
shared flat *57f* Wohngemeinschaft
sharp *116* scharf, deutlich, steil
shelter *54* (Obdachlosen-)Asyl,
Schutzraum, Unterschlupf
sheltered *57t* geschützt, behütet
shift *85t* Schicht(-)
to **shift sth to sb** *45t* etw auf jdn
abwälzen
to **shine** *86* glänzen, leuchten
shock wave *94* Druckwelle,
Erschütterung
to **shock** *94* schockieren
shocking *54* schockierend
shoes: to put yourself in sb's ~
71t sich in jds Lage versetzen
to **shoot** *94* *(Film)* drehen, Aufnah-
men machen
shooting *46f* Schießerei
shopkeeper *62* Ladenbesitzer/in
shoplifting *62* Ladendiebstahl
shortage *119f* Mangel, Knappheit
to **shout at** *39* anschreien
shy *25f* schüchtern, scheu

285

A–Z WORD LIST

sibling *34* Bruder/Schwester, Geschwisterkind *pl* Geschwister
sick: to be off ~ *71t* krankgeschrieben sein
side *33f* Seite
sieve *93f* Sieb
to sign up *104* sich anmelden
signal *44* Signal, Warnzeichen
significant(ly) *79* deutlich, spürbar, erheblich
silence *49* Schweigen, Stille
to silence *127* zum Schweigen bringen, abdämpfen
silicone *93t* Silikon
similar (to) *37f* ähnlich, vergleichbar
similarity *57* Ähnlichkeit
to simulate *27* simulieren
single: to be a ~ parent *9t* alleinerziehend sein
sit down: to sit in (on) *63* anwesend sein (bei)
site *46t (kurz für)* Website
site: building ~ *57f* Baustelle
situation *11* Situation, Lage
six-year-olds *10* Sechsjährige
skeletal *94* Skelett--, skelettartig
sketch *99* Skizze, Entwurf
to sketch *147* skizzieren
to ski *109f* skilaufen
skill *14* Fertigkeit, Fähigkeit
skilled *10* qualifiziert, Fach-
to skim *10* überfliegen
skin *66* Haut, Schale
skinny *90* mager, dürr
sky *127* Himmel
sleek *96* geschmeidig, schlank
to sleep rough *57t* im Freien übernachten, auf der Straße leben
sleeping pill *35f* Schlaftablette
sleepover *80* Pyjamaparty, Party mit Übernachtung
slide *45* Folie, Dia
slight(ly) *60* geringfügig, leicht
slim *94* schlank
sluggish *96* träge, schwerfällig
smallpox *126* Pocken
smart *72* intelligent, geschickt
smoker *37f* Raucher/in
to smooth (sth over sth) *93f* glätten, (etw über etw) streichen, gleichmäßig verteilen
smooth(ly) *71f* glatt, reibungslos, problemlos
to snigger *46t* kichern
to snow *109* schneien
soap (opera) *34* Seifenoper, TV-Serie
to soar *60* steigen, emporschnellen
so-called *70t* sogenannt
sociable *14* gesellig, verbindlich
social *6* gesellschaftlich, sozial, Sozial-

social administrator *6* Sozialverwalter/in, Sozialmanager/in
social care *20* Sozialfürsorge, Sozialwesen
social education worker *9* Sozialpädagoge/-pädagogin
social occasion *44* gesellschaftliches Ereignis
Social Studies *(pl)* *22* Sozialkunde, Sozialwissenschaften
social support service *8* soziale Leistung
society *10* Gesellschaft
socio-economic *95* sozioökonomisch *(sozial und wirtschaftlich)*
sock *84t* Socke
soft *84t* weich
solar-powered *132* solarbetrieben
solid *132* fest, solide
solidarity *119f* Solidarität
solution (to a problem) *12* Lösung (eines Problems, für ein Problem)
to solve (a task / a problem) *12* (eine Aufgabe) bewältigen, (ein Problem) lösen
sometime *107t* irgendwann
somewhat *132* etwas
as soon as *70f* sobald
to soothe sth *111* etw lindern, mildern
sorrow *127* Kummer, Leid
to sort *8* sortieren, ordnen
to sort out *32* klären, lösen
sound *33* Ton
source *92* Quelle
space *21f* Platz, Raum, Fläche
speaker *9* Redner/in, Sprecher/in
specialist *80* Fach-, Spezial-, Spezialist
to specialize (in) *60* sich spezialisieren (auf), sich spezialisiert haben (auf)
specific(ally) *56t* bestimmt, speziell, spezifisch
to speculate *93* spekulieren
speech *51* Rede, Vortrag
speech bubble *66* Sprechblase
speech impediment *82* Sprachfehler, Sprachstörung
to spell *107f* buchstabieren, schreiben
splint *108* Schiene *(med)*
to split sth down the middle *32* etw in der Mitte aufteilen/spalten
to split up *131f* sich trennen
spokesperson, *(pl)* **spokespersons/ spokespeople** *61* Sprecher/in
sponsor *58* Geldgeber/in, Sponsor/in
spontaneous *36* spontan
spoon *93f* Löffel
spot *99* (Werbe-)Spot
to spot *44* entdecken

spotlight *96* Rampenlicht, Scheinwerfer(licht)
spouse *45t* Gatte/Gattin
sprain *108* Verstauchung, Distorsion
to spread *129t* verteilen, verbreiten, sich ausbreiten
to sprinkle *93f* (be)streuen, (be)träufeln
sprint *97* (Kurzstrecken-)Lauf, Spurt
square one: to be back to ~ *72* wieder von vorne anfangen müssen
squat *97* Kniebeuge
to stab sb *47* auf jdn einstechen, jdn niederstechen
to stabilize *108* stabilisieren
stable *10* stabil, konstant
staff *9t* Personal, Belegschaft
stage *45* Stadium, Phase
stainless steel *93t* Edelstahl, rostfreier Stahl
to stamp sth out *47* etw ausmerzen
stand *140* Stand
to stand by *35* tatenlos zusehen
to stand in line (for) *72* Schlange stehen, sich anstellen (für/nach)
to stand up for sb/sth *81* sich für jdn/etw einsetzen, für jdn/etw eintreten
standard *140* Standard, Norm(al)-
starchy *92* stärkehaltig
to stare (at) *68* (an)starren
to start with *117t* zunächst, anfangs
to start sb off (on sth) *27* jdn auf etw bringen, jdm einen Einstieg geben (für etw)
starvation *94* Hunger(tod)
state *33; 133* Zustand; Land, Staat, staatlich
to state *21* erklären, angeben
statement *9* Aussage
statistical *114* statistisch
statistics *(pl)* *82* Statistik(en), statistische Angabe(n)
stay *104* Aufenthalt
to stay on *72* noch (da) bleiben
steadily *61* stetig, kontinuierlich
to steal *34* stehlen
step *11f* Schritt
stepfamily *32* Stieffamilie
stepfather *36* Stiefvater
stepmum *92* Stiefmutter
stereotype *83t* Klischee (vorstellung)
stereotypical *82* stereotyp, klischeehaft
to stick in one's mind *83t* im Gedächtnis haften (bleiben)
to stick to *9t* bleiben bei, festhalten an
stigmatized *46f* stigmatisiert
stimulation *82* Stimulierung, Anreiz

A–Z word list

sting *108* Biene-, Wespen-)Stich, Brennen

stomach *70* Magen, Bauch

storage *84t* Aufbewahrung, Lagerung

store: in ~ *145* vorgesehen, geplant

storeroom *84t* Lagerraum

strategy *58* Strategie

strength *24* Stärke

stress *12* Stress, Belastung

stress-buster *12* Stressbekämpfer

stressed *13f* gestresst

stressful *12* stressig

strict *9t* streng, strikt

strip *108t* Streifen

stroke *126* Schlaganfall

to **structure** *9t* strukturieren

to **be stuck (in)** *97f* festsitzen (in), stecken bleiben, nicht weiter- kommen

studies *(pl)* *7* Studium

stuff *46t* Zeug, Sachen

style *97f* Stil

style: (boot-camp) ~ *97f* im Stil (eines Ausbildungslagers)

to **submit** *109* einreichen

substance *6* Substanz, Stoff

substance abuse *6* Drogen- missbrauch

success: resounding ~ *61* durch- schlagender Erfolg

such as *21* wie (zum Beispiel)

to **suffer from sth** *12* an etw leiden

sufferer *94* Opfer, Kranke/r, Leidende/r

to **suggest** *27; 37f* vorschlagen; hinweisen auf, hindeuten auf

suggestion *7* Vorschlag

suggestive *68* zweideutig, anzüglich

suicidal *44* suizidal, selbstmord- gefährdet

suicide *43* Selbstmord

to **suit sb/sth** *80* jdm passen, jdm stehen, zu etw passen, etw entsprechen

suitable *26* geeignet, passend

to **summarize** *13* zusammenfassen

summary *21* Zusammenfassung

sunglasses *(pl)* *44* Sonnenbrille

sunny *126* sonnig

superior *73* Vorgesetzte/r

to **supersede** *132* verdrängen, ersetzen, ablösen

to **supervise** *9t* beaufsichtigen

supervision *12* Überwachung, Betreuung, Supervision

supervisor *12* Betreuer/in, Vorgesetzte/r

supplement *96* Ergänzung

support *8* Unterstützung

to **support** *8* unterstützen

supportive *14* hilfreich, verständnisvoll

supposed(ly) *96* angeblich

to **surface** *37f* auftauchen, aufkommen

surge of energy *45t* Energiewelle, Energiestoß

surname *107t* Nachname, Familienname

surprise: to come as a/no ~ *74* es ist eine/keine Überraschung

to **surround** *135* umgeben

survey *12* Umfrage, Erhebung

to **survey** *46f* untersuchen, erfassen

survey: long-running ~ *86* Langzeitstudie

to **survive** *117t* überleben

survivor *73* Überlebende/r

to **suspect** *95* vermuten

suspicious *58* misstrauisch

sustainability *104* Nachhaltigkeit

sustainable *132* nachhaltig, umweltgerecht

to **swallow** *48* (ver)schlucken

swamp *108* Sumpf

to **swap** *27* (aus)tauschen

sweat *24* Schweiß

sweater *46t* Pullover

to **sweep up** *127* auffegen, auskehren

swine *141t* Schwein, Schweine-

to **switch on/off** *12* an-/abschalten

symbol (of) *83t* Symbol (für), Siegel (z.B. Güte-, Bio-)

sympathetic *131f* verständnisvoll, wohlwollend

sympathy *127* Sympathie, Mitgefühl

symptom *44* Symptom, Anzeichen

syrup *98* Sirup

T

taboo subject *118* Tabuthema

to **tackle a problem** *58* ein Problem angehen

tailbone *94* Steißbein

tailor-made (for) *145* maßge- schneidert, zugeschnitten (auf)

to **take a break** *70f* (eine) Pause machen

to **take a look at** *7* (sich) ansehen

to **take a message** *107* eine Nach- richt entgegennehmen

to **take a seat** *25f* Platz nehmen, sich (hin)setzen

to **take advantage of** *46f* (sich) zunutze machen, ausnutzen

to **take exercise** *98* sich Bewegung verschaffen

to **take into account** *37* berück- sichtigen

to **take it in turns** *56* sich abwech- seln

to **take notes (on)** *56* (sich) Notizen machen (zu)

to **take part (in)** *20* teilnehmen (an)

to **take seriously** *9t* ernst nehmen

to **take sth off** *85t* etw ausziehen

to **take (time)** *45t* (Zeit) brauchen

to **take a tour of sth** *143* etw be- sichtigen, einen Rundgang machen durch etw

to **take along** *111* mitnehmen

to **take it easy** *71* es ruhig angehen, sich schonen

to **take on** *69* annehmen, übernehmen

to **take place** *25f* stattfinden

to **take sides** *49* Partei ergreifen

to **take sth up** *56t* etw aufnehmen, mit etw (neu) anfangen

to **take turns** *27* sich abwechseln

talk *11* Vortrag, Rede

to **talk sb through sth** *45t* etw mit jdm durchsprechen

to **talk sth over** *10* über etw reden, etw besprechen

talkative *14* gesprächig

tape *108* Band, Klebeband

target group *11f* Zielgruppe

to **target** *99* zielen auf, ins Visier nehmen

taste *145* Geschmack, Kostprobe

TBHQ *93* tert-Butylhydrochinon

to **teach** *12* lehren

teacher's pet *46t* Lieblingsschüler/ in, Streber/in

tear *126* Träne

to **tear** *49f* (zer)reißen

to **tease** *117t* (auf)reizen, ärgern

teaspoonful *93f* Teelöffel

technical *107f* technisch

technique *13* Methode, Technik

technological *142* technologisch

technology *71* Technik, Technologie

teen *8* Teenager, Jugendliche/r

teenaged *35t* im Teenager-Alter

television (TV) *34* Fernsehen

telework(ing) *72* Telearbeit

teleworker *72* Telearbeiter/in

temperature *93f* Temperatur

template *19* Muster, Vorlage, Schablone

temporary *22* vorübergehend, zeitlich befristet

to **tend to** *36* dazu neigen

tendency *119t* Neigung

tense *70f* angespannt, verkrampft

tension *70* Verspannung(en), Spannung

term *35p; 36* Trimester; Begriff

terminally ill *128* unheilbar krank

to **terminate** *38* beenden

termination *36* Schwangerschafts- abbruch, Beendigung

287

A–Z WORD LIST

in terms of ... 56t was ... angeht
thematic(ally) 135 thematisch
theme 106 Thema
therapeutic 128 therapeutisch
therapist 8 Therapeut/in
therapy 57t Therapie
thereby 132 dabei, dadurch
thin 93f dünn
to **think of sth** 109f sich etw überlegen, ausdenken
thorny 132 dornig, heikel
thought 7 Gedanke
thoughtless 46t gedankenlos, unbedacht
threat (to) 139 Bedrohung, Gefahr (für)
to **threaten** 42 (be)drohen
thriving 10 florierend, blühend
throughout 55 überall (in), in ganz
throughout ... 21 das ganze ... (hindurch), überall in ...
to **throw** 43 werfen
to **throw sth up** 96 aufwerfen, zu Tage bringen
tie 23 (Ver-)Bindung, Beziehung
till 47 bis
time: at the same ~ 69t; 129t zur selben Zeit, um die gleiche Zeit; gleichzeitig, zugleich
time: in two weeks' ~ 72 in zwei Wochen
times: at ~ 129t zeitweise
tin 93f Dose, Büchse
tip 81 Trinkgeld
to the right/left 84t nach rechts/links, zur Rechten/Linken
tobogganing 108 Schlittenfahren
today's 119t heutig, von heute
togetherness 85t Zusammengehörigkeit
token 20 symbolisch
tolerance 33f Toleranz, Verständnis
tomato, pl **tomatoes** 93f Tomate
to **tone** 96 straffen
tool 73 Werkzeug, Instrument
tooth, pl **teeth** 94 Zahn
top of sth: on ~ 93f auf etw (oben) drauf
topic 46 Punkt, Thema
topping 93f Überzug, Belag (z. B. Pizza)
torture 120 Folter
total 95 Gesamtbetrag, Summe
total: in ~ 95 insgesamt
to **touch** 68 berühren, anfassen
tough 46t hart, grob, brutal
tour 84 Rundgang, Führung
tour company 105f Touristikunternehmen
tourism 60t Tourismus
tourist attraction 81 Touristenattraktion

tourist industry 104 Tourismus-Industrie
town hall 135 Rathaus
trace 93t Spur
to **track** 142 (zurück-, nach)verfolgen, beobachten
trade fair 140 Handelsmesse
tradition 9t Tradition, Brauch
traditional 30 traditionell
trafficking: (drug) ~ 61 (Drogen-)Handel
to **train** 6 trainieren, ausbilden, ausgebildet werden
trained 6 ausgebildet
trainer 44 Ausbilder/in
training 11 Ausbildung, Training
tranquilizer 70 Beruhigungsmittel
transcript 71f Niederschrift, Protokoll
to **transfer (sb/sth)** 71f (jdn) versetzen, (etw) verlegen
transformation 96 Umwandlung, (grundlegende) Veränderung
transient 130t vorübergehend
translation 68 Übersetzung
transnational 140 transnational, grenzübergreifend
trap 45 Falle
traumatic 36 traumatisch
traumatized 120 traumatisiert
to **travel** 58 reisen
traveller 104 Reisende/r
to **treat** 35t behandeln
treatment 61 Behandlung
treetop 108 Baumkrone
trek 108 Reise, Treck
trial 140 Probe, Test, Versuch
to **trigger** 95 auslösen
to **triple** 142 (sich) verdreifachen
trisomy 80 Trisomie
trouble: to be in ~ 49f Ärger haben, in Schwierigkeiten stecken
troubled 55 mit Problemen belastet
trust 58 Vertrauen
to **trust** 13 (ver)trauen
tube 108t Rohr, Röhrchen
tune 99 Song, Lied
to **turn** 93f (um)drehen, kippen, stürzen (Teig)
to **turn (into)** 46t werden (zu)
to **turn left/right** 84t links/rechts abbiegen
to **turn sth into sth** 34 etw zu etw machen
to **turn to** 11 sich wenden an, (Seite) aufschlagen
turnaround 61 Aufschwung, Kehrtwendung
tweezers (pl) 108 Pinzette
typhoon 103 Taifun (tropischer Wirbelsturm)
typical (of) 56 typisch (für)

U

unable 12 unfähig, nicht in der Lage
unacceptable 57f unannehmbar, inakzeptabel
unclear 70 unklar
uncomfortable 57f ungemütlich, unwohl
unconscious 134 bewusstlos, unbewusst
underdeveloped 104 unterentwickelt
underground 108 unterirdisch
understanding 35t Verständnis
to **undertake** 10 unternehmen, in Angriff nehmen
uneducated 44 ungebildet
unemployed 6 arbeitslos
unfair (to sb) 71f unfair, ungerecht (jdm gegenüber)
uninteresting 49 uninteressant
to **unjumble** 50 (das Wirrwarr) ordnen
unknown 81 unbekannt
unlike 21 anders als, im Gegensatz zu
unlikely: to be ~ to do sth 61 etw wohl kaum tun werden
to **unlock** 133f freischalten, entsperren
unmarked 132 nicht gekennzeichnet, anonym
unnatural 93 unnatürlich
unpleasant 35f unangenehm, unerfreulich, unfreundlich
unqualified 120 un-, nicht qualifiziert, ungelernt
unreasonable 119f unvernünftig, unangemessen
unreliable 83t unzuverlässig
to **unroll** 108t ausrollen
unsolicited application 141 Initiativbewerbung, Blindbewerbung
unspoken 43 unausgesprochen
unsuitable 46t ungeeignet, unpassend
unsure 128 unsicher
unthreatening 49 nicht bedrohlich
unto 103 auf, zu, nach (archaisch)
unvarnished 94 unlackiert, ungeschminkt (Wahrheit, Bild)
unwanted 30 unerwünscht
unwilling to do sth 58 nicht bereit, etw zu tun
up to date 141t aktuell, auf dem/den neuesten Stand
up to sb: to be ~ 70f jds Sache sein
upbringing 37f Erziehung
to **upload** 46t hochladen
upset 71t aufgeregt, mitgenommen, bestürzt
upstairs 43 (nach) oben, im oberen Stockwerk

288

A–Z word list

used: it ~ to be *32* es war früher (*üblicherweise*)
usefulness *45* Nützlichkeit, Eignung
user *46f* (Be-)Nutzer/in

V

vacancy *141f* freie/offene Stelle
vaccination *141t* (Schutz-)Impfung
vaccine *93t* Impfstoff
value *26* Wert
vandalism *37f* Vandalismus
to vandalize *57t* mutwillig beschädigen, zerstören
variety *84* Vielfalt
various *97f* (mehrere) verschiedene
vegetarian *98* vegetarisch, Vegetarier/in
veneered *132* furniert
Venn diagram *34* Venndiagramm, Mengendiagramm
verbal *46f* verbal
verbal abuse *36* Beschimpfung(en)
versus, vs. *132* gegen
viable *132* realisierbar, durchführbar
vice versa *27* umgekehrt
victim *34* Opfer
victimization *43* Schikanierung
to victimize *46f* schikanieren
view *37f* Sicht
to view sth/sb *58* sich etw/jdn anschauen, etw/jdn betrachten
viewer *46t* Zuschauer/in
violation *120* Verstoß, Verletzung (von Gesetzen, Rechten)
violence *43* Gewalt
violent *46t* gewalttätig
virus, *pl* viruses *141t* Virus
visible *82* sichtbar
vision *10* Vision, Blick, Sehkraft
vision impairment *82* Beeinträchtigung der Sehkraft
visual *147* visuell, optisch
visual impairment *82* Sehbehinderung
visuals *(pl) 63* Anschauungsmaterial
vital(ly) *49* (lebens)wichtig
vitamin supplement *96* Vitaminpräparat
vocational college *BE 21* Fachoberschule, Berufskolleg
vocational school *57f* Berufsschule, berufsbildende Schule
vodka *57t* Wodka
voicemail *121* Anrufbeantworter
voice-over *81* Begleitkommentar
voluntary *56t* freiwillig, spontan
volunteer *102* freiwillig, ehrenamtlich, Freiwillige/r, Volontär/in
volunteer organization *102* Freiwilligenorganisation

to volunteer *26* sich freiwillig melden, ehrenamtlich arbeiten
vulnerable *82* verletzlich, verwundbar

W

wage *57f* Lohn, Gehalt
to wait in line (for) *72* Schlange stehen, sich anstellen (für/nach)
to wander *108* (umher-)wandern
war *120* Krieg
warning (against) *57t* Warnung (vor), Verwarnung
to waste *93* vergeuden, verschwenden
waste (of time) *70t* (Zeit-)Verschwendung
watchdog *94* Überwachungsbeauftragte/r, Überwachungsgremium
watercourse *132* Gewässer
wave *119f* Welle
way out *43* Ausweg, Ausgang
way: (in) a ... ~ *13* auf (eine) ... Art/Weise
weakness *24* Schwäche
weapon *46* Waffe
wear *24* Bekleidung
to wear off *45t* nachlassen
wearer *139* Träger/in
weather *25f* Wetter
weekly *106* wöchentlich
to weigh *47* wiegen
welcoming *84t* einladend
welfare *35* Wohl(fahrt), Fürsorge
welfare department *35* Sozialamt
well *104* Quelle, Brunnen
well known *59* bekannt
well: to do ~ *72* gut laufen, erfolgreich sein
well-known *95f* sehr bekannt, berühmt
wellness *140* Gesundsein, Wohlbefinden
western *32* westlich, West-
wheelchair *82* Rollstuhl
wherever *32* wo (auch) immer
to whisper *126* flüstern
white-water rafting *106* Wildwasserrafting
widely used *82* weitverbreitet
wife, *pl* wives *32* (Ehe-)Frau, Gattin
wild *132* wild
wildlife *110* Tiere (*in freier Wildbahn*), Tierwelt
willing *9t* bereit, willens, gewillt
to be with sb *38* mit jdm zusammen sein
withdrawn *44* zurückgezogen
witness *69t* Zeuge/Zeugin
to witness *46f* Zeuge sein, (mit)erleben

women's refuge *35* Frauenhaus
wood *127* Wald, Holz
wooden *132* hölzern, Holz-
woodland *132* Waldgebiet
word cloud *126* Schlagwortwolke
work experience *11* Praktikum/Praktika, Berufserfahrung
work permit *119f* Arbeitserlaubnis
to work on sth *72* arbeiten an
to work out *96* trainieren
to work up *49* verarbeiten, ausarbeiten
worker *8* Arbeiter/in
workforce *141t* Beschäftigte, Erwerbstätige, Belegschaft
working age *86* erwerbsfähiges Alter
working class *116* Arbeiterklasse, Arbeiter-
working hours *(pl) 141t* Arbeitszeit(en)
workout *96* (Fitness-)Training, Work-out
workplace *11* Arbeitsplatz
workshop *84* Werkstatt, Workshop
worldwide *82* weltweit
worried: You had me ~ (there). (*infml*) *93t* Sie haben mir einen Schrecken eingejagt.
worrying *46f* besorgniserregend
worse *46f* schlimmer
worship *118* Anbetung, Verehrung
worthwhile *9t* lohnend
wound *94* Wunde
wrinkle *90* Falte
to write up *59* verfassen
writer *13* Schreiber/in
wrong: to be ~ *127* sich irren
wrong: to go ~ *108* schiefgehen
wrong: What's ~ with ...? *71* Was stimmt nicht mit ...? / Was ist das Problem mit ...?

X

xenophobia *119f* Fremdenfeindlichkeit, Ausländerhass

Y

yeast *93f* Hefe
yet: not ... ~ *18* noch nicht
Yours faithfully *26* Mit freundlichen Grüßen
Yours sincerely *23* Mit freundlichen Grüßen
youth *6* Jugend(-), Jugendliche/r
youth court *57t* Jugendgericht
Youth offender institution *57f* Jugendgefängnis
yuck *93t* Ekel-, igitt!

Exam Skills and Strategies – answer key

1 Schwierige Texte lesen

Beispiel-Aufgabe
a The problems that Vincent faces daily are that his clients are all very different from each other, not always easy to deal with, frustrated, in pain, angry, and sometimes ungrateful.
b To deal with these problems, Vincent reminds himself that he's helping these people, tries not to take their outbursts personally, uses humour to make his patients laugh.
c In his free time, Vincent does things he enjoys, for example reading, working out at the gym, and socialising at a pub with friends.
d The reading that he does in his free time helps him with his work.
e Vincent does his job well and feels happy about it.

a Dem Autor zufolge lassen Führungskräfte in England kaum Nachdenken über Gefühle zu.
b Der/Die Vorgesetzte (*Supervisor*) führt die Gespräche durch.
c In England trifft sich der/die Vorgesetzte ein Mal im Monat mit jedem Mitarbeiter und spricht über die Tätigkeiten. Sie sprechen nicht über Emotionen.
d Die schwedische Art der Personalführung hat dem Autor geholfen, Selbstbewusstsein zu entwickeln und seine Beziehungen auf der Arbeit zu verbessern.
e Seiner Meinung nach ist es wichtig, dass die Menschen in seinem Beruf ihre Gefühle reflektieren, da ihre Arbeit komplex und herausfordernd ist und Sozialarbeiter ohnedies oft besorgt sind, ob sie die richtige Entscheidung getroffen haben.

2 Mit unbekannten Wörtern umgehen

a 6; b 1; c 4; d 2 (~~en~~sure); e 5 und/oder 2; f 2; nicht angewendet: 3

a False: Unemployment levels rose from 10.9% to 12%.
b Not given: Unemployment rose in Europe, but we don't know if that is true specifically for the UK.
c True: Austerity policies have had a negative impact on economic growth and employment.
d True: Young people do not have the skills employers are looking for.
e Not given: Although this may be true, here is no information about this in the text.
f False: The scheme is open to all young people after they have finished school or college.
g False: The scheme is for people who have just left school or college.
h True: Germany, Switzerland and Austria have low levels of unemployment and high levels of apprenticeship education.

3 Textproduktion: Umgang mit Operatoren

Beispiel-Aufgabe
a The main idea of the text is that families have always been diverse, and television programmes have always reflected this.
b Text plan/outline:

Types of diversity	Examples
Race	Upper-class black family (*The Cosby Show*)
Cultural diversity within family Racial diversity within family	Intercultural couples (*I Love Lucy, Modern Family*) Adopted daughter in *Modern Family*
Non-traditional family structure	Adoption (*Modern Family*), re-marriages and stepchildren (*Modern Family, Brady Bunch*)
Non-traditional couples Non-traditional age	Age difference (*I Love Lucy*), same-sex (*Modern Family*) Having children "late" in life (*I Love Lucy, Modern Family*)
Dysfunction	*The Simpsons*

Example answer:
One type of diversity in the text has to do with racial and cultural diversity. The text mentions a black family which is not typical because it is upper-class. It also mentions interracial couples and an adopted Asian daughter.
   There are also many examples of families which are non-traditional. They have adoption and re-marriages with stepchildren. Non-traditional couples are also mentioned. Here we see unusual age differences and same-sex partnerships. There are also examples of people not following tradition by having children late in life.
   There is also one example of a dysfunctional family.
c The author uses informal language to talk directly to the reader. For example, when he asks questions like "What is a 'normal family'?" at the start of the text. Informal phrases like "Let's look at …" and "Let's skip ahead to …" also speak directly to the reader and function as invitations to keep reading.
d TV production companies need to make money from their product. Therefore, they make programmes that people want to watch. Clearly, TV shows about unusual families are more interesting to viewers.
   Another reason may be that …

a The text talks generally about a "stereotypical family". This means a so-called nuclear family with a mother, father, two children (one boy, one girl), who live together in a nice house with a garden. There are no children from previous marriages, no obvious difficulties, disabilities, or differences, only harmony and peaceful relationships. Of course, very few families are really like this.
b The author depicts non-stereotypical families in short lists of adjectives. For example, the family in *I love Lucy* is described as an "inter-cultural, older-woman-younger-man couple". The Cosbys are

290

"successful, well-educated, and black". In general, families are "not homogenous or perfect". Each phrase forms a strong picture.
c Another TV show that portrays a family is *The Family Guy*. This family is quite traditional. The mother and father are married with three children and a dog. The mother works from home. I know many traditional families like this, so I think we can say that this is fairly representative of modern family life.

This family is somewhat dysfunctional. For example, they ignore and ridicule the daughter. The baby is evil and tries to kill the mother. Some dysfunction is normal in modern families, but not to this degree.

As a cartoon, there are many aspects of the family that are fantastical. I don't know any family that holds conversations with their dog. This is definitely not representative.

4 Mit Hör-/Sehverstehensaufgaben umgehen

Beispiel-Aufgabe
1 Die Selbstmordrate bei Männnern ist dreieinhalb Mal höher als die Rate bei Frauen.
2 Die gefährdetste Gruppe stellen Männer im Alter zwischen 40 und 45 Jahren dar.
3 Männer werden nicht ermutigt, in ihrer Situation Hilfe zu erbitten. Ihnen wird gesagt, stark zu sein und ihre Gefühle nicht zu zeigen.
4 In Großbritannien ist die Selbstmordrate bei Männern am höchsten im Nordosten Englands.
5 Es ist zu hoffen, dass durch diese Informationen Suizidpräventionsprogramme initiiert werden, die sich gezielt an Männer richten.

a Falsch: eins von vier Kindern ist Mobbing-Opfer.
b Richtig: Mobbing wiederholt sich, und der Täter verlässt die Situation mit einem Gefühl von Macht und Kontrolle.
c Falsch: Social Media hat zu mehr Mobbing geführt.
d Richtig: Viele Mobbing-Fälle ereignen sich auf dem Schulhof.
e Falsch: Dem Lehrer ist meist nicht bewusst, wie viel gemobbt wird.
f Zu Mobbern werden meist diejenigen, die entweder selbst einmal Opfer waren oder erlebt haben, wie eine andere Person gemobbt wurde, und so gesehen haben, dass die Situation auf eine Art gewinnbringend ist.
g Die Opfer wachsen für gewöhnlich in liebevollen, fürsorglichen Familien auf und sind rauen Umgang nicht gewohnt.
h Am besten kümmert man sich selbst um die Situation, und wenn das nicht hilft, sollte man sich Hilfe von einer anderen Person holen.

1. Anruf Name of caller: Nicky Reed; Date and time: Tuesday, 2.25p.m.; Message: Ms Reed is concerned about client Amanda Christie. Please call 0177 222 5843 today until 6p.m. or tomorrow after 9. **2. Anruf** Name of caller: Sandra; Date and time: Tuesday, 6.22p.m.; Message: Please call her on her mobile about Monday's meeting.
3. Anruf Name of caller: William Cole; Date and time: Wednesday, 8.03a.m.; Message: Mr Cole is calling about the job ad on the webpage. Please call 030 2254 6678 / 0163 341 7201 or email william.cole@gmail.com.

5 Einen Text zusammenfassen

This article is about young homeless people in Berlin. The text states that there are approximately 2,000 young people in this situation in Berlin. Often, these kids use drugs, face violence, have health problems, suffer from lack of sleep and infections. However, social workers from the Off Road Kids organization are trying to help these people by finding them a place to live, and educating them about health and hygiene. According to the author, the kids are educated to use condoms and, if they can't stop taking drugs, to use clean needles. It is believed that these measures will prevent a lot of young homeless people dying unnecessarily every year.

6 Mindmaps und Gliederungen erstellen

a–c maternity and paternity leave, women re-joining the workforce, family friendly working hours; **d–f** holiday entitlement, weekly hours, overtime; **g–i** equal pay for men and women, minimum wages, incentives

1 I disagree with this statement; **2–4** People who have children have an easier time organising their home lives. They have no stress from travelling to and from work, and a lot of time is saved. Employees enjoy having the communications technology at home. **5–7** The time they save travelling can be spent on their work. There are not as many distractions, because they don't get interrupted by colleagues. Telecommuting saves time for the worker, and saves money for the company (win-win situation).

Text plan / outline:
Introduction: The HR dept. is reponsible for organising and supporting the personnel of a company.
Paragraph 1
- hire good people
- train people to do their jobs properly
- fire people in a tactful way
Paragraph 2
- motivate employees
- support employees
- deal with conflicts
Conclusion: HR is responsible for the people, therefore very important.
Example answer:
In any company, the Human Resources Department is responsible for organising and supporting the personnel of a company. They deal with hiring, firing, training, motivation, support, dealing with conflicts, and any other tasks or problems that may arise.

Exam Skills and Strategies – answer key

One of the best ways to ensure that a company runs well is to hire the right person for the right job. HR employees should be good at spotting talent, and placing new employees in roles that are suited to them. After this, the HR department organizes training and development, so that people can do their jobs properly. However, if a bad decision is made, and the person is not suited to their job, HR is responsible for firing this person.

When employees are motivated to do their work and feel supported, they tend to be productive. Lack of motivation and support can lead to conflict within teams. HR personnel track the productivity of employees, and try to identify problems before they occur. And when problems arise, they are skilled in the art of negotiation and try to resolve conflict as quickly as possible. Common areas for problems at work are payment, working hours, and discrimination.

The most important part of a company is the people who work for it. As HR is responsible for finding and playing employees, training, and support, it is one of the most important departments in any company. If the HR department does its job properly, the entire company should run productively.

7 Einen Aufsatz oder eine Stellungnahme schreiben

Beispiel-Aufgabe (Stellungnahme)
Some employers are still reluctant to hire disabled workers. They argue that the costs of doing so will be too high. This excuse is unreasonable and I will argue against it. I will also name some benefits that come with employing disabled workers.

First, let's look at the "expense" excuse. Is it really very expensive to modify a workplace for a disabled person's needs? Not unless the company is so poor it cannot, for instance, afford a small amount of training, or some equipment – like a handrail. In other words, if any adjustments need to be made, the cost of these will probably be minimal. Therefore, concerns about the cost are not a good argument against hiring a disabled person, as any costs will be very small, and there might not even be any additional expenses.

Next, let's look at the tax breaks available to the company when they have a disabled member of staff. Companies can claim any expenses of modifying a workplace when they submit a tax return. All it takes is a couple of minutes of googling to find out further financial benefits. Furthermore, the publicity and notoriety companies gain from employing disabled people will improve their reputation, which can positively influence their end of year profits.

In conclusion, employers who are willing to challenge prejudice benefit in many ways. They receive tax breaks and good publicity. By performing a service to society, the company enhances its public image. The workplace benefits from diversity. This is why I believe all employers should include positive discrimination as part of their employment policy.

Text plan / outline:
Introduction: problem; purpose of text

Individual
- Advantages: acceptance, normality, normal wages
- Disadvantages: prejudice, not enough support

Businesses
- Advantages: tax breaks, diversity, good public image
- Disadvantages: need to modify workplace and train staff – cost?

Society
- Advantages: acceptance, inclusion, no need for disability pensions
- Disadvantages: changes to attitudes, social structures – need for education

Conclusion

Example answer:
Many people with cognitive disabilities are happy to work in a sheltered environment, but many would prefer to work in an ordinary company. There are some advantages and disadvantages to this wish, for the individual, businesses, and society in general.

For the individual, he or she would have the chance to participate in ordinary work life. They would have the chance of financial independence. However, depending on their disability, they may have problems dealing with complicated or unexpected situations, and would need extra support. This might not be available. And unfortunately, they could face prejudice from other colleagues.

Companies that employ people who are "disabled" usually get tax breaks. A diverse workforce gives employees the opportunity to learn new ways of dealing with different people, without attending education courses. Furthermore, the public image would improve. However, these advantages are not for free. Modifications to the company's building might need to be made. Staff may need extra training.

For society in general, inclusion and acceptance of different types of people is always a good thing. Many people who have cognitive disabilities get a disability pension. If they can earn money like everyone else, they will not need money from the state. However, there will need to be changes to attitudes and also social structures, and some people may feel resistant to changing themselves or their opinions.

All individuals should be able to choose how they live their lives. Many cognitively disabled people want to work in a normal company. Therefore, the advantages and disadvantages need to be examined so that the best solution for everyone can be found.

9 Bilder und Cartoons beschreiben und analysieren

Beispiel-Aufgabe
In the foreground there is a tourist with a large backpack. Behind him, there is a sign that says "World Heritage Site". The backpacker is walking through an ornate gateway. He is reading a brochure entitled "Low impact tourism". The tourist doesn't seem to be paying attention to where he is going. It looks as if he is completely absorbed in what he is reading. The tourist represents careless tourists in general.

The cartoon supports the information in the text, by showing the destruction that backpackers can cause.

Perhaps if tourists were banned from the destination in the picture, there would be less damage to the site. Together, the cartoon and text make me consider the impact I have when I go on holiday, because even tourists with good intentions can have a negative impact.

The cartoon shows an interview situation, with a man and a woman sitting together at a table. The woman who is being interviewed looks worried. The man interviewing her seems to be an insensitive, brutal sort of person. He is informing her that as a volunteer she can expect a lot of horrible things, including "exhaustion, emotional overload, lack of support, and … terror". The woman represents volunteers in general, and the man symbolizes the organizations that exploit volunteers. The point of the cartoon seems to be that people who work as volunteers will be exploited. In my opinion, the cartoonist exaggerates a lot. I think it is a mistake to generalize about all people who choose to work as volunteers, and the organizations that use them. Overall, I'm not sure what point the cartoonist wants to make. It has a negative effect on me, as if to say there is nothing positive or meaningful about volunteering, only exploitation and difficulties. (160 words)

Although both the cartoon and the text describe the hardships of volunteer work, the tone of the text is positive and encouraging. The people mentioned were helpful and willing to answer questions, as opposed to the man in the cartoon who is unhelpful and mean. The text gives a completely different opinion than the cartoon.

11 Schaubilder und Statistiken beschreiben und analysieren

Beispiel-Aufgabe

a This table indicates what percentage of customers believe in life after death. Nearly a third of non-religious customers said they believed in life after death, about 20% said they didn't believe in it, and roughly half said they weren't sure.
b This pie chart compares how often each type of sympathy gift is given. The most common gift is flowers. Food was more common than charitable gifts. The least common gifts are grouped together as "other". More than half of all people give flowers when someone dies.
c This line graph shows the share of customers who have chosen cremation over burial since the 1980s. Cremations increased steadily in the 1980s and 90s, with only a slight fluctuation. In the 2000s there was a significant drop, and for some time the rate stayed at the same level. Since then, cremations have soared and they are projected to keep doing so in the future.

a considerably higher; **b** gradual increase; **c** slowly decreased; **d** remained stable; **e** considerable fluctuation; **f** dropped suddenly; **g** rise sharply; **h** peaked; **i** dipped; **j** rising

The two bar charts show the causes of death in the European Union, by age group. The first chart shows middle-aged deaths, from ages 45 to 64. The second chart shows young adult deaths, from ages 20 to 44. The cause of most deaths in the middle-aged group is cancer. However, in young adults, the cause of most deaths is external causes. Cancer is the second biggest cause of death for young adults, whereas external causes account for just under 10% of deaths in middle aged people. In both groups, respiratory diseases make up considerably less than 10%. Digestive diseases also cause roughly the same number of deaths in both groups. In the older age group, the majority of deaths are caused by some form of health problem, whereas the younger group are more likely to die from external or other causes. (151 words)

12 Mediation

Beispiel-Aufgabe
Dear Colleagues

Recently, an article was printed in the newspaper about a robot called "Friend" that is being developed at the University of Bremen, with the aim of helping severely disabled people. The prototype is an electric wheelchair with a robot arm and eye camera. It is controlled by the user's head, with a chin joystick. The project leader said that the system did everything alone, but the user stayed in control. In addition to the robot friend, a reader is being developed that can turn the pages of a book with a vacuum and lever.

As you know, our patients are not able to do many things. This robot would give them the opportunity to do a great number of things by themselves. One user said it was incredible independence for her. Although it is still in the development stage, it is good to know such a machine has been invented. This may give hope to some of our patients.

I hope you found this information useful.
Best wishes
[Name]

Lieber Herr Mosel,
ich leite Ihnen hier eine E-Mail weiter, die unsere Teamleiterin Barbara Blasedale an alle von uns im Team geschrieben hat. Es geht um die Bedeutung, kulturelle Unterschiede zu respektieren, wenn wir im Ausland sind. Sie hat den Teammitgliedern ins Gedächtnis gerufen, dass sie Vertreter ihres jeweiligen Landes sind, und dass sie die Meinungen der Menschen bezüglich ihres Landes beeinflussen.

Sie hat geraten, neuen und andersartigen Situationen mit Offenheit zu begegnen, möglichst ohne zu urteilen. Sie hat auch davor gewarnt, zu verallgemeinern, da der Unterschied zwischen Meinung und Vorurteil nur gering ist. Schließlich hat sie das Team daran erinnert, sich gegenseitig zu unterstützen und zu ermutigen. Sie hat ihre Hilfe bei schwerwiegenden Problemen angeboten und dem Team viel Erfolg gewünscht.
Beste Grüße
[Name]

IRREGULAR VERBS

be	was/were	been	*sein*
beat	beat	beaten	*schlagen, besiegen*
become	became	become	*werden*
begin	began	begun	*anfangen, beginnen*
bend	bent	bent	*(sich) beugen*
blow	blew	blown	*wehen, blasen, ziehen*
break	broke	broken	*brechen*
breed	bred	bred	*sich vermehren, sich ausbreiten*
bring	brought	brought	*(mit)bringen*
build	built	built	*bauen*
burn	burnt/ burned	burnt/ burned	*(ver)brennen*
buy	bought	bought	*kaufen*
catch	caught	caught	*fangen, fassen, erreichen*
choose	chose	chosen	*(aus)wählen*
come	came	come	*kommen*
cost	cost	cost	*kosten*
cut	cut	cut	*schneiden*
deal (with)	dealt (with)	dealt (with)	*sich kümmern um, umgehen mit*
dig	dug	dug	*graben*
do	did	done	*tun, machen*
draw	drew	drawn	*zeichnen*
dream	dreamt/ dreamed	dreamt/ dreamed	*träumen*
drink	drank	drunk	*trinken*
drive	drove	driven	*fahren*
eat	ate	eaten	*essen*
fall	fell	fallen	*fallen*
feed	fed	fed	*füttern, ernähren*
feel	felt	felt	*(sich) fühlen, empfinden*
fight	fought	fought	*kämpfen*
find	found	found	*finden*
fit	fit/fitted	fit/fitted	*passen, anbringen, entsprechen*
fly	flew	flown	*fliegen*
forbid	forbade	forbidden	*verbieten*
forget	forgot	forgotten	*vergessen*
get	got	got (*AE* gotten)	*bekommen*
give	gave	given	*geben*
go	went	gone	*gehen, fahren*
grow	grew	grown	*wachsen*
hang	hung	hung	*hängen*
have	had	had	*haben*
hear	heard	heard	*hören*
hide	hid	hidden	*(sich) verstecken*
hit	hit	hit	*schlagen*
hold	held	held	*halten, festhalten*
hurt	hurt	hurt	*verletzen*
keep	kept	kept	*behalten*
know	knew	known	*kennen, wissen*
lay	laid	laid	*legen*
lead	led	led	*führen*
lean	leant/ leaned	leant/ leaned	*sich lehnen, sich beugen*
learn	learnt/ learned	learnt/ learned	*lernen*
leave	left	left	*abfahren, verlassen, weggehen*
let	let	let	*lassen*
lie	lay	lain	*liegen*
light	lit	lit	*anzünden, beleuchten*
lose	lost	lost	*verlieren*
make	made	made	*machen*
mean	meant	meant	*meinen, bedeuten*
meet	met	met	*treffen*
pay	paid	paid	*bezahlen*
put	put	put	*setzen, stellen, legen*
quit	quit/ quitted	quit/ quitted	*verlassen, aufhören*
read	read	read	*lesen*
ride	rode	ridden	*reiten, fahren*
ring	rang	rung	*anrufen, läuten*
rise	rose	risen	*(an)steigen*
run	ran	run	*laufen, rennen*
say	said	said	*sagen*
see	saw	seen	*sehen*
seek	sought	sought	*suchen*
sell	sold	sold	*verkaufen*
send	sent	sent	*senden, schicken*
set	set	set	*setzen, stellen*
shake	shook	shaken	*schütteln*
shine	shone	shone	*scheinen, glänzen*
show	showed	shown	*zeigen*
shrink	shrank	shrunk	*schrumpfen, zurück- gehen*
shut	shut	shut	*schließen*
sing	sang	sung	*singen*
sink	sank	sunk	*sinken*
sit	sat	sat	*sitzen*
sleep	slept	slept	*schlafen*
slide	slid	slid	*(ab)rutschen, (ab) sacken*
smell	smelt/ smelled	smelt/ smelled	*riechen*
speak	spoke	spoken	*sprechen*
spell	spelt/ spelled	spelt/ spelled	*buchstabieren*
spend	spent	spent	*ausgeben, verbringen*
spread	spread	spread	*(sich) verbreiten*
stand	stood	stood	*stehen*
steal	stole	stolen	*stehlen*
swim	swam	swum	*schwimmen*
take	took	taken	*nehmen*
teach	taught	taught	*unterrichten, beibringen*
tell	told	told	*sagen, erzählen*
think	thought	thought	*denken*
throw	threw	thrown	*werfen*
understand	understood	understood	*verstehen*
wake	woke	woken	*aufwachen, -wecken*
wear	wore	worn	*tragen*
win	won	won	*gewinnen*
write	wrote	written	*schreiben*